CONTEMPORARY ETHICS
Selected Readings

Edited by

James P. Sterba
University of Notre Dame

Prentice Hall, Englewood Cliffs, New Jersey 07632

LIBRARY OF CONGRESS
Library of Congress Cataloging-in-Publication Data

Contemporary ethics : selected readings / James P. Sterba.
    p.   cm.
  Bibliography: p.
  ISBN 0-13-169897-4
  1. Ethics.   I. Sterba, James P.
BJ1012.C658 1989
170--dc19   88-25243
                                                           CIP

Editorial/production supervision:
WordCrafters Editorial Services, Inc.
Cover design: Diane Saxe
Manufacturing buyer: Peter Havens

 © 1989 by Prentice-Hall,
A Division of Simon & Schuster, Inc.
Englewood Cliffs, New Jersey 07632

Printed in the United States of America
10   9   8   7   6   5   4   3   2   1

ISBN 0-13-169897-4

Prentice-Hall International (UK) Limited, *London*
Prentice-Hall of Australia Pty. Limited, *Sydney*
Prentice-Hall Canada Inc., *Toronto*
Prentice-Hall Hispanoamericana, S.A., *Mexico*
Prentice-Hall of India Private Limited, *New Delhi*
Prentice-Hall of Japan, Inc., *Tokyo*
Simon & Schuster Southeast Asia Pte. Ltd., *Singapore*
Editora Prentice-Hall do Brasil, Ltda., *Rio de Janeiro*

To Kurt Baier and John Rawls
whose work made this book possible

CONTENTS

IV ALTERNATIVE PERSPECTIVES IN NORMATIVE ETHICS

V MORAL DILEMMAS AND MORAL REALISM

PREFACE

This anthology is designed to be a basic text for a second course in philosophy for students whose first course provided them with some familiarity with ethical theory. The anthology introduces such students to four major topics in contemporary ethics. The first three topics, the Nature of Ethics, The Justification of Ethics, and Alternative Perspectives in Ethics have been standard topics from G. E. Moore to the present. The fourth topic, Moral Dilemmas and Ethical Realism, is a more recent topic that has generated a host of articles in philosophical journals and a few specialized anthologies. With respect to the three standard topics, I have combined so-called contemporary classics with some of the most recent articles on the topic. For the fourth topic, I have focused on providing selections from some of the best-known people in the field. For all four topics, I have included a broad selection of opposing articles. In the Introduction, I have attempted to show how all four topics are interrelated.

It is possible to teach a course covering just some of these topics or a course covering just some of the articles under each topic. As far as I can tell, such courses are being taught at a wide range of colleges and universities by professors (many of them friends of mine) who are weary from carrying large piles of photocopied materials to their classes. This anthology provides a better alternative.

For their help in putting this anthology together, I wish to thank my graduate and undergraduate students at Notre Dame and at the University of Rochester; my colleagues at Notre Dame, in particular Michael DePaul, Jorge Garcia, and David Solomon; and the secretarial staff at Notre Dame, in particular Cheryl Reed. I also want to especially thank Joe Heider, Philosophy Editor at Prentice Hall, for his constant encouragement and support.

James P. Sterba

PART I   Introduction

There are many facets to contemporary ethics, but there are only a few central questions that philosophers have returned to time and time again. These questions are: What is the nature of ethics? What is its justification? Its requirements? This anthology seeks to explore answers given by contemporary philosophers to these and other related questions.

THE NATURE OF ETHICS

Virtually everyone agrees that contemporary ethics begins with G. E. Moore's inquiry into the nature of ethics (selection 1). In previous inquiries, the domain of ethics was limited to the domain of human conduct. By contrast, Moore sought to broaden the domain to include a general inquiry into what is good. But Moore was not looking to provide a catalog of items that are good. Rather he sought to determine how good is to be defined. His surprising answer to that question was that good is not to be defined at all. For Moore, good is an indefinable nonnatural property. By characterizing good as indefinable, Moore meant that good is a simple rather than a complex property and thus not analyzable into other simples. By his own admission, Moore was never clear what he meant to convey by calling good a nonnatural property.[1] Initially, he claimed that the property did not belong to the subject matter of the natural sciences or psychology or alternatively that it was incapable of existing by itself in time.[2] Later he claimed that it was not an intrinsic property of natural objects but rather a property that depended on or was supervenient upon such intrinsic properties.[3] According to Moore, throughout the history of ethics many philosophers have confused the property of goodness with the intrinsic properties of natural objects thereby committing what he called the "naturalistic fallacy."

To expose philosophers who have committed this fallacy, Moore employed what came to be called the "open-question argument." Thus suppose someone proposed a definition of "good." For example, suppose someone claimed that "good" means "productive of pleasure." Moore claimed that such a definition could be effectively challenged by asking the question, "Is what is productive of pleasure good?" Because this question is intelligible and not like asking, "Is an unmarried male a bachelor?" Moore claimed this showed that the proposed definition is inadequate and its proponents guilty of the naturalistic fallacy.

Now many have challenged Moore's use of the open-question argument claiming that the argument calls into question perfectly adequate definitions like "water is H$_2$O" and "temperature is mean kinetic energy." But this challenge fails because such definitions are only adequate for scientific purposes and fail to capture other essential qualities of what they purport to define.

William Frankena in a justly celebrated article has proposed yet another challenge to Moore's view (selection 2). Frankena contends that the naturalistic fallacy could not be a logical fallacy since it may be committed even when a logically valid argument is used. Frankena further contends that if the naturalistic fallacy is a fallacy at all, it is a species of a more general definist fallacy of confusing one property with some other distinct property. But Frankena's most significant challenge is his contention that the only way to establish that the naturalistic fallacy has been committed is by showing that we are all aware of good as a distinct indefinable property. This last criticism, however, ignores the role that the open-question argument plays in Moore's view. According to Moore, to establish that the naturalistic fallacy has been committed, it suffices to show that the open-question argument undercuts any proposed definition of good; there is no need to show that we are all aware of good as a distinct indefinable property.

But does the open-question argument undercut all definitions of "good"? Consider the following definition: "Good" means "perfective of the nature of a thing."[4] Suppose we try to use the open-question argument against this definition and ask, "Is what is

perfective of the nature of a thing good?" It seems that this question is no more intelligible than the question, "Is a bachelor an unmarried male?" Now Moore might have responded by claiming that this is simply an arbitrary verbal definition that fails to show that "good" is a complex notion that is analyzable in terms of simples. Nevertheless, the definition is useful by suggesting how "good" may be linked to the features of natural objects.

A much more radical response to Moore, however, was presented by Charles Stevenson. Rejecting the idea that "good" referred to some objective property, Stevenson claimed that "good" serves an emotive or expressive function. In selection 3, Stevenson suggests that "X is good" can be approximately defined as "we like X" or "I do like X, do so as well." In later work, Stevenson favored the definition, "X has properties A B C. Hence, I approve of X, do so as well."[5]

The main advantages of defining "good" in this way are twofold. First, the definition makes clear the dynamic or action-guiding character of moral terms. Second, the definition shows how there can be disagreement in ethics. People can disagree in their beliefs about what are relevant natural properties (A, B, C, etc.) possessed by X or they can disagree in their attitudes toward X even when they agree about what are the relevant properties possessed by X. For example, people can disagree concerning their evaluation of political candidates because they disagree over what policies the candidates, in fact, support (disagreement in belief), or they can disagree simply in their evaluation of those policies (disagreement in attitude).

To many philosophers, however, the disadvantages of the emotivist account far outweigh its advantages. In selection 4, Brand Blanshard raises a number of problems for the emotivist analysis. In general, Blanshard objects to tying "good" or "bad" to our judgments of approval or disapproval. Blanshard contends that things can be good or bad independently of whether we actually approve or disapprove of them and independently of the degree to which we approve or disapprove. For example, Blanshard argues that the suffering of a rabbit in a trap can be bad even when no one actually disapproves of it. But even if Blanshard's objections are telling against the emotivist account formulated by Stevenson, it does seem possible to avoid objections of this sort by substituting a more idealized account. For suppose we define "X is good" as "An ideal observer with all the relevant information would approve of X." Obviously it would be necessary to specify in what respects this agent was to be idealized and what counts as relevant information, but it seems that this could be done in a way that would avoid Blanshard's objections. One could even combine this definition with the one proposed earlier as follows: "X is good" means "An ideal observer with all the relevant information would approve of X because X has the qualities that are perfective of its nature."

Although the preceding definition suggests that for every X there are some set of good-making properties, it does not tell us specifically how to determine what those properties are for X. To do so would seem to ultimately involve deriving an evaluative conclusion from descriptive premises, and many philosophers believe that to attempt such a derivation would entail committing the naturalistic fallacy. However, John R. Searle argues in selection 5 that such a derivation can be achieved without committing the naturalistic fallacy if we begin with facts about social institutions. He offers the following derivation:

1. Jones uttered the words "I hereby promise to pay you, Smith, five dollars."
1a. Under conditions C anyone who utters the words "I hereby promise to pay you, Smith, five dollars" promises to pay Smith five dollars.
1b. Conditions C obtain.
2. Jones promised to pay Smith five dollars.
2a. All promises are acts of placing oneself under an obligation to do the thing promised.

3. Jones placed herself under an obligation to pay Smith five dollars.
3a. All those who place themselves under an obligation are, other things being equal, under an obligation.
3b. Other things are equal.
4. Jones is under an obligation to pay Smith five dollars.
4a. Other things being equal, one ought to do what one is under an obligation to do.
4b. Other things are equal.
5. Jones ought to pay Smith five dollars.

In selection 6, Anthony Flew contends that the premises of Searle's argument would only be purely descriptive if they are interpreted as part of a detached anthropological report about the institution of promising. Searle admits that his premises could be interpreted in this fashion but contends that it is not the interpretation he intends. As Searle interprets them, his premises are asserted by a participant speaking from within the institution of promising. However, when they are interpreted in this way, as Flew points out, the premises are evaluative as well as descriptive. Searle would not deny this, he would simply add that most of our institutional commitments are like that.

Of course, there is the further question of whether committing ourselves to the institution of promising leads to obligations in just the way Searle claims. Searle holds that performing the speech act of uttering "I hereby promise" in the absence of any moral constraints still leads to a prima facie obligation to keep the promise. But suppose an underworld figure "promises" to eliminate a noncooperative, duly elected public official. Surely such a promise would not generate a prima facie *moral* obligation to kill an innocent person. What such a case shows is that there are either moral constraints that determine when we can effectively promise or moral constraints that determine when our promises generate prima facie moral obligations. In subsequent work, Searle seems to endorse this second alternative, claiming that in his argument he was not trying to derive a *moral* "ought" from an "is."[6] Interpreted in this way, however, Searle's argument seems less interesting because many philosophers would grant that obligations that may not be moral can be generated by our involvement in social institutions.

In selection 7, Philippa Foot attempts to establish a stronger conclusion than that defended by Searle against nonnaturalists, like Flew and R. M. Hare, who deny that evaluative properties are logically linked to the natural (descriptive) properties of objects. Foot attempts to refute what she takes to be two central claims by such nonnaturalists. These claims are:

1. Evaluation can be based on eccentric evidence without a special explanation.
2. Any evidence can be rejected as a basis for evaluation.

To show that claim 1 should be rejected, Foot argues that no one could maintain that someone is good because she clasps and unclasps her hands three times an hour without giving a special explanation of why the person is good. But while Foot's view here seems incontrovertible, nonnaturalists need not disagree. For instance, Hare allows that in Foot's example a special explanation *is required* of why a person who clasps and unclasps her hands three times a day is good.[7]

With respect to claim 2, Foot rejects the view that one could coherently describe something as injurious yet withhold a negative evaluation or coherently describe some behavior as courageous yet withhold a positive evaluation. By contrast, nonnaturalists think that it is logically possible to withhold evaluations in such cases. Thus, for example, Hare claims that a person can admit that something is poisonous yet deny that it ought not to be chosen to eat.[8] Yet here nonnaturalists are only denying that these descriptions entail evaluations that are conclusive; they are not denying that they entail

prima facie evaluations. Of course, nonnaturalists also claim that it is, *in principle*, possible to provide some pure descriptions of the underlying condition that is injurious or the underlying behavior that is courageous from which not even prima facie evaluations follow.[9] Naturalists, like Foot, would presumably deny that this is possible, but even if nonnaturalists were right that such pure descriptions could be provided, there may be no reason to do so. For all practical purposes, we may be able to begin our moral arguments with at least partially evaluative premises that all parties hold in common. What this would show is that the descriptive–evaluative gap (or the is–ought gap) is, in fact, irrelevant to the task of conducting effective moral arguments in everyday life.

In the final reading of this section (selection 8), Alasdair MacIntyre claims that contemporary moral philosophy is characterized by radical disagreement, interminable arguments, and incommensurable premises, citing a number of examples of current moral disputes whose proposed solutions have various historical origins. According to MacIntyre, since contemporary moral philosophy purports to provide objective solutions to such disputes, it cannot be characterized by an emotivism of meaning as Stevenson attempted to do. Nevertheless, MacIntyre argues that contemporary moral philosophy can be characterized by an emotivism of use because it fails to effectively resolve these disputes.

One might try to respond to MacIntyre by showing how the particular disputes that he cites can be resolved in ways that should be acceptable to all parties, but since MacIntyre could always cite other disputes, an effective response requires an adequate justification for morality against those who would reject morality altogether along with an adequate defense of some particular normative perspective against those who favor other moral perspectives. The next two sections of the anthology treat each of these topics in turn.

THE JUSTIFICATION OF ETHICS

Stephen Toulmin pioneered what has been called the good-reasons approach to justification in ethics (selection 9). In Toulmin's approach, good reasons are determined ultimately by reference to the very function of ethics. That function, Toulmin claims, is "to correlate our feelings and behavior in such a way as to make the fulfillment of everyone's aims and desires as far as possible compatible."[10] Frequently, however, there is no need to appeal directly to the function of ethics. For example, where there is no conflict of duties, it suffices to appeal to the applicable conventional rules, such as the rules of the road, to determine what are the relevant good reasons. Thus facts that constitute good reasons in Toulmin's view do not do so in virtue of anything to which they refer but rather in virtue of the use to which they are put in supporting judgments that ultimately serve the very function of ethics.

But couldn't the function of ethics be different from what it is? Toulmin does not think that this is possible without ethics ceasing to be ethics, just as the function of science could not be other than "to alter expectations" without science ceasing to be science.[11]

Yet surely we could ask, assuming that the function of ethics is fixed in this way, why should we engage in ethics? According to Toulmin, the only answer that we can give to this question is that we *are engaged* in ethics; it is not possible to give any further justification. For to ask for a further justification for ethics could not be a request for a moral reason to be moral since that would simply be redundant. And if it is a request for a nonmoral reason to be moral, what sort of justification could be given? For example, Toulmin argues that we couldn't give a self-interest justification for ethics.

It is just at this point that Kurt Baier disagrees with Toulmin concerning the development of a good-reasons approach to ethics. For Baier (selection 10) contends that it is possible to provide a justification for

ethics that is compelling to all reasonable agents.

Baier reformulates his justification for morality in terms of a number of requirements of practical reason, the most important of which are the following:

Universality
Since a fact F is a reason for someone to do A in virtue of her satisfying certain conditions D, F must be a reason to do A for anyone who satisfies D.

Empirical Substantiation
The soundness of the belief that C is the criterion that is to determine whether or not F is a reason for a certain strength for X to do A is to be determined by the way acceptance of this criterion affects the satisfactoriness of the relevant lives.

Universalizability
If F is a reason to do A for anyone who satisfies D, then F must also be capable of being a reason to do A for everyone who satisfies D.

Baier contends that only when moral reasons are taken to be supreme can these three requirements of practical reason be met since only then would each person have the best reason grounded in the satisfactoriness of the person's own life that every person (not any person) can possibly have.

Kai Nielson agrees with Baier against Toulmin that "Why be moral?" is a meaningful question (selection 11). According to Nielson, even in contexts when it is not in one's self-interest to be moral, there may be aesthetic, economic, or political reasons for being moral, and other philosophers claim that there can also be logical reasons, like consistency and nonarbitrariness, for being moral. Nielson, however, denies that such reasons suffice to justify morality over self-interest. Nielson thinks that there are compelling reasons why we collectively should be moral but not necessarily compelling reasons why each of us individually should be moral. Given particular circumstances, it may be in one's overall self-interest to act immorally, and there may be no compelling reason against doing so. Even more frequently, it may serve one's overall self-interest to be a "classic amoralist," that is, someone who maintains reciprocal relationships only with the members of one's own class, and there may be no compelling reason against doing so. In either of these ways, Nielson contends that it is possible to show that acting immorally is not contrary to reason. In effect, Nielson is rejecting the universalizability condition of Baier's argument. He is denying that amoralists must believe that it is always a good thing for others to behave as the amoralists themselves are behaving.

In selection 12, Alan Gewirth proposes yet another justification for morality. The central premises of Gewirth's argument can be summarized as follows:

1. All agents regard their purposes as good according to whatever criteria are involved in their actions to fulfill them.
2. Therefore, all agents must affirm a right to the freedom and well-being necessary to achieve their purposes.
3. All agents must affirm such a right on the basis of simply being prospective, purposive agents.
4. Hence, all agents must affirm that every prospective, purposive agent has a right to freedom and well-being.

Gewirth claims that the universalized right affirmed in the conclusion of his argument is a *moral* right and that every agent has to endorse that right under pain of self-contradiction.

There appears to be an interpretation of Gewirth's conclusion that does follow from his premises; unfortunately, it is not the interpretation Gewirth intends. For from the generally acceptable premises of his argument, it does follow that all agents must affirm that every prospective, purposive agent has a right to freedom and well-being, but the universalized right so deduced is still a prudential and not a moral right.

What a prudential right to freedom and well-being implies is an asymmetrically action-guiding "ought." This means that when an agent says that every prospective, purposive agent has a prudential right to freedom and well-being, the action-guiding implications are that the agent ought to take the steps necessary to secure or to retain the agent's own freedom and well-being, but not that the agent ought to take steps to secure or even steps not to interfere with the freedom and well-being of any other agent, except insofar as it is necessary for securing or retaining the agent's own freedom and well-being. And similarly for every other agent. This asymmetrically action-guiding ought is often said to be analogous to the oughts found in the most ordinary cases of competitive games—cases that we otherwise would have thought conform to the requirements of practical reason. For example, in football a defensive player might think that the opposing team's quarterback ought to pass on third down with five yards to go, while not wanting the quarterback to do so and hoping to foil any such attempt the quarterback makes.

Unfortunately, the success of Gewirth's argument for the justification of morality depends on the impossibility of interpreting the universalized right to freedom and well-being in his conclusion as anything other than a moral right, that is, a right that is symmetrically action guiding and entails that others at least ought not to interfere with the right-holder's exercising his or her right. Since, as we have seen, it is possible to interpret this universalized right as a prudential right, Gewirth's argument for the justification of morality in terms of the demands of practical reason cannot succeed as formulated.

Hoping to succeed where others have failed, Stephen Darwall begins his defense of morality in selection 13 by appealing to the following seemingly uncontroversial principle:

A rational agent ought to act at *t* as there is, all things considered, reason for her to act at *t*.

Darwall then goes on to claim that there is a reason for a person to act at *t* if that person would, by a dispassionate reflection on the relevant evidence at *t,* retain or acquire that reason at *t.* For Darwall this reflection takes place either from a personal or from an impersonal standpoint. From a personal standpoint, such reflection gives rise to self-regarding reasons. From an impersonal standpoint, such reflection gives rise to other-regarding reasons. According to Darwall, both sorts of reasons are relevant to the rational assessment of conduct.

Now there are two difficulties with Darwall's specification of the class of relevant reasons. First, Darwall does not provide an argument for why the rational egoist who takes self-interested reasons to be supreme should recognize as relevant those reasons that are derived from an impersonal standpoint. Second, Darwall treats as irrelevant to the rational assessment of conduct reasons a person could only have acquired in the past. For example, on Darwall's account, that people could have acquired certain reasons to oppose the racist and sexist practices in their society but now because of their insensitivity can no longer acquire such reasons is irrelevant to the assessment of the reasonableness of their conduct.

Nevertheless, the major difficulty with Darwall's defense of morality concerns not his interpretation of what is to count as a relevant reason but rather his interpretation of what is to count as a rational weighing of such reasons. According to Darwall, since a rational weighing of such reasons applies to everyone, it must ultimately be made from an impersonal and, hence, impartial standpoint, thus resulting in reasons that are symmetrically action-guiding for all rational agents. Such reasons entail that other rational agents at least ought not to interfere with an agent's acting as there is reason for the agent to act, all things considered. Unfortunately, Darwall never considers why a rational weighing of the relevant reasons, even if it is to apply to everyone, could not be made from a personal standpoint, thus resulting in reasons that are asymmetrically action-guiding like the oughts in competitive games. Such reasons would not entail that other rational agents at least ought not to interfere with an agent's acting as there is reason for the agent to act, all things considered.

This latter interpretation, of course, is the one the defender of rational egoism would endorse, and Darwall needs to argue that this interpretation would beg the question against the defender of morality. But even given such an argument, it wouldn't thereby follow, at least not directly, that an *impartial* weighing of the relevant reasons is rationally required. One needs to argue first that some type of a compromise between conflicting self-regarding and other-regarding reasons is rationally required. Only then could one reasonably proceed to argue that the type of compromise that is needed should be impartial. Even then it would be surprising if the impartiality that is rationally required turned out to be, as Darwall claims, the same impartiality that is found in John Rawls's original position. For that would mean that moral perspectives that incorporated weaker notions of impartiality would all be contrary to reason.

In selection 14, Philippa Foot rejects all attempts, like those of Baier, Gewirth, and Darwall, to justify morality as a requirement of practical reason. Foot argues that morality has been mistakenly thought to have some inescapable categorical force when, in fact, it is a system of hypothetical imperatives dependent for its justification on the reasons, wants, and interests people just happen to have. According to Foot, it is possible for people not to have any reason to be moral, and thus to act immorally, without acting contrary to reason. Of course, Foot grants that moral rules are generally thought to have force independent of the reasons people happen to have, and, on this account, are thought to be categorical imperatives. However, to show that this view is mistaken, Foot simply points out that the rules of etiquette are also thought to have the same independent force although we do not classify them as categorical imperatives.

Obviously, the only way to fully respond to Foot's critique is to provide just the sort of justification for morality that she claims can't be done, and this is what most of the selections included in this section attempt to do. Nevertheless, it should be noted that the contrast between morality and etiquette only works with respect to that part of etiquette that is not grounded upon moral rules. For the rest of etiquette, its nonhypothetical character is explainable by the nonhypothetical character of morality itself.

While others have attempted to justify morality as a requirement of rationality, David Gauthier (selection 15) has constructed an elaborate argument designed to show that acquiring a disposition to act morally can be justified in terms of self-interest, or as he would put it, that adopting a strategy of constrained maximization can be justified in terms of the maximization of individual utility. Gauthier contends that the disposition of a rational individual to comply with a strategy of constrained maximization is conditional upon the person's expectation that "she will benefit in comparison with the utility she could expect were no one to cooperate."[12] Thus, in order for a strategy of constrained maximization to be justified on the basis of maximizing individual utility, it must be the case that constrained maximizers can tell beforehand whether they are interacting with other constrained maximizers or with straightforward maximizers. Only in this way can they avoid being taken advantage of by straightforward maximizers. Happily, this obstacle can be overcome, Gauthier argues, provided that constrained maximizers are present in sufficient numbers and that people's dispositions to cooperate may be ascertained by others "not with certainty but as more than mere guesswork."[13]

A final condition not mentioned in this selection that must be met before a strategy of constrained maximization is said to be justified on grounds of maximizing individual utility is that its adoption proceed from a noncoercive starting point.[14] The test for such a starting point is that, other things being equal, no one is made worse off by the actions of others than they would be if those others had never existed. Thus, for example, to arrive at such a noncoercive starting point, it would not be enough for slaveholders to simply free their slaves; they must also compensate them so that they are no longer worse off than they would be had the slaveholders never existed. Without such a noncoercive starting point, Gauthier contends, it would not be rational for someone to freely adopt a strategy of constrained maximization. Thus, on Gauthier's view, "morals arise in and from the rational agreement of equals."[15]

But does Gauthier's argument succeed in showing that morality can be justified in terms of self-interest? What his argument clearly succeeds in showing is that a limited disposition to take into account the interests of others can be justified on grounds of self-interest, or put another way, that at least sometimes acting from duty, that is, from the motive of doing one's duty, can be required by self-interest. This is a significant result. But whether it succeeds as a justification for morality depends upon how we go on to further specify our definition of morality.

For Gauthier morality takes into account the interests of everyone alike, but it does so only within a voluntary system of mutual benefit. Thus, for example, attempts by slaveholders to retain their slaves or attempts by South African whites to retain their privileged status, when no other course of action would better serve their individual utility, are not immoral on Gauthier's account. Rather they are simply beyond the pale of morality. On more standard accounts of morality, however, such instances of coercive exploitation constitute some of our clearest examples of immorality. Moreover, on Gauthier's account of morality, we cannot even morally approve of the actions of those who violently throw off the shackles of coercive exploitation in order to establish a more just society against the interest of their former slaveholders or rulers. But again, on more standard accounts of morality, such cases are among our clearest examples of justified moral action.

Thus, while Gauthier's justification for morality is successful within a limited domain, too much still falls outside of Gauthier's account of morality for it to be a fully adequate justification of morality in terms of self-interest.

In the final reading of this section (selection 16) I survey a number of attempts to justify morality. Rejecting yet drawing upon these attempts, I present a justification based on the requirements of practical reason that, I claim, demonstrates that the rational egoist acts contrary to reason. What I argue is that a non-question-begging conception of rationality requires the following:

1. In evaluating people's conduct we take into account not only the relevant reasons they have but also the relevant reasons they could have.
2. In weighing these relevant reasons we opt for a compromise between self-interested and altruistic reasons that constitutes morality.

Now one could object to the first requirement on the grounds that the class of relevant reasons has not been adequately specified. But while the specification of the class of relevant reasons is admittedly inadequate, it can be improved upon, and any competing account would have to do the same.[16] One might also object to the second requirement on the grounds that there are many possible compromises between self-interested and altruistic reasons not all of which would support the requirements of morality. In response, I need to show that only a morally acceptable range of compromises can be shown to satisfy the requirements of a non-question-begging conception of rationality.[17]

ALTERNATIVE PERSPECTIVES IN NORMATIVE ETHICS

In the previous section, the readings explored the question of the justification of morality, and a number of the readings attempted to show just how morality can be justified. But whether such attempts to justify morality succeed or fail, most people do, in fact, want to be moral. So even in the absence of an adequate justification for morality, given people's actual commitments, we can still raise the question of which particular moral perspective they should endorse. Accordingly, in this section we shall consider a range of alternative moral perspectives each of which appeals to a different ultimate moral and political ideal. Now each of these moral perspectives has its consequentialist and nonconsequentialist defenders. This means that some defenders see the perspective they endorse as justified on the basis of its consequences while others do not. What this shows is that while the consequentialist/nonconsequentialist distinction may be of some theoretical use, it is not of much practical use in coming to terms with the moral perspectives that people actually endorse.

One such perspective that people actually endorse is libertarianism. Libertarians such as John Hospers (selection 17) take liberty to be the ultimate moral and political ideal and typically define "liberty" as "the state of being unconstrained by other persons from doing what one wants." This definition limits the scope of liberty in two ways. First, not all constraints, whatever the source, count as a restriction on liberty; the constraints must come from other persons. For example, people who are constrained by natural forces from getting to the top of Mount Everest do not lack liberty in this regard. Second, the constraints must run counter to people's wants. Thus, people who do not want to hear Beethoven's Fifth Symphony do not feel their liberty is restricted when other people forbid its performance, even though the proscription does in fact constrain what they are able to do.

Of course, libertarians may argue that these constraints do restrict a person's liberty because people normally want to be unconstrained by others. But other philosophers have claimed that such constraints point to a serious defect in the libertarian's definition of liberty, which can only be remedied by defining "liberty" more broadly as "the state of being unconstrained by other persons from doing what one is able to do." If we apply this revised definition to the previous example, we find that people's liberty to hear Beethoven's Fifth Symphony would be restricted even if they did not want to hear it (and even if, perchance, they did not want to be unconstrained by others) because other people would still be constraining them from doing what they are able to do.

Confident that problems of defining liberty can be overcome in some satisfactory manner, libertarians go on to characterize their moral and political ideal as requiring that each person should have the greatest amount of liberty commensurate with the same liberty for all. From this ideal, libertarians claim that a number of more specific requirements, in particular a right to life, a right to freedom of speech, press, and assembly, and a right to property can be derived.

It is important to note that the libertarian's right to life is not a right to receive from others the goods and resources necessary for preserving one's life; it is simply a right not to be killed. So understood, the right to life is not a right to receive welfare. In fact, there are no welfare rights in the libertarian view. Accordingly, the libertarian's understanding of the right to property is not a right to receive from others the goods and resources necessary for one's welfare, but rather a right to acquire goods and resources either by initial acquisition or by voluntary agreement.

Obviously, by defending rights such as these, libertarians can only support a limited role for government. That role is simply to prevent and punish initial acts of coercion—the only wrongful actions for libertarians.

Libertarians do not deny that it is a good thing for people to have sufficient goods and resources to meet at least their basic nutritional needs, but libertarians do deny that government has a duty to provide for such needs. Some good things, such as the provision of welfare to the needy, are requirements of charity rather than justice, libertarians claim. Accordingly, failure to make such provisions is neither blameworthy nor punishable.

In selection 18, I argue that a libertarian ideal of liberty, which appears to reject the rights of a welfare state, can be seen to support such rights through an application of the "ought" implies "can" principle to conflicts between the rich and the poor. In one interpretation, the principle supports such rights by favoring the liberty of the poor over the liberty of the rich. In another interpretation, the principle supports such rights by favoring a conditional right to property over an unconditional right to property. In either interpretation, what is crucial in the derivation of these rights is the claim that it would be unreasonable to ask the poor to deny their basic needs and accept anything less than these rights as the condition for their willing cooperation.

In contrast with libertarians, welfare liberals, such as John Rawls (selection 19), take contractual fairness to be the ultimate moral and political ideal and contend that the fundamental rights and duties in a society are those that people would agree to under fair conditions.

Note that welfare liberals do not say that the fundamental rights and duties in a society are those to which people actually do agree because these might not be fair at all. For example, people might agree to a certain system of fundamental rights and duties only because they have been forced to do so or because their only alternative is starving to death. Thus, actual agreement is not sufficient, nor is it even necessary, for determining an adequate conception of justice. According to welfare liberals, what is necessary and sufficient is that people would agree to such rights and duties under fair conditions.

But what are fair conditions? According to John Rawls, fair conditions can be expressed by an "original position" in which people are concerned to advance their own interests behind a "veil of ignorance." The effect of the veil of ignorance is to deprive people in the original position of the knowledge they would need to advance their own interests in ways that are morally arbitrary. Rawls presents the principles of justice he believes would be derived in the original position in two successive formulations. The first formulation is as follows:

I. Special conception of justice
   1. Each person is to have an equal right to the most extensive basic liberty compatible with a similar liberty for others.
   2. Social and economic inequalities are to be arranged so that they are (a) reasonably expected to be to everyone's advantage and (b) attached to positions and offices open to all.
II. General conception of justice
   All social values—liberty and opportunity, income and wealth, and the bases of self-respect—are to be distributed equally unless an unequal distribution of any or all of these values is to everyone's advantage.

Later these principles are more accurately formulated as:

I. Special conception of justice
   1. Each person is to have an equal right to the most extensive total system of equal basic liberties compatible with a similar system of liberty for all.
   2. Social and economic inequalities are to be arranged so that they are (a) to the greatest benefit of the least advantaged, consistent with the just savings principle and (b) attached to offices and positions open to all under conditions of fair equality of opportunity.
II. General conception of justice
   All social goods—liberty and opportunity, income and wealth, and the bases of self-respect—are to be distributed equally unless an unequal distribution of any or all of

these goods is to the advantage of the least favored.

Under both formulations, the general conception of justice differs from the special conception of justice by allowing trade-offs between liberty and other social goods. According to Rawls, persons in the original position would want the special conception of justice to be applied in place of the general conception of justice whenever social conditions allowed all representative persons to exercise their basic liberties.

Rawls holds that these principles of justice would be chosen in the original position because persons so situated would find it reasonable to follow the conservative dictates of a "maximin strategy" and thereby secure for themselves the highest minimum payoff.

Rawls's defense of a welfare liberal conception of justice has been challenged in a variety of ways. Some critics have endorsed Rawls's contractual approach while disagreeing with Rawls over what principles of justice would be derived thereby. These critics usually attempt to undermine the use of a maximin strategy in the original position.[18] Other critics, however, have found fault with the contractual approach itself. Libertarians, for example, have challenged the moral adequacy of the very ideal of contractual fairness.

This second challenge to the ideal of contractual fairness is potentially the more damaging because, if valid, it would force supporters to embrace some other political ideal. This challenge, however, fails if it can be shown that the libertarian's own ideal of liberty, when correctly interpreted, leads to much the same practical requirements as are usually associated with the welfare liberal's ideal of contractual fairness, as I attempt to do in selection 18.

According to R. M. Hare (selection 20), one way to avoid the challenges that have been directed at the welfare liberal ideal of contractual fairness is to begin with an account of the logical properties of moral judgments, that is, their universalizability and their prescriptivity. Moral judgments are said to be universalizable in the same sense in which descriptive judgments are universalizable. If I say that something is red or solid, then, according to Hare, I am committed to the view that anything that is like it in the relevant respects would also be red or solid. Similarly, if I say that I ought to imprison A in order to make her pay her debt, then I am committed to the view that others in similar circumstances ought to imprison debtors in order to make them pay their debts. For Hare, a moral judgment is universalizable in the sense that it "logically commits the speaker to making a similar judgment about anything which is exactly like the subject of the original judgment or like it in the relevant respects. The relevant respects are those which formed the grounds of the original judgment."[19] By virtue of their prescriptivity, moral judgments are said to entail imperatives and normally lead to action from which it follows that, "if a man does what he says he ought not to, though perfectly able to resist the temptation to do it, then there is something wrong with what he says, as well as with what he does."[20] Thus, in Hare's view, a moral judgment not only presupposes a principle (the universalizability requirement), it also leads to action (the prescriptivity requirement).

Hare contends that the logical properties of moral judgments require equal consideration of the interests of all the affected parties and thereby secure the same impartiality as Rawls's veil of ignorance.[21] But even granting the usefulness of Hare's distinction between level 1 moral principles (for use in everyday moral thinking) and level 2 principles (arrived at under ideal conditions of knowledge and reflection), there is a problem with Hare's reformulation of Rawls's original position to arrive at acceptable level 1 moral principles. According to Hare, all that is needed in the original position to secure impartiality is "an economical veil" of ignorance that only deprives persons so situated of the knowledge of each person's particular nature and circumstances (including the knowledge of

whether they are contemporaries) while giving them complete knowledge of the course of history and the present conditions of society, as well as unlimited general information.[22] Confident that this economical view is sufficient for impartiality, Hare sees no justification for Rawls's thicker veil of ignorance, which also deprives persons in the original position of the knowledge of the course of history and the present conditions of society.

Yet consider the choice facing persons behind Hare's economical veil. Persons behind Hare's economical veil with their knowledge of the course of history and the present conditions of society could determine when it was possible to secure considerable utility for the overwhelming majority in society by enslaving or denying basic rights to certain minority groups. They could decide when the possibility of turning up as members of certain disadvantaged minority groups themselves would be an acceptable risk, in virtue of the high probability of their belonging to the majority. As a result, it would be in the interest of persons behind Hare's economical veil to choose principles that denied the basic needs and desires of certain minority groups when this benefited the overwhelming majority in society. In contrast, Rawls's decision procedure firmly guarantees basic rights to minorities. The thicker veil of ignorance in Rawls's theory deprives persons in the original position of the knowledge that is necessary to assess with confidence the probabilities of their being in particular positions in society, thus making it in their interest to secure a high minimum for each and every person in society.

Nevertheless, resolving the debates among libertarians and welfare liberals will not provide an acceptable moral and political ideal— at least not if socialists are correct. Socialists maintain that libertarians and welfare liberals both fail (although to varying degrees) to recognize the ultimate moral significance of an ideal of equality.

More specifically, socialists defend an ideal that calls for equality of need fulfillment. As Kai Nielson contends in selection 21, radical egalitarianism is justified because it produces the conditions for the most extensive satisfaction of the needs of everyone.

At first hearing, this ideal might sound simply crazy to someone brought up in a capitalist society. The obvious problem is how to get persons to put forth their best effort if income will be distributed on the basis of individual need rather than individual contribution.

The socialist answer is to make the work that must be done enjoyable in itself, as much as is possible. As a result, people will want to do the work they are capable of doing because they find it intrinsically rewarding. For a start, socialists might try to convince workers to accept lower salaries for presently existing jobs that are intrinsically rewarding. For example, they might ask top executives to work for $300,000 a year rather than $600,000. Yet socialists ultimately hope to make all jobs intrinsically as rewarding as possible so that, after people are no longer working primarily for external rewards when making their best contributions to society, distribution can proceed on the basis of need.

Socialists propose to implement their ideal of equality by giving workers democratic control over the workplace. They believe that if workers have more to say about how they do their work, they will find their work intrinsically more rewarding. As a consequence, they will be more motivated to work since their work itself will be meeting their needs. Socialists also believe that extending democracy to the workplace will necessarily lead to socialization of the means of production and the end of private property.

However, even with democratic control of the workplace, some jobs, such as collecting garbage or changing bedpans, probably can't be made intrinsically rewarding. Now what socialists propose to do with respect to such jobs is to divide them up in some equitable manner. Some people might, for example, collect garbage one day a week and then work at intrinsically rewarding jobs for the rest of the week. Others would change bedpans or do some other slop job one day a week and then work at an intrinsically rewarding job the other days of the week. By making jobs intrinsically as rewarding as possible, in part through democratic control of the workplace and an equitable assignment of unrewarding tasks, socialists believe people will contribute according to their ability even when distribution proceeds according to need.

Finally, it is important to note that the socialist ideal of equality does not accord with what exists in such countries as the Soviet Union or Albania. Judging the acceptability of the socialist ideal of equality by what takes place in those countries would be as unfair as judging the acceptability of the libertarian ideal of liberty by what takes place in countries like Chile or South Africa where citizens are arrested and imprisoned without cause. By analogy, it would be like judging the merits of college football by the way Vanderbilt's or Northwestern's teams play rather than by the way Alabama's or Notre Dame's teams play. Actually, a fairer comparison would be to judge the socialist ideal of liberty by what takes place in countries like Sweden or Yugoslavia and to judge the libertarian ideal of liberty by what takes place in the United States. Even these comparisons, however, are not wholly appropriate because none of these countries fully conforms to those ideals.

To justify the ideal of equality, Kai Nielson argues that it is required by liberty or at least by a fair distribution of liberty. By "liberty" Nielsen means both "positive liberty to receive certain goods" and "negative liberty not to be interfered with," so his argument from liberty will not have much weight with libertarians, who only value negative liberty. Rather, his argument is directed primarily at welfare liberals, who value both positive and negative liberty as well as a fair distribution of liberty.

Another basic difficulty with Nielson's socialist solution to the problem of distributive justice concerns the proclaimed necessity of abolishing private property and socializing the means of production. It seems perfectly possible to give workers more control over their workplace while at the same time the means of production remain privately owned. Of course, private ownership would have a somewhat different character in a society with democratic control of the workplace, but it need not cease to be private ownership. After all, private ownership would also have a somewhat different character in a society where private holdings, and hence bargaining power, were distributed more equally than is found in most capitalist societies, yet it would not cease to be private ownership. Accordingly, we could imagine a society where the means of production are privately owned but where—because ownership is so widely dispersed throughout the society (e.g., nearly everyone owns ten shares of major industrial stock and no one more than twenty shares) and because of the degree of democratic control of the workplace—many of the valid criticisms socialists make of existing capitalist societies would no longer apply.

Another prominent moral and political ideal defended by contemporary philosophers is the communitarian ideal of the common good. As one might expect, many defenders of this ideal regard it as rooted in Aristolelian moral theory. Like Aristotle, communitarians endorse a fundamental contrast between human beings as they are and human beings as they could be if they realized their essential nature. Ethics is then viewed as a science that enables human beings to understand how they can make the transition from the former state to the latter. This view of ethics requires some account of potency to act and some account of the essence of human beings and the end or telos they seek. Moreover, for human beings to make this transition from potency to act, a particular set of virtues is needed, and people who fail to acquire these virtues cannot realize their true nature and reach their true end.

According to John Finnis, the common good is a set of conditions that enables the members of communities to attain for themselves the basic goods for the sake of which they have reason to collaborate with each other in their communities.[23] Finnis characterizes these basic goods as life, knowledge, play, aesthetic experience, friendship, religion, and practical reasonableness. Any other goods we might recognize and pursue, Finnis argues, will turn out to represent or be constituted by some or all of these basic goods.

In pursuing these basic goods, Finnis claims that we must adhere to a number of requirements of practical reasonableness, the most important of which are the following:

1. No arbitrary preferences among these basic goods.
2. Consequences should have limited relevance in moral decision making.
3. Every basic good must be respected in every act.

In large part, Finnis defends these requirements by attacking utilitarianism of the sort defended by R. M. Hare in selection 20. Finnis seems to think that once utilitarianism is seen to be defective as a moral theory, the merits of his own view become apparent.

Finnis also contrasts his own account of basic human goods with Rawls's thin theory of the good. In Rawls's theory, basic human goods are generally useful means for the pursuit of whatever ends one may have. For Finnis, basic human goods are the ends for which we strive. But while this contrast does exist, there seems to be no reason why both Rawls and Finnis could not incorporate each other's account of basic human goods without affecting any substantial change in their conceptions of justice.

Where Finnis and Rawls do seem to disagree, however, is not with respect to the nature of basic human goods themselves but rather with respect to the principles that apply to the pursuit of such goods. In particular, Finnis's requirements of practical reasonableness rule out the sacrifice of any basic good to achieve a greater total of basic goods. Thus, for Finnis, one may never do evil that good may come of it. By contrast, persons in Rawls's original position would reject an absolute prohibition on doing evil that good may come of it because there are cases where the evil or intended harm is either

1. trivial (e.g., as in the case of stepping on someone's foot to get out of a crowded subway),
2. easily reparable (e.g., as in the case of lying to a temporarily depressed friend to keep her from committing suicide), or
3. sufficiently outweighed by the consequences of the action (e.g., as in the case of shooting 1 of 200 civilian hostages to prevent in the only way possible the execution of all 200).

Finnis's main justification for maintaining an absolute prohibition at least in the most morally difficult cases is to appeal to divine command theory.[24] Unfortunately, when divine command theory is used to resolve morally difficult cases, it can only do so by embracing an anything-could-be-right-if-God-commanded-it view, with all the absurdities that are traditionally associated with that view.[25] Consequently, there just does not appear to be any reasonable alternative to a nonabsolutist stance that allows moral requirements to bend but not break in difficult cases.

In the final reading of this section (selection 23), Annette C. Baier draws on the work of Carol Gilligan to suggest that women favor an ethic of love and caring in contrast to the ethic of obligation favored by men.[26] In Gilligan's own work, the contrast that is drawn is between a caring perspective and a justice perspective. According to Gilligan, these two perspectives are analogous to the alternative ways we tend to organize ambiguous perceptual patterns, for example, seeing a figure first as a square then as a diamond depending upon its relationship to the surrounding frame. More specifically, she claims:

From a justice perspective, the self as moral agent stands as the figure against a ground of social relationships, judging the conflicting claims of self and others against a standard of equality or equal respect (the Categorical Imperative, the Golden Rule). From a care perspective, the relationship becomes the figure, defining self and others. Within the context of relationship, the self as a moral agent perceives and responds to the perception of need. The shift in moral perspective is manifest by a change in the moral question from "What is just?" to "How to respond?"[27]

Using these perspectives as classificatory tools, Gilligan reports that 69 percent of her sample raised considerations of both justice and care while 67 percent focused their attention on one set of concerns (with focus defined as 75 percent or more of the considerations raised pertaining either to justice or to care).[28] Significantly, with one exception, all of the men who focused, focused on justice. The women were divided, with roughly one third focusing on care and one third on justice.

The conclusion that Gilligan wants to draw from this research is that the care perspective is an equally valid moral perspective that has tended to be disregarded in moral theory and psychological research alike because of male bias. To determine whether this conclusion is justified, however, we would need to get clearer about the contrast between the two perspectives. If women and men differ with regard to the perspectives on which they tend to focus, it must be possible to clearly distinguish between the two perspectives. Otherwise bias could enter into the researcher's classification of people's reasons as belonging to one or the other perspective.[29]

Yet rather than try to further distinguish the perspectives, Baier attempts to integrate them under the notion of "appropriate trust." Baier sketches how a theory that employs the notion of appropriate trust might deal with various topics in a way that brings together the concerns of both perspectives. In a subsequent article, Baier goes on to define a relationship of appropriate trust as one that is based upon neither threats nor the successful coverup of breaches of trust.[30]

One advantage of Baier's approach is that it fits nicely into a general reconciliationist strategy with respect to alternative ethical perspectives. Such a strategy attempts to show that the practical differences between alternative ethical perspectives are not as great as might initially seem to be the case. In selection 18, I pursued this strategy with respect to the libertarian and welfare liberal perspectives, and it may be possible to do the same for the other ethical perspectives we have considered in this section.[31]

MORAL DILEMMAS AND MORAL REALISM

Yet to many philosophers any strategy of reconciling alternative ethical perspectives would be undermined by the existence of moral dilemmas. The existence of moral dilemmas is also thought by some philosophers to be incompatible with moral realism. In this section, the readings focus on each of these topics and discuss their implications for ethical theory.

With respect to moral dilemmas, the key question is whether there are any. Consider the following definition:

A moral dilemma is a situation in which one morally ought to do A and morally ought to do B but cannot do both because doing A precludes doing B.

Given this definition, you would be facing a moral dilemma if you ought to take care of your ailing mother and you ought to pursue your career but given the circumstances you cannot do both.

In selection 24, Ruth Barcan Marcus is concerned with showing that moral dilemmas, so understood, do not presuppose inconsistent moral rules. Marcus argues that moral rules can be consistent yet compatible with the existence of moral dilemmas provided that there is some possible world in which they are obeyable in all circumstances in that world. Of course, this allows for the possibility that in the actual world moral

rules may conflict and thereby give rise to moral dilemmas. Since when faced with a moral dilemma, one cannot do all that one ought, Marcus also sees the need to reject the standard "ought" implies "can" principle in favor of the following:

One ought to act in such a way that if one ought to do A and one ought to do B then one can do both A and B.

However, this principle is only a regulative principle and cannot always be acted upon.

Marcus's main reason for favoring the existence of moral dilemmas is that she thinks that it is often appropriate when faced with a dilemma to feel guilt or remorse with regard to the action not performed. Such a response, Marcus thinks, would have to be regarded as inappropriate by those who reject moral dilemmas. Yet Earl Conee (selection 25), who denies the existence of moral dilemmas, allows that guilt or remorse can be appropriate in just the kind of situations Marcus discusses. Consequently, while denying that there are moral dilemmas, Conee seems to take away Marcus's main reason for affirming their existence.

But what reason does Conee have for denying that there are moral dilemmas? Conee does find fault with the principle that Marcus substitutes for the "ought" implies "can" principle. Conee argues that it is not the case that we should always avoid putting ourselves in situations where our duties will conflict. He gives the example of a spy whose success depends upon placing herself in situations where her (prima facie) duties will conflict. Yet Conee's main reason for denying the existence of moral dilemmas is that he believes that in situations of moral conflict between doing A and doing B either (1) S morally ought, all things considered, to do A or (2) S morally ought, all things considered, to do B or (3) S morally ought, all things considered, to do A or B but not both. Alan Donagan in selection 26 also denies the existence of moral dilemmas for the very same reason. He simply adds that with respect to alternative 3 there can be nonmoral considerations that break the moral tie between doing A and doing B.

In contrast, those who like Marcus think that there are moral dilemmas hold that in situations of moral conflict between doing A and doing B it is the case that (1) S morally ought, all things considered, to do A *and* (2) S morally ought, all things considered, to do B. Moreover, using a principle of agglomeration, 1 and 2 imply 3—S ought, all things considered, to do A and B. And given our definition of a moral dilemma, one cannot do A and B; one can only do A or B. That is why Marcus rejects the "ought" implies "can" principle. However, other philosophers have opted to reject the principle of agglomeration instead.[32] But Donagan objects to this move on the grounds that it mistakenly models morality after a system of positive laws. Donagan argues that laws that derive from political authorities can conflict in ways that moral rules cannot.

Yet overall the differences between those who affirm the existence of moral dilemmas and those who deny their existence may not be as great as they seem. This is because those who affirm and those who deny the existence of moral dilemmas can still agree that if you were faced with a conflict between caring for your ailing mother and pursuing your career, one alternative may be preferable to the other. For example, both Marcus and Donagan contend that there can be nonmoral reasons for such a preference. The crucial difference is that only those who affirm the existence of moral dilemmas maintain that there is an, all things considered, moral requirement to do the nonpreferred alternative.

Of course, if there are moral dilemmas, there would be no *moral* reason for doing A rather than doing B, even if there are nonmoral reasons for doing so. So there would be no alternative that was clearly *morally* preferable. Yet unless moral realism is understood to preclude the possibility of "moral ties," it would certainly be compatible with the existence of moral dilemmas. So the question of moral realism—that is, the question of whether there are moral facts or objective moral values that are accessible to us—cannot be answered by determining whether there are moral dilemmas.[33]

Nevertheless, in selection 27, J. L. Mackie advances two other arguments against moral realism. The first is an argument from relativity (that the variation in moral codes is best explained by the subjectivity of values). The second is an argument from queerness (that objective values would have to be metaphysically odd because they would have to be necessarily action guiding and epistemologically odd because they would have to be known by a special intuition).

In selection 28, David O. Brink responds to each of these arguments in turn. In response to the argument from relativity, Brink points out (1) that many moral disputes are rooted in resolvable nonmoral disagreements, (2) that a coherentist strategy has assets for reaching agreement not recognized by Mackie, and (3) that moral realism need not presuppose that all moral disputes are resolvable, even in principle. In response to the argument from queerness, Brink denies that moral facts are necessarily action-guiding. In fact, Brink rejects all forms of internalism (the view that the recognition of moral facts is internally related to the performance of human actions). Brink claims that only some form of externalism (the view that the recognition of moral facts is externally related to the performance of human actions) can provide an adequate understanding of morality. However, internalism and externalism come in many forms, and while the extreme form of internalism that Mackie uses to characterize morality is clearly objectionable for the reasons Brink gives, weaker forms of internalism, like the form defended by Stephen Darwall in selection 13, need not be. In fact, many so-called internalists and externalists seem to hold roughly the same view about the relationship between the recognition of moral facts and the performance of human actions. So Brink's criticism of Mackie needs to be separated from his rejection of all forms of internalism.

In selection 29, Gilbert Harman proposes still another argument against moral realism. Harman compares the role of observation in ethics to its role in science. He argues that to explain the occurrence of observations that support scientific theories we need to make assumptions about physical facts, but that to explain the occurrence of observations that support moral theories we do not need to make any comparable assumptions about moral facts. Rather with respect to moral theories, it suffices to make assumptions about people's psychologies, in particular the moral sensibilities they happen to have. For example, when a physicist sees a vapor trail in a cloud chamber and judges, "There goes a proton," our best explanation of this observation, Harman claims, appeals beyond people's psychologies to a physical fact about the world, that is, that there was a proton going through a cloud chamber causing a vapor trail. By contrast, when we see children setting a cat on fire and judge, "That is wrong," our best explanation of this observation, Harman claims, need not appeal to any moral facts about the world beyond people's moral sensibilities.

In the final reading of this section (selection 30), Nicholas L. Sturgeon criticizes Harman's argument against moral realism. Sturgeon claims that moral facts do play a role in explaining our moral observations. For example, the fact that Hitler was depraved is appealed to in order to support our judgment that Hitler's behavior was morally wrong. To account for this judgment, we do not appeal to our moral sensibilities alone. Of course, our appeal to the fact that Hitler was depraved to explain our moral observations may be mistaken. But in the same way our appeal to the fact there was a photon to explain our scientific observations may be mistaken. Thus, Sturgeon concludes that, as far as Harman's argument is concerned, moral realism is on a par with scientific realism.

In more recent work, however, Harman no longer contends that appeals to moral facts are "totally irrelevant" to the explanation of our moral beliefs and observations.[34]

Nevertheless, he still rejects moral realism because he contends that our moral claims cannot be empirically tested in all the ways scientific claims can be empirically tested, at least until some naturalistic analysis of moral terms has been provided. This is because in the absence of some such naturalistic analysis, Harman contends that it is always possible to reject moral realism by appealing to an emotivist analysis of our moral claims. In response, Sturgeon has argued that no naturalistic analysis is needed in order to support moral realism.[35] Rather he claims that the kinds of moral explanations we endorse are sufficient grounds for moral realism. In fact, Sturgeon contends that any naturalistic analysis of moral terms would presuppose the adequacy of just such explanations.

Yet even if Sturgeon is right that a naturalistic analysis of moral terms is not needed to show how moral facts figure in the explanations we endorse, such an analysis would certainly be helpful to turn aside critiques that do not begin by assuming that there are moral facts.[36] For this reason, the earlier debate between naturalists and nonnaturalists discussed in the readings in Section II is clearly relevant to a resolution of the debate over moral realism.

It may also be the case that some headway can be made in both debates by beginning with a partial analysis sufficient to distinguish a moral from a nonmoral perspective.[37] For example, consider the following:

Moral requirements are such that they are not contrary to reason to ask everyone affected to accept.

This analysis has its roots in an interpretation of the "ought" implies "can" principle that has been thought to be constitutive of a moral perspective. In fact, to reject this principle, so interpreted, is to imply that people can be morally required to do what is contrary to reason for them to do, which is absurd. Of course, accepting this analysis may not suffice to resolve the debate between utilitarians and contractarians.[38] But, as I have argued in selection 18, it should suffice to move libertarians to endorse different practical requirements from those they usually favor. Moreover, there may be other ways to resolve the debate between contractarians and utilitarians over practical requirements.[39] In any case, this seems to be at least one promising way to carry on the debate in contemporary ethics over the nature of ethics, its justification, and its requirements.

NOTES

1. G. E. Moore, "A Reply to My Critics," in *The Philosophy of G. E. Moore,* ed. Paul Schilpp, 3rd ed. (La Salle: Open Court, 1968), 582ff.

2. G. E. Moore, *Principia Ethica* (London: Cambridge University Press, 1903), 40–1.

3. G. E. Moore, "The Conception of Intrinsic Value," in *Philosophical Studies* (Totowa: Littlefield, Adams & Col, 1968), 260ff.

4. Notice that when something is a tool answering to human purposes, what is perfective of its nature will also answer to those purposes. Notice also that things that might be considered intrinsically good, such as pleasure, are so regarded because they are perfective of the nature of a thing.

5. Charles L. Stevenson, *Ethics and Language* (New Haven: Yale University Press, 1944), chapter IX.

6. J. R. Searle, "Reply to 'The Promising Game,'" in *Readings in Contemporary Ethical Theory,* ed. Kenneth Pahel and Marvin Schiller (Englewood Cliffs: Prentice-Hall, 1970), 182.

7. R. M. Hare, "Descriptivism," *Proceedings of the British Academy,* 49 (1963), 117–134.

8. Ibid.

9. Ibid. See also selection 6.

10. Stephen Toulmin, *An Examination of the Place of Reason in Ethics* (Cambridge: Cambridge University Press, 1950), 137.

11. Ibid., 98–101, 160–3.

12. David Gauthier, *Morals by Agreement* (Oxford: Oxford University Press, 1986), 169.

13. Ibid., 174.

14. Ibid., 200.

15. Ibid., 204.

16. James P. Sterba, *How to Make People Just* (Totowa: Rowman and Littlefield, 1988), chapter 11.

17. Ibid.

18. See, for example, James P. Sterba, "Distributive Justice," *American Journal of Jurisprudence* (1977): 55–79 and John C. Harsanyi, *Essays on Ethics, Social Behavior and Scientific Behavior* (Boston: D. Reidel Publishing, 1976), 37–85.

19. R. M. Hare, *Freedom and Reason* (Oxford: Oxford University Press, 1963), 139–140.

20. Ibid., 82–83.

21. R. M. Hare, "Rawls' Theory of Justice I and II," *Philosophical Quarterly* 23 (1973), 144–55, 241–52.

22. Ibid., 150–1, 155.

23. John Finnis, *Natural Law and Natural Right* (Oxford: Clarenden Press, 1980), 165.

24. Ibid., especially Part 3.

25. See John Chandler, "Divine Command Theories and the Appeal to Love," *American Philosophical Quarterly* 22 (1985): 231–9.

26. Carol Gilligan, *In a Different Voice* (Cambridge: Harvard University Press, 1982); "Moral Orientation and Moral Development," in *Women and Moral Theory,* ed. Eva Kittay and Diana Meyers (Totowa: Rowman and Littlefield, 1987), 19–36.

27. Gilligan, "Moral Orientation and Moral Development," 23.

28. Ibid., 5.

29. For more discussion of this point, see Sterba, *How to Make People Just,* chapter 12.

30. Annette Baier, "Trust and Antitrust," *Ethics* (1986), 255.

31. Sterba, *How to Make People Just,* Part II.

32. Bernard Williams, "Ethical Consistency," in *Problems of the Self* (Cambridge: Cambridge University Press, 1973), 166–86.

33. For an opposing view, see Bernard Williams, "Consistency and Realism," in *Problems of the Self,* 187–206; Walter Sinnott-Armstrong, "Moral Realisms and Moral Dilemmas," *The Journal of Philosophy* 85 (1987): 263–276.

34. Gilbert Harman, "Moral Explanations of Natural Facts—Can Moral Claims be Tested Against Moral Reality?" *The Southern Journal of Philosophy* 24, Supplement (1986): 57–68.

35. Nicholas L. Sturgeon, "Harman on Moral Explanations of Natural Facts," *The Southern Journal of Philosophy* 24, Supplement (1986): 69–78.

36. It is unclear whether Harman's critique assumes the existence of moral facts. However, Sturgeon interprets it as assuming the existence of such facts.

37. For further discussion, see James P.

Sterba, *Morality in Practice,* 2nd. ed. (Belmont: Wadsworth Publishing, 1988), 1–13.

38. For an argument that it does, see T. M. Scanlon, "Contractualism and Utilitarianism," in *Utilitarianism and Beyond,* ed. Amartya Sen and Bernard Williams (Cambridge: Cambridge University Press, 1982), 103–128.

39. Sterba, *How To Make People Just,* Part 2.

1
THE SUBJECT-MATTER OF ETHICS

G. E. Moore

... But our question 'What is good?' may have still another meaning. We may mean to ask, not what thing or things are good, but how 'good' is to be defined. This is an enquiry which belongs only to Ethics, not to Casuistry; and this is the enquiry which will occupy us first.

It is an enquiry to which most special attention should be directed; since this question, how 'good' is to be defined, is the most fundamental question in all Ethics. That which is meant by 'good' is, in fact, except its converse 'bad,' the *only* simple object of thought which is peculiar to Ethics. Its definition is, therefore, the most essential part in the definition of Ethics; and moreover a mistake with regard to it entails a far larger number of erroneous ethical judgments than any other. Unless this first question be fairly understood, and its true answer clearly recognised, the rest of Ethics is as good as useless from the point of view of systematic knowledge. True ethical judg-

ments, of the two kinds last dealt with, may indeed be made by those who do not know the answer to this question as well as by those who do; and it goes without saying that the two classes of people may lead equally good lives. But it is extremely unlikely that the *most general* ethical judgments will be equally valid, in the absence of a true answer to this question: I shall presently try to show that the gravest errors have been largely due to beliefs in a false answer. And, in any case, it is impossible that, till the answer to this question be known, any one should know *what is the evidence* for any ethical judgment whatsoever. But the main object of Ethics, as a systematic science, is to give correct *reasons* for thinking that this or that is good; and, unless this question be answered, such reasons cannot be given. Even, therefore, apart from the fact that a false answer leads to false conclusions, the present enquiry is a most necessary and important part of the science of Ethics.

What, then, is good? How is good to be defined? Now, it may be thought that this is a verbal question. A definition does indeed

From *Principia Ethica*, Cambridge University Press, 1903, pp. 5–17. Reprinted by permission.

often mean the expressing of one word's meaning in other words. But this is not the sort of definition I am asking for. Such a definition can never be of ultimate importance in any study except lexicography. If I wanted that kind of definition I should have to consider in the first place how people generally use the word 'good'; but my business is not with its proper usage, as established by custom. I should, indeed, be foolish, if I tried to use it for something which it did not usually denote: if, for instance, I were to announce that, whenever I used the word 'good,' I must be understood to be thinking of that object which is usually denoted by the word 'table.' I shall, therefore, use the word in the sense in which I think it is ordinarily used; but at the same time I am not anxious to discuss whether I am right in thinking that it is so used. My business is solely with that object or idea, which I hold, rightly or wrongly, that the word is generally used to stand for. What I want to discover is the nature of that object or idea, and about this I am extremely anxious to arrive at an agreement.

But, if we understand the question in this sense, my answer to it may seem a very disappointing one. If I am asked 'What is good?' my answer is that good is good, and that is the end of the matter. Or if I am asked 'How is good to be defined?' my answer is that it cannot be defined, and that is all I have to say about it. But disappointing as these answers may appear, they are of the very last importance. To readers who are familiar with philosophic terminology, I can express their importance by saying that they amount to this: That propositions about the good are all of them synthetic and never analytic; and that is plainly no trivial matter. And the same thing may be expressed more popularly, by saying that, if I am right, then nobody can foist upon us such an axiom as that 'Pleasure is the only good' or that 'The good is the desired' on the pretence that this is 'the very meaning of the word.'

Let us, then, consider this position. My point is that 'good' is a simple notion, just as 'yellow' is a simple notion; that, just as you cannot, by any manner of means, explain to any one who does not already know it, what yellow is, so you cannot explain what good is. Definitions of the kind that I was asking for, definitions which describe the real nature of the object or notion denoted by a word, and which do not merely tell us what the word is used to mean, are only possible when the object or notion in question is something complex. You can give a definition of a horse, because a horse has many different properties and qualities, all of which you can enumerate. But when you have enumerated them all, when you have reduced a horse to his simplest terms, then you can no longer define those terms. They are simply something which you think of or perceive, and to any one who cannot think of or perceive them, you can never, by any definition, make their nature known. It may perhaps be objected to this that we are able to describe to others, objects which they have never seen or thought of. We can, for instance, make a man understand what a chimaera is, although he has never heard of one or seen one. You can tell him that it is an animal with a lioness's head and body, with a goat's head growing from the middle of its back, and with a snake in place of a tail. But here the object which you are describing is a complex object; it is entirely composed of parts, with which we are all perfectly familiar—a snake, a goat, a lioness; and we know, too, the manner in which these parts are to be put together, because we know what is meant by the middle of a lioness's back, and where her tail is wont to grow. And so it is with all objects, not previously known, which we are able to define: they are all complex; all composed of parts, which may themselves, in the first instance, be capable of similar definition, but which must in the end be reducible to simplest parts, which can no longer be defined. But yellow and good, we say, are not complex: they are notions of that simple kind, out of which definitions are composed and with which the power of further defining ceases.

When we say, as Webster says, 'The definition of horse is "A hoofed quadruped of the genus Equus,"' we may, in fact, mean three different things. (1) We may mean merely: 'When I say "horse," you are to understand that I am talking about a hoofed quadruped of the genus Equus.' This might be called the arbitrary verbal definition: and I do not mean that good is indefinable in that sense. (2) We may mean, as Webster ought to mean: 'When most English people say "horse," they mean a hoofed quadruped of the genus Equus.' This may be called the verbal definition proper, and I do not say that good is indefinable in this sense either; for it is certainly possible to discover how people use a word: otherwise, we could never have known that 'good' may be translated by 'gut' in German and by 'bon' in French. But (3) we may, when we define horse, mean something much more important. We may mean that a certain object, which we all of us know, is composed in a certain manner: that it has four legs, a head, a heart, a liver, etc., etc., all of them arranged in definite relations to one another. It is in this sense that I deny good to be definable. I say that it is not composed of any parts, which we can substitute for it in our minds when we are thinking of it. We might think just as clearly and correctly about a horse, if we thought of all its parts and their arrangement instead of thinking of the whole: we could, I say, think how a horse differed from a donkey just as well, just as truly, in this way, as now we do, only not so easily; but there is nothing whatsoever which we could so substitute for good; and that is what I mean, when I say that good is indefinable.

But I am afraid I still have not removed the chief difficulty which may prevent acceptance of the proposition that good is indefinable. I do not mean to say that *the* good, that which is good, is thus indefinable; if I did think so, I should not be writing on Ethics, for my main object is to help towards discovering that definition. It is just because I think there will be less risk of error in our search for a definition of 'the good,' that I am now insisting that *good* is indefinable. I must try to explain the difference between these two. I suppose it

may be granted that 'good' is an adjective. Well 'the good,' 'that which is good,' must therefore be the substantive to which the adjective 'good' will apply: it must be the whole of that to which the adjective will apply, and the adjective must *always* truly apply to it. But if it is that to which the adjective will apply, it must be something different from that adjective itself; and the whole of that something different, whatever it is, will be our definition of *the* good. Now it may be that this something will have other adjectives, beside 'good,' that will apply to it. It may be full of pleasure, for example; it may be intelligent: and if these two adjectives are really part of its definition, then it will certainly be true, that pleasure and intelligence are good. And many people appear to think that, if we say 'Pleasure and intelligence are good,' or if we say 'Only pleasure and intelligence are good,' we are defining 'good.' Well, I cannot deny that propositions of this nature may sometimes be called definitions; I do not know well enough how the word is generally used to decide upon this point. I only wish it to be understood that that is not what I mean when I say there is no possible definition of good, and that I shall not mean this if I use the word again. I do most fully believe that some true proposition of the form 'Intelligence is good and intelligence alone is good' can be found; if none could be found, our definition of *the* good would be impossible. As it is, I believe *the* good to be definable; and yet I still say that good itself is indefinable.

'Good,' then, if we mean by it the quality which we assert to belong to a thing, when we say that the thing is good, is incapable of any definition, in the most important sense of that word. The most important sense of 'definition' is that in which a definition states what are the parts which invariably compose a certain whole; and in this sense 'good' has no definition because it is simple and has no parts. It is one of those innumerable objects of thought which are themselves incapable of definition, because they are the ultimate terms by reference to which whatever *is* capable of definition must be defined. That there must be an indefinite number of such terms is obvious, on reflection; since we cannot define anything except by analysis, which, when carried as far as it will go, refers us to something, which is simply different from anything else, and which by that ultimate difference explains the peculiarity of the whole which we are defining: for every whole contains some parts which are common to other wholes also. There is, therefore, no intrinsic difficulty in the contention that 'good' denotes a simple and indefinable quality. There are many other instances of such qualities.

Consider yellow, for example. We may try to define it, by describing its physical equivalent; we may state what kind of light-vibrations must stimulate the normal eye, in order that we may perceive it. But a moment's reflection is sufficient to shew that those light-vibrations are not themselves what we mean by yellow. *They* are not what we perceive. Indeed we should never have been able to discover their existence, unless we had first been struck by the patent difference of quality between the different colours. The most we can be entitled to say of those vibrations is that they are what corresponds in space to the yellow which we actually perceive.

Yet a mistake of this simple kind has commonly been made about 'good.' It may be true that all things which are good are *also* something else, just as it is true that all things that are yellow produce a certain kind of vibration in the light. And it is a fact, that Ethics aims at discovering what are those other properties belonging to all things which are good. But far too many philosophers have thought that when they named those other properties they were actually defining good; that these properties, in fact, were simply not 'other,' but absolutely and entirely the same with goodness. This view I propose to call the 'naturalistic fallacy" and of it I shall now endeavour to dispose.

Let us consider what it is such philosophers say. And first it is to be noticed that they do not agree among themselves. They not only say that they are right as to what good is, but they endeavour to prove that other people who say that it is something else, are wrong. One, for instance, will affirm that good is pleasure, another, perhaps, that good is that which is desired; and each of these will argue eagerly to prove that the other is wrong. But how is that possible? One of them says that good is nothing but the object of desire, and at the same time tries to prove that it is not pleasure. But from his first assertion, that good just means the object of desire, one of two things that must follow as regards his proof:

(1) He may be trying to prove that the object of desire is not pleasure. But, if this be all, where is his Ethics? The position he is maintaining is merely a psychological one. Desire is something which occurs in our minds, and pleasure is something else which also occurs; and our would-be ethical philosopher is merely holding that the latter is not the object of the former. But what has that to do with the question in dispute? His opponent held the ethical position that pleasure was the good, and although he should prove a million times over the psychological proposition that pleasure is not the object of desire, he is no nearer proving his opponent to be wrong. The position is like this. One man says a triangle is a circle: another replies 'A triangle is a straight line, and I will prove to you that I am right: *for*' (this is the only argument) 'a straight line is not a circle.' 'That is quite true,' the other may reply; 'but nevertheless a triangle is a circle, and you have said nothing whatever to prove the contrary. What is proved is that one of us is wrong, for we agree that a triangle cannot be both a straight line and a circle: but which is wrong, there can be no earthly means of proving, since you define triangle as straight line and I define it as a circle'—Well, that is one alternative which any naturalistic Ethics has to face; if good is *defined* as something else, it is then impossible either to prove that any other definition is wrong or even to deny such definition.

(2) The other alternative will scarcely be more welcome. It is that the discussion is

after all a verbal one. When A says 'Good means pleasant' and B says 'Good means desired,' they may merely wish to assert that most people have used the word for what is pleasant and for what is desired respectively. And this is quite an interesting subject for discussion: only it is not a whit more an ethical discussion than the last was. Nor do I think that any exponent of naturalistic Ethics would be willing to allow that this was all he meant. They are all so anxious to persuade us that what they call the good is what we really ought to do. 'Do, pray, act so, because the word "good" is generally used to denote actions of this nature': such, on this view, would be the substance of their teaching. And in so far as they tell us how we ought to act, their teaching is truly ethical, as they mean it to be. But how perfectly absurd is the reason they would give for it! 'You are to do this, because most people use a certain word to denote conduct such as this.' 'You are to say the thing which is not, because most people call it lying.' That is an argument just as good!—My dear sirs, what we want to know from you as ethical teachers, is not how people use a word; it is not even, what kind of actions they approve, which the use of this word 'good' may certainly imply: what we want to know is simply what *is* good. We may indeed agree that what most people do think good, is actually so; we shall at all events be glad to know their opinions: but when we say their opinions about what *is* good, we do mean what we say; we do not care whether they call that thing which they mean 'horse' or 'table' or 'chair,' 'gut' or 'bon' or 'ἀγαθίς'; we want to know what it is that they so call. When they say 'Pleasure is good,' we cannot believe that they merely mean 'Pleasure is pleasure' and nothing more than that.

Suppose a man says 'I am pleased'; and suppose that is not a lie or a mistake but the truth. Well, if it is true, what does that mean? It means that his mind, a certain definite mind, distinguished by certain definite marks from all others, has at this moment a certain definite feeling called pleasure. 'Pleased' *means* nothing but having

pleasure, and though we may be more pleased or less pleased, and even, we may admit for the present, have one or another kind of pleasure; yet in so far as it is pleasure we have, whether there be more or less of it, and whether it be of one kind or another, what we have is one definite thing, absolutely undefinable, some one thing that is the same in all the various degrees and in all the various kinds of it that there may be. We may be able to say how it is related to other things: that, for example, it is in the mind, that it causes desire, that we are conscious of it, etc., etc. We can, I say, describe its relations to other things, but define it we can *not*. And if anybody tried to define pleasure for us as being any other natural object; if anybody were to say, for instance, that pleasure *means* the sensation of red, and were to proceed to deduce from that that pleasure is a colour, we should be entitled to laugh at him and to distrust his future statements about pleasure. Well, that would be the same fallacy which I have called the naturalistic fallacy. That 'pleased' does not mean 'having the sensation of red,' or anything else whatsoever, does not prevent us from understanding what it does mean. It is enough for us to know that 'pleased' does mean 'having the sensation of pleasure,' and though pleasure is absolutely indefinable, though pleasure is pleasure and nothing else whatever, yet we feel no difficulty in saying that we are pleased. The reason is, of course, that when I say 'I am pleased,' I do *not* mean that 'I' am the same thing as 'having pleasure.' And similarly no difficulty need be found in my saying that 'pleasure is good' and yet not meaning that 'pleasure' is the same thing as 'good,' that pleasure *means* good, and that good *means* pleasure. If I were to imagine that when I said 'I am pleased,' I meant that I was exactly the same thing as 'pleased,' I should not indeed call that a naturalistic fallacy, although it would be the same fallacy as I have called naturalistic with reference to Ethics. The reason for this is obvious enough. When a man confuses two natural objects with one another, defining the one by the other, if for instance, he confuses himself, who is one natural object, with 'pleased' or with 'pleasure' which are others, then there is no reason to call the fallacy naturalistic. But if he confuses 'good,' which is not in the same sense a natural object, with any natural object whatever, then there is a reason for calling that a naturalistic fallacy; its being made with regard to 'good' marks it as something quite specific, and this specific mistake deserves a name because it is so common. As for the reasons why good is not to be considered a natural object, they may be reserved for discussion in another place. But, for the present, it is sufficient to notice this: Even if it were a natural object, that would not alter the nature of the fallacy nor diminish its importance one whit. All that I have said about it would remain quite equally true: only the name which I have called it would not be so appropriate as I think it is. And I do not care about the name: what I do care about is the fallacy. It does not matter what we call it, provided we recognise it when we meet with it. It is to be met with in almost every book on Ethics; and yet it is not recognised: and that is why it is necessary to multiply illustrations of it, and convenient to give it a name. It is a very simple fallacy indeed. When we say that an orange is yellow, we do not think our statement binds us to hold that 'orange' means nothing else than 'yellow,' or that nothing can be yellow but an orange. Supposing the orange is also sweet! Does that bind us to say that 'sweet' is exactly the same thing as 'yellow,' that 'sweet' must be defined as 'yellow'? And supposing it be recognised that 'yellow' just means 'yellow' and nothing else whatever, does that make it any more difficult to hold that oranges are yellow? Most certainly it does not: on the contrary, it would be absolutely meaningless to say that oranges were yellow, unless yellow did in the end mean just 'yellow' and nothing else whatever—unless it was absolutely indefinable. We should not get any very clear notion about things, which are yellow—we should not get very far with our science, if we were bound to hold that everything which was yellow, *meant* exactly the same thing as yellow. We should find we had to hold that an orange was exactly the same thing as a stool, a piece of paper, a lemon, anything you like. We could prove any number of absurdities; but should we be the nearer to the truth? Why, then, should it be different with 'good'? Why, if good is good and indefinable, should I be held to deny that pleasure is good? Is there any difficulty in holding both to be true at once? On the contrary, there is no meaning in saying that pleasure is good, unless good is something different from pleasure. It is absolutely useless, so far as Ethics is concerned, to prove, as Mr Spencer tries to do, that increase of pleasure coincides with increase of life, unless good *means* something different from either life or pleasure. He might just as well try to prove that an orange is yellow by shewing that it always is wrapped up in paper.

In fact, if it is not the case that 'good' denotes something simple and indefinable, only two alternatives are possible: either it is a complex, a given whole, about the correct analysis of which there may be disagreement; or else it means nothing at all, and there is no such subject as Ethics. In general, however, ethical philosophers have attempted to define good, without recognising what such an attempt must mean. They actually use arguments which involve one or both of the absurdities considered above. We are, therefore, justified in concluding that the attempt to define good is chiefly due to want of clearness as to the possible nature of definition. There are, in fact, only two serious alternatives to be considered, in order to establish the conclusion that 'good' does denote a simple and indefinable notion. It might possibly denote a complex, as 'horse' does; or it might have no meaning at all. Neither of these possibilities has, however, been clearly conceived and seriously maintained, as such, by those who presume to define good; and both may be dismissed by a simple appeal to facts.

(1) The hypothesis that disagreement about the meaning of good is disagreement

with regard to the correct analysis of a given whole, may be most plainly seen to be incorrect by consideration of the fact that, whatever definition be offered, it may be always asked, with significance, of the complex so defined, whether it is itself good. To take, for instance, one of the more plausible, because one of the more complicated, of such proposed definitions, it may easily be thought, at first sight, that to be good may mean to be that which we desire to desire. Thus if we apply this definition to a particular instance and say 'When we think that A is good, we are thinking that A is one of the things which we desire to desire,' our proposition may seem quite plausible. But, if we carry the investigation further, and ask ourselves 'Is it good to desire to desire A?' it is apparent, on a little reflection, that this question is itself as intelligible, as the original question 'Is A good?'—that we are, in fact, now asking for exactly the same information about the desire to desire A, for which we formerly asked with regard to A itself. But it is also apparent that the meaning of this second question cannot be correctly analysed into 'Is the desire to desire A one of the things which we desire to desire?': we have not before our minds anything so complicated as the question 'Do we desire to desire to desire to desire A?' Moreover any one can easily convince himself by inspection that the predicate of this proposition— 'good'—is positively different from the notion of 'desiring to desire' which enters into its subject: 'That we should desire to desire A is good' is *not* merely equivalent to 'That A should be good is good.' It may indeed be true that what we desire to desire is always also good; perhaps, even the converse may be true: but it is very doubtful whether this is the case, and the mere fact that we understand very well what is meant by doubting it, shews clearly that we have two different notions before our minds.

(2) And the same consideration is sufficient to dismiss the hypothesis that 'good' has no meaning whatsoever. It is very natural to make the mistake of supposing that what is universally true is of such a nature that its negation would be self-contradictory: the importance which has been assigned to analytic propositions in the history of philosophy shews how easy such a mistake is. And thus it is very easy to conclude that what seems to be a universal ethical principle is in fact an identical proposition; that, if, for example, whatever is called 'good' seems to be pleasant, the proposition 'Pleasure is the good' does not assert a connection between two different notions, but involves only one, that of pleasure, which is easily recognised as a distinct entity. But whoever will attentively consider with himself what is actually before his mind when he asks the question 'Is pleasure (or whatever it may be) after all good?' can easily satisfy himself that he is not merely wondering whether pleasure is pleasant. And if he will try this experiment with each suggested definition in succession, he may become expert enough to recognise that in every case he has before his mind a unique object, with regard to the connection of which with any other object, a distinct question may be asked. Every one does in fact understand the question 'Is this good?' When he thinks of it, his state of mind is different from what it would be, were he asked 'Is this pleasant, or desired, or approved?' It has a distinct meaning for him, even though he may not recognise in what respect it is distinct. Whenever he thinks of 'intrinsic value,' or 'intrinsic worth,' or says that a thing 'ought to exist,' he has before his mind the unique object— the unique property of things—which I mean by 'good.' Everybody is constantly aware of this notion, although he may never become aware at all that it is different from other notions of which he is also aware. But, for correct ethical reasoning, it is extremely important that he should become aware of this fact; and, as soon as the nature of the problem is clearly understood, there should be little difficulty in advancing so far in analysis.

2
THE NATURALISTIC FALLACY

William K. Frankena

The future historian of "thought and expression" in the twentieth century will no doubt record with some amusement the ingenious trick, which some of the philosophical controversialists of the first quarter of our century had, of labeling their opponents' views "fallacies." He may even list some of these alleged fallacies for a certain sonority which their inventors embodied in their titles: the fallacy of initial predication, the fallacy of simple location, the fallacy of misplaced concreteness, the naturalistic fallacy.

Of these fallacies, real or supposed, perhaps the most famous is the naturalistic fallacy. For the practitioners of a certain kind of ethical theory, which is dominant in England and capably represented in America, and which is variously called objectivism, non-naturalism, or intuitionism, have frequently charged their opponents with committing the naturalistic fallacy. Some of these opponents have strongly repudiated the charge of fallacy, others have at least

commented on it in passing, and altogether the notion of a naturalistic fallacy has had a considerable currency in ethical literature. Yet, in spite of its repute, the naturalistic fallacy has never been discussed at any length, and, for this reason, I have elected to make a study of it in this paper. I hope incidentally to clarify certain confusions which have been made in connection with the naturalistic fallacy, but my main interest is to free the controversy between the intuitionists and their opponents of the notion of a logical or quasi-logical fallacy, and to indicate where the issue really lies.

The prominence of the concept of a naturalistic fallacy in recent moral philosophy is another testimony to the great influence of the Cambridge philosopher, Mr. G. E. Moore, and his book, *Principia Ethica*. Thus Mr. Taylor speaks of the "vulgar mistake" which Mr. Moore has taught us to call "the naturalistic fallacy,"[1] and Mr. G. S. Jury, as if to illustrate how well we have learned this lesson, says, with reference to naturalistic definitions of value, "All such definitions stand charged with Dr. Moore's 'naturalistic

From *Mind,* Vol. 48 (1939), pp. 464–77. Reprinted by permission.

fallacy'."[2] Now, Mr. Moore coined the notion of the naturalistic fallacy in his polemic against naturalistic and metaphysical systems of ethics. "The naturalistic fallacy is a fallacy," he writes, and it "must not be committed." All naturalistic and metaphysical theories of ethics, however, "are *based* on the naturalistic fallacy, in the sense that the commission of this fallacy has been the main cause of their wide acceptance."[3] The best way to dispose of them, then, is to expose this fallacy. Yet it is not entirely clear just what is the status of the naturalistic fallacy in the polemics of the intuitionists against other theories. Sometimes it is used as a weapon, as when Miss Clarke says that if we call a thing good simply because it is liked we are guilty of the naturalistic fallacy.[4] Indeed, it presents this aspect to the reader in many parts of *Principia Ethica* itself. Now, in taking it as a weapon, the intuitionists use the naturalistic fallacy as if it were a logical fallacy on all fours with the fallacy of composition, the revelation of which disposes of naturalistic and metaphysical ethics and leaves intuitionism standing triumphant. That is, it is taken as a fallacy in advance, for use in controversy. But there are signs in *Principia Ethica* which indicate that the naturalistic fallacy has a rather different place in the intuitionist scheme, and should not be used as a weapon at all. In this aspect, the naturalistic fallacy must be proved to be a fallacy. It cannot be used to settle the controversy, but can only be asserted to be a fallacy when the smoke of the battle has cleared. Consider the following passages: (a) "the naturalistic fallacy consists in the contention that good *means* nothing but some simple or complex notion, that can be defined in terms of natural qualities"; (b) "the point that good is indefinable and that to deny this involves a fallacy, is a point capable of strict proof."[5] These passages seem to imply that the fallaciousness of the naturalistic fallacy is just what is at issue in the controversy between the intuitionists and their opponents and cannot be wielded as a weapon in that controversy. One of the points I wish to make in this paper is that the charge of committing the naturalistic fallacy can be made, if at all, only as a conclusion from the discussion and not as an instrument of deciding it.

The notion of a naturalistic fallacy has been connected with the notion of a bifurcation between the "ought" and the "is", between value and fact, between the normative and the descriptive. Thus Mr. D. C. Williams says that some moralists have thought it appropriate to chastise as the naturalistic fallacy the attempt to derive the Ought from the Is.[6] We may begin, then, by considering this bifurcation, emphasis on which, by Sidgwick, Sorley, and others, came largely as a reaction to the procedures of Mill and Spencer. Hume affirms the bifurcation in his *Treatise:* "I cannot forbear adding to these reasonings an observation, which may, perhaps, be found of some importance. In every system of morality which I have hitherto met with, I have always remarked, that the author proceeds for some time in the ordinary way of reasoning, and establishes the being of a God, or makes observations concerning human affairs; when of a sudden I am surprised to find, that instead of the usual copulations of propositions, *is,* and *is not,* I meet with no proposition that is not connected with an *ought,* or an *ought not.* This change is imperceptible; but is, however, of the last consequence. For as this *ought,* or *ought not,* expresses some new relation or affirmation, it is necessary that it should be observed and explained; and at the same time that a reason should be given, for what seems altogether inconceivable, how this new relation can be a deduction from others, which are entirely different from it. But as authors do not commonly use this precaution, I shall presume to recommend it to the readers; and am persuaded, that this small attention would subvert all the vulgar systems of morality, and let us see that the distinction of vice and virtue is not founded merely on the relations of objects, nor is perceived by reason."[7]

Needless to say, the intuitionists *have* found this observation of some importance.[8] They agree with Hume that it subverts all the vulgar systems of morality, though, of course, they deny that it lets us see that the distinction of virtue and vice is not founded on the relations of objects, nor is perceived by reason. In fact, they hold that a small attention to it subverts Hume's own system also, since this gives naturalistic definitions of virtue and vice and of good and evil.[9]

Hume's point is that ethical conclusions cannot be drawn validly from premises which are non-ethical. But when the intuitionists affirm the bifurcation of the 'ought' and the 'is', they mean more than that ethical propositions cannot be deduced from non-ethical ones. For this difficulty in the vulgar systems of morality could be remedied, as we shall see, by the introduction of definitions of ethical notions in non-ethical terms. They mean, further, that such definitions of ethical notions in non-ethical terms are impossible. "The essential point," says Mr. Laird, "is the irreducibility of values to non-values."[10] But they mean still more. Yellow and pleasantness are, according to Mr. Moore, indefinable in non-ethical terms, but they are natural qualities and belong on the 'is' side of the fence. Ethical properties, however, are not, for him, mere indefinable natural qualities, descriptive or expository. They are properties of a different *kind*—non-descriptive or non-natural.[11] The intuitionist bifurcation consists of three statements:

1. Ethical propositions are not deducible from non-ethical ones.[12]
2. Ethical characteristics are not definable in terms of non-ethical ones.
3. Ethical characteristics are different in kind from non-ethical ones.

Really it consists of but one statement, namely, (3), since (3) entails (2) and (2) entails (1). It does not involve saying that any ethical characteristics are absolutely indefinable. That is another question, although this is not always noticed.

What, now, has the naturalistic fallacy to do with the bifurcation of the 'ought' and the 'is'? To begin with, the connection is this: many naturalistic and metaphysical moralists proceed as if ethical conclusions can be deduced from premises all of which are non-ethical, the classical examples being Mill and Spencer. That is, they violate (1). This procedure has lately been referred to as the "factualist fallacy" by Mr. Wheelwright and as the "valuational fallacy" by Mr. Wood.[13] Mr. Moore sometimes seems to identify it with the naturalistic fallacy, but in the main he holds only that it involves, implies, or rests upon this fallacy.[14] We may now consider the charge that the procedure in question is or involves a fallacy.

It may be noted at once that, even if the deduction of ethical conclusions from non-ethical premises is in no way a fallacy, Mill certainly did commit a fallacy in drawing an analogy between visibility and desirability in his argument for hedonism; and perhaps his committing *this* fallacy, which, as Mr. Broad has said, we all learn about at our mothers' knees, is chiefly responsible for the notion of a naturalistic *fallacy*. But is it a fallacy to deduce ethical conclusions from non-ethical premises? Consider the Epicurean argument for hedonism which Mill so unwisely sought to embellish: pleasure is good, since it is sought by all men. Here an ethical conclusion is being derived from a non-ethical premise. And, indeed, the argument, taken strictly as it stands, *is* fallacious. But it is not fallacious because an *ethical* term occurs in the conclusion which does not appear in the premise. It is fallacious because any argument in the form "A is B, therefore A is C" is invalid, if taken strictly as it stands. For example, it is invalid to argue that Croesus is rich because he is wealthy. Such arguments are, however, not intended to be taken strictly as they stand. They are enthymemes and contain a suppressed premise. And, when this suppressed premise is made explicit, they are valid and involve no logical fallacy.[15] Thus the Epicurean inference from psychological to ethical hedonism is valid when the suppressed premise is added to the effect that what is sought by all men is good. Then the only question left is whether the premises are true.

It is clear, then, that the naturalistic fallacy

is not a logical fallacy, since it may be involved even when the argument is valid. How does the naturalistic fallacy enter such "mixed ethical arguments"[16] as that of the Epicureans? Whether it does or not depends on the nature of the suppressed premise. This may be either an induction, an intuition, a deduction from a "pure ethical argument," a definition, or a proposition which is true by definition. If it is one of the first three, then the naturalistic fallacy does not enter at all. In fact, the argument does not then involve violating (1), since one of its premises will be ethical. But if the premise to be supplied is a definition or a proposition which is true by definition, as it probably was for the Epicureans, then the argument, while still valid, involves the naturalistic fallacy, and will run as follows:

a. Pleasure is sought by all men.
b. What is sought by all men is good (by definition).
c. Therefore, pleasure is good.

Now I am not greatly interested in deciding whether the argument as here set up violates (1). If it does not, then no 'mixed ethical argument' actually commits any factualist or valuational fallacy, except when it is unfairly taken as complete in its enthymematic form. If it does, then a valid argument may involve the deduction of an ethical conclusion from non-ethical premises and the factualist or valuational fallacy is not really a fallacy. The question depends on whether or not (b) and (c) are to be regarded as ethical propositions. Mr. Moore refuses to so regard them, contending that, by hypothesis, (b) is analytic or tautologous, and that (c) is psychological, since it really says only that pleasure is sought by all men.[17] But to say that (b) is analytic and not ethical and that (c) is not ethical but psychological is to prejudge the question whether 'good' can be defined; for the Epicureans would contend precisely that if their definition is correct then (b) is ethical but analytic and (c) ethical though psychological. Thus, unless the question of the definability of

goodness is to be begged, (b) and (c) must be regarded as ethical, in which case our argument does not violate (1). However, suppose, if it be not nonsense, that (b) is non-ethical and (c) ethical, then the argument will violate (1), but it will still obey all of the canons of logic, and it is only confusing to talk of a 'valuational logic' whose basic rule is that an evaluative conclusion cannot be deduced from non-evaluative premises.[18]

For the only way in which either the intuitionists or postulationists like Mr. Wood can cast doubt upon the conclusion of the argument of the Epicureans (or upon the conclusion of any parallel argument) is to attack the premises, in particular (b). Now, according to Mr. Moore, it is due to the presence of (b) that the argument involves the naturalistic fallacy. (b) involves the identification of goodness with 'being sought by all men', and to make this or any other such identification is to commit the naturalistic fallacy. The naturalistic fallacy is not the procedure of violating (1). It is the procedure, implied in many mixed ethical arguments and explicitly carried out apart from such arguments by many moralists, of defining such characteristics as goodness or of substituting some other characteristic for them. To quote some passages from *Principia Ethica:*—

(a) " . . . far too many philosophers have thought that when they named those other properties [belonging to all things which are good] they were actually defining good; that these properties, in fact, were simply not 'other', but absolutely and entirely the same with goodness. This view I propose to call the 'naturalistic fallacy' . . . ."[19]

(b) "I have thus appropriated the name Naturalism to a particular method of approaching Ethics . . . . This method consists in substituting for 'good' some one property of a natural object or of a collection of natural objects. . . ."[20]

(c) " . . . the naturalistic fallacy [is] the fallacy which consists in identifying the simple notion which we mean by 'good' with some other notion."[21]

Thus, to identify 'better' and 'more evolved', 'good' and 'desired', etc., is to commit the naturalistic fallacy.[22] But just why is such a procedure fallacious or erroneous? And is it a fallacy only when applied to good? We must now study Section 12 of *Principia Ethica*. Here Mr. Moore makes some interesting statements:

" . . . if anybody tried to define pleasure for us as being any other natural object; if anybody were to say, for instance, that pleasure *means* the sensation of red. . . Well, that would be the same fallacy which I have called the naturalistic fallacy. . . . I should not indeed call that a naturalistic fallacy, although it is the same fallacy as I have called naturalistic with reference to Ethics. . . . When a man confuses two natural objects with one another, defining the one by the other . . . then there is no reason to call the fallacy naturalistic. But if he confuses 'good', which is not . . . a natural object, with any natural object whatever, then there is reason for calling that a naturalistic fallacy. . . ."[23]

Here Mr. Moore should have added that, when one confuses "good,' which is not a metaphysical object or quality, with any metaphysical object or quality, as metaphysical moralists do, according to him, then the fallacy should be called the metaphysical fallacy. Instead he calls it a naturalistic fallacy in this case too, though he recognizes that the case is different since metaphysical properties are non-natural[24]—a procedure which has misled many readers of *Principia Ethica*. For example, it has led Mr. Broad to speak of "theological naturalism."[25]

To resume: "Even if [goodness] were a natural object, that would not alter the nature of the fallacy nor diminish its importance one whit."[26] From these passages it is clear that the fallaciousness of the procedure which Mr. Moore calls the naturalistic fallacy is not due to the fact that it is applied to good or to an ethical or non-natural characteristic. When Mr. R. B. Perry defines 'good' as 'being an object of interest' the trouble is not merely that he is defining *good*. Nor is the trouble that he is defining an *ethical* characteristic in terms of *non-ethical* ones. Nor is the trouble that he is regarding a *non-natural characteristic* as a *natural* one. The trouble is more generic than that. For clarity's sake I shall speak of the definist fallacy as the generic fallacy which underlies the naturalistic fallacy. The naturalistic fallacy will then, by the above passages, be a species or form of the definist fallacy, as would the metaphysical fallacy if Mr. Moore had given that a separate name.[27] That is, the naturalistic fallacy, as illustrated by Mr. Perry's procedure, is a fallacy, not because it is naturalistic or confuses a non-natural quality with a natural one, but solely because it involves the definist fallacy. We may, then, confine our attention entirely to an understanding and evaluation of the definist fallacy.

To judge by the passages I have just quoted, the definist fallacy is the process of confusing or identifying two properties, of defining one property by another, or of substituting one property for another. Furthermore, the fallacy is always simply that two properties are being treated as one, and it is irrelevant, if it be the case, that one of them is natural or non-ethical and the other non-natural or ethical. One may commit the definist fallacy without infringing on the bifurcation of the ethical and the non-ethical, as when one identifies pleasantness and redness or rightness and goodness. But even when one infringes on that bifurcation in committing the definist fallacy, as when one identifies goodness and pleasantness or goodness and satisfaction, then the *mistake* is still not that the bifurcation is being infringed on, but only that two properties are being treated as one. Hence, on the present interpretation, the definist *fallacy* does not, in any of its forms, consist in violating (3), and has no essential connexion with the bifurcation of the 'ought' and the 'is'.

This formulation of the definist fallacy explains or reflects the motto of *Principia Ethica*, borrowed from Bishop Butler: "Everything is what it is, and not another thing." It follows from this motto that goodness is what it is and not another thing. It follows that views which try to identify it with something else are making a mistake of an elementary sort. For it *is* a mistake to confuse or identify two properties. If the properties really are two, then they simply are not identical. But do those who define ethical notions in non-ethical terms make this mistake? They will reply to Mr. Moore that they are not identifying two properties; what they are saying is that two words or sets of words stand for or mean one and the same property. Mr. Moore was being, in part, misled by the material mode of speech, as Mr. Carnap calls it, in such sentences as "Goodness is pleasantness," "Knowledge is true belief," etc. When one says instead, "The word 'good' and the word 'pleasant' mean the same thing," etc., it is clear that one is not identifying two things. But Mr. Moore kept himself from seeing this by his disclaimer that he was interested in any statement about the use of words.[28]

The definist fallacy, then, as we have stated it, does not rule out any naturalistic or metaphysical definitions of ethical terms. Goodness is not identifiable with any 'other' characteristic (if it is a characteristic at all). But the question is: *which* characteristics are other than goodness, which names stand for characteristics other than goodness? And it is begging the question of the definability of goodness to say out of hand that Mr. Perry, for instance, is identifying goodness with something else. The point is that goodness is what it is, even if it is definable. That is why Mr. Perry can take as the motto of his naturalistic *Moral Economy* another sentence from Bishop Butler: "Things and actions are what they are, and the consequences of them will be what they will be; why then should we desire to be deceived?" The motto of *Principia Ethica* is a tautology, and should be expanded as follows: Everything is what it is, and not another thing, unless it is another thing, and even then it is what it is.

On the other hand, if Mr. Moore's motto (or the definist fallacy) rules out any definitions, for example of 'good', then it rules out all definitions of any term whatever. To be effective at all, it must be understood to mean, "Every term means what it means, and not what is meant by any other term." Mr. Moore seems implicitly to understand his motto in this way in Section 13, for he proceeds as if 'good' has no meaning, if it has no unique meaning. If the motto be taken in this way, it will follow that 'good' is an indefinable term, since no synonyms can be found. But it will also follow that no term is definable. And then the method of analysis is as useless as an English butcher in a world without sheep.

Perhaps we have misinterpreted the definist fallacy. And, indeed, some of the passages which I quoted earlier in this paper seem to imply that the definist fallacy is just the error of defining an indefinable characteristic. On this interpretation, again, the definist fallacy has, in all of its forms, no essential connection with the bifurcation of the ethical and the non-ethical. Again, one may commit the definist fallacy without violating that bifurcation, as when one defines pleasantness in terms of redness or goodness in terms of rightness (granted Mr. Moore's belief that pleasantness and goodness are indefinable). But even when one infringes on that bifurcation and defines goodness in terms of desire, the *mistake* is not that one is infringing on the bifurcation by violating (3), but only that one is defining an indefinable characteristic. This is possible because the proposition that goodness is indefinable is logically independent of the proposition that goodness is non-natural: as is shown by the fact that a characteristic may be indefinable and yet natural, as yellowness is; or non-natural and yet definable, as rightness is (granted Mr. Moore's views about yellowness and rightness).

Consider the definist fallacy as we have just stated it. It is, of course, an error to define an indefinable quality. But the question, again, is: which qualities are indefinable? It is begging the question in favor of intuitionism to say in advance that the quality goodness is indefinable and that, therefore, all naturalists commit the definist fallacy. One must know that goodness is indefinable before one can argue that the definist fallacy *is* a fallacy. Then, however, the definist fallacy can enter only at the end of the controversy between intuitionism and definism, and cannot be used as a weapon in the controversy.

The definist fallacy may be stated in such a way as to involve the bifurcation between the 'ought' and the 'is'.[29] It would then be committed by anyone who offered a definition of any ethical characteristic in terms of non-ethical ones. The trouble with such a definition, on this interpretation, would be that an *ethical* characteristic is being reduced to a *non-ethical* one, a *non-natural* one to a *natural* one. That is, the definition would be ruled out by the fact that the characteristic being defined is ethical or non-natural and therefore cannot be defined in non-ethical or natural terms. But on this interpretation, too, there is danger of a *petitio* in the intuitionist argumentation. To assume that the ethical characteristic is exclusively ethical is to beg precisely the question which is at issue when the definition is offered. Thus, again, one must know that the characteristic is non-natural and indefinable in natural terms before one can say that the definists are making a mistake.

Mr. Moore, McTaggart, and others formulate the naturalistic fallacy sometimes in a way somewhat different from any of those yet discussed. They say that the definists are confusing a universal synthetic proposition about *the good* with a definition of *goodness*.[30] Mr. Abraham calls this the "fallacy of misconstrued proposition."[31] Here again the difficulty is that, while it is true that it is an error to construe a universal synthetic proposition as a definition, it is a *petitio* for the intuitionists to say that what the definist is taking for a definition is really a universal synthetic proposition.[32]

At last, however, the issue between the intuitionists and the definists (naturalistic or metaphysical) is becoming clearer. The definists are all holding that certain propositions involving ethical terms are analytic, tautologous, or true by definition, e.g., Mr. Perry so regards the statement, "All objects of desire are good." The intuitionists hold that such statements are synthetic. What underlies this difference of opinion is that the intuitionists claim to have at least a dim awareness of a simple unique quality or relation of goodness or rightness which appears in the region which our ethical terms roughly indicate, whereas the definists claim to have no awareness of any such quality or relation in that region, which is different from all other qualities and relations which belong to the same context but are designated by words other than 'good' and 'right' and their obvious synonyms.[33] The definists are in all honesty claiming to find but one characteristic where the intuitionists claim to find two, as Mr. Perry claims to find only the property of being desired where Mr. Moore claims to find both it and the property of being good. The issue, then, is one of inspection or intuition, and concerns the awareness or discernment of qualities and relations.[34] That is why it cannot be decided by the use of the notion of a fallacy.

If the definists may be taken at their word, then they are not actually confusing two characteristics with each other, nor defining an indefinable characteristic, nor confusing definitions and universal synthetic propositions—in short they are not committing the naturalistic or definist fallacy in any of the interpretations given above. Then the only fallacy which they commit—the real naturalistic or definist fallacy—is the failure to descry the qualities and relations which are central to morality. But this is neither a logical fallacy nor a logical confusion. It is not even, properly speaking, an error. It is rather a kind of blindness, analogous to color-blindness. Even this moral blindness can be ascribed to the definists only if they are correct in their claim to have no awareness of any unique ethical characteristics and if the intuitionists are correct in affirming the existence of such characteristics, but certainly to call it a 'fallacy', even in a loose sense, is both unamiable and profitless.

On the other hand, of course, if there are no such characteristics in the objects to which we attach ethical predicates, then the intuitionists, if we may take them at their word, are suffering from a corresponding moral hallucination. Definists might then call this the intuitionistic or moralistic fallacy, except that it is no more a 'fallacy' than is the blindness just described. Anyway, they do not believe the claim of the intuitionists to be aware of unique ethical characteristics, and consequently do not attribute to them this hallucination. Instead, they simply deny that the intuitionists really do find such unique qualities or relations, and then they try to find some plausible way of accounting for the fact that very respectable and trustworthy people think they find them.[35] Thus they charge the intuitionists with verbalism, hypostatisation, and the like. But this half of the story does not concern us now.

What concerns us more is the fact that the intuitionists do not credit the claim of the definists either. They would be much disturbed, if they really thought that their opponents were morally blind, for they do not hold that we must be regenerated by grace before we can have moral insight, and they share the common feeling that morality is something democratic even though not all men are good. Thus they hold that "we are all aware" of certain unique characteristics when we use the terms 'good', 'right', etc., only due to a lack of analytic clearness of mind, abetted perhaps by a philosophical prejudice, we may not be aware at all that they are different from other characteristics of which we are also aware.[36] Now, I have been arguing that the intuitionists cannot charge the definists with committing any fallacy unless and until they have shown that we are all, the definists included, aware of the disputed unique characteristics. If, however, they were to show this, then, at least at the end of the controversy, they could accuse the definists of the error of confusing two characteristics, or of the error of defining an indefinable one, and these errors might, since the term is somewhat loose in its habits, be called 'fallacies', though they are not logical fallacies in the sense in which an invalid argument is. The fallacy of misconstrued proposition depends on the error of confusing two characteristics, and hence could also on our present supposition, be ascribed to the definists, but it is not really a *logical* confusion,[37] since it does not actually involve being confused about the difference between a proposition and a definition.

Only it is difficult to see how the intuitionists can prove that the definists are at least vaguely aware of the requisite unique characteristics.[38] The question must surely be left to the inspection or intuition of the definists themselves, aided by whatever suggestions the intuitionists may have to make. If so, we must credit the verdict of their inspection, especially of those among them who have read the writings of the intuitionists reflectively, and, then, as we have seen, the most they can be charged with is moral blindness.

Besides trying to discover just what is meant by the naturalistic fallacy, I have tried to show that the notion that a logical or quasi-logical fallacy is committed by the definists only confuses the issue between the intuitionists and the definists (and the issue between the latter and the emotivists or postulationists), and misrepresents the way in which the issue is to be settled. No logical fallacy need appear anywhere in the procedure of the definists. Even fallacies in any less accurate sense cannot be implemented to decide the case against the definists; at best they can be ascribed to the definists only after the issue has been decided against them on independent grounds. But the only defect which can be attributed to the definists, *if* the intuitionists are right in affirming the existence of unique indefinable ethical characteristics, is a peculiar moral blindness, which is not a fallacy even in the looser sense. The issue in question must be decided by whatever method we may find satisfactory for determining whether or not a word stands for a characteristic at all, and, if it does, whether or not it stands for a unique characteristic. What method is to be employed is, perhaps, in one form or another, the basic problem of contemporary philosophy, but no generally satisfactory solution of the problem has yet been reached. I shall venture to say only this: it does seem to me that the issue is not to be decided against the intuitionists by the application *ab extra* to ethical judgments of any empirical or ontological meaning dictum.[39]

NOTES

The Naturalistic Fallacy

1. A. E. Taylor, *The Faith of a Moralist,* vol. I, p. 104 n.

2. *Value and Ethical Objectivity,* p. 58.

3. *Principia Ethica,* pp. 38, 64.

4. M. E. Clarke, "Cognition and Affection in the Experience of Value," *Journal of Philosophy* (1938).

5. *Principia Ethica,* pp. 73, 77. See also p. xix.

6. "Ethics as Pure Postulate," *Philosophical Review* (1933). See also T. Whittaker, *The Theory of Abstract Ethics,* pp. 19 f.

7. Book III, part ii, section i.

8. See J. Laird, *A Study in Moral Theory,* pp. 16 f.; Whittaker, *op. cit.,* p. 19.

9. See C. D. Broad, *Five Types of Ethical Theory,* ch. iv.

10. *A Study in Moral Theory,* p. 94 n.

11. See *Philosophical Studies,* pp. 259, 273 f.

12. See J. Laird, *op. cit.,* p. 318. Also pp. 12 ff.

13. P. E. Wheelwright, *A Critical Introduction to Ethics,* pp. 40–51, 91 f.; L. Wood, "Cognition and Moral Value," *Journal of Philosophy* (1937), p. 237.

14. See *Principia Ethica,* pp. 114, 57, 43, 49. Whittaker identifies it with the naturalistic fallacy and regards it as a "logical" fallacy, *op. cit.,* pp. 19 f.

15. See *ibid.,* pp. 50, 139; Wheelwright, *loc. cit.*

16. See C. D. Broad, *The Mind and its Place in Nature,* pp. 488 f.; Laird, *loc. cit.*

17. See *op. cit.,* pp. 11 f.; 19, 38, 73, 139.

18. See L. Wood, *loc. cit.*

19. P. 10.

20. P. 40.

21. P. 58, *cf.* pp. xiii, 73.

22. *Cf.* pp. 49, 53, 108, 139.

23. P. 13.

24. See pp. 38–40, 110–112.

25. *Five Types of Ethical Theory,* p. 259.

26. P. 14.

27. As Whittaker has, *loc. cit.*

28. See *op. cit.,* pp. 6, 8, 12.

29. See J. Wisdom, *Mind* (1931), p. 213, note 1.

30. See *Principia Ethica,* pp. 10, 16, 38; *The Nature of Existence,* vol. ii, p. 398.

31. Leo Abraham, "The Logic of Intuitionism," *International Journal of Ethics* (1933).

32. As Mr. Abraham points out, *loc. cit.*

33. See R. B. Perry, *General Theory of Value,* p. 30; *cf. Journal of Philosophy* (1931), p. 520.

34. See H. Osborne, *Foundations of the Philosophy of Value,* pp. 15, 19, 70.

35. Cf. R. B. Perry, *Journal of Philosophy* (1931), pp. 520 ff.

36. *Principia Ethica,* pp. 17, 38, 59, 61.

37. But see H. Osborne, *op. cit.,* pp. 18 f.

38. For a brief discussion of their arguments, see *ibid.,* p. 67; L. Abraham, *op. cit.* I think they are all inconclusive, but cannot show this here.

39. See *Principia Ethica,* pp. 124 f., 140.

3

THE EMOTIVE MEANING OF ETHICAL TERMS

Charles L. Stevenson

Ethical questions first arise in the form "is so and so good?" or "is this alternative better than that?" These questions are difficult partly because we don't quite know what we are seeking. We are asking, "is there a needle in the haystack?" without even knowing just what a needle is. So the first thing to do is to examine the questions themselves. We must try to make them clearer, either by defining the terms in which they are expressed or by any other method that is available.

The present essay is concerned wholly with this preliminary step of making ethical questions clear. In order to help answer the question "is X good?" we must *substitute* for it a question that is free from ambiguity and confusion.

It is obvious that in substituting a clearer question we must not introduce some utterly

From *Mind,* Vol. 46 (1937). Reprinted by permission.

different kind of question. It won't do (to take an extreme instance of a prevalent fallacy) to substitute for "is X good?" the question "is X pink with yellow trimmings?" and then point out how easy the question really is. This would beg the original question, not help answer it. On the other hand, we must not expect the substituted question to be strictly "identical" with the original one. The original question may embody hypostatization, anthropomorphism, vagueness, and all the other ills to which our ordinary discourse is subject. If our substituted question is to be clearer it must remove these ills. The questions will be identical only in the sense that a child is identical with the man he later becomes. Hence we must not demand that the substitution strike us, on immediate introspection, as making no change in meaning.

Just how, then, must the substituted question be related to the original? Let us assume (inaccurately) that it must result from replacing "good" by some set of terms that define it. The question then resolves itself to this:

How must the defined meaning of "good" be related to its original meaning?

I answer that it must be *relevant.* A defined meaning will be called "relevant" to the original meaning under these circumstances: Those who have understood the definition must be able to say all that they then want to say by using the term in the defined way. They must never have occasion to use the term in the old, unclear sense. (If a person did have to go on using the word in the old sense, then to this extent his meaning would not be clarified and the philosophical task would not be completed.) It frequently happens that a word is used so confusedly and ambiguously that we must give it *several* defined meanings, rather than one. In this case only the whole set of defined meanings will be called "relevant," and any one of them will be called "partially relevant." This is not a rigorous treatment of *relevance,* by any means, but it will serve for the present purposes.

Let us now turn to our particular task— that of giving a relevant definition of "good." Let us first examine some of the ways in which others have attempted to do this.

The word "good" has often been defined in terms of *approval,* or similar psychological attitudes. We may take as typical examples: "good" means *desired by me* (Hobbes); and "good" means *approved by most people* (Hume, in effect).[1] It will be convenient to refer to definitions of this sort as "interest theories," following R. B. Perry, although neither "interest" nor "theory" is used in the most usual way.[2]

Are definitions of this sort relevant?

It is idle to deny their *partial relevance.* The most superficial inquiry will reveal that "good" is exceedingly ambiguous. To maintain that "good" is *never* used in Hobbes' sense, and never in Hume's, is only to manifest an insensitivity to the complexities of language. We must recognize, perhaps, not only these senses, but a variety of similar ones, differing both with regard to the kind of interest in question and with regard to the people who are said to have the interest. But that is a minor matter. The essential

question is not whether interest theories are *partially* relevant, but whether they are *wholly* relevant. This is the only point for intelligent dispute. Briefly: Granted that some senses of "good" may relevantly be defined in terms of interest, is there some *other* sense which is *not* relevantly so defined? We must give this question careful attention. For it is quite possible that when philosophers (and many others) have found the question "is X good?" so difficult, they have been grasping for this *other* sense of "good" and not any sense relevantly defined in terms of interest. If we insist on defining "good" in terms of interest, and answer the question when thus interpreted, we may be begging *their* question entirely. Of course this *other* sense of "good" may not exist, or it may be a complete confusion; but that is what we must discover.

Now many have maintained that interest theories are *far* from being completely relevant. They have argued that such theories neglect the very sense of "good" that is most typical of ethics. And certainly, their arguments are not without plausibility.

Only—what *is* this typical sense of "good"? The answers have been so vague and so beset with difficulties that one can scarcely determine.

There are certain requirements, however, with which the typical sense has been expected to comply—requirements which appeal strongly to our common sense. It will be helpful to summarize these, showing how they exclude the interest theories:

In the first place, we must be able sensibly to *disagree* about whether something is "good." This condition rules out Hobbes' definition. For consider the following argument: "This is good." "That isn't so; it's not good." As translated by Hobbes, this becomes: "I desire this." "That isn't so, for *I* don't." The speakers are not contradicting one another, and think they are only because of an elementary confusion in the use of pronouns. The definition, "good" means *desired by my community,* is also excluded, for how could people from different communities disagree?[3]

In the second place, "goodness" must have, so to speak, a magnetism. A person who recognizes X to be "good" must ipso facto acquire a stronger tendency to act in its favor than he otherwise would have had. This rules out the Humian type of definition. For according to Hume, to recognize that something is "good" is simply to recognize that the majority approve of it. Clearly, a man may see that the majority approve of X without having, himself, a stronger tendency to favor it. This requirement excludes any attempt to define "good" in terms of the interest of people *other* than the speaker.[4]

In the third place, the "goodness" of anything must not be verifiable solely by use of the scientific method. "Ethics must not be psychology." This restriction rules out all of the traditional interest theories without exception. It is so sweeping a restriction that we must examine its plausibility. What are the methodological implications of interest theories which are here rejected?

According to Hobbes' definition a person can prove his ethical judgments with finality by showing that he is not making an introspective error about his desires. According to Hume's definition one may prove ethical judgments (roughly speaking) by taking a vote. *This* use of the empirical method, at any rate, seems highly remote from what we usually accept as proof and reflects on the complete relevance of the definitions that imply it.

But are there not more complicated interest theories that are immune from such methodological implications? No, for the same factors appear; they are only put off for a while. Consider, for example, the definition: "X is good" means *most people would approve of X if they knew its nature and consequences.* How, according to this definition, could we prove that a certain X was good? We should first have to find out, empirically, just what X was like and what its consequences would be. To this extent the empirical method as required by the definition seems beyond intelligent objection. But what remains? We should next have to

discover whether most people would approve of the sort of thing we had discovered X to be. This could not be determined by popular vote—but only because it would be too difficult to explain to the voters, beforehand, what the nature and consequences of X really were. Apart from this, voting would be a pertinent method. We are again reduced to counting noses as a *perfectly final* appeal.

Now we need not scorn voting entirely. A man who rejected interest theories as irrelevant might readily make the following statement: "If I believed that X would be approved by the majority, when they knew all about it, I should be strongly *led* to say that X was good." But he would continue: "*Need I say that X was good, under the circumstances? Wouldn't my acceptance of the alleged 'final proof' result simply from my being democratic? What about the more aristocratic people?* They would simply say that the approval of most people, even when they knew all about the object of their approval, simply had nothing to do with the goodness of anything, and they would probably add a few remarks about the low state of people's interests." It would indeed seem, from these considerations, that the definition we have been considering has presupposed democratic ideals from the start; it has dressed up democratic propaganda in the guise of a definition.

The omnipotence of the empirical method, as implied by interest theories and others, may be shown unacceptable in a somewhat different way. G. E. Moore's familiar objection about the open question is chiefly pertinent in this regard. No matter what set of scientifically knowable properties a thing may have (says Moore, in effect), you will find, on careful introspection, that it is an open question to ask whether anything having these properties is *good*. It is difficult to believe that this recurrent question is a totally confused one, or that it seems open only because of the ambiguity of "good." Rather, we must be using some sense of "good" which is not definable, relevantly, in terms of anything scientifically knowable. That is, the scientific method is not sufficient for ethics.[5]

These, then, are the requirements with which the "typical" sense of "good" is expected to comply: (1) goodness must be a topic for intelligent disagreement; (2) it must be "magnetic"; and (3) it must not be discoverable solely through the scientific method.

2

I can now turn to my proposed analysis of ethical judgments. First let me present my position dogmatically, showing to what extent I vary from tradition.

I believe that the three requirements given above are perfectly sensible, that there is some *one* sense of "good" which satisfies all three requirements, and that no traditional interest theory satisfies them all. But this does not imply that "good" must be explained in terms of a Platonic Idea, or of a categorical imperative, or of a unique, unanalyzable property. On the contrary, the three requirements can be met by a *kind* of interest theory. *But we must give up a presupposition that all the traditional interest theories have made.*

Traditional interest theories hold that ethical statements are *descriptive* of the existing state of interests—that they simply *give information* about interests. (More accurately, ethical judgments are said to describe what the state of interests is, was, or will be, or to indicate what the state of interests *would* be under specified circumstances.) It is this emphasis on description, on information, which leads to their incomplete relevance. Doubtless there is always *some* element of description in ethical judgments, but this is by no means all. Their major use is not to indicate facts but to *create an influence*. Instead of merely describing people's interests they *change* or *intensify* them. They *recommend* an interest in an object, rather than state that the interest already exists.

For instance: When you tell a man that he ought not to steal, your object is not merely to let him know that people disapprove of stealing. You are attempting, rather, to get *him* to disapprove of it. Your ethical judgment has a quasi-imperative force which, operating through suggestion and intensified by your tone of voice, readily permits you to begin to *influence*, to *modify*, his interests. If in the end you do not succeed in getting *him* to disapprove of stealing, you will feel that you have failed to convince him that stealing is wrong. You will continue to feel this, even though he fully acknowledges that you disapprove of it and that almost everyone else does. When you point out to him the consequences of his actions—consequences which you suspect he already disapproves of—these *reasons* which support your ethical judgment are simply a means of facilitating your influence. If you think you can change his interests by making vivid to him how others will disapprove of him, you will do so, otherwise not. So the consideration about other people's interests is just an additional means you may employ in order to move him and is not a part of the ethical judgment itself. Your ethical judgment does not merely describe interests to him, it directs his very interests. The difference between the traditional interest theories and my view is like the difference between describing a desert and irrigating it.

Another example: A munitions maker declares that war is a good thing. If he merely meant that he approved of it, he would not have to insist so strongly nor grow so excited in his argument. People would be quite easily convinced that he approved of it. If he merely meant that most people approved of war, or that most people would approve of it if they knew the consequences, he would have to yield his point if it were proved that his was not so. But he would not do this, nor does consistency require it. He is not *describing* the state of people's approval; he is trying to *change* it by his influence. If he found that few people approved of war, he might insist all the more strongly that it was good, for there would be more changing to be done.

This example illustrates how "good" may

be used for what most of us would call bad purposes. Such cases are as pertinent as any others. I am not indicating the *good* way of using "good." I am not influencing people but am describing the way this influence sometimes goes on. If the reader wishes to say that the munitions maker's influence is bad—that is, if the reader wishes to awaken people's disapproval of the man, and to make him disapprove of his own actions—I should at another time be willing to join in this undertaking. But this is not the present concern. I am not using ethical terms but am indicating how they *are* used. The munitions maker, in his use of "good," illustrates the pervasive character of the word just as well as does the unselfish man who, eager to encourage in each of us a desire for the happiness of all, contends that the supreme good is peace.

Thus ethical terms are *instruments* used in the complicated interplay and readjustment of human interests. This can be seen plainly from more general observations. People from widely separated communities have different moral attitudes. Why? To a great extent because they have been subject to different social influences. Now clearly this influence does not operate through sticks and stones alone; words play a great part. People praise one another to encourage certain inclinations and blame one another to discourage others. Those of forceful personalities issue commands which weaker people, for complicated instinctive reasons, find it difficult to disobey, quite apart from fears of consequences. Further influence is brought to bear by writers and orators. Thus social influence is exerted, to an enormous extent, by means that have nothing to do with physical force or material reward. The ethical terms facilitate such influence. Being suited for use in *suggestion*, they are a means by which men's attitudes may be led this way or that. The reason, then, that we find a greater similarity in the moral attitudes of one community than in those of different communities is largely this: ethical judgments propagate themselves. One man says "this is good"; this may influence the ap-

proval of another person, who then makes the same ethical judgment, which in turn influences another person, and so on. In the end, by a process of mutual influence, people take up more or less the same attitudes. Between people of widely separated communities, of course, the influence is less strong; hence different communities have different attitudes.

These remarks will serve to give a general idea of my point of view. We must now go into more detail. There are several questions which must be answered: How does an ethical sentence acquire its power of influencing people—why is it suited to suggestion? Again, what has this influence to do with the *meaning* of ethical terms? And finally, do these considerations really lead us to a sense of "good" which meets the requirements mentioned in the preceding section?

Let us deal first with the question about *meaning*. This is far from an easy question, so we must enter into a preliminary inquiry about meaning in general. Although a seeming digression this will prove indispensable.

3

Broadly speaking, there are two different *purposes* which lead us to use language. On the one hand we use words (as in science) to record, clarify, and communicate *beliefs*. On the other hand we use words to give vent to our feelings (interjections), or to create moods (poetry), or to incite people to actions or attitudes (oratory).

The first use of words I shall call "descriptive," the second, "dynamic." Note that the distinction depends solely upon the *purpose* of the *speaker*.

When a person says "hydrogen is the lightest known gas," his purpose *may* be simply to lead the hearer to believe this, or to believe that the speaker believes it. In that case the words are used descriptively. When a person cuts himself and says "damn," his purpose is not ordinarily to record, clarify, or communicate any belief. The word is used dynamically. The two ways of using words, however, are by no means mutually exclusive. This is obvious from the fact that our purposes are often complex. Thus when one says "I want you to close the door," part of his purpose, ordinarily, is to lead the hearer to believe that he has this want. To that extent the words are used descriptively. But the major part of one's purpose is to lead the hearer to *satisfy* the want. To that extent the words are used dynamically.

It very frequently happens that the same sentence may have a dynamic use on one occasion and not on another, and that it may have different dynamic uses on different occasions. For instance: A man says to a visiting neighbor, "I am loaded down with work." His purpose may be to let the neighbor know how life is going with him. This would *not* be a dynamic use of words. He may make the remark, however, in order to drop a hint. This *would* be dynamic usage (as well as descriptive). Again, he may make the remark to arouse the neighbor's sympathy. This would be a *different* dynamic usage from that of hinting.

Or again, when we say to a man, "of course you won't make those mistakes any more," we *may* simply be making a prediction. But we are more likely to be using "suggestion," in order to encourage him and hence *keep* him from making mistakes. The first use would be descriptive, the second, mainly dynamic.

From these examples it will be clear that we cannot determine whether words are used dynamically or not merely by reading the dictionary—even assuming that everyone is faithful to dictionary meanings Indeed, to know whether a person is using a word dynamically we must note his tone of voice, his gestures, the general circumstances under which he is speaking, and so on.

We must now proceed to an important question: What has the dynamic use of words to do with their *meaning*? One thing is clear—we must not define "meaning" in a way that would make meaning vary with dynamic usage. If we did, we should have no use for the term. All that we could say

about such "meaning" would be that it is very complicated and subject to constant change. So we must certainly distinguish between the dynamic use of words and their meaning.

It does not follow, however, that we must define "meaning" in some nonpsychological fashion. We must simply restrict the psychological field. Instead of identifying meaning with *all* the psychological causes and effects that attend a word's utterance, we must identify it with those that it has a *tendency* (causal property, dispositional property) to be connected with. The tendency must be of a particular kind, moreover. It must exist for all who speak the language; it must be persistent and must be realizable more or less independently of determinate circumstances attending the word's utterance. There will be further restrictions dealing with the interrelations of word in different contexts. Moreover, we must include, under the psychological responses which the words tend to produce, not only immediate introspective experiences but *dispositions* to react in a given way with appropriate stimuli. I hope to go into these matters in a subsequent essay.[6] Suffice it now to say that I think "meaning" may be thus defined in a way to include "propositional" meaning as an important kind.

The definition will readily permit a distinction between meaning and dynamic use. For when words are accompanied by dynamic purposes, it does not follow that they *tend* to be accompanied by them in the way mentioned above. E.g. there need be no tendency realizable more or less independently of the determinate circumstances under which the words are uttered.

There will be a kind of meaning, however, in the sense above defined, which has an intimate relation to dynamic usage. I refer to "emotive" meaning (in a sense roughly like that employed by Ogden and Richards).[7] The emotive meaning of a word is a tendency of a word, arising through the history of its usage, to produce (result from) *affective* responses in people. It is the immediate aura of feeling which hovers about a word.[8] Such tendencies to produce affective responses cling to words very tenaciously. It would be difficult, for instance, to express merriment by using the interjection "alas." Because of the persistence of such affective tendencies (among other reasons) it becomes feasible to classify them as "meanings."

Just *what* is the relation between emotive meaning and the dynamic use of words? Let us take an example. Suppose that a man tells his hostess, at the end of a party, that he thoroughly enjoyed himself, and suppose that he was in fact bored. If we consider his remark an innocent one, are we likely to remind him, later, that he "lied" to his hostess? Obviously not, or at least, not without a broad smile; for although he told her something that he believed to be false, and with the intent of making her believe that it was true—those being the ordinary earmarks of a lie—the expression, "you lied to her," would be emotively too strong for our purposes. It would seem to be a reproach, even if we intended it not to be a reproach. So it will be evident that such words as "lied" (and many parallel examples could be cited) become suited, on account of their emotive meaning, to a certain kind of dynamic use—so well suited, in fact, that the hearer is likely to be misled when we use them in any other way. The more pronounced a word's emotive meaning is, the less likely people are to use it purely descriptively. Some words are suited to encourage people, some to discourage them, some to quiet them, and so on.

Even in these cases, of course, the dynamic purposes are not to be identified with any sort of meaning; for the emotive meaning accompanies a word much more persistently than do the dynamic purposes. But there is an important contingent relation between emotive meaning and dynamic purpose: the former assists the latter. Hence if we define emotively laden terms in a way that neglects their emotive meaning, we become seriously confused. *We lead people to think that the terms defined are used dynamically less often than they are.*

4

Let us now apply these remarks in defining "good." This word may be used morally or nonmorally. I shall deal with the nonmoral usage almost entirely, but only because it is simpler. The main points of the analysis will apply equally well to either usage.

As a preliminary definition let us take an inaccurate approximation. It may be more misleading than helpful but will do to begin with. Roughly, then, the sentence "X is good" means *we like X.* ("We" includes the hearer or hearers.)

At first glance this definition sounds absurd. If used, we should expect to find the following sort of conversation: A. "This is good." B. "But I *don't* like it. What led you to believe that I did?" The unnaturalness of B's reply, judged by ordinary word usage, would seem to cast doubt on the relevance of my definition.

B's unnaturalness, however, lies simply in this: he is assuming that "we like it" (as would occur implicitly in the use of "good") is being used descriptively. This will not do. When "we like it" is to take the place of "this is good," the former sentence must be used not purely descriptively, but dynamically. More specifically, it must be used to promote a very subtle (and for the nonmoral sense in question, a very easily resisted) kind of *suggestion.* To the extent that "we" refers to the hearer it must have the dynamic use, essential to suggestion, of leading the hearer to *make* true what is said, rather than merely to believe it. And to the extent that "we" refers to the speaker, the sentence must have not only the descriptive use of indicating belief about the speaker's interest, but the quasi-interjectory, dynamic function of giving direct expression to the interest. (This immediate expression of feelings assists in the process of suggestion. It is difficult to disapprove in the face of another's enthusiasm.)

For an example of a case where "we like this" is used in the dynamic way that "this is good" is used, consider the case of a mother who says to her several children, "one thing is certain, *we all like to be neat.*" If she really believed this, she would not bother to say so. But she is not using the words descriptively. She is *encouraging* the children to like neatness. By telling them that they like neatness, she will lead them to *make* her statement true, so to speak. If, instead of saying "we all like to be neat" in this way, she had said "it's a good thing to be neat," the effect would have been approximately the same.

But these remarks are still misleading. Even when "we like it" is used for suggestion, it is not quite like "this is good." The latter is more subtle. With such a sentence as "this is a good book," for example, it would be practically impossible to use instead "we like this book." When the latter is used it must be accompanied by so exaggerated an intonation, to prevent its becoming confused with a descriptive statement, that the force of suggestion becomes stronger and ludicrously more overt than when "good" is used.

The definition is inadequate, further, in that the definiens has been restricted to dynamic usage. Having said that dynamic usage was different from meaning, I should not have to mention it in giving the *meaning* of "good."

It is in connection with this last point that we must return to emotive meaning. The word "good" has a laudatory emotive meaning that fits it for the dynamic use of suggesting favorable interest. But the sentence "we like it" has no such emotive meaning. Hence my definition has neglected emotive meaning entirely. Now to neglect emotive meaning serves to foster serious confusions, as I have previously intimated; so I have sought to make up for the inadequacy of the definition by letting the restriction about dynamic usage take the place of emotive meaning. What I should do, of course, is to find a definiens whose emotive meaning, like that of "good," simply does *lead* to dynamic usage.

Why did I not do this? I answer that it is not possible if the definition is to afford us increased clarity. No two words, in the first place, have quite the same emotive meaning. The most we can hope for is a rough approximation. But if we seek for such an approximation for "good," we shall find nothing more than synonyms, such as "desirable" or "valuable"; and these are profitless because they do not clear up the connection between "good" and favorable interest. If we reject such synonyms, in favor of nonethical terms, we shall be highly misleading. For instance "this is good" has something like the meaning of "I *do* like this; do so as well." But this is certainly not accurate. For the imperative makes an appeal to the conscious efforts of the hearer. Of course he cannot like something just by trying. He must be led to like it through suggestion. Hence an ethical sentence differs from an imperative in that it enables one to make changes in a much more subtle, less fully conscious way. Note that the ethical sentence centers the hearer's attention not on his interests but on the object of interest, and thereby facilitates suggestion. Because of its subtlety, moreover, an ethical sentence readily permits counter-suggestion and leads to the give and take situation that is so characteristic of arguments about values.

Strictly speaking, then, it is impossible to define "good" in terms of favorable interest if emotive meaning is not to be distorted. Yet it is possible to say that "this is good" is *about* the favorable interest of the speaker and the hearer or hearers, and that it has a laudatory emotive meaning which fits the words for use in suggestion. This is a rough description of meaning, not a definition. But it serves the same clarifying function that a definition ordinarily does, and that, after all, is enough.

A word must be added about the moral use of "good." This differs from the above in that it is about a different kind of interest. Instead of being about what the hearer and speaker *like,* it is about a stronger sort of approval. When a person *likes* something, he is pleased when it prospers and disappointed when it does not. When a person *morally approves* of something he experiences a rich feeling of security when it prospers and is indignant or "shocked" when it does not. These are rough and inaccurate examples of the many factors which one would have to mention in distinguishing the two kinds of interest. In the moral usage, as well as in the nonmoral, "good" has an emotive meaning which adapts it to suggestion.

And now, are these considerations of any importance? Why do I stress emotive meanings in this fashion? Does the omission of them really lead people into errors? I think, indeed, that the errors resulting from such omissions are enormous. In order to see this, however, we must return to the restrictions, mentioned in Section 1, with which the typical sense of "good" has been expected to comply.

5

The first restriction, it will be remembered, had to do with disagreement. Now there is clearly some sense in which people disagree on ethical points, but we must not rashly assume that all disagreement is modeled after the sort that occurs in the natural sciences. We must distinguish between "disagreement in belief" (typical of the sciences) and "disagreement in interest." Disagreement in belief occurs when A believes p and B disbelieves it. Disagreement in interest occurs when A has a favorable interest in X and when B has an unfavorable one in it. (For a full-bodied disagreement, neither party is content with the discrepancy.)

Let me give an example of disagreement in interest. A. "Let's go to a cinema tonight." B. "I don't want to do that. Let's go to the symphony." A continues to insist on the cinema, B on the symphony. This is disagreement in a perfectly conventional sense. They cannot agree on where they want to go, and each is trying to redirect the other's interest. (Note that imperatives are used in the example.)

It is disagreement in *interest* which takes place in ethics. When C says "this is good" and D says "no, it's bad," we have a case of suggestion and counter-suggestion. Each man is trying to redirect the other's interest.

There obviously need be no domineering, since each may be willing to give ear to the other's influence; but each is trying to move the other nonetheless. It is in this sense that they disagree. Those who argue that certain interest theories make no provision for disagreement have been misled, I believe, simply because the traditional theories, in leaving out emotive meaning, give the impression that ethical judgments are used descriptively only; and of course when judgments are used purely descriptively, the only disagreement that can arise is disagreement *in belief*. Such disagreement may be disagreement in belief *about* interests, but this is not the same as disagreement *in* interest. My definition does not provide for disagreement in belief about interests any more than does Hobbes'; but that is no matter, for there is no reason to believe, at least on common sense grounds, that this kind of disagreement exists. There is only disagreement *in* interest. (We shall see in a moment that disagreement in interest does not remove ethics from sober argument— that this kind of disagreement may often be resolved through empirical means.)

The second restriction, about "magnetism," or the connection between goodness and actions, requires only a word. This rules out only those interest theories that do *not* include the interest of the speaker in defining "good." My account does include the speaker's interest, hence is immune.

The third restriction, about the empirical method, may be met in a way that springs naturally from the above account of disagreement. Let us put the question in this way: When two people disagree over an ethical matter, can they completely resolve the disagreement through empirical considerations, assuming that each applies the empirical method exhaustively, consistently, and without error?

I answer that sometimes they can and sometimes they cannot, and that at any rate, even when they can, the relation between empirical knowledge and ethical judgments is quite different from the one that traditional interest theories seem to imply.

This can best be seen from an analogy. Let us return to the example where A and B could not agree on a cinema or a symphony. The example differed from an ethical argument in that imperatives were used, rather than ethical judgments, but was analogous to the extent that each person was endeavoring to modify the other's interest. Now how would these people argue the case, assuming that they were too intelligent just to shout at one another?

Clearly, they would give "reasons" to support their imperatives. A might say, "But you know, Garbo is at the Bijou." His hope is that B, who admires Garbo, will acquire a desire to go to the cinema when he knows what film will be there. B may counter, "but Toscanini is guest conductor tonight, in an all-Beethoven program." And so on. Each supports his imperative (*"let's* do so and so") by reasons which may be empirically established.

To generalize from this: disagreement in interest may be rooted in disagreement in belief. That is to say, people who disagree in interest would often cease to do so if they knew the precise nature and consequences of the object of their interest. To this extent disagreement in interest may be resolved by securing agreement in belief, which in turn may be secured empirically.

This generalization holds for ethics. If A and B, instead of using imperatives, had said, respectively, "it would be *better* to go to the cinema," and "it would be better to go to the symphony," the reasons which they would advance would be roughly the same. They would each give a more thorough account of the object of interest, with the purpose of completing the redirection of interest which was begun by the suggestive force of the ethical sentence. On the whole, of course, the suggestive force of the ethical statement merely exerts enough pressure to start such trains of reasons, since the reasons are much more essential in resolving disagreement in interest than the persuasive effect of the ethical judgment itself.

Thus the empirical method is relevant to ethics simply because our knowledge of the world is a determining factor to our interests. But note that empirical facts are not inductive grounds from which the ethical judgment problematically follows. (This is what traditional interest theories imply.) If someone said "close the door," and added the reason "we'll catch cold," the latter would scarcely be called an inductive ground of the former. Now imperatives are related to the reasons which support them in the same way that ethical judgments are related to reasons.

Is the empirical method *sufficient* for attaining ethical agreement? Clearly not. For empirical knowledge resolves disagreement in interest only to the extent that such disagreement is rooted in disagreement in belief. Not all disagreement in interest is of this sort. For instance: A is of a sympathetic nature and B is not. They are arguing about whether a public dole would be good. Suppose that they discovered all the consequences of the dole. Is it not possible, even so, that A will say that it is good and B that it is bad? The disagreement in interest may arise not from limited factual knowledge but simply from A's sympathy and B's coldness. Or again, suppose in the above argument that A was poor and unemployed and that B was rich. Here again the disagreement may not be due to different factual knowledge. It would be due to the different social positions of the men, together with their predominant self-interest.

When ethical disagreement is not rooted in disagreement in belief, is there *any* method by which it may be settled? If one means by "method" a *rational* method, then there is no method. But in any case there is a "way." Let us consider the above example again, where disagreement was due to A's sympathy and B's coldness. Must they end by saying, "well, it's just a matter of our having different temperaments"? Not necessarily. A, for instance, may try to *change* the temperament of his opponent. He may pour out his enthusiasm in such a moving way—present the sufferings of the poor with such appeal—that he will lead his opponent to see life through different eyes. He may build up by the contagion of his feelings an influence which will modify B's temperament and create in him a sympathy for the poor which did not previously exist. This is often the only way to obtain ethical agreement, if there is any way at all. It is persuasive, not empirical or rational; but that is no reason for neglecting it. There is no reason to scorn it, either, for it is only by such means that our personalities are able to grow, through our contact with others.

The point I wish to stress, however, is simply that the empirical method is instrumental to ethical agreement only to the extent that disagreement in interest is rooted in disagreement in belief. There is little reason to believe that all disagreements are of this sort. Hence the empirical method is not sufficient for ethics. In any case, ethics is not psychology, since psychology does not endeavour to *direct* our interests; it discovers facts about the ways in which interests are or can be directed, but that is quite another matter.

To summarize this section: my analysis of ethical judgments meets the three requirements for the typical sense of "good" that were mentioned in Section 1. The traditional interest theories fail to meet these requirements simply because they neglect dynamic usage, and the sort of disagreement that results from such usage, together with the method of resolving the disagreement. I may add that my analysis answers Moore's objection about the open question. Whatever scientifically knowable properties a thing may have, it *is* always open to question whether a thing having these (enumerated) qualities is good. For to ask whether it is good is to ask for *influence*. And whatever I may know about an object, I can still ask, quite pertinently, to be influenced with regard to my interest in it.

6

And now, have I really pointed out the "typical" sense of "good"?

I suppose that many will still say "no," claiming that I have simply failed to set down *enough* requirements that this sense must meet, and that my analysis, like all others given in terms of interest, is a way of begging the issue. They will say: "when we ask 'is X good?' we don't want mere influence, mere advice. We decidedly don't want to be influenced through persuasion, nor are we fully content when the influence is supported by a wide scientific knowledge of X. The answer to our question will, of course, modify our interests. But this is only because a unique sort of truth will be revealed to us—a truth that must be apprehended a priori. We want our interests to be guided by this truth and by nothing else. To substitute for this special truth mere emotive meaning and mere factual truth is to conceal from us the very object of our search."

I can only answer that I do not understand. What is this truth to be *about*? For I recollect no Platonic Idea, nor do I know what to *try* to recollect. I find no indefinable property nor do I know what to look for. And the "self-evident" deliverances of reason, which so many philosophers have mentioned, seem on examination to be deliverances of their respective reasons only (if of anyone's) and not of mine.

I strongly suspect, indeed, that any sense of "good" which is expected both to unite itself in synthetic a priori fashion with other concepts and to influence interests as well, is really a great confusion. I extract from this meaning the power of influence alone, which I find the only intelligible part. If the rest is confusion, however, then it certainly deserves more than the shrug of one's shoulders. What I should like to do is to *account* for the confusion—to examine the psychological needs which have given rise to it and show how these needs may be satisfied in another way. This is *the* problem, if confusion is to be stopped at its source. But it is an enormous problem and my reflections on it, which are at present worked out only roughly, must be reserved until some later time.

I may add that if "X is good" has the meaning that I ascribe to it, then it is not a judgment that professional philosophers and only professional philosophers are qualified to make. To the extent that ethics predicates the ethical terms of anything, rather than explains their meaning, it becomes more than a purely intellectual study. Ethical judgments are social instruments. They are used in a cooperative enterprise that leads to a mutual readjustment of human interests. Philosophers have a part in this; but so too do all men.

NOTES

1. The definition ascribed to Hume is oversimplified, but not, I think, in a way that weakens the force of the observations that I am about to make. Perhaps the same should be said of Hobbes.

A more accurate account of Hume's Ethics is given in *Ethics and Language* (New Haven, 1944), pp. 273–76.

2. In *General Theory of Value* (New York, 1926) Perry used "interest" to refer to any sort of favoring or disfavoring, or any sort of disposition to be for or against something. And he used "theory" where he might, alternatively, have used "proposed definition," or "proposed analysis of a common sense meaning."

In most of the (chronologically) later essays in the present volume the term "interest" systematically gives place to the term "attitude." The purpose of the change was solely to provide a more transparent terminology: it was not intended to repudiate Perry's *conception* of interest.

3. See G. E. Moore, *Philosophical Studies* (New York, 1922), pp. 332–34.

4. See G. C. Field, *Moral Theory* (London, 1921) pp. 52, 56–57.

5. See G. E. Moore, *Principia Ethica* (Cambridge, 1903), ch. 1. I am simply trying to preserve the spirit of Moore's objection and not the exact form of it.

6. The "subsequent essay" became, instead, Chapter 3 of *Ethics and Language*, which among other points defends those that follow:

(1) When used in a generic sense that emphasizes what C. W. Morris calls the *pragmatic* aspects of language, the term "meaning" designates a tendency of words to express or evoke states of mind in the people who use the words. The tendency is of a special kind, however, and many qualifications are needed (including some that bear on syntax) to specify its nature.

(2) When the states of mind in question are cognitive, the meaning can conveniently be called *descriptive;* and when they are feelings, emotions, or attitudes, the meanings can conveniently be called *emotive.*

(3) The states of mind (in a rough and tentative sense of that term) are normally quite complicated. They are not necessarily images or feelings but may in their turn be further tendencies—tendencies to respond to various stimuli that may subsequently arise. A word may have a constant meaning, accordingly, even though it is accompanied, at various times that it is used, by different images or feelings.

(4) Emotive meaning is something more than a by-product of descriptive meaning. When a term has both sorts of meaning, for example, a change in its descriptive meaning may not be attended by a change in emotive meaning.

(5) When a speaker's use of emotive terms evokes an attitude in a hearer (as it sometimes may not, since it has only a *tendency* to do so), it must not be conceived as merely adding to the hearer's attitude in the way that a spark might add its heat to the atmosphere. For a more appropriate analogy, in many cases, we must think rather of a spark that ignites tinder.

7. See C. K. Ogden and I. A. Richards, *The Meaning of Meaning* (2nd ed. London, 1927). On p. 125 there is a passage on ethics which is the source of the ideas embodied in this essay.

8. In *Ethics and Language* the phrase "aura of feeling" was expressly repudiated. If the present essay had been more successful in anticipating the analysis given in that later work, it would have introduced the notion of emotive meaning in some such way as this:

The emotive meaning of a word or phrase is a strong and persistent tendency, built up in the course of linguistic history, to give direct expression (quasi-interjectionally) to certain of the speaker's feelings or emotions or attitudes; and it is also a tendency to evoke (quasi-imperatively) corresponding feelings, emotions, or attitudes in those to whom the speaker's remarks are addressed. It is the emotive meaning of a word, accordingly, that leads us to characterize it as *laudatory* or *derogatory*—that rather generic characterization being of particular interest when we are dealing with terms like "good" and "bad" or "right and wrong." But emotive meanings are of great variety: they may yield terms that express or evoke horror, amazement, sadness, sympathy, and so on.

4

THE NEW SUBJECTIVISM IN ETHICS

Brand Blanshard

By the new subjectivism in ethics I mean the view that when anyone says "this is right" or "this is good," he is only expressing his own feeling; he is not asserting anything true or false, because he is not asserting or judging at all; he is really making an exclamation that expresses a favorable feeling.

This view has recently come into much favor. With variations of detail, it is being advocated by Russell, Wittgenstein, and Ayer in England, and by Carnap, Stevenson, Feigl, and others, in this country. Why is it that the theory has come into so rapid a popularity? Is it because moralists of insight have been making a fresh and searching examination of moral experience and its expression? No, I think not. A consideration of the names just mentioned suggests a truer reason. All these names belong, roughly speaking, to a single school of thought in the theory of knowledge. If the new view has become popular in ethics, it is because certain persons who were

From Brand Blanshard, "The New Subjectivism in Ethics," *Philosophy and Phenomenological Research,* IX, No. 3 (1949), 504–511. Reprinted by permission.

at work in the theory of knowledge arrived at a new view *there*, and found, on thinking it out, that it required the new view in ethics; the new view comes less from ethical analysis than from logical positivism.

These writers, as positivists or near-positivists, held that every judgment belongs to one or other of two types. On the one hand, it may be *a priori* or necessary. But then it is always analytic, i.e., it unpacks in its predicate part or all of its subject. Can we safely say that 7 + 5 make 12? Yes, because 12 is what we mean by "7 + 5." On the other hand, the judgment may be too empirical, and then, if we are to verify it, we can no longer look to our meanings only; it refers to sense experience and there we must look for its warrant. Having arrived at this division of judgments, the positivists raised the question of where value judgments fall. The judgment that knowledge is good, for example, did not seem to be analytic; the value that knowledge might have did not seem to be part of our concept of knowledge. But neither was the statement empirical, for goodness was not a quality like red or squeaky that could be seen or heard. What were they to do, then, with these awkward judgments of value? To find a place for them in their theory of knowledge would require them to revise the theory radically, and yet that theory was what they regarded as their most important discovery. It appeared that the theory could be saved in one way only. If it could be shown that judgments of good and bad were not judgments at all, that they asserted nothing true or false, but merely expressed emotions like "Hurrah" or "Fiddlesticks," then these wayward judgments would cease from troubling and weary heads could be at rest. This is the course the positivists took. They explained value judgments by explaining them away.

Now I do not think their view will do. But before discussing it, I should like to record one vote of thanks to them for the clarity with which they have stated their case. It has been said of John Stuart Mill that he wrote so clearly that he could be found out. This theory has been put so clearly and precisely that it deserves criticism of the same kind, and this I will do my best to supply. The theory claims to show by analysis that when we say "That is good," we do not mean to assert a character of the subject of which we are thinking. I shall argue that we do mean to do just that.

Let us work through an example, and the simpler and commoner the better. There is perhaps no value statement on which people would more universally agree than the statement that intense pain is bad. Let us take a set of circumstances in which I happen to be interested on the legislative side and in which I think every one of us might naturally make such a statement. We come upon a rabbit that has been caught in one of the brutal traps in common use. There are signs that it has struggled for days to escape and that in a frenzy of hunger, pain, and fear, it has all but eaten off its own leg. The attempt failed: the animal is now dead. As we think of the long and excruciating pain it must have suffered, we are very likely to say: "It was a bad thing that the little animal should suffer so." The positivist tells us when we say

this we are only expressing our present emotion. I hold, on the contrary, that we mean to assert something of the pain itself, namely that it was bad— bad when and as it occurred.

Consider what follows from the positivist view. On that view, nothing good or bad happened in the case until I came on the scene and made my remark. For what I express in my remark is something going on in me at the time, and that of course did not exist until I did come on the scene. The pain of the rabbit was not itself bad; nothing evil was happening when the pain was being endured; badness, in the only sense in which it is involved at all, waited for its appearance till I came and looked and felt. Now that this is at odds with our meaning may be shown as follows. Let us put to ourselves the hypothesis that we had not come on the scene and that the rabbit never was discovered. Are we prepared to say that in that case nothing bad had occurred in the sense in which we said it did? Clearly not. Indeed we should say, on the contrary, that the accident of our later discovery made no difference whatever to the badness of the animal's pain, that it would have been every whit as bad whether a chance passer-by happened later to discover the body and feel repugnance or not. If so, then it is clear that in saying the suffering was bad we are not expressing our feelings only. We are saying that the pain was bad when and as it occurred and before anyone took an attitude toward it.

The first argument is thus an ideal experiment in which we use the method of difference. It removes our present expression and shows that the badness we meant would not be affected by this, whereas on positivist grounds it should be. The second argument applies the method in the reverse way. It ideally removes the past event, and shows that this would render false what we mean to say, whereas on positivist grounds it should not. Let us suppose that the animal did not in fact fall into the trap and did not suffer at all, but that we mistakenly believe it did, and say as before that its suffering was an evil thing.

On the positivist theory, everything I sought to express by calling it evil in the first case is still present in the second. In the only sense in which badness is involved at all, whatever was bad in the first case is still present in its entirety, since all that is expressed in either case is a state of feeling, and that feeling is still there. And our question is, is such an implication consistent with what we meant? Clearly it is not. If anyone asked us, after we made the remark that the suffering was a bad thing, whether we should think it relevant to what we said to learn that the incident had never occurred and no pain had been suffered at all, we should say that it made all the difference in the world, that what we were asserting to be bad was precisely the suffering we thought had occurred back there, that if this had not occurred, there was nothing left to be bad, and that our assertion was in that case mistaken. The suggestion that in saying something evil had occurred we were after all making no mistake, because we had never meant anyhow to say anything about the past suffering, seems to me merely frivolous. If we did not mean to say this, why should we be so relieved on finding that the suffering had not occurred? On the theory before us, such relief would be groundless, for in that suffering itself there would be nothing to be relieved about. The positivist theory would here distort our meaning beyond recognition.

So far as I can see, there is only one way out for the positivist. He holds that goodness and badness lie in feelings of approval or disapproval. And there is a way in which he might hold that badness did in this case precede our own feeling of disapproval without belonging to the pain itself. The pain itself was neutral; but unfortunately the rabbit, on no grounds at all, took up toward this neutral object an attitude of disapproval, and that made it for the first time, and in the only intelligible sense, bad. This way of escape is theoretically possible, but since it has grave difficulties of its own and has not, so far as I know, been urged by positivists, it is perhaps best not to spend time over it.

I come now to a third argument, which again is very simple. When we come upon the rabbit and make our remark about its suffering being a bad thing, we presumably make it with some feeling; the positivists are plainly right in saying that such remarks do usually express feeling. But suppose that a week later we revert to the incident in thought and make our statement again. And suppose that the circumstances have now so changed that the feeling with which we made the remark in the first place has faded. The pathetic evidence is no longer before us; and we are now so fatigued in body and mind that the feeling is, as we say, quite dead. In these circumstances, since what was expressed by the remark when first made is, on the theory before us, simply absent, the remark now expresses nothing. It is as empty as the word "Hurrah" would be when there was no enthusiasm behind it. And this seems to me untrue. When we repeat the remark that such suffering was a bad thing, the feeling with which we made it last week may be at or near the vanishing point, but if we were asked whether we meant to say what we did before, we should certainly answer Yes. We should say that we made our point with feeling the first time and little or no feeling the second time, but that it was the same point we were making. And if we can see that what we meant to say remains the same, while the feeling varies from intensity to near zero, it is not the feeling that we primarily meant to express.

I come now to a fourth consideration. We all believe that toward acts or effects of a certain kind one attitude is fitting and another not; but on the theory before us such a belief would not make sense. Broad and Ross have lately contended that this fitness is one of the main facts of ethics, and I suspect they are right. But this is not exactly my point. My point is this: whether there is such fitness or not, we all assume that there is, and if we do, we express in moral judgments more than the subjectivists say we do. Let me illustrate.

In his novel *The House of the Dead*, Dostoevsky tells of his experiences in a Siberian prison camp. Whatever the unhappy inmates of such camps are like today, Dostoevsky's companions were about as grim a lot as can be imagined. "I have heard stories," he writes, "of the most terrible, the most unnatural actions, of the most monstrous murders, told with the most spontaneous, childishly merry laughter." Most of us would say that in this delight at the killing of others or the causing of suffering there is something very unfitting. If we were asked why we thought so, we should say that these things involve great evil and are wrong, and that to take delight in what is evil or wrong is plainly unfitting. Now on the subjectivist view, this answer is ruled out. For before someone takes up an attitude toward death, suffering, or their infliction, they have no moral quality at all. There is therefore nothing about them to which an attitude of approval or condemnation could be fitting. They are in themselves neutral, and, so far as they get a moral quality, they get it only through being invested with it by the attitude of the onlooker. But if that is true, why is any attitude more fitting than any other? Would applause, for example, be fitting if, apart from the applause, there was nothing good to applaud? Would condemnation be fitting if, independently of the condemnation, there were nothing bad to condemn? In such a case, any attitude would be as fitting or unfitting as any other, which means that the notion of fitness has lost all point.

Indeed we are forced to go much farther. If goodness and badness lie in attitudes only and are brought into being by them, those men who greeted death and misery with childishly merry laughter are taking the only sensible line. If there is nothing evil in these things, if they get their moral complexion only from our feeling about them, why shouldn't they be greeted with a cheer? To greet them with repulsion would turn what before was neutral into something bad; it would needlessly bring badness into the world; and even on subjectivist assumptions that does not seem very bright. On the other hand, to greet them with delight would

convert what before was neutral into something good; it would bring goodness into the world. If I have murdered a man and wish to remove the stain, the way is clear. It is to cry, "Hurrah for murder."

What is the subjectivist to reply? I can only guess. He may point out that the inflicting of death is *not* really neutral before the onlooker takes his attitude, for the man who inflicted the death no doubt himself took an attitude, and thus the act had a moral quality derived from this. But that makes the case more incredible still, for the man who did the act presumably approved it, and if so it was good in the only sense in which anything is good, and then our conviction that the laughter is unfit is more unaccountable still. It may be replied that the victim, too, had his attitude and that since this was unfavorable, the act was not unqualifiedly good. But the answer is plain. Let the killer be expert at his job; let him dispatch his victim instantly before he has time to take an attitude, and then gloat about his perfect crime without ever telling anyone. Then, so far as I can see, his act will be good without any qualification. It would become bad only if someone found out about it and disliked it. And that would be a curiously irrational procedure, since the man's approving of his own killing is in itself just as neutral as the killing that it approves. Why then should anyone dislike it?

It may be replied that we can defend our dislike on this ground that, if the approval of killing were to go unchecked and spread, most men would have to live in insecurity and fear, and these things are undesirable. But surely this reply is not open; these things are not, on the theory, undesirable, for nothing is; in themselves they are neutral. Why then should I disapprove men's living in this state? The answer may come that if other men live in insecurity and fear, I shall in time be infected myself. But even in my own insecurity and fear there is, on the theory before us, nothing bad whatever, and therefore, if I disapprove them, it is without a shadow of ground and with no more fitness in my attitude than if I cordially cheered them. The theory thus conflicts with our judgments of fitness all along the line.

I come now to a fifth and final difficulty with the theory. It makes mistakes about values impossible. There is a whole nest of inter-connected criticisms here, some of which have been made so often that I shall not develop them again, such as that I can never agree or disagree in opinion with anyone else about an ethical matter, and that in these matters I can never be inconsistent with others or with myself. I am not at all content with the sort of analysis which says that the only contradictions in such cases have regard to facts and that contradictions about value are only differences of feeling. I think that if anyone tells me that having a bicuspid out without an anaesthetic is not a bad experience and I say it is a very nasty experience indeed, I am differing with him in opinion, and differing about the degree of badness of the experience. But without pressing this further, let me apply the argument in what is perhaps a fresh direction.

There is an old and merciful distinction that moralists have made for many centuries about conduct—the distinction between what is subjectively and what is objectively right. They have said that in any given situation there is some act which, in view of all the circumstances, would be the best act to do; and this is what would be objectively right. The notion of an objectively right act is the ground of our notion of duty; our duty is always to find and do this act if we can. But of course we often don't find it. We often hit upon and do acts that we think are the right ones, but we are mistaken; and then our act is only subjectively right. Between these two acts the disparity may be continual; Professor Prichard suggested that probably few of us in the course of our lives ever succeed in doing *the* right act.

Now so far as I can see, the new subjectivism would abolish this difference at a stroke. Let us take a case. A boy abuses his small brother. We should commonly say,

"That is wrong, but perhaps he doesn't know any better. By reason of bad teaching and a feeble imagination, he may see nothing wrong in what he is doing, and may even be proud of it. If so, his act may be subjectively right, though it is miles away from what is objectively right." What concerns me about the new subjectivism is that it prohibits this distinction. If the boy feels this way about his act, then it is right in the only sense in which anything is right. The notion of an objective right lying beyond what he has discovered, and which he ought to seek and do is meaningless. There might, to be sure, be an act that would more generally arouse favorable feelings in others, but that would not make it right for him unless he thought of it and approved it, which he doesn't. Even if he did think of it, it would not be obligatory for him to feel about it in any particular way, since there is nothing in any act, as we have seen, which would make any feeling more suitable than any other.

Now if there is no such thing as an objectively right act, what becomes of the idea of duty? I have suggested that the idea of duty rests on the idea of such an act, since it is always our duty to find that act and do it if we can. But if whatever we feel approval for at the time is right, what is the point of doubting and searching further? Like the little girl in Boston who was asked if she would like to travel, we can answer, "Why should I travel when I'm already there?" If I am reconciled in feeling to my present act, no act I could discover by reflection could be better, and therefore why reflect or seek at all? Such a view seems to me to break the mainspring of duty, to destroy the motive for self-improvement, and to remove the ground for self-criticism. It may be replied that by further reflection I can find an act that would satisfy my feelings more widely than the present one, and that this is the act I should seek. But this reply means either that such general satisfaction is objectively better, which would contradict the theory, or else that, if at the time I don't feel it better, it isn't better, in which case I have no motive for seeking it. When certain self-righteous persons took an inflexible line with Oliver Cromwell, his very Cromwellian reply was, "Bethink ye, gentlemen, by the bowels of Christ, that ye may be mistaken." It was good advice. I hope nobody will take from me the privilege of finding myself mistaken. I should be sorry to think that the self of thirty years ago was as far along the path as the self of today, merely because he was a smug young jackanapes, or even that the paragon of today has as little room for improvement as would be allowed by his myopic complacency.

One final remark. The great problems of the day are international problems. Has the new subjectivism any bearing upon these problems? I think it has, and a somewhat sinister bearing. I would not suggest, of course, that those who hold the theory are one whit less public-spirited than others; surely there are few who could call themselves citizens of the world with more right (if "rights" have meaning any longer) than Lord Russell. But Lord Russell has confessed himself discontented with his ethical theory, and in view of his breadth of concern, one cannot wonder. For its general acceptance would, so far as one can see, be an international disaster. The assumption behind the old League and the new United Nations was that there is such a thing as right and wrong in the conduct of a nation, a right and wrong that do not depend on how it happens to feel at the time. It is implied, for example, that when Japan invaded Manchuria in 1931 she might be wrong, and that by discussion and argument she might be shown to be wrong. It was implied that when the Nazis invaded Poland they might be wrong, even though German public sentiment overwhelmingly approved it. On the theory before us, it would be meaningless to call these nations mistaken; if they felt approval for what they did, then it was right with as complete a justification as could be supplied for the disapproval felt by the rest of the world. In the present tension between Russia and ourselves over eastern Europe, it is nonsense to speak of the right or rational course for either of us to take; if with all the facts before the two parties, each feels approval for its own course, both attitudes are equally justified or unjustified; neither is mistaken; there is no common reason to which they can take an appeal; there are no principles by which an international court could pronounce on the matter; nor would there be any obligation to obey the pronouncement if it were made. This cuts the ground from under any attempt to establish one's case as right or anyone else's case as wrong. So if our friends the subjectivists still hold their theory after I have applied my little ruler to their knuckles, which of course they will, I have but one request to make of them: Don't advertise it to the people in the Kremlin.

5
HOW TO DERIVE 'OUGHT' FROM 'IS'

John R. Searle

I

It is often said that one cannot derive an 'ought' from an 'is'. This thesis, which comes from a famous passage in Hume's *Treatise,* while not as clear as it might be, is at least clear in broad outline: there is a class of statements of fact which is logically distinct from a class of statements of value. No set of statements of fact by themselves entails any statement of value. Put in more contemporary terminology, no set of *descriptive* statements can entail an *evaluative* statement without the addition of at least one evaluative premise. To believe otherwise is to commit what has been called the naturalistic fallacy.

I shall attempt to demonstrate a counter-example to this thesis.[2] It is not of course to be supposed that a single counter-example can refute a philosophical thesis, but in the present instance if we can present a plausible counter-example and can in addition give some account or explanation of how and why it is a counter-example, and if we can further offer a theory to back up our counter-example—a theory which will generate an indefinite number of counter-examples—we may at the very least cast considerable light on the original thesis; and possibly, if we can do all these things, we may even incline ourselves to the view that the scope of that thesis was more restricted than we had originally supposed. A counter-example must proceed by taking a statement or statements which any proponent of the thesis would grant were purely factual or 'descriptive' (they need not actually contain the word 'is') and show how they are logically related to a statement which a proponent of the thesis would regard as clearly 'evaluative'. (In the present instance it will contain an 'ought'.)[3]

Consider the following series of statements:

1. Jones uttered the words 'I hereby promise to pay you, Smith, five dollars.'
2. Jones promised to pay Smith five dollars.

From *Philosophical Review,* Vol. 73 (1964), 43–58. Reprinted by permission.

3. Jones placed himself under (undertook) an obligation to pay Smith five dollars.
4. Jones is under an obligation to pay Smith five dollars.
5. Jones ought to pay Smith five dollars.

I shall argue concerning this list that the relation between any statement and its successor, while not in every case one of 'entailment', is none the less not just a contingent relation; and the additional statements necessary to make the relationship one of entailment do not need to involve any evaluative statements, moral principles, or anything of the sort.

Let us begin. How is (1) related to (2)? In certain circumstances, uttering the words in quotation marks in (1) is the act of making a promise. And it is a part of or a consequence of the meaning of the words in (1) that in those circumstances uttering them is promising. 'I hereby promise' is a paradigm device in English for performing the act described in (2), promising.

Let us state this fact about English usage in the form of an extra premise:

(1a) Under certain conditions C anyone who utters the words (sentence) 'I hereby promise to pay you, Smith, five dollars' promises to pay Smith five dollars.

What sorts of things are involved under the rubric 'conditions C?' What is involved will be all those conditions, those states of affairs, which are necessary and sufficient conditions for the utterance of the words (sentence) to constitute the successful performance of the act of promising. The conditions will include such things as that the speaker is in the presence of the hearer Smith, they are both conscious, both speakers of English, speaking seriously. The speaker knows what he is doing, is not under the influence of drugs, not hypnotised or acting in a play, not telling a joke or reporting an event, and so forth. This list will no doubt be somewhat indefinite because the boundaries of the concept of a promise, like the boundaries of most con-

cepts in a natural language, are a bit loose.[4] But one thing is clear; however loose the boundaries may be, and however difficult it may be to decide marginal cases, the conditions under which a man who utters 'I hereby promise' can correctly be said to have made a promise are straightforwardly empirical conditions.

So let us add as an extra premise the empirical assumption that these conditions obtain.

(1b) Conditions C obtain.

From (1), (1a), and (1b) we derive (2). The argument is of the form: If C then (if U then P): C for conditions, U for utterance, P for promise. Adding the premises U and C to this hypothetical we derive (2). And as far as I can see, no moral premises are lurking in the logical woodpile. More needs to be said about the relation of (1) to (2), but I reserve that for later.

What is the relation between (2) and (3)? I take it that promising is, by definition, an act of placing oneself under an obligation. No analysis of the concept of promising will be complete which does not include the feature of the promiser placing himself under or undertaking or accepting or recognising an obligation to the promisee, to perform some future course of action, normally for the benefit of the promisee. One may be tempted to think that promising can be analysed in terms of creating expectations in one's hearers, or some such, but a little reflection will show that the crucial distinction between statements of intention on the one hand and promises on the other lies in the nature and degree of commitment or obligation undertaken in promising.

I am therefore inclined to say that (2) entails (3) straight off, but I can have no objection if anyone wishes to add—for the purpose of formal neatness—the tautological premise:

(2a) All promises are acts of placing oneself under (undertaking) an obligation to do the thing promised.

How is (3) related to (4)? If one has placed oneself under an obligation, then, other things being equal, one is under an obligation. That I take it also is a tautology. Of course it is possible for all sorts of things to happen which will release one from obligations one has undertaken and hence the need for the *ceteris paribus* rider. To get an entailment between (3) and (4) we therefore need a qualifying statement to the effect that:

(3a) Other things are equal.

Formalists, as in the move from (2) to (3), may wish to add the tautological premise:

(3b) All those who place themselves under an obligation are, other things being equal, under an obligation.

The move from (3) to (4) is thus of the same form as the move from (1) to (2): If E then (if PUO then UO): E for other things are equal, PUO for place under obligation and UO for under obligation. Adding the two premises E and PUO we derive UO.

Is (3a), the *ceteris paribus* clause, a concealed evaluative premise? It certainly looks as if it might be, especially in the formulation I have given it, but I think we can show that, though questions about whether other things are equal frequently involve evaluative considerations, it is not logically necessary that they should in every case. I shall postpone discussion of this until after the next step.

What is the relation between (4) and (5)? Analogous to the tautology which explicates the relation of (3) and (4) there is here the tautology that, other things being equal, one ought to do what one is under an obligation to do. And here, just as in the previous case, we need some premise of the form:

(4a) Other things are equal.

We need the *ceteris paribus* clause to eliminate the possibility that something extraneous to the relation of 'obligation' to 'ought'

might interfere.[5] Here, as in the previous two steps, we eliminate the appearance of enthymeme by pointing out that the apparently suppressed premise is tautological and hence, though formally neat, it is redundant. If, however, we wish to state it formally, this argument is of the same form as the move from (3) to (4): If E then (if UO then O); E for other things are equal, UO for under obligation, O for ought. Adding the premises E and UO we derive O.

Now a word about the phrase 'other things being equal' and how it functions in my attempted derivation. This topic and the closely related topic of defeasibility are extremely difficult and I shall not try to do more than justify my claim that the satisfaction of the condition does not necessarily involve anything evaluative. The force of the expression 'other things being equal' in the present instance is roughly this. Unless we have some reason (that is, unless we are actually prepared to give some reason) for supposing the obligation is void (step 4) or the agent ought not to keep the promise (step 5), then the obligation holds and he ought to keep the promise. It is not part of the force of the phrase 'other things being equal' that in order to satisfy it we need to establish a universal negative proposition to the effect that no reason could ever be given by anyone for supposing the agent is not under an obligation or ought not to keep the promise. That would be impossible and would render the phrase useless. It is sufficient to satisfy the condition that no reason to the contrary can in fact be given.

If a reason is given for supposing the obligation is void or that the promiser ought not to keep the promise, then characteristically a situation calling for evaluation arises. Suppose, for example, we consider a promised act wrong, but we grant that the promiser did undertake an obligation. Ought he to keep the promise? There is no established procedure for objectively deciding such cases in advance, and an evaluation (if that is really the right word) is in order. But unless we have some reason to the contrary, the *ceteris paribus* condition is satisfied, no evaluation is necessary, and the question whether he ought to do it is settled by saying 'he promised.' It is always an open possibility that we may have to make an evaluation in order to derive 'he ought' from 'he promised', for we may have to evaluate a counter-argument. But an evaluation is not logically necessary in every case, for there may as a matter of fact be no counter-arguments. I am therefore inclined to think that there is nothing necessarily evaluative about the *ceteris paribus* condition, even though deciding whether it is satisfied will frequently involve evaluations.

But suppose I am wrong about this: would that salvage the belief in an unbridgeable logical gulf between 'is' and 'ought'? I think not, for we can always rewrite my steps (4) and (5) so that they include the *ceteris paribus* clause as part of the conclusion. Thus from our premises we would then have derived 'Other things being equal Jones ought to pay Smith five dollars', and that would still be sufficient to refute the tradition, for we would still have shown a relation of entailment between descriptive and evaluative statements. It was not the fact that extenuating circumstances can void obligations that drove philosophers to the naturalistic fallacy fallacy; it was rather a theory of language, as we shall see later on.

We have thus derived (in as strict a sense of 'derive' as natural languages admit of) an 'ought' from an 'is'. And the extra premises which were needed to make the derivation work were in no cause moral or evaluative in nature. They consisted of empirical assumptions, tautologies, and descriptions of word usage. It must be pointed out also that the 'ought' is a 'categorical' not a 'hypothetical' ought. (5) does not say that Jones ought to pay up if he wants such and such. It says he ought to pay up, period. Note also that the steps of the derivation are carried on in the third person. We are not concluding 'I ought' from 'I said "I promise"', but 'he ought' from 'he said "I promise"'.

The proof unfolds the connection between the utterance of certain words and the speech act of promising and then in turn unfolds promising into obligation and

moves from obligation to 'ought'. The step from (1) to (2) is radically different from the others and requires special comment. In (1) we construe 'I hereby promise . . . ' as an English phrase having a certain meaning. It is a consequence of that meaning that the utterance of that phrase under certain conditions is the act of promising. Thus by presenting the quoted expressions in (1) and by describing their use in (1a) we have as it were already invoked the institution of promising. We might have started with an even more ground-floor premise than (1) by saying:

(1b) Jones uttered the phonetic sequence:/ai⁺hir⁺bai⁺pramis⁺təpei⁺yu⁺smiθ⁺faiv⁺dəl ərz/

We would then have needed extra empirical premises stating that this phonetic sequence was associated in certain ways with certain meaningful units relative to certain dialects.

The moves from (2) to (5) are relatively easy. We rely on definitional connections between 'promise', 'obligate', and 'ought', and the only problem which arises is that obligations can be overridden or removed in a variety of ways and we need to take account of that fact. We solve our difficulty by adding further premises to the effect that there are no contrary considerations, that other things are equal.

II

In this section I intend to discuss three possible objections to the derivation.

First Objection

Since the first premise is descriptive and the conclusion evaluative, there must be a concealed evaluative premise in the description of the conditions in (2b).

So far, this argument merely begs the question by assuming the logical gulf between descriptive and evaluative which the derivation is designed to challenge. To make the objection stick, the defender of the distinction would have to show how exactly (2b) must contain an evaluative premise and what sort of premise it might be. Uttering certain words in certain conditions just *is* promising and the description of these conditions needs no evaluative element. The essential thing is that in the transition from (1) to (2) we move from the specification of a certain utterance of words to the specification of a certain speech act. The move is achieved because the speech act is a conventional act; and the utterance of words, according to the conventions, constitutes the performance of just that speech act.

A variant of this first objection is to say: all you have shown is that 'promise' is an evaluative, not a descriptive, concept. But this objection again begs the question and in the end will prove disastrous to the original distinction between descriptive and evaluative. For that a man uttered certain words and that these words have the meaning they do are surely objective facts. And if the statement of these two objective facts plus a description of the conditions of the utterance is sufficient to entail the statement (2) which the objector alleges to be an evaluative statement (Jones promised to pay Smith five dollars), then an evaluative conclusion is derived from descriptive premises without even going through steps (3), (4), and (5).

Second Objection

Ultimately the derivation rests on the principle that one ought to keep one's promises and that is a moral principle, hence evaluative.

I don't know whether 'one ought to keep one's promises' is a 'moral' principle, but whether or not it is, it is also tautological; for it is nothing more than a derivation from the two tautologies:

All promises are (create, are undertakings of, are acceptances of) obligations,
and
One ought to keep (fulfil) one's obligations.

What needs to be explained is why so many philosophers have failed to see the tautological character of this principle. Three things I think have concealed its character from them.

The first is a failure to distinguish external questions about the institution of promising from internal questions asked within the framework of an institution. The questions 'Why do we have such an institution as promising?' and 'Ought we to have such institutionalised forms of obligation as promising?' are external questions asked about and not within the institution of promising. And the question 'Ought one to keep one's promises?' can be confused with or can be taken as (and I think has often been taken as) an external question roughly expressible as 'Ought one to accept the institution of promising?' But taken literally, as an internal question, as a question about promises and not about the institution of promising, the question 'Ought one to keep one's promises?' is as empty as the question 'Are triangles three-sided?' To recognise something as a promise is to grant that, other things being equal, it ought to be kept.

A second fact which has clouded the issue is this. There are many situations, both real and imaginable, where one ought not to keep a promise, where the obligation to keep a promise is overridden by some further considerations, and it was for this reason that we needed those clumsy *ceteris paribus* clauses in our derivation. But the fact that obligations can be overridden does not show that there were no obligations in the first place. On the contrary. And these original obligations are all that is needed to make the proof work.

Yet a third factor is the following. Many philosophers still fail to realise the full force of saying that 'I hereby promise' is a performative expression. In uttering it one performs but does not describe the act of promising. Once promising is seen as a speech act of a kind different from describing, then it is easier to see that one of the features of the act is the undertaking of an obligation. But if one thinks the utterance of 'I promise' or 'I hereby promise' is a peculiar kind of description—for example, of one's mental state—then the relation between promising and obligation is going to seem very mysterious.

Third Objection

The derivation uses only a factual or inverted-commas sense of the evaluative terms employed. For example, an anthropologist observing the behaviour and attitudes of the Anglo-Saxons might well go through these derivations, but nothing evaluative would be included. Thus step (2) is equivalent to 'He did what they call promising' and step (5) to 'According to them he ought to pay Smith five dollars.' But since all of the steps (2) to (5) are in *oratio obliqua* and hence disguised statements of fact, the fact-value distinction remains unaffected.

This objection fails to damage the derivation, for what it says is only that the steps *can* be reconstrued as in *oratio obliqua*, that we can construe them as a series of external statements, that we can construct a parallel (or at any rate related) proof about reported speech. But what I am arguing is that, taken quite literally, without any *oratio obliqua* additions or interpretations, the derivation is valid. That one can construct a similar argument which would fail to refute the fact-value distinction does not show that this proof fails to refute it. Indeed it is irrelevant.

NOTES

1. Earlier versions of this paper were read before the Stanford Philosophy Colloquium and the Pacific Division of the American Philosophical Association. I am indebted to many people for helpful comments and criticisms, especially Hans Herzberger, Arnold Kaufmann, Benson Mates, A. I. Melden, and Dagmar Searle.

2. In its modern version. I shall not be concerned with Hume's treatment of the problem.

3. If this enterprise succeeds, we shall have bridged the gap between 'evaluative' and 'descriptive' and consequently have demonstrated a weakness in this very terminology. At present, however, my strategy is to play along with the terminology, pretending that the notions of evaluative and descriptive are fairly clear. At the end of the paper I shall state in what respects I think they embody a muddle.

4. In addition the concept of a promise is a member of a class of concepts which suffer from looseness of a peculiar kind, viz. defeasibility. Cf. H. L. A. Hart, 'The Ascription of Responsibility and Rights', *Logic and Language*, first series, ed. A. Flew (Oxford 1951).

5. The *ceteris paribus* clause in this step excludes somewhat different sorts of cases from those excluded in the previous step. In general we say, 'He undertook an obligation, but none the less he is not (now) under an obligation' when the obligation has been *removed*, e.g. if the promisee says, 'I release you from your obligation.' But we say, 'He is under an obligation, but none the less ought not to fulfil it' in cases where the obligation is *overridden* by some other consideration, e.g. a prior obligation.

6

ON NOT DERIVING 'OUGHT' FROM 'IS'

Antony Flew

... The word nevertheless seems to have gone round that the idea that there is a radical difference between *ought* and *is* is old hat, something which though still perhaps cherished by out-group back-woodsmen has long since been seen through and discarded by all with-it mainstream philosophers. For instance, in a penetrating article on 'Do illocutionary forces exist?'[1] Mr L. Jonathan Cohen offers some provocative asides:'the statement-evaluation dichotomy, whatever it may be, is as erroneous on my view as on Austin's; and 'Indeed there is a case for saying that Austin's recommendation about the word "good" is itself a hangover from the fact-value dichotomy.' Cohen gives no hint as to where and how this dichotomy was so decisively liquidated. But a recent paper by Mr John R. Searle, on 'How to derive "ought" from "is" '[2] can perhaps be seen as an attempt to plug the gap. Searle's stated aim is to show that the Naturalistic Fallacy is not a fallacy, and he gives many signs of

From *Analysis* 25 (1964):25–32. Reprinted by permission.

thinking of his aspirations in Austinian terms. My object is to show that Searle is entirely unsuccessful, and to suggest that anyone who hopes to succeed where he has failed will have to find other and more powerful arguments.

2.The first point to remark about Searle's article is that he chooses to start from his own characterisation of what the Naturalistic Fallacy is supposed to consist in; and that he neither quotes nor gives precise references to any statements by the philosophers with whom he wishes to disagree. His characterisation runs:

It is often said that one cannot derive an 'ought' from an 'is'. This thesis, which comes from a famous passage in Hume's *Treatise*, while not as clear as it might be, is at least clear in broad outline: there is a class of statements of fact which is logically distinct from a class of statements of value. No set of statements of fact by themselves entails any statement of value. Put in more contemporary terminology, no set of *descriptive* statements can entail an *evaluative* statement without the addition of at least one evaluative premise. To believe otherwise is to commit the naturalistic fallacy. (Italics here and always as in original.)

Let us consider alongside this paragraph from Searle some sentences written by a contemporary protagonist of the view which Searle is supposed to be challenging. These quotations come from K. R. Popper and—significantly—they come from *The Open Society* (1945):

The breakdown of magic tribalism is closely connected with the realization that taboos are different in various tribes, that they are imposed and enforced by man, and that they may be broken without unpleasant repercussions if one can only escape the sanctions imposed by one's fellow-men. . . . These experiences may lead to a conscious differentiation between the man-enforced normative laws or conventions, and the natural regularities which are beyond his power. . . . In spite of the fact that this position was reached a long time ago by the Sophist Protagoras . . . it is still so little understood that it seems necessary to explain it in some detail. . . . It is we who impose our standards upon nature, and who introduce in this way morals into the natural world, in spite of the fact that we are part of this world. . . . It is important for the understanding of this attitude to realize that decisions can never be derived from facts (or statements of facts), although they pertain to facts. The decision, for instance to oppose slavery does not depend upon the fact that all men are born free and equal, and no man is born in chains . . . even if they were born in chains, many of us might demand the removal of these chains. . . . The making of a decision, the adoption of a standard, is a fact. But the norm which has been adopted, is not. That most people agree with the norm 'Thou shalt not steal' is a sociological fact. But the norm 'Thou shalt not steal' is not a fact; and it can never be inferred from sentences describing facts. . . . *It is impossible to derive a sentence stating a norm or a decision from a sentence stating a fact;* this is only another way of saying that it is impossible to derive norms or decisions from facts. (Vol. I, pp. 50–3)

Popper's account even in this abbreviated form, is of course much fuller than that given by Searle; and, partly for that reason, it says or suggests many things which are not comprised in Searle's short paragraph. It presents the idea of the Naturalistic Fallacy as involved in the clash of world-outlooks and personal commitments; and it is governed throughout by the notion that 'we are free to form our own moral opinions in a much stronger sense than we are free to form our own opinions as to what the facts are.[2] But the most relevant and important difference is that Popper at least suggests, what is true, that the fundamental discrimination in terms of which the Naturalistic Fallacy is being characterised is not, and does not have to be thought to be, a clearcut feature of all actual discourse. It is not something which you cannot fail to observe everywhere as already there and given, if once you have learnt what to look for. There is, rather, a differentiation which has to be made and insisted upon; and the distinction is one the development of which may go against the grain of set habits and powerful inclinations. Our situation in this case is not at all like that represented in the second chapter of the book of *Genesis,* where God presents to Adam the beasts of the field and the fowl of the air, leaving it to him merely to supply names for each natural kind.

Searle's account of the opposing position seems to suggest, what his later criticism appears to be assuming, that its misguided spokesmen must be committed to the notion: that an *is/ought* dichotomy is something which the alert natural historian of utterances could not fail to notice, as somehow already given; and that no utterances can either combine, or be ambiguous as between, these two sorts of claim. Yet when we turn to Popper, and allow him to speak for himself, we find in his account nothing at all to suggest any commitment to the erroneous ideas: that all the utterances which are actually made must already be clearly and unambiguously either statements of fact or expressions of value; or that every actual utterance is either purely a statement of fact or purely normative. What Popper emphasises is, rather, the epoch-marking importance of the development of this sort of distinction, the great need to insist upon it, and the difficulty of appreciating fully what it does and what it does not imply.

It is perhaps possible that Searle here, like so many others elsewhere, has been misled by Hume's irony; notwithstanding that Searle himself disclaims concern with 'Hume's treatment of the problem.' For Hume does indeed write as if he was quite modestly claiming only to have noticed, and to have become seized of the vast importance of, a distinction which, however unwittingly, everyone was always and systematically making already:[3]

I cannot forbear adding to these reasonings an observation, which may, perhaps, be found of some importance. In every system of morality, which I have hitherto met with, I have always remarked, that the author proceeds for some time in the ordinary way of reasoning, and establishes the being of a God, or makes observations concerning human affairs; when of a sudden I am surprised to find, that instead of the usual copulations of propositions *is,* and *is not,* I meet with no proposition that is not connected with an *ought,* or an *ought not.*

3. After this somewhat protracted introduction, designed to refresh memories about what is and is not involved in the position which Searle is supposed to be attacking, we can now at last turn to his arguments. He works with the example of promising: 'The proof unfolds the connection between the utterance of certain words and the speech act of promising and then in turn unfolds promising into obligation and moves from obligation to "ought"'. The idea is to start with a purely descriptive premise such as 'Jones uttered the words "I hereby promise to pay you, Smith, five dollars"', or that Jones uttered the corresponding phonetic sequence, and to proceed by a series of deductive moves to the purely normative conclusion 'Jones ought to pay Smith five dollars'. Considerable elaboration is necessary, and is provided, in the attempt to deal with the complications arising: because the utterance of such words or sounds will not always rate as a making of the promise; and because the prima facie

obligation to keep a promise can be nullified or overridden.

It will, in the light of what has been said in section 2, be sufficiently obvious what sort of moves the critic must make if he hopes to drive a wedge into such a proposed proof. He has to distinguish normative and descriptive elements in the meaning of words like *promise;* and to insist that, however willing we may be to accept the package deal in this particular uncontentious case of promising, it is nevertheless still not possible to deduce the normative from the descriptive part of the combination. The best place to insert the wedge in Searle's argument seems to be where he maintains: 'one thing is clear; however loose the boundaries may be, and however difficult it may be to decide marginal cases, the conditions under which a man who utters 'I hereby promise' can correctly be said to have made a promise are straightforwardly empirical conditions'. The weakness becomes glaring if we summon for comparison some obnoxious contentions of the same form. Terms such as *nigger* or *Jewboy, apostate* or *infidel, colonialist* or *kulak* no doubt carry, at least when employed in certain circles, both normative and descriptive meanings; and, presumably, the descriptive element of that meaning can correctly be said to apply whenever the appropriate 'straightforwardly empirical conditions' are satisfied. But in these parallel cases most of us, I imagine, would be careful to use one of the several linguistic devices for indicating that we do not commit ourselves to the norms involved, or that we positively repudiate them. Thus, to revert to Searle's example, one could, without any logical impropriety, say of the man who had in suitable circumstances uttered the words 'I hereby promise . . .' that he had done what is called (by those who accept the social institution of promising) promising. The oddity of this non-committal piece of pure description would lie simply in the perversity of suggesting a policy of non-involvement in an institution which is surely essential to any tolerable human social life.

4. It remains to ask either why these

moves do not impinge on Searle as considerable objections or how he thinks to dispose of them. We have already in section 2 offered suggestions bearing on these questions. But more light is to be found by considering in the second part of his article ₁is discussion of 'three possible objections to the derivation'.

(a) The first of these objections consists in simply asserting that 'Since the first premise is descriptive and the conclusion evaluative, there must be a concealed evaluative premise in the description of the conditions. . . .'. To which Searle replies that as it stands this objection just begs the question: it requires to be supplemented with some account of the precise location and nature of the concealed evaluative premise. So far, so unexceptionable. The crunch comes when he continues: 'Uttering certain words in certain conditions just *is* promising and the description of these conditions needs no evaluative element'. For, as we have been urging in section 3, the normative element enters: not with the neutral description of the conditions in which those who accept the social institution of promise-making and promise-keeping would say that someone had made what they call a promise; but at the moment when, by using the word *promise* without reservation, we commit ourselves to that institution.

(b) The second objection considered runs: 'Ultimately the derivation rests on the principle that one ought to keep one's promises and that is a moral principle, hence evaluative.' To this Searle responds that, whether or not this is a moral principle, 'it is also tautological'. He then proceeds to offer three suggestions to explain 'why so many philosophers have failed to see the tautological character of this principle'. This is, perhaps, to go rather too fast. For the sentence 'One ought to keep one's promises' is not in itself and unequivocally either tautological or not. It could without too much strain be given either tautological or substantial or even equivocal employments. If the user is prepared to accept that the absence of obligation is a sufficient reason for withdrawing the word *promise*, then the employment is clearly tautological. But if he is to be taken to be referring to certain specific descriptive conditions, and maintaining that, granted those, certain specific things ought to be done, then, surely, the employment is substantial. And if he is insisting that, granted these specific descriptive conditions, then necessarily those things ought to be done; then he would seem to be equivocating between a substantial and a tautological employment.

The first of Searle's suggestions is that some of his opponents have failed 'to distinguish external questions about the institution of promising from internal questions asked within the framework of the institution'. No doubt some have: though it would be slightly surprising and wholly deplorable to find that many philosophers in an Humean tradition had neglected a distinction of a kind for which one of the classical sources is to be found in the third appendix of the second *Inquiry*. Even so this particular charge rings very badly in the present context. For, as we were urging in section 3, the weakness of Searle's attempted derivation lies precisely in the refusal to allow that the acceptance of a social institution must come between any statement of the purely descriptive conditions for saying that a promise was made, and the drawing of the normative conclusion that something ought to be done.

A more subtle version of the same fault can be seen in Searle's reply to a variant of his first proposed objection, which would protest: 'all you have shown is that "promise" is an evaluative, not a descriptive, concept.' This variant, he claims, 'in the end will prove disastrous to the original distinction between descriptive and evaluative. For that a man uttered certain words and that these words have the meaning that they do are surely objective facts. And if the statement of these two objective facts plus a description of the conditions of the utterance is sufficient to entail the statement . . . which the objector alleges to be an evaluative statement . . . then an evaluative conclusion is derived from descriptive premises . . . '. But here again it is both necessary and decisive to insist on distinguishing: between a detached report on the meanings which some social group gives to certain value words; and the unreserved employment of those words by an engaged participant. For it is between the former and the latter that there comes exactly that commitment to the incapsulated values which alone warrants us to draw the normative conclusions.

Searle's other two suggestions both refer to peculiarities which make his chosen example especially tricky to handle: the second notices the difficulties which arise because the prima facie obligation to keep a promise made may sometimes properly be overridden by other claims: and the third takes cognisance of the fact that the first person present tense 'I promise' is performative. It is not perhaps altogether clear why failure to take the measure of this insight—for which again a classical source can be found in Hume[5]—is supposed to encourage the idea that 'One ought to keep one's promises' is not tautological. What Searle says is:'If one thinks the utterance of "I promise" or "I hereby promise" is a peculiar kind of description . . . then the relation between promising and obligation is going to seem very mysterious'. Certainly if one thinks that, then there will be a mystery as to why the utterance of these words is construed, by anyone who accepts the institution of promising, as involving the incurring of an obligation. But this is no reason at all for saying that the same misguided person must also by the same token find something mysterious about the notion that, supposing that someone has promised, it follows necessarily that he is obliged.

This is a good occasion to say that where we have spoken of a descriptive element in the meaning of *promise*, we were, of course, intending to include only uses other than the first person present performative. Fortunately the complications connected with that use can for present purposes be largely ignored. For in Searle's candidate proof 'I promise' is mentioned, not used; and so our criticism insists that the normative premise is to be found at the point where the performance is characterised, unreservedly, as a promise.

(c)The third objection considered is that: 'The derivation uses only a factual or inverted-commas sense of the evaluative terms employed.' This discussion is the most interesting for us. It is here that Searle comes nearest to recognising, and to trying to deal with, the rather obvious sort of criticism which we have been deploying. In formulating this objection Searle recognises the distinction: between the employment of a term like *promise* in a detached anthropological description of a social practice; and the use of the same term, without reservation, by a committed participant. His reply is: 'This objection fails to damage the derivation, for what it says is only that the steps *can* be reconstrued as in *oratio obliqua* . . . . That one can construct a similar argument which would fail to refute the fact-value distinction does not show that this proof fails to refute it. Indeed it is irrelevant'.

This, of course, is true. And if all spokesmen for the opposition were such men of straw it would be a very easy matter to consign them to the garbage dump. What is so extraordinary is that, having apparently allowed the crucial distinction, Searle fails to notice the decisive objection: that his step from 1, 'Jones uttered the words "I hereby promise to pay you, Smith, five dollars" ' to 2, 'Jones promised to pay Smith five dollars' is fallacious; unless, that is, we are supposed, as we are not, to construe 2 as being purely descriptive, as being, as it were, in *oratio obliqua*.

To explain Searle's oversight the only philosophically relevant suggestions we can offer are those indicated in section 2. Yet it really is extremely hard to believe that he is attributing to his opponents the assumptions: that all our discourse is already divided into elements which are either purely normative or exclusively descriptive; and that no legitimate expression could combine in its meaning both normative and descriptive components. For, though such misconceptions could conceivably be derived from a wooden and unsophisticated reading of some of those sentences in the *Treatise,* such a construction must at once make a mystery of any claim that attention to this distinction 'would subvert all the vulgar systems of morality'. This sort of thing could scarcely even be thought—as quite clearly it has been thought by many of the most distinguished protagonists of the idea of the Naturalistic Fallacy—if what was at stake really was just a matter of noticing a division already clearly and universally obtaining; rather than, as of course it is, a matter of insisting on making discriminations where often there is every sort of combination and confusion . . .

NOTES

1. *Philosophical Quarterly, 14(1964).*
2. R. M. Hare, *Freedom and Reason* (Oxford 1963) p. 2. The same author's *The Language of Morals* (Oxford 1952) is another excellent source for the sophisticated and flexible handling of the idea of the Naturalistic Fallacy; and Hare is, of course, perfectly well aware that the same terms and expressions may combine both descriptive and normative meanings—and hence that normative standards are incapsulated in certain uses of such terms.
3. D. Hume, *Treatise,* III. i. I.
4. *Treatise,* III. ii. 5, 'Of the obligation of promises'.

7
MORAL BELIEFS

Philippa Foot

1

To many people it seems that the most notable advance in moral philosophy during the past fifty years or so has been the refutation of naturalism; and they are a little shocked that at this late date such an issue should be reopened. It is easy to understand their attitude: given certain apparently unquestionable assumptions, it would be about as sensible to try to reintroduce naturalism as to try to square the circle. Those who see it like this have satisfied themselves that they know in advance that any naturalistic theory must have a catch in it somewhere, and are put out at having to waste more time exposing an old fallacy. This paper is an attempt to persuade them to look critically at the premises on which their arguments are based.

It would not be an exaggeration to say that the whole of moral philosophy, as it is

From *Proceedings of the Aristotelian Society* Vol. 59(1958—1959). ©The Aristotelian Society 1959. Reprinted by courtesy of the Editor.

now widely taught, rests on a contrast between statements of fact and evaluations, which runs something like this: 'The truth or falsity of statements of fact is shown by means of evidence; and what counts as evidence is laid down in the meaning of the expressions occurring in the statement of fact. (For instance, the meaning of "round" and "flat" made Magellan's voyages evidence for the roundness rather than the flatness of the Earth; someone who went on questioning whether the evidence was evidence could eventually be shown to have made some linguistic mistake.) It follows that no two people can make the same statement and count completely different things as evidence; in the end one at least of them could be convicted of linguistic ignorance. It also follows that if a man is given good evidence for a factual conclusion he cannot just refuse to accept the conclusion on the ground that in his scheme of things this evidence is not evidence at all. With evaluations, however, it is different. An evaluation is not connected logically with the factual statements on which it is based. One man may say that a thing is good because of some fact about it, and another may refuse to take that fact as any evidence at all, for nothing is laid down in the meaning of "good" which connects it with one piece of "evidence" rather than another. It follows that a moral eccentric could argue to moral conclusions from quite idiosyncratic premises; he could say, for instance, that a man was a good man because he clasped and unclasped his hands, and never turned NNE after turning SSW. He could also reject someone else's evaluation simply by denying that his evidence was evidence at all.

'The fact about "good" which allows the eccentric still to use this term without falling into a morass of meaninglessness, is its "action-guiding" or "practical" function. This it retains; for like everyone else he considers himself bound to choose the things he calls "good" rather than those he calls "bad". Like the rest of the world he uses "good" in connection only with a "pro-attitude"; it is only that he has pro-attitudes to quite different things, and therefore calls them good.'

There are here two assumptions about 'evaluations', which I will call assumption (1) and assumption (2).

Assumption (1) is that some individual may, without logical error, base his beliefs about matters of value entirely on premises which no one else would recognise as giving any evidence at all. Assumption (2) is that, given the kind of statement which other people regard as evidence for an evaluative conclusion, he may refuse to draw the conclusion because *this* does not count as evidence for *him*.

Let us consider assumption (1). We might say that this depends on the possibility of keeping the meaning of 'good' steady through all changes in the facts about anything which are to count in favour of its goodness. (I do not mean, of course, that a man can make changes as fast as he chooses; only that, whatever he has chosen, it will not be possible to rule him out of order.) But there is a better formulation, which cuts out

trivial disputes about the meaning which 'good' happens to have in some section of the community. Let us say that the assumption is that the evaluative function of 'good' can remain constant through changes in the evaluative principle; on this ground it could be said that even if no one can call a man *good* because he clasps and unclasps his hands, he can commend him or express his *pro-attitude* towards him, and if necessary can invent a new moral vocabulary to express his unusual moral code.

Those who hold such a theory will naturally add several qualifications. In the first place, most people now agree with Hare, against Stevenson, that such words as 'good' only apply to individual cases through the application of general principles, so that even the extreme moral eccentric must accept principles of commendation. In the second place 'commending', 'having a pro-attitude', and so on, are supposed to be connected with doing and choosing, so that it would be impossible to say, e.g. that a man was a good man only if he lived for a thousand years. The range of evaluation is supposed to be restricted to the range of possible action and choice. I am not here concerned to question these supposed restrictions on the use of evaluative terms, but only to argue that they are not enough.

The crucial question is this. Is it possible to extract from the meaning of words such as 'good' some element called 'evaluative meaning' which we can think of as externally related to its objects? Such an element would be represented, for instance, in the rule that when any action was 'commended' the speaker must hold himself bound to accept an imperative 'let me do these things'. This is externally related to its object because, within the limitation which we noticed earlier, to possible actions, it would make sense to think of anything as the subject of such 'commendation'. On this hypothesis a moral eccentric could be described as commending the clasping of hands as the action of a good man, and we should not have to look for some background to give this supposition sense. That is to say, on this hypothesis the clasping of hands could be commended without any explanation; it could be what those who hold such theories call 'an ultimate moral principle'.

I wish to say that this hypothesis is untenable, and that there is no describing the evaluative meaning of 'good', evaluation, commending, or anything of the sort, without fixing the object to which they are supposed to be attached. Without first laying hands on the proper object of such things as evaluation, we shall catch in our net either something quite different, such as accepting an order or making a resolution, or else nothing at all.

Before I consider this question, I shall first discuss some other mental attitudes and beliefs which have this internal relation to their object. By this I hope to clarify the concept of internal relation to an object, and incidentally, if my examples arouse resistance, but are eventually accepted, to show how easy it is to overlook an internal relation where it exists.

Consider, for instance, pride.

People are often surprised at the suggestion that there are limits to the things a man can be proud of, about which indeed he can feel pride. I do not know quite what account they want to give of pride; perhaps something to do with smiling and walking with a jaunty air, and holding an object up where other people can see it; or perhaps they think that pride is a kind of internal sensation, so that one might naturally beat one's breast and say 'pride is something I feel *here*'. The difficulties of the second view are well known; the logically private object cannot be what a name in the public language is the name of.[1] The first view is the more plausible, and it may seem reasonable to say that given certain behaviour a man can be described as showing that he is proud of something, whatever that something may be. In one sense this is true, and in another sense not. Given any description of an object, action, personal characteristic, etc., it is not possible to rule it out as an object of pride. Before we can do so we need to know what would be said about it by the man who is to be proud of it, or feels proud of it; but if he does not hold the right beliefs about it then whatever his attitude is it is not pride. Consider, for instance, the suggestion that someone might be proud of the sky or the sea: he looks at them and what he feels is *pride*, or he puffs out his chest and gestures with *pride* in their direction. This makes sense only if a special assumption is made about his beliefs, for instance, that he is under some crazy delusion and believes that he has saved the sky from falling, or the sea from drying up. The characteristic object of pride is something seen (*a*) as in some way a man's own, and (*b*) as some sort of achievement or advantage; without this object pride cannot be described. To see that the second condition is necessary, one should try supposing that a man happens to feel proud because he has laid one of his hands on the other, three times in an hour. Here again the supposition that it is pride that he feels will make perfectly good sense if a special background is filled in. Perhaps he is ill, and it is an achievement even to do this; perhaps this gesture has some religious or political significance, and he is a brave man who will so defy the gods or the rulers. But with no special background there can be no pride, not because no one could psychologically speaking feel pride in such a case, but because whatever he did feel could not logically be pride. Of course, people can see strange things as achievements, though not just anything, and they can identify themselves with remote ancestors, and relations, and neighbours, and even on occasions with Mankind. I do not wish to deny there are many far-fetched and comic examples of pride.

We could have chosen many other examples of mental attitudes which are internally related to their object in a similar way. For instance, fear is not just trembling, and running, and turning pale; without the thought of some menacing evil no amount of this will add up to fear. Nor could anyone be said to feel dismay about something he did not see as bad; if his thoughts about it were that it was altogether a good thing, he could not say that (oddly enough) what he felt about it was dismay. 'How odd, I feel dismayed when I ought to be pleased' is the prelude to a hunt for the adverse aspect of the thing, thought of as lurking behind the pleasant façade. But someone may object that pride and fear and dismay are feelings or emotions and therefore not a proper analogy for 'commendation', and there will be an advantage in considering a different kind of example. We could discuss, for instance, the belief that a certain thing is dangerous, and ask whether this could logically be held about anything whatsoever. Like 'this is good', 'this is dangerous' is an assertion, which we should naturally accept or reject by speaking of its truth or falsity; we seem to support such statements with evidence, and moreover there may seem to be a 'warning function' connected with the word 'dangerous' as there is supposed to be a 'commending function' connected with the word 'good'. For suppose that philosophers, puzzled about the property of dangerousness, decided that the word did not stand for a property at all, but was essentially a practical or action-guiding term, used for *warning*. Unless used in an 'inverted comma sense' the word 'dangerous' was used to warn, and this meant that anyone using it in such a sense committed himself to avoiding the things he called dangerous, to preventing other people from going near them, and perhaps to running in the opposite direction. If the conclusion were not obviously ridiculous, it would be easy to infer that a man whose application of the term was different from ours throughout might say that the oddest things were dangerous without fear of disproof; the idea would be that he could still be described as 'thinking them dangerous', or at least as 'warning', because by his attitude and actions he would have fulfilled the conditions for these things. This is nonsense because without its proper object *warning*, like *believing dangerous*, will not be there. It is logically impossible to warn

about anything not thought of as threatening evil, and for danger we need a particular kind of serious evil such as injury or death.

There are, however, some differences between thinking a thing dangerous and feeling proud, frightened or dismayed. When a man says that something is dangerous he must support his statement with a special kind of evidence; but when he says that he feels proud or frightened or dismayed the description of the object of his pride or fright or dismay does not have quite this relation to his original statement. If he is shown that the thing he was proud of was not his after all, or was not after all anything very grand, he may have to say that his pride was not justified, but he will not have to take back the statement that he was proud. On the other hand, someone who says that a thing is dangerous, and later sees that he made a mistake in thinking that an injury might result from it, has to go back on his original statement and admit that he was wrong. In neither case, however, is the speaker able to go on as before. A man who discovered that it was not his pumpkin but someone else's which had won the prize could only say that he still felt proud, if he could produce some other ground for pride. It is in this way that even feelings are logically vulnerable to facts.

It will probably be objected against these examples that for part of the way at least they beg the question. It will be said that indeed a man can only be proud of something he thinks a good action, or an achievement, or a sign of noble birth; as he can only feel dismay about something which he sees as bad, frightened at some threatened evil; similarly he can only warn if he is also prepared to speak, for instance, of injury. But this will only limit the range of possible objects of those attitudes and beliefs if the range of these terms is limited in its turn. To meet this objection I shall discuss the meaning of 'injury' because this is the simplest case. Anyone who feels inclined to say that anything could be counted as an achievement, or as the evil of which people were afraid, or about which they felt dismayed, should just try this out. I wish to consider the proposition that anything could be thought of as dangerous, because if it causes injury it is dangerous, and anything could be counted as an injury. I shall consider bodily injury because this is the injury connected with danger; it is not correct to put up a notice by the roadside reading 'Danger!' on account of bushes which might scratch a car. Nor can a substance be labelled 'dangerous' on the ground that it can injure delicate fabrics; although we can speak of the danger that it may do so, that is not the use of the word which I am considering here.

When a body is injured it is changed for the worse in a special way, and we want to know which changes count as injuries. First of all, it matters how an injury comes about; e.g. it cannot be caused by natural decay. Then it seems clear that not just any kind of thing will do, for instance, any unusual mark on the body, however much trouble a man might take to have it removed. By far the most important class of injuries are injuries to a part of the body, counting as injuries because there is interference with the function of that part; injury to a leg, an eye, an ear, a hand, a muscle, the heart, the brain, the spinal cord. An injury to an eye is one that affects, or is likely to affect, its sight; an injury to a hand one which makes it less well able to reach out and grasp, and perform other operations of this kind. A leg can be injured because its movements and supporting power can be affected; a lung because it can become too weak to draw in the proper amount of air. We are most ready to speak of an injury where the function of a part of the body is to perform a characteristic operation, as in these examples. We might hesitate to say that a skull can be injured, and might prefer to speak of damage to it, since although there is indeed a function (a protective function) there is no operation. But thinking of the protective function of the skull we may want to speak of injury here. In so far as the concept of *injury* depends on that of *function* it is narrowly limited, since not even every use to which a part of the body is put will count as its function. Why is it that, even if it is the means by which they earn their living, we would never consider the removal of the dwarf's hump or the bearded lady's beard as a bodily injury? It will be tempting to say that these things are disfigurements, but this is not the point; if we suppose that a man who had some invisible extra muscle made his living as a court jester by waggling his ears, the ear would not have been injured if this were made to disappear. If it were natural to men to communicate by movements of the ear, then ears would have the function of signalling (we have no word for this kind of 'speaking') and an impairment of this function would be an injury; but things are not like this. This court jester would use his ears to make people laugh, but this is not the function of ears.

No doubt many people will feel impatient when such facts are mentioned, because they think that it is quite unimportant that this or that *happens* to be the case, and it seems to them arbitrary that the loss of the beard, the hump, or the ear muscle would not be called an injury. Isn't the loss of that by which one makes one's living a pretty catastrophic loss? Yet it seems quite natural that these are not counted as injuries if one thinks about the conditions of human life, and contrasts the loss of a special ability to make people gape or laugh with the ability to see, hear, walk, or pick things up. The first is only needed for one very special way of living; the other in any foreseeable future for any man. This restriction seems all the more natural when we observe what other threats besides that of injury can constitute danger: of death, for instance, or mental derangement. A shock which could cause mental instability or impairment of memory would be called dangerous, because a man needs such things as intelligence, memory, and concentration as he needs sight or hearing or the use of hands. Here we do not speak of injury unless it is possible to connect the impairment with some physical change, but we speak of danger because there is the same loss of a capacity which any man needs.

There can be injury outside the range we have been considering; for a man may sometimes be said to have received injuries where no part of his body has had its function interfered with. In general, I think that any blow which disarranged the body in such a way that there was lasting pain would inflict an injury, even if no other ill resulted, but I do not know of any other important extension of the concept.

It seems therefore that since the range of things which can be called injuries is quite narrowly restricted, the word 'dangerous' is restricted in so far as it is connected with injury. We have the right to say that a man cannot decide to call just anything dangerous, however much he puts up fences and shakes his head.

So far I have been arguing that such things as pride, fear, dismay, and the thought that something is dangerous have an internal relation to their object, and hope that what I mean is becoming clear. Now we must consider whether those attitudes or beliefs which are the moral philosopher's study are similar, or whether such things as 'evaluation' and 'thinking something good' and 'commendation' could logically be found in combination with any object whatsoever. All I can do here is to give an example which may make this suggestion seem implausible, and to knock away a few of its supports. The example will come from the range of trivial and pointless actions such as we were considering in speaking of the man who clasped his hands three times an hour, and we can point to the oddity of the suggestion that this can be called a good action. We are bound by the terms of our question to refrain from adding any special background, and it should be stated once more that the question is about what can count in favour of the goodness or badness of a man or an action, and not what could be, or be thought, good or bad with a special background. I believe that the view I am attacking often seems plausible only because

the special background is surreptitiously introduced.

Someone who said that clasping the hands three times in an hour was a good action would first have to answer the question 'How do you mean?' For the sentence 'this is a good action' is not one which has a clear meaning. Presumably, since our subject is moral philosophy, it does not here mean 'that was a good thing to do' as this might be said of a man who had done something sensible in the course of any enterprise whatever; we are to confine our attention to 'the moral use of "good" '. I am not clear that it makes sense to speak of a 'moral use of "good" ', but we can pick out a number of cases which raise moral issues. It is because these are so diverse and because 'this is a good action' does not pick out any one of them, that we must ask 'How do you mean?' For instance, some things that are done fulfil a duty, such as the duty of parents to children or children to parents. I suppose that when philosophers speak of good actions they would include these. Some come under the heading of a virtue such as charity, and they will be included too. Others again are actions which require the virtues of courage or temperance, and here the moral aspect is due to the fact that they are done in spite of fear or the temptation of pleasure; they must indeed be done for the sake of some real or fancied good, but not necessarily what philosophers would want to call a moral good. Courage is not *particularly* concerned with saving other people's lives, or temperance with leaving them their share of the food and drink, and the goodness of *what is done* may here be all kinds of usefulness. It is because there are these very diverse cases included (I suppose) under the expression 'a good action' that we should refuse to consider applying it without asking what is meant, and we should now ask what is intended when someone is supposed to say that 'clasping the hands three times in an hour is a good action'. Is it supposed that this action fulfils a duty? Then in virtue of what does a man have this duty, and to whom does he owe it? We have promised not to slip in a special background, but he cannot possibly have a *duty* to clasp his hands unless such a background exists. Nor could it be an act of charity, for it is not thought to do anyone any good, nor again a gesture of humility unless a special assumption turns it into this. The action could be courageous, but only if it were done both in the face of fear and for the sake of a good; and we are not allowed to put in special circumstances which could make this the case.

I am sure that the following objection will now be raised. 'Of course clasping one's hands three times in an hour cannot be brought under one of the virtues which we recognise, but that is only to say that it is not a good action by our current moral code. It is logically possible that in a quite different moral code quite different virtues should be recognised, for which we have not even got a name.' I cannot answer this objection properly, for that would need a satisfactory account of the concept of a virtue. But anyone who thinks it would be easy to describe a new virtue connected with clasping the hands three times in an hour should just try. I think he will find that he has to cheat, and suppose that in the community concerned the clasping of hands has been given some special significance, or is thought to have some special effect. The difficulty is obviously connected with the fact that without a special background there is no possibility of answering the question 'What's the point?' It is no good saying that here would be a point in doing the action because the action was a morally good action: the question is how it can be given any such description if we cannot first speak about the point. And it is just as crazy to suppose that we can call *anything* the point of doing something without having to say what the point of *that* is. In clasping one's hands one may make a slight sucking noise, but what is the point of that? It is surely clear that moral virtues must be connected with human good and harm, and that it is quite impossible to call anything you like good or harm. Consider, for instance, the suggestion that a man might say he had

been harmed because a bucket of water had been taken out of the sea. As usual it would be possible to think up circumstances in which this remark would make sense; for instance, when coupled with a belief in magical influences; but then the harm would consist in what was done by the evil spirits, not in the taking of the water from the sea. It would be just as odd if someone were supposed to say that harm had been done to him because the hairs of his head had been reduced to an even number.[2]

I conclude that assumption (1) is very dubious indeed, and that no one should be allowed to speak as if we can understand 'evaluation', 'commendation' or 'pro-attitude', whatever the actions concerned.

II

I propose now to consider what was called assumption (2), which said that a man might always refuse to accept the conclusion of an argument about values, because what counted as evidence for other people did not count for him. Assumption (2) could be true even if assumption (1) were false, for it might be that once a particular question of values—say a moral question—had been accepted, any disputant was bound to accept particular pieces of evidence as relevant, the same pieces as everyone else, but that he could always refuse to draw any moral conclusions whatsoever or to discuss any questions which introduced moral terms. Nor do we mean 'he might refuse to draw the conclusion' in the trivial sense in which anyone can perhaps refuse to draw *any* conclusion; the point is that any statement of value always seems to go beyond any statement of fact, so that he might have a reason for accepting the factual premises but refusing to accept the evaluative conclusion. That this is so seems to those who argue in this way to follow from the practical implications of evaluation. When a man uses a word such as 'good' in an 'evaluative' and not an 'inverted comma' sense, he is supposed to commit his will. From this it has seemed to follow inevitably that there is a logical gap between fact and value; for is it not one thing to say that a thing is so, and another to have a particular attitude towards its being so; one thing to see that certain effects will follow from a given action, and another to care? Whatever account was offered of the essential feature of evaluation—whether in terms of feelings, attitudes, the acceptance of imperatives or what not—the fact remained that with an evaluation there was a committal in a new dimension, and that this was not guaranteed by any acceptance of facts.

I shall argue that this view is mistaken; that the practical implication of the use of moral terms has been put in the wrong place, and that if it is described correctly the logical gap between factual premises and moral conclusion disappears.

In this argument it will be useful to have as a pattern the practical or 'action-guiding' force of the word 'injury', which is in some, though not all, ways similar to that of moral terms. It is clear I think that an injury is necessarily something bad and therefore something which as such anyone always has a reason to avoid, and philosophers will therefore be tempted to say that anyone who uses 'injury' in its full 'action-guiding' sense commits himself to avoiding the things he calls injuries. They will then be in the usual difficulties about the man who says he knows he ought to do something but does not intend to do it; perhaps also about weakness of the will. Suppose that instead we look again at the kinds of things which count as injuries, to see if the connection with the will does not start here. As has been shown, a man is injured whenever some part of his body, in being damaged, has become less well able to fulfil its ordinary function. It follows that he suffers a disability, or is liable to do so; with any injured hand he will be less well able to pick things up, hold onto them, tie them together or chop them up, and so on. With defective eyes there will be a thousand other things he is unable to do, and in both cases we should naturally say

that he will often be unable to get what he wants to get or avoid what he wants to avoid.

Philosophers will no doubt seize on the word 'want', and say that if we suppose that a man happens to want the things which an injury to his body prevents him from getting, we have slipped in a supposition about a 'pro-attitude' already; and that anyone who does not happen to have these wants can still refuse to use 'injury' in its prescriptive, or 'action-guiding' sense. And so it may seem that the only way to make a *necessary* connection between 'injury' and the things that are to be avoided, is to say that it is only used in an 'action-guiding' sense when applied to something the speaker intends to avoid. But we should look carefully at the crucial move in that argument, and query the suggestion that someone might happen not to want anything for which he would need the use of hands or eyes. Hands and eyes, like ears and legs, play a part in so many operations that a man could only be said not to need them if he had no wants at all. That such people exist, in asylums, is not to the present purpose at all; the proper use of his limbs is something a man has reason to want if he wants anything.

I do not know just what someone who denies this proposition could have in mind. Perhaps he is thinking of changing the facts of human existence, so that merely wishing, or the sound of the voice, will bring the world to heel? More likely he is proposing to rig the circumstances of some individual's existence within the framework of the ordinary world, by supposing for instance that he is a prince whose servants will sow and reap and fetch and carry for him, and so use their hands and eyes in his service that he will not need the use of his. Let us suppose that such a story could be told about a man's life; it is wildly implausible, but let us pretend that it is not. It is clear that in spite of this we could say that any man had a reason to shun injury; for even if at the end of his life it could be said that by a strange set of circumstances he had never needed the use of his eyes, or his hands, this could not possibly be foreseen. Only by once more changing the facts of human existence, and supposing every vicissitude foreseeable, could such a supposition be made.

This is not to say that an injury might not bring more incidental gain than necessary harm; one has only to think of times when the order has gone out that able-bodied men are to be put to the sword. Such a gain might even, in some peculiar circumstances, be reliably foreseen, so that a man would have even better reason for seeking than for avoiding injury. In this respect the word 'injury' differs from terms such as 'injustice'; the practical force of 'injury' means only that anyone has *a* reason to avoid injuries, not that he has an overriding reason to do so.

It will be noticed that this account of the 'action-guiding' force of 'injury' links it with reasons for acting rather than with actually doing something. I do not think, however, that this makes it a less good pattern for the 'action-guiding' force of moral terms. Philosophers who have supposed that actual action was required if 'good' were to be used in a sincere evaluation have got into difficulties over weakness of will, and they should surely agree that enough has been done if we can show that any man has reason to aim at virtue and avoid vice. But is this impossibly difficult if we consider the kinds of things that count as virtue and vice? Consider, for instance, the cardinal virtues, prudence, temperance, courage and justice. Obviously any man needs prudence, but does he not also need to resist the temptation of pleasure when there is harm involved? And how could it be argued that he would never need to face what was fearful for the sake of some good? It is not obvious what someone would mean if he said that temperance or courage were not good qualities, and this not because of the 'praising' sense of these *words,* but because of the things that courage and temperance are.

I should like to use these examples to show the artificiality of the notions of 'commendation' and of 'pro-attitudes' as these are commonly employed. Philosophers who talk about these things will say

that after the facts have been accepted—say that X is the kind of man who will climb a dangerous mountain, beard an irascible employer for a rise in pay, and in general face the fearful for the sake of something he thinks worth while—there remains the question of 'commendation' or 'evaluation'. If the word 'courage' is used they will ask whether or not the man who speaks of another as having courage is supposed to have commended him. If we say 'yes' they will insist that the judgement about courage *goes beyond the facts,* and might therefore be rejected by someone who refused to do so; if we say 'no' they will argue that 'courage' is being used in a purely descriptive or 'inverted commas sense', and that we have not got an example of the evaluative use of language which is the moral philosopher's special study. What sense can be made, however, of the question 'does he commend?' What is this extra element which is supposed to be present or absent after the facts have been settled? It is not a matter of liking the man who has courage, or of thinking him altogether good, but of 'commending him for his courage'. How are we supposed to do that? The answer that will be given is that we only commend someone else in speaking of him as courageous if we accept the imperative 'let me be courageous' for ourselves. But this is quite unnecessary. I can speak of someone else as having the virtue of courage, and of course recognise it as a virtue in the proper sense, while knowing that I am a complete coward, and making no resolution to reform. I know that I should be better off if I were courageous, and so have a reason to cultivate courage, but I may also know that I will do nothing of the kind.

If someone were to say that courage was not a virtue he would have to say that it was not a quality by which a man came to act well. Perhaps he would be thinking that someone might be worse off for his courage, which is true, but only because an incidental harm might arise. For instance, the courageous man might have underestimated a risk, and run into some disaster which a cowardly man would have avoided because he was not prepared to take any risk at all. And his courage, like any other virtue, could be the cause of harm to him because possessing it he fell into some disastrous state of pride.[3] Similarly, those who question the virtue of temperance are probably thinking not of the virtue itself but of men whose temperance has consisted in resisting pleasure for the sake of some illusory good, or those who have made this virtue their pride. . . .

NOTES

1. See L. Wittgenstein, *Philosophical Investigations* (1967), especially sections 243–315.

2. In face of this sort of example many philosophers take refuge in the thicket of aesthetics. It would be interesting to know if they are willing to let their whole case rest on the possibility that there might be aesthetic objections to what was done.

3. Cf. Aquinas, *Summa Theologica,* I–II, q. 55, Art. 4.

8

MORAL DISAGREEMENT TODAY AND THE CLAIMS OF EMOTIVISM

Alasdair MacIntyre

The most striking feature of contemporary moral utterance is that so much of it is used to express disagreements; and the most striking feature of the debates in which these disagreements are expressed is their interminable character. I do not mean by this just that such debates go on and on and on—although they do—but also that they apparently can find no terminus. There seems to be no rational way of securing moral agreement in our culture. Consider three examples of just such contemporary moral debate framed in terms of characteristic and well-known rival moral arguments:

1 (a) A just war is one in which the good to be achieved outweighs the evils involved in waging the war and in which a clear distinction can be made between combatants—whose lives are at stake—and innocent noncombatants. But in a modern war calculation of future escalation is never

From *After Virtue: A Study in Moral Philosophy* pp.6–18. © 1984 by the University of Notre Dame Press, Notre Dame, IN 46556. Reprinted by permission.

reliable and no practically applicable distinction between combatants and noncombatants can be made. Therefore no modern war can be a just war and we all now ought to be pacifists.

(b) If you wish for peace, prepare for war. The only way to achieve peace is to deter potential aggressors. Therefore you must build up your armaments and make it clear that going to war on any particular scale is not necessarily ruled out by your policies. An inescapable part of making *this* clear is being prepared both to fight limited wars and to go not only to, but beyond, the nuclear brink on certain types of occasion. Otherwise you will not avoid war *and* you will be defeated.

(c) Wars between the Great Powers are purely destructive; but wars waged to liberate oppressed groups, especially in the Third World, are a necessary and therefore justified means for destroying the exploitative domination which stands between mankind and happiness.

2 (a) Everybody has certain rights over his or her own person, including his or her own body. It follows from the nature of these rights that at the stage when the embryo is

essentially part of the mother's body, the mother has a right to make her own uncoerced decision on whether she will have an abortion or not. Therefore abortion is morally permissible and ought to be allowed by law.

(b) I cannot will that my mother should have had an abortion when she was pregnant with me, except perhaps if it had been certain that the embryo was dead or gravely damaged. But if I cannot will this in my own case, how can I consistently deny to others the right to life that I claim for myself? I would break the so-called Golden Rule unless I denied that a mother has in general a right to an abortion. I am not of course thereby committed to the view that abortion ought to be legally prohibited.

(c) Murder is wrong. Murder is the taking of innocent life. An embryo is an identifiable individual, differing from a newborn infant only in being at an earlier stage on the long road to adult capacities and, if any life is innocent, that of an embryo is. If infanticide is murder, as it is, abortion is murder. So abortion is not only morally wrong, but ought to be legally prohibited.

3 (a) Justice demands that every citizen should enjoy, so far as is possible, an equal opportunity to develop his or her talents and his or her other potentialities. But prerequisites for the provision of such equal opportunity include the provision of equal access to health care and to education. Therefore justice requires the governmental provision of health and educational services, financed out of taxation, and it also requires that no citizen should be able to buy an unfair share of such services. This in turn requires the abolition of private schools and private medical practice.

(b) Everybody has a right to incur such and only such obligations as he or she wishes, to be free to make such and only such contracts as he or she desires and to determine his or her own free choices. Physicians must therefore be free to practice on such terms as they desire and patients must be free to choose among physicians; teachers must be free to teach on such terms as they choose and pupils and parents to go where they wish for education. Freedom thus requires not only the existence of private practice in medicine and private schools in education, but also the abolition of those restraints on private practice which are imposed by licensing and regulation by such bodies as universities, medical schools, the A.M.A. and the state.

These arguments have only to be stated to be recognized as being widely influential in our society. They have of course their articulate expert spokesmen: Herman Kahn and the Pope, Che Guevara and Milton Friedman are among the authors who have produced variant versions of them. But it is their appearance in newspaper editorials and high-school debates, on radio talk shows and letters to congressmen, in bars, barracks and board-rooms, it is their typicality that makes them important examples here. What salient characteristics do these debates and disagreements share?

They are of three kinds. The first is what I shall call, adapting an expression from the philosophy of science, the conceptual incommensurability of the rival arguments in each of the three debates. Every one of the arguments is logically valid or can be easily expanded so as to be made so; the conclusions do indeed follow from the premises. But the rival premises are such that we possess no rational way of weighing the claims of one as against another. For each premise employs some quite different normative or evaluative concept from the others, so that the claims made upon us are of quite different kinds. In the first argument, for example, premises which invoke justice and innocence are at odds with premises which invoke success and survival; in the second, premises which invoke rights are at odds with those which invoke universalizability; in the third it is the claim of equality that is matched against that of liberty. It is precisely because there is in our society no established way of deciding between these claims that moral argument appears to be necessarily interminable. From our rival conclusions we can argue back to our rival premises; but when we do arrive at our premises argument ceases and the invocation of one premise against another becomes a matter of pure assertion and counter-assertion. Hence perhaps the slightly shrill tone of so much moral debate.

But that shrillness may have an additional source. For it is not only in arguments with others that we are reduced so quickly to assertion and counter-assertion; it is also in the arguments that we have within ourselves. For whenever an agent enters the forum of public debate he has already presumably, explicitly or implicitly, settled the matter in question in his own mind. Yet if we possess no unassailable criteria, no set of compelling reasons by means of which we may convince our opponents, it follows that in the process of making up our own minds we can have made no appeal to such criteria or such reasons. If I lack any good reasons to invoke against you, it must seem that I lack any good reasons. Hence it seems that underlying my own position there must be some non-rational decision to adopt that position. Corresponding to the interminability of pubic argument there is at least the appearance of a disquieting private arbitrariness. It is small wonder we become defensive and therefore shrill.

A second, equally important, but contrasting, characteristic of these arguments is that they do none the less purport to be *impersonal* rational arguments and as such are usually presented in a mode appropriate to that impersonality. What is that mode? Consider two different ways in which I may provide backing for an injunction to someone else to perform some specific action. In the first type of case I say, 'Do so-and-so'. The person addressed replies, 'Why should I do so-and-so?' I reply, 'Because I wish it.' Here I have given the person addressed no reason to do what I command or request unless he or she independently possesses some particular reason for paying regard to my wishes. If I am your superior officer—in the police, say, or the army—or otherwise have power or authority over you, or if you love me or fear me or want something from me, then by saying 'Because I wish it' I have

indeed given *you* a reason, although not perhaps a sufficient reason, for doing what it is that I enjoin. Notice that in this type of case whether my utterance gives you a reason or not depends on certain characteristics possessed at the time of hearing or otherwise learning of the utterance by you. What reason-giving force the injunction has depends in this way on the personal context of the utterance.

Contrast with this the type of case in which the answer to the question 'Why should I do so-and-so?' (after someone has said 'Do so-and-so') is not 'Because I wish it', but some such utterance as 'Because it would give pleasure to a number of people' or 'Because it is your duty'. In this type of case the reason given for action either is or is not a good reason for performing the action in question independently of who utters it or even of whether it is uttered at all. Moreover the appeal is to a type of consideration which is independent of the relationship between speaker and hearer. Its use presupposes the existence of *impersonal* criteria—the existence, independently of the preferences or attitudes of speaker and hearer, of standards of justice or generosity or duty. The particular link between the context of utterance and the force of the reason-giving which always holds in the case of expressions of personal preferences or desire is severed in the case of moral and other evaluative utterances.

This second characteristic of contemporary moral utterance and argument, when combined with the first, imparts a paradoxical air to contemporary moral disagreement. For if we attended solely to the first characteristic, to the way in which what at first appears to be argument relapses so quickly into unargued disagreement, we might conclude that there is nothing to such contemporary disagreements but a clash of antagonistic wills, each will determined by some set of arbitrary choices of its own. But this second characteristic, the use of expressions whose distinctive function in our language is to embody what purports to be an appeal to objective standards, suggests otherwise. For even if the surface appearance of argument is only a masquerade, the question remains 'Why *this* masquerade?' What is it about rational argument which is so important that it is the nearly universal appearance assumed by those who engage in moral conflict? Does not this suggest that the practice of moral argument in our culture expresses at least an aspiration to be or to become rational in this area of our lives?

A third salient characteristic of contemporary moral debate is intimately related to the first two. It is easy to see that the different conceptually incommensurable premises of the rival arguments deployed in these debates have a wide variety of historical origins. The concept of justice in the first argument has its roots in Aristotle's account of the virtues; the second argument's genealogy runs through Bismarck and Clausewitz to Machiavelli; the concept of liberation in the third argument has shallow roots in Marx, deeper roots in Fichte. In the second debate a concept of rights which has Lockean antecedents is matched against a view of universalizability which is recognizably Kantian and an appeal to the moral law which is Thomist. In the third debate an argument which owes debts to T.H. Green and to Rousseau competes with one which has Adam Smith as a grandfather. This catalogue of great names is suggestive; but it may be misleading in two ways. The citing of individual names may lead us to underestimate the complexity of the history and the ancestry of such arguments; and it may lead us to look for that history and that ancestry only in the writings of philosophers and theorists instead of in those intricate bodies of theory and practice which constitute human culture, the beliefs of which are articulated by philosophers and theorists only in a partial and selective manner. But the catalogue of names does suggest how wide and heterogeneous the variety of moral sources is from which we have inherited. The surface rhetoric of our culture is apt to speak complacently of moral pluralism in this connection, but the notion of pluralism is too imprecise. For it may equally well apply to an ordered dialogue of intersecting viewpoints and to an unharmonious melange

of ill-assorted fragments. The suspicion—and for the moment it can only be a suspicion—that it is the latter with which we have to deal is heightened when we recognize that all those various concepts which inform our moral discourse were originally at home in larger totalities of theory and practice in which they enjoyed a role and function supplied by contexts of which they have now been deprived. Moreover the concepts we employ have in at least some cases changed their character in the past three hundred years; the evaluative expressions we use have changed their meaning. In the transition from the variety of contexts in which they were originally at home to our own contemporary culture 'virtue' and 'justice' and 'piety' and 'duty' and even 'ought' have become other than they once were. How ought we to write the history of such changes?

It is in trying to answer this question that the connection between these features of contemporary moral debate and my initial hypothesis becomes clear. For if I am right in supposing that the language of morality passed from a state of order to a state of disorder, this passage will surely be reflected in—in part indeed will actually consist in—just such changes of meaning. Moreover, if the characteristics of our own moral arguments which I have identified—most notably the fact that we simultaneously and inconsistently treat moral argument as an exercise of our rational powers and as mere expressive assertion—are symptoms of moral disorder, we ought to be able to construct a true historical narrative in which at an earlier stage moral argument is very different in kind. Can we?

One obstacle to our so doing has been the persistently unhistorical treatment of moral philosophy by contemporary philosophers in both the writing about and the teaching of the subject. We all too often still treat the moral philosophers of the past as contributors to a single debate with a relatively unvarying subject-matter, treating Plato and Hume and Mill as contemporaries both of ourselves and of each other. This leads to an abstraction of these writers from the cultural and social milieus in which they lived and thought and so the history of their thought acquires a false independence from the rest of the culture. Kant ceases to be part of the history of Prussia, Hume is no longer a Scotsman. For from the standpoint of moral philosophy as *we* conceive it these characteristics have become irrelevances. Empirical history is one thing, philosophy quite another. But are we right in understanding the division between academic disciplines in the way that we conventionally do? Once again there seems to be a possible relationship between the history of moral discourse and the history of the academic curriculum.

Yet at this point it may rightly be retorted: You keep speaking of possibilities, of suspicions, of hypotheses. You allow that what you are suggesting will initially seem implausible. You are in this at least right. For all this resort to conjectures about history is unnecessary. The way in which you have stated the problem is misleading. Contemporary moral argument is rationally interminable, because *all* moral, indeed all evaluative argument is and always must be rationally interminable. Contemporary moral disagreements of a certain kind cannot be resolved, because *no* moral disagreements of that kind in any age, past, present or future, can be resolved. What you present as a contingent feature of our culture, standing in need of some special, perhaps historical explanation, is a necessary feature of all cultures which possess evaluative discourse. This is a challenge which cannot be avoided at an early stage in this argument. Can it be defeated?

One philosophical theory which this challenge specifically invites us to confront is emotivism. Emotivism is the doctrine that all evaluative judgments and more specifically all moral judgments are *nothing but* expressions of preference, expressions of attitude or feeling, insofar as they are moral or evaluative in character. Particular judgments may of course unite moral and factual elements. 'Arson, being destructive of property, is wrong' unites the factual judgment that arson destroys property with the moral judgment that arson is wrong. But the moral element in such a judgment is always to be sharply distinguised from the factual. Factual judgments are true or false; and in the realm of fact there are rational criteria by means of which we may secure agreement as to what is true and what is false. But moral judgments, being expressions of attitude or feeling, are neither true nor false; and agreement in moral judgment is not to be secured by any rational method, for there are none. It is to be secured, if at all, by producing certain non-rational effects on the emotions or attitudes of those who disagree with one. We use moral judgments not only to express our own feelings and attitudes, but also precisely to produce such effects in others. . . .

The emotive theory, . . ., purports to be a theory about the meaning of sentences; but the expression of feeling or attitude is characteristically a function not of the meaning of sentences, but of their use on particular occasions. The angry schoolmaster, to use one of Gilbert Ryle's examples, may vent his feelings by shouting at the small boy who has just made an arthimetical mistake, 'Seven times seven equals forty-nine!' But the use of this sentence to express feelings or attitudes has nothing whatsoever to do with its meaning. This suggests that we should not simply rely on these objections to reject the emotive theory, but that we should rather consider whether it ought not to have been proposed as a theory about the *use*—understood as purpose or function—of members of a certain class of expressions rather than about their *meaning*—understood as including all that Frege intended by 'sense' and 'reference'.

Clearly the argument so far shows that when someone utters a moral judgment, such as 'This is right' or 'This is good', it does not mean the same as 'I approve of this, do so as well' or 'Hurrah for this!' or any of the other attempts at equivalence suggested by emotive theorists; but even if the meaning of such sentences were quite other than emotive theorists supposed, it might be plausibly claimed, if the evidence was adequate, that in using such sentences to *say* whatever they mean, the agent was in fact *doing* nothing other than expressing his feelings or attitudes and attempting to influence the feelings and attitudes of others. If the emotive theory thus interpreted were correct it would follow that the meaning and the use of moral expressions were, or at the very least had become, radically discrepant with each other. Meaning and use would be at odds in such a way that meaning would tend to conceal use. We could not safely infer what someone who uttered a moral judgment was doing merely by listening to what he said. Moreover the agent himself might well be among those for whom use was concealed by meaning. He might well, precisely because he was self-conscious about the meaning of the words that he used, be assured that he was appealing to independent impersonal criteria, when all that he was in fact doing was expressing his feelings to others in a manipulative way. . . .

. . . Emotivism on this account turns out to be an empirical thesis, or rather a preliminary sketch of an empirical thesis, presumably to be filled out later by psychological and sociological and historical observations, about those who continue to use moral and other evaluative expressions, as if they were governed by objective and impersonal criteria, when all grasp of any such criterion has been lost. We should therefore expect emotivist types of theory to arise in a specific local circumstance as a response to types of theory and practice which share certain key features of Moore's intuitionism. Emotivism thus understood turns out to be, as a cogent theory of use rather than a false theory of meaning, connected with one specific stage in moral development or decline, a stage which our own culture entered early in the present century.

Suggested Readings

BLANSHARD, BRAND, *Reason and Goodness*, London: George Allen & Unwin Ltd., 1961.

BRANDT, RICHARD, *Ethical Theory*, Englewood Cliffs: Prentice-Hall, 1959.

BRUENING, WILLIAM, *The Is-Ought Problem*, Washington, D.C.: University Press of America, 1978.

FOOT, PHILIPPA, *Virtues and Vices*, Berkeley: University of California Press, 1978.

FRANKENA, WILLIAM K., *Ethics*, Englewood Cliffs: Prentice Hall, 1973.

HANCOCK, ROGER N., *Twentieth Century Ethics*, New York: Columbia University Press, 1974.

HARE, R.M., *The Language of Morals*, Oxford: The Clarendon Press, 1952.

HUDSON, W. D., *The Is-Ought Question*, London: Macmillan, 1969.

HUSDON, W. D., *A Century of Moral Philosophy*, New York: St. Martin's Press, 1980.

HUDSON, W. D., *Modern Moral Philosophy*, New York: St. Martin's Press, 1983.

KERNER, GEORGE C., *The Revolution in Ethical Theory*, London: Oxford University Press, 1966.

MACINTYRE, ALASDAIR, *Whose Justice? Which Rationality?* Notre Dame: University of Notre Dame Press, 1988.

MOORE, G. E., *Ethics*, London: Oxford University Press, 1912.

ROSS, W. D., *The Right and the Good*, The Clarendon Press, 1930.

SCHILPP, PAUL ARTHUR, ED., *The Philosophy of G. E. Moore*, LaSalle: Open Court, 1968.

STEVENSON, C. L., *Ethics and Language*, New Haven: Yale University Press, 1944.

WALLACE, G., AND WALKER, A.D.M., *The Definition of Morality*, London: Methuen & Co. Ltd., 1970.

WARNOCK, MARY, *Ethics Since 1900*, London: Oxford University Press, 1966.

9
THE LOGIC OF MORAL REASONING

Stephen Toulmin

QUESTIONS ABOUT THE RIGHTNESS OF ACTIONS

Consider, first, the simplest and commonest ethical question, 'Is this the right thing to do?' We are taught when young to behave in ways laid down as appropriate to the situations we are in. Sometimes there is a doubt whether or not a proposed action conforms to the moral code. It is to resolve such doubts that we are taught to use the question, 'Is this the right thing to do?,' and, provided the code contains a relevant principle, the answer is 'Yes' or 'No,' according as the proposed action does or does not conform. Questions like, 'What is the right thing to do?,' 'What ought really to have been done?' and 'Was this the correct decision?' do similar jobs, and can be understood in similar ways.

In consequence, if someone complains, 'That wasn't the thing to do' or 'That was

From *An Examination of the Place of Reason in Ethics* (Cambridge: Cambridge University Press), pp. 312–334. Reprinted by permission.

hardly the way of going about things, was it?,' his remark may have a genuinely ethical force. And this remains the case, although the only *fact* at issue is whether the action in question belongs to a class of actions generally approved of in the speaker's community. Some people have been misled by this into arguing that many so-called 'ethical' statements are just disguised statements of fact; that 'what seems to be an ethical judgment is very often a factual classification of an action.'[1] But this is a mistake. What makes us call a judgement 'ethical' is the fact that it is used to harmonise people's actions (rather than to give a recognisable description of a state of affairs, for instance); judgements of the kind concerned are unquestionably 'ethical' by this standard; and the fact that the action belongs to a certain class of actions is not so much the 'disguised meaning of' as the 'reason for' the ethical judgement.

Furthermore, the test for answering questions of this simple kind remains the accepted practice, even though the particular action may have unfortunate results. Suppose that I am driving along a winding, country road, and deliberately keep on the left-hand side going round the blind corners. It may happen that a driver going the other way is cutting his corners, so that we collide head-on; but this does not affect the propriety of my driving. My care to keep to the left remains 'right,' my decision not to take any risks on the corners remains 'correct,' in spite of the fact that the consequences, in the event, were unfortunate. Provided that I had no reason to expect such an upset, provided that I was not to know how the other man was behaving—knowledge which would have made a material difference to my decision, and would have taken my situation out of the straightforward class to which the rule applies—the existence of the Rule of the Road is all that is needed to make my decision 'correct.'

REASONING ABOUT THE RIGHTNESS OF ACTIONS

This brings us to questions about one's 'reasons' for a decision or an action.

If the policeman investigating the accident asks the other driver, 'Why were you driving on the right-hand side of the road?,' he will have to produce a long story in order to justify himself. If, however, I am asked why I was driving on the *left,* the only answer I can give is that the left-hand side is the one on which one *does* drive in England—that the Rule of the Road *is* to drive on the left.

Again, the schoolboy who gets his colours through favouritism may ask, 'And why shouldn't I have been given them?' If he does so, his schoolfellows will point out that it is the practice (and in fact the whole point of colours) for them to go to the best cricketers; and that there were better cricketers to whom they could have been given. And this will be all the justification needed.

Finally, an example in which the logical structure of this type of 'reasoning' is fully set out: suppose that I say, 'I feel that I ought to take this book and give it back to Jones' (so reporting on my feelings). You

may ask me, 'But ought you really to do so?' (turning the question into an ethical one), and it is up to me to produce my 'reasons,' if I have any. To begin with, then, I may reply that I ought to take it back to him, 'because I promised to let him have it back before midday'—so classifying my position as one of type S_1. 'But ought you *really*?,' you may repeat. If you do, I can relate S_1 to a more general S_2, explaining, 'I ought to, because I promised to let him have it back.' And if you continue to ask, 'But why ought you really?,' I can answer, in succession, 'Because I ought to do whatever I promise him to do' (S_3), 'Because I ought to do whatever I promise anyone to do' (S_4), and 'Because anyone ought to do whatever he promises anyone else that he will do' or 'Because it was a promise' (S_5). Beyond this point, however, the question cannot arise: there is no more general 'reason' to be given beyond one which relates the action in question to an accepted social practice.

CONFLICTS OF DUTIES

This straightforward method of answering the questions, 'Is this the right thing to do?' and 'Why ought you to do that?,' can apply only in situations to which a rule of action is unambiguously appropriate. The most interesting practical questions, however, always arise in those situations in which one set of facts drives us one way, and another pulls us in the opposite direction.

If the muck-heap at the bottom of my garden bursts into flames in midsummer, and someone says, 'There's nothing to be surprised at in that: it's a simple case of spontaneous combustion. Surely you've heard of ricks burning in the same kind of way?,' his explanation may satisfy me: the analogy between the burning of my muck-heap and the spontaneous combustion of a hayrick is close enough for it to be plausible. But, if it is late January, I may reject the explanation, and protest, 'That's all very well in July or August, but not in midwinter: whoever heard of a hayrick catching fire with snow on the ground?,' and, unless he can assure me that it does quite frequently happen, I shall continue to hanker after a different explanation.

In much the same way, the fact that I promised to let Jones have his book back will seem to me reason enough for taking it to him on time—if that is all that there is to it. But, if I have a critically ill relative in the house, who cannot be left, the issue is complicated. The situation is not sufficiently unambiguous for reasoning from the practice of promise-keeping to be conclusive: I may therefore argue, 'That's all very well in the ordinary way, but not when I've got my grandmother to look after: whoever heard of risking someone else's life just to return a borrowed book?' Unless evidence is produced that the risks involved in breaking my promise to Jones are even greater than those attending my grandmother, if she is left alone, I shall conclude that it is my duty to remain with her.

Given two conflicting claims, that is to say, one has to weigh up, as well as one can, the risks involved in ignoring either, and choose 'the lesser of the two evils.' Appeal to a single current principle, though the primary test of the rightness of an action, cannot therefore be relied on as a universal test: where this fails, we are driven back upon our estimate of the probable consequences. And this is the case, not only where there is a conflict of duties, but also, for instance, in circumstances in which, although no matter of principle is involved, some action of ours can nevertheless meet another's need. Here again we naturally and rightly conclude that the action is one that we 'ought' to perform, but we record in our usage the difference between such circumstances and those in which a matter of principle *is* involved: although we should say that we 'ought' to perform the action, we should not usually say that we had a 'moral obligation' to perform it, or even that it was our 'duty.' We here appeal to consequences in the absence of a relevant principle, or 'duty.'[2]

So it comes about that we can, in many cases, justify an individual action by reference to its estimated consequences. Such a reference is no substitute for a principle, where any principle is at issue: but moral reasoning is so complex, and has to cover such a variety of types of situation, that no one logical test (such as 'appeal to an accepted principle') can be expected to meet every case.

REASONING ABOUT THE JUSTICE OF SOCIAL PRACTICES

All these types of question are intelligible by reference to the primitive stage in the development of ethics. As soon as we turn to the second stage, however, there is room for questions of a radically different type.

Recall our analysis of 'explanation.' There I pointed out that, although on most occasions the question, 'Is this really straight?,' has a use, situations might be encountered in which the question, in its ordinary sense, simply cannot be asked. These occasions were of two kinds:

(i)   those on which the criterion of straightness is itself questioned, within the framework of a particular theory, and
(ii) those on which the criteria of straightness used in alternative theories are found to be different.

The same kinds of situation arise (and, indeed, are more familiar) in ethics. To give an example of the first: so long as one confines oneself to a particular moral code, no more general 'reason' can be given for an action than one which relates it to a practice (or principle) within that code. If an astronomer, who is discussing light-rays in outer space in terms of non-Euclidean geometry, is asked what reason he has for saying that they are straight, he can only reply, 'Well, they just *are*': in the same way, if I am asked why one ought to keep a particular promise, all that I can say is, 'Well, one just *ought*.' Within the framework of a particular scientific theory, one can ask of most things, 'Is *this* really straight?,' but the *criterion* of straightness cannot be questioned: within the framework of a particular moral code, one can ask of most individual actions, 'Is *this* really right?,' but the *standards* of rightness cannot be questioned.

As an example of the second type of situation: the question, 'Which is it really right to do—to have only one wife like a Christian, or to have anything up to four like the Mohammedans,' is odd in the same way as the question, 'Is a light-ray going past the sun really straight, as a non-Euclidean theorist declares, or deflected, as a Euclidean theorist says?' If corresponding standards in two moral codes are found to be different, the question, 'Which of these is really right?,' cannot arise. Or rather (to put the same thing in another way), if the question *does* arise, it arises in a very different way, serves a different purpose, and requires an answer of a different sort.

What kind of purpose does it serve, and what kind of answer does it require? In science, if I insist on asking of the standard of straightness, 'But is *it* really straight?,' I am going outside the framework of that particular scientific theory. To question the standard is to question the theory—to criticise the theory *as a whole*—not to ask for an explanation of the phenomenon ostensibly under discussion (the properties of light-rays in outer space). So again in ethics: if I ask of the behavior prescribed in any standard of conduct, 'Is *it* really right?,' I am going outside the moral code; and my question is a criticism of the practice *as a practice*, not a request for a justification of a particular case of promise-keeping (or whatever it may be).

To question the rightness of a particular action is one thing: to question the justice of a practice *as a practice* is another. It is this second type of question which becomes intelligible when we turn to the second stage of development. If a society has a developing moral code, changes in the economic, social, political or psychological situation may lead people to regard the existing practices as unnesessarily restrictive, or as dangerously lax. If this happens, they may come to ask, for instance, 'Is it right that women should be debarred from smoking in public?,' or 'Would it not be better if there were no mixed bathing after dark?,' in each case questioning the practice concerned *as a whole*. The answer to be given will (remembering the function of ethics) be reached by estimating the probable consequences

(i) of retaining the present practice, and
(ii) of adopting the suggested alternative.

If, as a matter of fact, there is good reason to suppose that the sole consequences of making the proposed change would be to avoid some existing distresses, then, as a matter of ethics, there is certainly a good reason for making the change. As usual, however, the logically straightforward case is a comparatively uninteresting one: in practice, the interesting problems are those which arise when the happy consequences of the change are not so certain, or when they are likely to be accompanied by new, though perhaps less serious, distresses. And what stake may reasonably be risked for any particular likelihood of gain is something only to be settled with confidence—if then—by appeal to experience.

THE TWO KINDS OF MORAL REASONING

Two cautions are necessary. Although, as a matter of logic, it makes sense to discuss the justice of any social practice, some practices will in fact always remain beyond question. It is inconceivable (for instance) that any practice will ever be suggested, to replace promising and promise-keeping, which would be anything like as effective. Even in the most 'advanced' stages of morality, therefore, promise-keeping will remain right.

Again, the fact that I can discuss the rightness of promise-keeping as a practice, in this way, does not imply that there is any way of calling in question the rightness of keeping individual promises. In arguing that promise-keeping will remain right at all stages, 'because its abolition would lead to suffering,' I am doing something different in important respects from what I am doing, if I say that I ought to take this book back to Jones now, 'because I promised to.' I can justify the latter statement by pointing out that I am in any of the situations S_1 to S_5: and such reasons will be acceptable in any community which expects promises to be fulfilled. But I cannot further justify it by saying, 'Because one must not inflict avoidable suffering': this kind of reason is appropriate only when discussing whether a social practice should be retained or changed.

The two kinds of moral reasoning which we have encountered are, therefore, distinct. Each provides its own logical criteria—criteria which are appropriate to the criticism of individual actions, or social practices, but not both. It was this distinction between the 'reasons' for an individual action and the 'reasons' for a social practice which Socrates made as he waited for the hemlock: he was ready to die rather than repudiate it—refusing, when given the chance, to escape from the prison and so avoid execution. As an Athenian citizen, he saw that it was his duty (regardless of the actual consequences in his particular case) to respect the verdict and the sentence of the court. To have escaped would have been to ignore this duty. By doing so, he would not merely have questioned the justice of the verdict in his case: he would have renounced the Athenian constitution and moral code as a whole. This he was not prepared to do.

The history of Socrates illustrates the nature of the distinction, and the kind of situation in which it is important: the kind of situation in which it ceases to be of value can be seen from the story of Hampden and the 'ship-money.' It is those principles which we recognise as just which we have to respect most scrupulously: if we are prepared to dispute the justice of a principle, everything is altered. One of the most striking ways of disputing the justice of a principle is, indeed, by refusing to conform on a particular occasion: and such refusals give rise, in law

and morality alike, to the notion of a 'test case.'

Over 'test cases,' the distinction between the two sorts of moral reasoning vanishes. In justifying the action concerned, one no longer refers to the current practice: it is the injustice of the accepted code, or the greater justice of some alternative proposal, which is now important. The justification of the action is made 'a matter of principle' and the change in the logical criteria appropriate follows accordingly. In making an action a test case one must, however, take care that one's intentions are clear. If this is not done, the action may be criticised on the wrong level. It may be condemned, either by reference to the very principle it was intended to dispute, or as self-interested, or both; and the question of principle may go against one by default. There is an element of pathos about a test case which goes wrong for this reason; but those men whose protests are carried off successfully are often remembered as heroes. . . .

IS ANY 'JUSTIFICATION' OF ETHICS NEEDED?

In talking about the logic of ethical reasoning in the light of the function of ethics, I have tried to indicate two things:

(i) the different types of question which naturally arise in ethical contexts, and the ways in which they are answered; and

(ii) the limits of ethical reasoning—that is, the kinds of occasion on which questions and considerations of an ethical kind can no longer arise.

So far, however, I have not given an explicit answer to the question from which we set out: namely, 'What is it, in an ethical discussion, that makes a reason a good reason, or an argument a valid argument?'

In previous chapters this question has always caused trouble. When discussing the objective doctrine of ethics, we found it impossible even to reach it without first mastering some highly mysterious arguments about 'non-natural' properties; even more surprisingly, the advocates of the subjective and imperative doctrines tried to dismiss it as vain. But now we are in the opposite position. In this chapter, I have not attempted to give a 'theory of ethics'; I have simply tried to describe the occasions, on which we are in fact prepared to call judgements 'ethical' and decisions 'moral,' and the part which reasoning plays on such occasions. This description has led us to see how, in *particular types* of ethical question and argument, good reasoning is distinguished from bad, and valid argument from invalid—to be specific, by applying to individual judgements the test of principle, and to principles the test of general fecundity.

Now we have to ask, 'Is any further answer needed? Given particular rules applicable to different kinds of ethical judgement and question, have we not all we want? And, if any more were needed, could it not be supplied from an account, more detailed and accurate than has been given, but of the same kind?'

I myself do not feel the need for any *general* answer to the question, 'What makes some ethical reasoning "good" and some ethical arguments "valid"?': answers applicable to particular types of argument are enough. In fact, it seems to me that the demand for any such general answer (however it is to be obtained) must lead one to paradox as surely as did the corresponding demand over science. For either such a general answer will, in particular cases, be equivalent to the rules which we have found, or it will contradict them. In the first case, it can do one of two things. Either it can distort our account, so that one of the criteria alone seems important; or else it can point out, in a more or less roundabout way, the advantages—indeed, 'the absolute necessity to the existence of society'³—of harmonious co-operation. Instead, however, it may contradict our results. What then? What if we try to adopt the new rules for criticising arguments about conduct, which this general answer lays down?

If we do adopt these new criteria, then it will no longer be 'ethical' reasoning, 'moral' considerations, arguments from 'duty' and questions about what we 'ought' to do that we are criticising: it will be questions, arguments and considerations of quite another kind—in fact, a different mode of reasoning. This can be shown quite quickly. For suppose that, far from radically changing our criteria, all that the new rules do is to select one of them as the *universal* criterion. If the test of principle is chosen, so that we are never to be allowed to question the pronouncements of those who administer the moral code, then it is not 'morality' to which they apply—it is 'authority,' and authority of a kind which may reasonably be expected to develop rapidly into tyranny. And conversely, if the test of principle is itself ruled out in favour of a universal test of consequence (of the estimated effects on others), then we are faced with something which is no more 'morality' than the other—it would now be better described as 'expediency.' But arguments from expediency and arguments from authority are no more 'ethical' than experienced guess-work is 'scientific.' Consequently, even if all we do is to give up one or other of our present logical criteria, we turn ethics into something other than it is. And if this is the case there is no need for us to go on and consider more drastic alterations: they can be ruled out at once.

No doubt those philosophers who search for more general rules will not be satisfied. No doubt they will still feel that they want an explicit and unique answer to our central question. And no doubt they will object that, in all this, I have not even 'justified' our using reason in ethics at all. 'It's all very well your laying down the law about particular types of ethical argument,' they will say; 'but what is the justification for letting *any* reasoning affect how we decide to behave? Why *ought* one to do what is right, anyway?'

They are sufficiently answered by the peculiarity of their own questions. For let us consider what kind of answer they want when they ask, 'Why ought one to do what is right?' There is no room *within* ethics for such a question. Ethical reasoning may be able to show why we ought to do this action as opposed to that, or advocate this social practice as opposed to that, but it is no help where there can be no choice. And their question does not present us with genuine alternatives at all. For, since the notions of 'right' and of 'obligation' originate in the same situations and serve similar purposes, it is a self-contradiction (taking 'right' and 'ought' in their simplest senses) to suggest that we 'ought' to do anything but what is 'right.' This suggestion is as unintelligible as the suggestion that some emerald objects might not be green, and the philosophers' question is on the level with the question, 'Why are all scarlet things red?' We can therefore parry it only with another question—'What else "ought" one to do?'

Similar oddities are displayed by all their questions—as long as we take them literally. Ethics may be able to 'justify' one of a number of courses of action, or one social practice as opposed to another: but it does not extend to the 'justification' of all reasoning about conduct. One course of action can be opposed to another: one social practice can be opposed to another. But to what are we expected to oppose 'ethics-as-a-whole'? There can be no discussion about the proposition, 'Ethics is ethics'; any argument treating 'ethics' as something other than it is must be false; and, if those who call for a 'justification' of ethics want 'the case for morality,' as opposed to 'the case for expediency,' etc., then they are giving philosophy a job which is not its own. To show that you ought to choose certain actions is one thing: to make you *want to do* what you ought to do is another, and not a philosopher's task.

REASON AND SELF-LOVE

Hume ran sharply into this difficulty. He had, in fact, to confess (of a man in whom self-love overpowered the sense of right),

'It would be a little difficult to find any [reasoning] which will appear to him satisfactory and convincing.'[4] This confession of his was, however, a masterpiece of understatement. The difficulty he speaks of is of no 'little' one: indeed, it is an 'absolute and insuperable' one, an 'impossibility.' But note the reason: it is not a *practical* impossibility at all, but a *logical* one. A man's ignoring all ethical arguments is just the kind of thing which would lead us to say that his self-love *had* overpowered his sense of right. As long, and only as long, as he continued to ignore all moral reasoning, we should say that his self-love continued in the ascendant: but once he began to accept such considerations as a guide to action, we should begin to think that 'the sense of right' had won.

It is always possible that, when faced with a man whose self-love initially overpowered his sense of right, we might hit upon some reasoning which appeared to him 'satisfactory and convincing.' The result, however, would not be 'a man in whom self-love was dominant, but who was satisfied and convinced by ethical reasoning' (for this is a contradiction in terms); it would be 'a man in whom self-love was dominant, until reasoning beat it down and reinstated the sense of right.'

NOTES

1. Ayer, *Language, Truth and Logic* (2nd ed.), p. 21.

2. We can, and sometimes do, employ the language of 'duty' in this case also, by treating the reference to consequences as a reference to a completely general 'duty' to help one another when in need. For our present purposes, the difference between these two ways of putting it is purely verbal.

3. Hume, *Natural History of Religion*, § XIII, *ad fin*.

4. Hume, *Enquiries* (ed. Selby-Bigge), p. 283.

10
MORAL REASONS

Kurt Baier

. . . To construct the ideal of rationality we must allow two moves. The first is the rather "formal" proposition that perfect rationality consists in performing without flaw the three tasks of practical reasoning: acting in accordance with the outcome of one's deliberation (a task for the will); taking into account and giving proper weight to all the relevant reasons (a task of calculation with counters made available by one's social order); and, lastly, subjecting these socially provided counters to the relevant critical scrutiny, that is, making sure that what are generally accepted as, really are, reasons. It is plain that this last task is the most difficult and obscure, and one for which different people may have very unequal aptitudes. These remarks in any case make it clear that perfect rationality is not to be identified with the attainment of those goals for the attainment of which we employ these quasi-calculative methods. Perfect rationality does not guarantee success, it merely gives the

From *Midwest Studies in Philosophy* Vol. III (1978), 62–74. Reprinted by permission.

best chance of success by way of the methods thought up by a given culture, one's own, or if one knows a better one, that culture.

The second move is to inquire into the goal for whose attainment practical reasoning is the method. The brief answer is, of course: the good. To make this clearer, it will be helpful to look more closely at the question of *what actually are practical reasons*. To this end we must keep apart three different questions which hide under that single interrogative: (i) Of what sorts of things can we say that they are practical reasons? (ii) What are we saying of these things when we call them such reasons? (iii) On what grounds can we call them practical reasons?

The first question is easy enough. It is facts about Jones' doing A which are reasons for Jones *to* do or *not to* do A. They are such reasons for him whether or not he is aware of these facts. It is not enough that he should, rightly or mistakenly *believe* something to be such a fact: for in that case, he merely believes, rightly or mistakenly, that there is, or that he has, a reason to act in a certain way. Of course, a fact could not be *his* reason *for* doing something unless he knew or believed it to be a fact.

We have already given one answer to question (ii), but it was rather uninformative: to call a fact a reason for someone to do a thing, is to imply that a perfectly rational being *would* and human beings *ought* to give this fact some weight in their deliberations about what to do. Just what weight they would or ought to give it does of course depend on how *weighty* or *strong* a reason it is. Not every reason has the same weight and very few are weighty enough to be adequate or sufficient reasons for doing what they favor, irrespective of what other reasons may also be applicable. A theory of perfect rationality thus involves not only knowledge of the facts to which the perfectly rational being would give weight in his deliberations but also how much weight, at least relative to other relevant facts.

But this takes us to the third and most important question, concerning the grounds on the basis of which we can call a fact a reason for or against doing a certain thing, and the grounds on the basis of which we call one a stronger reason than another. Plainly, our everyday beliefs on these matters are rather unsystematic. We believe that facts, such as that doing A would give us pleasure, would be in our interest, is required by law, would give others pleasure, is in other people's interest, would be a good thing all round, is our duty, and many more such facts, are reasons for us to do A. And the corresponding negative facts are regarded as reasons for us not to do A. For this loose assortment of beliefs to constitute a substantive theory of what are practical reasons, and thereby of perfect rationality, we would have to add at least the following further principles.

(i) *A principle of unity.* By this I mean a principle establishing the systematic unity among specific substantive claims to the effect that some fact, F, is a reason of a certain strength, for people satisfying certain conditions, to do A. One possible and popular version of

such a principle would be something like the principle of Rational Egoism: *only* facts showing that X's doing A would be in X's best interest are to constitute reasons for X to do A.[1] Other ways would be to offer several such ultimate principles which each individual might then trade off against one another in some personal preferential choice.[2] I shall shortly offer my own suggestion for such a systematization.

(ii) *A principle of empirical substantiation.* By this I mean a principle determining how human experience is to be regarded as bearing on the substantive propositions of the theory. This is perhaps the most important and certainly the least understood aspect of normative theory. The irrelevance of sense experience as understood by the British Empiricists and the nonconclusiveness of facts about what a given individual or group of individuals feels, desires or needs, has driven many contemporary philosophers into a non-empirical, anti-naturalist position. Here I can do no more than assert, dogmatically, that the undeniable *nonconclusiveness* of someone's pleasure and pain, or the satisfaction and frustration of his desires and needs, or even his happiness and unhappiness, is perfectly compatible with their *relevance* to the good and so to rationality. For what can still be decisive is the satisfactoriness of the relevant lives, that is, the lives of those who are guided by such a system of practical reasons and perhaps other sentient creatures affected by them. The principle of empirical substantiation might be something like the following: The soundness of the belief that C is the criterion (for example, self-interest) which is to determine whether or not F is a reason of a certain strength for X to do A is to be determined by the way the acceptance of this criterion affects the satisfactoriness of the relevant lives.

(iii) *A principle of universality.* As we have seen, the idea of practical rationality involves the performance of three tasks, a task for the will, a calculative task, and a critical task. The calculative task consists in applying a set of relatively unchanging general directives to a great variety of particular practical problems. The idea is that every member of the community can be taught to superimpose, upon his inclinations, decisions in accordance with such publicly available guidelines and so to avoid the disadvantages consequent upon acting simply on inclination, however well informed. If the community is to have such practical reasoning, then it should have universal directives, though they need not be completely general. That is to say, it is desirable only that such reasons should be capable of guiding *all* individuals satisfying certain conditions, say, nursing mothers, diabetics, school teachers, and so on. They need not apply to *all* human beings as such. There is a further reason why universality is desirable. The consequences of the acceptance of something as a guideline for a class of people can be determined much more easily, accurately, and reliably, if *all* members of the relevant class follow it than if some do, others don't. We can, therefore, formulate our principle of universality in something like the following way: Since a fact F, is a reason for someone to do A in virtue of his satisfying certain conditions D, F must be a reason to do A for anyone who satisfies D.

(iv) *A principle of universalizability.* It follows from the ideal of rationality that if F is a reason to do A for *anyone* who satisfies D, then F must also be capable of being a reason to do A for *everyone* who satisfies D. For if we did not accept this constraint on what can be a reason, we should have to give up the claim that it would be a good thing for everyone to be perfectly rational, but this is absurd. This does not show Rational Egoism to be self-contradictory, for the Rational Egoist can (and must) accept the corollary of this principle, namely, that where the promotion of his own good conflicts with that of another, there is no rational way of settling the issue. But the Rational Egoist has to accept this as not a bad thing, at least overall, while most people would regard it as a bad thing. If it can be shown to be a bad thing, this would amount to a refutation of Rational Egoism, though not on the grounds of inconsistency.[3]

So far, our inquiry into the nature of practical reasons and practical reasoning has shown it to be an ideal of individual self-determination superimposed upon and capable of deviating from actual intention-formation, however well informed. The implied method of self-determination makes reference to and relies on the existence of a given culture which yields the general principles for the solution of recurring and novel individual practical problems. So far, the role of society is merely that of the most suitable agent for pooling, storing, and using the cumulative experience of its members, for the purpose of giving to each a well-tested set of practical directives for solving his practical problems for himself. On this model of practical reasoning, each individual can employ only what I shall call "independent reasons," that is to say, reasons designed to accomplish optimal outcomes, *taking the conduct of others as being independent of one's own.* Such independent reasons are the only kind available whenever a person is not willing to, or cannot, or does not want to *depend on* others being willing to participate in a cooperative scheme under which the conduct of others is dependent on his own. I want now to show the respects in which such a system of independent reasons is unsatisfactory, and what this has to do with moral reasons and reasoning.

II

The unsatisfactoriness of such a system of independent reasons is most easily seen in connection with the doctrine of Rational Egoism, that is, the doctrine that

(v) Only facts showing that X's doing A would be in X's best interest constitute reasons for X to do A.

or

(vi) Facts showing that X's doing A would be in X's best interest are the *supreme* reasons for X to do A.

For our purposes it makes no difference which of these two versions we adopt, since the same difficulty arises for both of them.

The difficulty I have in mind is the well-known individually and collectively nonoptimal outcome, in certain situations, for people who act in accordance with reasons based on the theory of Rational Egoism. The most fully explored such situation is the so-called Prisoners' Dilemma (PD). The story is that two prisoners, A and B, accused of jointly committed crimes are told that if both confess they will receive 10 years in prison, if neither confesses 2 years, and if one confesses while the other does not, the one who confesses will get off scot free, while the other will get 20 years.

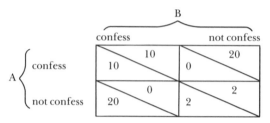

Now if both prisoners subscribe to Rational Egoism, *and if what A does will not affect what B does,* then the rational course for each is to confess. For if we assume, as is natural, that it is in their interest to get the shortest possible prison term, then confessing achieves that, whatever the other does, each prisoner will do better by confessing than by not confessing. If B confesses, A will get only 10 years if he (A) confesses, but 20 if he does not. And if B does not confess, A will get off scot free if he (A) confesses but will get two years if he does not confess. Nevertheless, the outcome is less satisfactory for both than it need be since, by confessing, both get 10 years, while by not confessing they would get only two years. The paradoxical result is that *each* does better by confessing than by not confessing, but *both* do better by not confessing than by confessing.

It seems to follow that it would be better if they did not use independent reasons, but used some other form of reasoning which directed both not to confess. In general, there are two difficulties in the way of such an alternative system of reasoning. The first is the so-called "Assurance Problem": the knowledge that although it would be better for both not to confess, it would be worse for either if he did not confess while the other

did, and best for either if he confessed while the other did not. Each thus needs assurance that the other will not do what independent reasons advise (namely, confess) because doing so (confessing) does not involve the (considerable) risk of the greatest loss and holds out some (small) chance of the greatest gain. The problem is how to provide this assurance.

The second difficulty, not serious in the case of PD, is what is called the Coordination Problem, that is, the problem of making clear to everyone concerned which of the various possible solutions is the one to be chosen by all. In the case of PD it is plain that this is nonconfession by both, since it disadvantages neither and is better for both than confession. But in other real-life situations there may be many solutions.

Hobbes' solution (and perhaps Bentham's)[4] is the introduction of a sovereign who authoritatively solves the various social coordination problems by laying down public directives (laws) binding on all, and solves the assurance problem by attaching stringent sanctions to these directives, thus making it profitable for all to follow these directives, and so giving the necessary assurance to everybody subject to the law. Hobbes thought that by conferring on the sovereign near absolute power, each subject brought about a situation which was in his best interest and in which it was in his best interest or at least in accordance with reason to follow the sovereign's directives. The difference between these last two claims is important, for if it may sometimes *be* in one's interest to break the law, then the creation of the sovereign is not a foolproof solution to Prisoners' Dilemma. Hobbes attempts to patch up this hole in his solution by a game-theoretic argument to the effect that though it may turn out to have been in one's interest to break the law, it could never be in accordance with reason to think in advance that it would turn out to be so.[5] But this argument depends on two claims only one of which is sound, namely, that anyone violating the law can gain from his violation only by "the errors of other men." The second, namely, that one "could not foresee, nor reckon upon" such errors, and therefore in breaking the law one always necessarily acts contrary to reason, is unsound. For surely in most societies, perhaps in all, it is not always impossible or unlikely that a person should be able to tell with very great certainty, and with comparatively little risk to himself should he be mistaken, that he will not be caught. Hobbes cannot, therefore, clinch his point that in a society with a sovereign and a legal order no member ever has adequate reason to disobey the law.

If I am right in this, then Hobbesians have to concede that Rational Egoists, on their theory, sometimes have adequate reason to break the law. Furthermore, a community of such egoists suspecting one another of being such, have on their theory adequate reason to strengthen their own position so as to be able to break the law with impunity and to ensure that others will never be in that position. They have reason to ensure, by stringent policies of "law and order," that crime does not pay *other people*. At the same time they have reason to attempt, perhaps by bribes, threats, and other methods, to bend the law to their own advantage. Their egoistic officials, whose task it is to ensure that the rules are enforced, have reason to enrich themselves by bending the law, for a consideration. Given the unequal abilities of different people to promote their interest, such a social order will tend towards an increasingly unjust absolutism. But as the society moves more and more in that direction, it will be more and more in the interest of, and therefore in accordance with reason for, more and more people to try and break the law, even at greater risk to themselves. Such Rational Egoist societies will, in other words, tend to be unstable, with periodic revolutions and many of the drawbacks of the Hobbesian state of nature.

Where exactly does the Hobbesian solution go wrong? The two most popular answers hinge on what seem to me inadequate diagnoses of the shortcomings with which the Hobbesian solution is designed to cope. One is psychological. It argues either that Hobbes is mistaken about human psychology—we are not as egoistic as he makes out; or that, though Hobbes is quite right, and though we really now are too egoistic, we need not and ought not to be. Now, it seems to me, though I cannot argue this here,[6] that no humanly achievable amount of psychological change in the direction of greater altruism can solve Hobbes' problem. For the proportion of people about whom one cares significantly less than about oneself must surely remain high. But as long as it remains high, the Hobbesian problems also remain.

The other diagnosis focuses on an inadequacy of the Rational Egoist theory of practical reasons. Recommended remedies are either to include altruistic reasons in the system of practical reasons, that is, to include the substantive claim that the fact that doing A is in someone else's interest is a reason for one to do A, or to insist on reasons as objective, that is, the view that reasons are not person-relative, so that the fact that doing A is in *someone's* interest is a reason for *anyone* and *everyone* to do A.[7] However, these remedies seem to me equally inadequate, though again I cannot argue this here. It must suffice to say that they cannot provide the needed principle by which to adjudicate conflict of egoistic and altruistic reasons, or conflicts of interest if, as will often be the case, a person will have equally good objective reason to do A and not to do A when doing A is in N's, and not doing A in M's interest.

It seems to me that the crucial flaw in the Hobbesian state of nature, or in PD, is the limitation to independent reasons. The Hobbesian solution does not correct this flaw. Hobbesians must regard the social mores, custom and law, as merely a necessary evil. Necessary, that is, for the solution of the coordination and assurance problems. In particular, everybody has reason to support the existence of the social sanctions, only because nothing else can assure him that others will abide by the socially prescribed form of coordination, rather than depart from it in order to derive, at the expense of others, even greater gains for themselves. Such an attitude to the social order permits, indeed requires, each individual to try to change law and custom so as to favor him and his loved ones more than is currently the case, and to violate law and custom whenever he can advantageously do that.[8]

If this is the real flaw and cause of instability and dissatisfaction, then the solution lies in having law and custom regarded in the society as "binding" on all members, as constituting adequate reasons to act as they require, that is, as reasons which override independent reasons when they come into conflict with them. We could call such a theory "Rational Conventionalism." It can be expressed in the formula,

(vii) The requirements of the social order are to be regarded by its members as reasons for acting accordingly and, where they come into conflict with independent reasons, as *overriding* them.

Rational Conventionalism has an important corollary which I shall call "the principle of determinate universalizability":

(viii) If F is a reason to do A, for anyone falling into a recognized category D, then F must be a reason to do A for everyone falling into this category.

This is a stronger principle than the principle of universalizability ((iv) above). It differs from (iv) in that it authoritatively spells out the conditions, D, on account of which a given fact, F, is a reason for someone. What is more, such reasons *ex hypothesi override* whatever independent reasons against doing A someone satisfying D may have. And in virtue of the social sanctions rightly attached to them, they are also "binding" on everyone who satisfied D; everyone, that is, who is subject to and a beneficiary of the relevant social order. Rational Conventionalism explains well enough why we think we have duties to do more for our fellow countrymen than for those living in other societies.

Rational Conventionalism is prima facie attractive since it seems to solve the recalcitrant problem of instability, but it cannot be a sound theory of practical reasons. Surely, a slave in a slave society would not rightly regard all the coercive rules of his society, at least not all those concerning slavery, as adequate reasons to act as they require of him. The law relating to run-away slaves does not give him an adequate reason to return. Exactly why is it a mistake, we must ask, to move from the fact that life would be better for everyone living under such an order—it might well be better even for the slave—if its requirements *were* regarded as overriding reasons than if that were not so, to the conclusion that the requirements of any such coercive social order are rightly regarded and so really constitute, adequate reasons for members of such an order to act accordingly?

The mistake is this. If these requirements are really to be overriding reasons, then everyone must have adequate independent reasons to want them generally so regarded. Now if my argument was sound, then it may well be the case that whatever (within certain limits) the nature of the social order, everyone is better off under it than in a state of nature, and still better off if the social requirements are regarded as overriding reasons than if they are regarded as necessary but irksome obstacles or in some such way. Nevertheless, this shows only that everyone has *some* reason but not that he has *adequate* reason to want these requirements regarded as overriding reasons.

What, then, would make them adequate? Clearly, the society would have to meet certain standards of excellence. A very high standard which would certainly yield adequate reasons would be a society so organized that everyone had *the best possible independent* reason anyone could in reason demand for wanting the social requirements regarded as overriding reasons, namely, the best possible reasons *everyone* could have. A person would have the better an independent reason for wanting the social requirements so regarded the more favorable the social rules are to him and those he cares about. Of course, a person could always ask for better independent reasons than he already has, for there seems to be no limit to the advantages and privileges the society may grant him. It does seem, however, that the principle of universalizability sets a rational limit: he cannot *in reason* demand a better reason than *everyone* can have. It would seem that the best independent reason anyone can in reason demand for wanting the social requirements generally regarded as overriding reasons, that is, the best independent reason *everyone* can have, is that the social order be not simply for the good of everyone (almost any social order would achieve that) but for the good of everyone alike—that it be *equitable*. If the order comes up to this standard, then everyone has adequate independent reason to want the social requirements generally recognized as overriding reasons. And in that case they are rightly so regarded, and therefore really are such overriding reasons. This incidentally also answers the question why I (anyone) ought to obey the requirements of an equitable social order even if doing so is irksome or against my (his) best interest.

It is plain, however, that less than that must be regarded as constituting adequate reason. The advantages of having the requirements so recognized are great and must be allowed to outweigh some of the disadvantages to those against whom the social order discriminates. Obviously, the claim of a social order which falls short of equitability to have its social requirements recognized as overriding reasons will be the stronger the *better* its institutional machinery for rectifying such inequitabilities.

By now, my answer to the question, "what are moral reasons"? should be clear. They are the reasons constituted by the principles, rules, and precepts of a morality, whether an individual's or a society's. When, as outsiders, say anthropologists, we talk about people's moral reasons for doing things, we may mean simply those of their reasons which they would take to be, perhaps actually call moral reasons. We then imply only that *they* take them to be *sound* moral reasons, without ourselves endorsing them as such. But when, as insiders, we speak of people's or our own moral reasons for doing something, or when

we speak of certain facts, say, that doing A is against the law or would be the breach of a promise, as moral reasons against doing A, we imply that these are reasons of *our* morality and that *we* think them sound reasons. And I believe that this means (whether we know it or not) that they are facts about doing A which show that doing A violates the principles, rules, or precepts of a part of our social order which everyone in it has adequate independent reason to recognize as reasons overriding all other relevant reasons and binding on all and possibly only those subject to and beneficiaries of that social order. It seems to me that this account can accommodate all the deep convictions we have about the nature of morality and moral reasons and can therefore explain and justify the seeming self-evidence of these convictions: they are conceptually based, conceptual truths derivable from the concepts of morality and reason.[9]

NOTES

1. For a systematization of this sort, see for example, Russell Grice, *The Grounds of Moral Judgments* (Cambridge, 1967).

2. See, for example, Henry Sidgwick, *The Methods of Ethics*, 7th ed.,(1907), esp. pp. 111–112 or *Political Argument* (London, 1965).

3. For a defense of Rational Egoism against this charge, see, for example, Jesse Kalin, "In Defense of Egoism" in David P. Gauthier, ed., *Morality and Rational Self-Interest* (Englewood Cliffs, 1970), esp. sections IV and V.

4. See David Lyons, *In the Interest of the Governed* (Oxford,1973).

5. *Leviathan*, ch.XV.

6. I have done so elsewhere, for example, in "Rationality and Morality," *Erkenntnis*, 11, (1977), 197–223.

7. See, for example, Thomas Nagel, *The Possibility of Altruism* (Oxford, 1970).

8. This was clearly seen by Plato in the famous "out-doing" argument against Thrasymachus in the *Republic*.

9. I was enabled to write this paper by an NEH Fellowship for Independent Study and Research during the winter term of 1977, which I hereby gratefully acknowledge.

11
WHY SHOULD I BE MORAL? REVISITED

Kai Nielsen

To ask "Why should I be moral?" is to ask "Why should I do what is right?". . .

Some philosophers have resisted the very posing of this question. They have taken it to be a pseudo-question. I first want to respond to them in a rather brisk manner. That is, I will respond to those who want to reject the question not because it is immoral to ask it but for the reason that it is—or so they believe—senseless to ask it. It makes about as much sense, they claim, as asking "Why are all scarlet things red?" If we reflect carefully on the occurrence of the word "should" in the putative question "Why should I be moral" we will come to see, the claim goes, that we are trying to ask for the logically impossible: we are asking for a moral reason to accept any moral reasons at all.

That objection evaporates as soon as we reflect on the fact that not all intelligible uses of "should" are moral uses of the term. When I ask, "Should I put a bandage on that cut?" I

am not normally asking a moral question and the "should" does not here have a moral use. When I ask, "Why should I be moral?" I am not asking, if I have my wits about me, "What moral reason or reasons have I for being moral?" That indeed is like asking "Why are all scarlet things red?" Rather, I am asking, can I, everything considered, give a reason sufficiently strong—a non-moral reason clearly—for my always giving an overriding weight to moral considerations, when they conflict with other considerations, such that I could be shown to be acting irrationally, or at least less rationally than I otherwise would be acting, if I did not give such pride of place to moral considerations?

Those who want to reject the very question can in turn respond. The very context of the situation, where the question "Why be moral?" could be raised, is a context, as the above in effect shows, in which it is assumed that acting morally is not in the interest of the agent asking that question, but, if that is so, the question is, after all, senseless, because it is asking for a reason which must be a self-interested reason for

---

From *American Philosophical Quarterly*, Vol. 21, No. 1 (January 1984):81–91. Reprinted by permission.

being moral, while, at the same time, it is assumed that being moral is not in the agent's self-interest. But that comes to asking for a self-interested reason for doing what is not in his self-interest and that plainly is nonsense. In asking the question the questioner is asking something which is incoherent for he is asking for a reason of self-interest for doing what is contrary to his self-interest.

It could be, and indeed it has been, denied that it only makes sense to ask the question "Why should I be moral?" when it is assumed that acting morally is not in the questioner's self-interest. But, that response aside, there are the following difficulties with that attempt to exhibit the meaninglessness of that question. It is not a logical or conceptual truth (if indeed it is true at all) that, everything considered, the most rational thing for an individual, any individual at all, to do is always to do that which will promote his self-interest. It is not true by definition and it also appears not to be a "universal law of rationality" for it appears to be the case at any rate—to take what would be a disconfirming instance—that there are circumstances in which it would not be in an individual's short term or long term self-interest to donate a kidney, yet it still would not be irrational or contrary to reason for him to do so. If there are cases of this sort (as there most certainly appear at least to be), then it cannot be the case that *the* rational thing for an individual to do is always to do that which is in his self-interest. There are rational individuals, for example some kidney donaters, who are neither being irrational nor acting irrationally in donating a kidney. There are things which are not *required* by reason which are still plainly not *contrary* to reason. Kidney donating, even against your self-interest, can sometimes be one of them.

Moreover, in asking "Why should I be moral?", in contexts where it is not in my self-interest to be moral, it is not clear that, if I am not confusedly asking for a moral reason for not doing what, everything considered, I regard as immoral and indeed

actually is immoral, I must then be asking for a self-interested reason for not doing it. It might instead be an aesthetic reason, an economic reason, a political reason such as acting out of pure class solidarity, or indeed the questioner may not be quite sure what kind of reason he will take as overriding— that itself is one of the elements in the question. So that road is also blocked in the attempt to show that the question is a pseudo-question.

Alternatively, it can be argued that the question is a pseudo-question because, as we have seen, to ask "Why should I be moral?" is to ask "Why should I do what is right?" and that putative question, it is claimed, is a senseless question, because, saying that an act is right just means that one should do it. This is, some will say, the final answer to a challenger of the hegemony of morality. And this, it will be claimed, obtains even for an individual agent in an ongoing moral society. For questions concerning what to do, the moral point of view just is the ultimately overriding point of view. The short of the matter is that if one understands what it is for an act to be right or wrong, it is senseless, for one to try to turn around and ask why one should do what one acknowledges, and acknowledges correctly, is right and avoid what is wrong. Doing what is right is just what one should do and indeed must do or at least try to do.

This is plainly not "the short of the matter," for indeed to try to settle the matter thus is utterly to fail to appreciate the force and the point of the putative question. Not all "shoulds", as we have seen, are moral "shoulds." In asking why he should take moral reasons as overriding, a person is asking "Why take the moral point of view?" or, at least, "Why always take the moral point of view as always the overriding guide for all his actions where moral considerations are relevant?" The person asking that question can perfectly well understand that, *from the moral point of view*, "I should do what, everything considered, I regard as right" is analytic or at least unchallengeable. But while not for a moment challenging that, he can perfectly relevantly point out that he is concerned with a different matter. He is asking why take the moral point of view at all? Whatever discoveries we might make about what the moral point of view requires will not *ipso facto,* or perhaps not at all, answer that question. Knowing, assuming now that we can know such a thing, that an act is right or is morally required, is, from the point of view of the person contemplating so acting, a sufficient reason for his doing it, only if the person in question is already committed to acting morally. What is a *morally* justifying reason may be neither a *motivating* reason nor a *justifying* reason *sans phrase.* But the question "Why should I be moral?" is to be construed as a request for reasons to justify that commitment to morality. From the moral point of view, moral reasons are taken as the overriding reasons for action, but why should he, as an individual, accept them as such, or, what comes to the same thing, reason in accordance with the moral point of view? That is the question we are trying to ask and it can't be, non-question beggingly answered or dismissed, by simply telling us that morally speaking it is the right thing to do.

Suppose an individual acknowledges that putting limits on the pursuit of rational self-interest just is acting morally. But he can still ask, "Why should I do that rather than pursue my rational self-interest without any limit?" This is one prominent form of the question "Why should I be moral?" and it has not been shown to be a senseless question.

So let us now proceed on the assumption that the question is not a pseudo-question. Still, "Why be moral?" is indeed a strange question which requires a reasonably determinate reading or set of readings if any headway is to be made with it. We have already done some of that but we still need to refine it a bit.

One, at least seemingly straightforward way of asking it, is to ask: why move beyond self-interest? Why adopt the so-called, or perhaps even the not so so-called, impartial, universal moral point of view? Some will, on various grounds, deny that there is such an impartial, or even partially impartial, moral point of view. But let us grant here, for the sake of the discussion at least, that we have a coherent conception of such an impartial moral point of view and then ask the hard "Why-be-moral? question": so what, why should I adopt it?

It is plainly and unequivocally in our collective interests that we have a morality and that people generally act in accordance with it. Life in a world without reasonably functioning moral institutions would in Hobbes's famous phrase be nasty, brutish and short. In living we all need moral institutions. Even if the particular morality is only a conventional morality that we as rational egoists bargain ourselves into, it is much better than no morality at all. It is plainly in our interests to have moral institutions and practices in place and functioning. But that shows why *we* should have a morality, why it is in *our* interests to have a functioning morality, it does not answer the question of why *I* should be moral.

That *we* should be moral—that taken collectively we require moral institutions—does not show why an individual in a society with reasonably funtioning moral institutions should himself be a person of moral principle. He should simulate such behavior all right, but why should he not be a free-rider and give the appearance of moral commitment while always, or at least typically, feathering his own nest when it is safe to do so? The correct answer to the question "Why should *we* be moral?" is not necessarily the correct answer to "Why *I* should be moral?".

Some will respond that it is. That an answer to the question of why people should be moral is automatically an answer to why an individual should be moral because of the very nature of what a reason is or what reason is. If to preserve my health is a good reason for me to exercise, it is a good reason for any person like me in circumstances like mine to exercise as well, so if X is a good reason for Y to do Z then it is also a good reason for anyone else like Y in Y's circumstances to do *Z*. Moreover, if some things, *A*, *B*, *C* and *D*, are such that for anyone in any circumstance there is good reason to have them, then there is trivially reason for each of them to have them. Reasons are general; we can't sensibly say of two similarly inclined and generally relevantly similar people in identical circumstances that *X* is a good reason for *Y* to *Z* and not a good reason for *W* to *Z*. Contrary to what I have said above, if we have a good answer, as we do, to why *we* should be moral, we also have a good answer to why *I* should be moral—why any given individual in an ongoing tolerably moral society should be moral. This response fails, among other things, to keep in mind the distinction between an *agent-neutral viewpoint* and an *agent-relative viewpoint*. Both may be concerned with what happens or what is done or is to be done. But they view these questions from a very different vantage point (perspective). When our aims are held in common, they are agent-neutral. The above critical response to my argument for splitting the "Why should I be moral?" and "Why should we be moral?" question is from a resolutely agent-neutral viewpoint. If *X* is a reason for *Y* to do *Z* it is plainly a reason for anyone else relevantly like *Y* and similarly inclined and situated to do *Z*. If there is reason for me to protect my interests in a certain circumstance, I cannot consistently deny that it is a reason for you to protect your interests as well, if you are like me and similarly circumstanced. But all the while we are viewing things from an agent-neutral viewpoint. The immoralist free-rider on morality grants that that plainly is what to do from an agent-neutral viewpoint but he is in effect asking "Why should I take an agent-neutral viewpoint rather than an agent-relative viewpoint?" From an agent-neutral viewpoint, there is as much a reason for you to do something as for me to do it. I can't deny that you have a reason to do it if I do, unless I can show some relevant difference between you and me. But when I am viewing things from an agent-relative viewpoint, I can with perfect consistency ignore that and I can relevantly ask why should I abandon that

agent-relative viewpoint. And that plainly is the viewpoint the person who is asking why he should be moral is asking that question from, if he at all has his wits about him. No non-question begging reason has been given why he must override that viewpoint or shift to an agent-neutral viewpoint to remain a rational individual rationally acting in the world. That, morally speaking, he must simply beg the question for he is asking "Why take the moral point of view?".

Is it not at least logically possible that the immoralist (amoralist if you will) might be satisfied with his life? Can it be shown that, no matter who I am, no matter what preference schedules I happen to have, that my long-term self-interest is more likely to be satisfied if I, in conjunction with everyone else or even with the greater majority of the people, am doing what morally speaking is the right thing to do, than, if everybody else or even (perhaps) most people are so acting, and I, undetected, am not so acting? Must a prudent intelligent immoralist make himself unhappy or harm even his own long-term self-interest by continuing to be such an immoralist?

Such an at least putatively rational immoralist will be an adroit free-rider. He will have an interest in other people being moral, since other people's immorality, particularly when they are close by, will, or at least very likely may, adversely effect his own life, and the lives of people he just happens to care about. He, no more than the moralist, will want a Hobbesian state of nature. He will also, and for the same reasons, have an interest in the effective enforcement of the principles and precepts of morality. He will, if he is thoroughly rational and reflective, want others to restrict their exclusive pursuit of their self-interest. But what he reflectively wants for himself is another matter. . . .

We human beings, it will be said, are socialized in such a way that we inevitably will come to have a moral conscience "telling" us in specific situations what is right and wrong and nagging us, indeed not infrequently whipping us, for not doing what our conscience tells us we must do. We cannot, the claim goes, safely ignore the dictates of our conscience and remain happy. Even if we are very clever indeed at simulating moral commitment, we will, though publicly unreprobated, still pay heavily in psychic suffering if we violate the dictates of our conscience.

Suppose my conscience is bothering me because I am really acting without what I acknowledge is, morally speaking, a proper regard for others. Must I, in such a circumstance, be acting against my true interests? Must I be unhappy or less happy than I otherwise would be? Must I remain, if I don't rationalize, a person who is so bothered by his conscience? And must all rational persons in such circumstance so react?

Many people—perhaps most people—are captured by tribal taboos and tribal loyalties and are held hostage, in varying degrees, to neurotic compulsions about duties and the like. They will be, again in varying degrees, miserable if they do not act in accordance with what they believe morality enjoins. But people can free themselves from such superstitions and compulsions. Where they can, they will not for *these* reasons be made unhappy, if they are prudently immoral at least in terms of the morality that previously held sway over them.

Do we, all the same, have good reason to believe that they will be less happy than people of good will? How do we know, or do we know, that the immoralist cannot live in such a way that he will be truly happy? (We must beware of an unwitting intellectual cheating here, through an implicit persuasive definition of "*truly* happy" or "*true* interests.")

It is true that an individual who rather systematically behaves in a thoroughly unprincipled way is very likely to be found out, even when he is clever and tolerably prudent about it. And when he is found out people will generally turn against him—some very sharply—and it is very unlikely, in such a circumstance, that his life will be (to put it minimally) a very happy one. Morality—or at least behavior sufficiently like morality not to occasion such reprobation—will, in such a circumstance, pay off.

Still this will not show that occasional quite deliberate patterns of prudent and intelligent immorality might not, on some occasions, handsomely pay off for the perpetrator of those acts. Still, we have not yet squarely faced questions concerning the psychological effects of the pangs of conscience. We should ask ourselves this question. Is it not possible for those who recognize that the dictates of conscience are not the dictates of reason, to come to repudiate the *authority* of conscience and to come to regard their conscience as simply their superego: an irrational or at least non-rational censor whose authority they no longer acknowledge?

However, it will in turn be responded, that this is too rationalistic a way of looking at the matter. We can reject the *authority* of conscience and it can still (as reformed teetotalers know) have a hold over one. Such conditioning—a socializing into the having of a conscience—is, under most circumstances, humanly speaking, or sociologically speaking, inescapable, and a rational immoralist could not wish the general conditioning circumstance changed because he recognizes, à la Hobbes, the plain value of moral institutions for *us*. He, as we have seen, is asking "Why should *I* be moral?" not "Why should *we* be moral?".

To this it could, in turn, be replied, that even in tolerably stable, well-ordered societies certain individuals are not so afflicted with sharp pangs of conscience. There is a not inconsiderable amount of unprincipled behavior about, some of it plainly stupid and counter-productive even for its perpetrators, some of it more marginally stupid and counter-productive and some of it with at least the appearance of being intelligent, controlled and plainly advantage producing for the perpetrator of the immorality. It is a banal falsehood that crime never pays. It surely appears at least to be the case, that the burden of proof falls very heavily on the moralist who would maintain that deep down any such immoralist must be unhappy, must be acting against his "true self" or at least his "true interests."

Still isn't he? He, being human, could not but value friendship, love, comradeship and fraternity. But all those things would be impossible for him, at least in their more genuine forms, if he lived the life of an immoralist. But, in not having them, he loses a lot—loses more than he could ever gain in a trade off with the goods he gained by his immoralism. The very central human goods (friendship, love, comradeship, fraternity), goods resting on a non-calculating reciprocity, will not be available to him, it is natural to argue, if he does not take the moral point of view. So, taking that point of view is, after all, a necessary though not a sufficient condition for his happiness. Not even psychoanalysis can, or will even try to, obliterate the voice of the superego. It can at most diminish its excessive demands. Our conditioning was too early and too pervasive for there to be any reasonable question of turning our backs on it now. We cannot so easily cast off these ancient internalized demands.

You cannot, so the claim goes, act without regard to the dictates of morality if you really want to be happy. Yet in our societies not a few people, some of them apparently contentedly and without evident harmful consequences to themselves, wear their consciences very lightly indeed. Is that appearance really deceiving? Are they all secretly miserable? Is it so clear that immorality never pays? Do we have good grounds for believing, persuasive definitions aside, that for us as individuals it is always in our best interests to do what morality requires?

I am inclined to think that the belief that it is is a philosopher's myth. A consoling story some moral philosophers tell themselves. Even if a policy of *systematic* immoralism would make friendship, love and comradeship impossible—things we plainly have reason to want—it need not be that to gain these things requires any thorough-

going moral integrity on our part. The immoralist can be selectively and prudently immoral—and this without a lot of rationalistic calculation. He need not be systematically or paranoidly immoral and, like Macbeth, drive everyone from him.

Whether or not it is in your true interests to be moral depends on what sort of person you happen to be. Beware of those moralizing moralists—those keepers of the true faith—who read their own sentiments into all humankind and conclude that all immoralists must be unhappy.

There is, of course, the not unreasonable worry that a person lacking in moral integrity will face social ostracism: loss of love, contempt of family, friends, colleagues and the like. I have suggested, in turn, that, where the person is intelligent and prudently in control of himself (as an immoralist could be), this danger is typically exaggerated by people understandably anxious to preserve the utter hegemony of morality.

There are further twists to the skein of the argument over immoralism. Even if it is the case that there are no ultimate non-questions begging grounds, in such general situations, for an individual's acting in accordance with the moral point of view rather than from a purely self-interested point of view and even if it is the case that no ultimate non-question begging reason can be given for taking an agent-neutral perspective rather than agent-relative perspective, still these things do not show that we have vindicated an individual's having moral commitments. Rather what we should conclude is that, in this type circumstance, justification has come to an end and that we must simply *decide* for ourselves how we should act and what sort of persons we will strive to be or to become. What all of this points to is that here at least decision is king.

If the above line of reasoning, about the incommensurability of the moral point of view and the self-interested point, is on the mark, then there can be no rational considerations showing us that we must, on pain of simply being irrational, be moral. If we are going to be through and through tough-minded and not be taken in by mythologies, we will conclude that, in the last analysis (whatever exactly that means), we must just decide to act in one way or another without having reasons sufficient to show that one course of action rather than another is *required* by reason.

To reinforce the above line of argument consider the situation of what I shall call a classist amoralist in our class societies. I mean by "a classist amoralist" a) a person who is part of the dominant elite in such a society, b) a person who only extends his disinterested caring to his own peers and to those under-lings (servants, mistresses, and the like) he just happens to care about, and c) a person who treats all other people manipulatively, deploying morality as moral ideology to keep those people in line in such a way that the interests of his class, and with that his own interests, are furthered. He has genuine moral relations with his own peers—the members of the elite class. Between such people there can be genuine love, disinter-ested concern, justice: the genuine recipro-cities that partly constitute morality; but this is not extended, by the classist amoralists in that elite, to their relations with the vast dominated class. They, or at least most of them, are treated manipulatively. For them, our classist amoralist believes, moral ideol-ogy with its artful semblance of morality is enough. The thing to do with them, he avers, is, with the adroit use of the consciousness industry, to do a real snow job on them. But there is for the classist amoralist no question of treating them morally as equal members of a Kantian kingdom of ends. An artful disguise of morality is all that is required or desirable from the perspective of his classist amoralism.

It is not evident that such a society need be unstable or at least less stable than a society in which the moral point of view prevails. It is true that most members of ruling elites concoct comforting myths for themselves which conveniently reinforce their sense of their own class superiority. But it is not clear that all such classist amoralists must be so myth-prone. Slave societies existed in a stable manner for a long time. Is it really plausible to believe that all slave owners thought that they were somehow innately superior to their slaves? Do all Afrikaners today, who are wholehearted supporters of their system of apartheid, believe that Whites are superior to the Blacks they so cruelly exploit? Is it not vastly more probable that *some* of the more intelligent and reflective slave owners or defenders of apartheid would have con-cluded or will conclude, as the case may be, both that there, but by the wheel of fortune, go they; and that the thing to do is to continue, within reason, doing what they can to protect their own good fortune. Such persons, so reasoning, could still have the usual resources of love, trust, companion-ship and relatedness. A person, so reasoning and so acting, is unfair, and knows he is unfair, but, *among his peers*, he could very well be scrupulously fair, and, after all, he could say, perfectly correctly, that he didn't make the world. He just grew up in a society so structured. After all do not many of us in uncomfortable situations tell ourselves analo-gously comforting stories and make our little adjustments?

It looks like the burden of proof falls heavily on a moralist to prove that such a classist amoralist or immoralist need in any-way be less happy, live a less self-fulfilling life, than the person of moral principle or moral integrity. Indeed in some circum-stances—circumstances in which the world we live in is particularly swinish—he might even be happier or more self-fulfilled. And we have no good grounds for believing that such an immoralist in such a circumstance must be less rational or even, in a non-question begging sense, less reasonable than the person of firm and functional moral commitment.

Such a classist amoralist, note, is not as vulnerable as an immoralist who is an indi-vidual egoist. While many of us can and surely do get away with occasional thoroughly selfish and unprincipled acts, a deliberate, persistent policy of selfishness, even when it is intelligently cunning, is very likely to bring on guilt feelings, punishment, estrangement from others as well as their contempt and hostility. Classist amoralism with the reciprocity to be found in its class solidarity is far more secure than individual egoism. It is far less likely that the classist amoralist will find his sources of security, comfort, and happiness undermined. In such a society the classist amoralist (assuming he has the good fortune to belong to the dominant class) can have securely available to him, as the individual egoist cannot, things all of us, at least on reflection, want, namely companionship, love, approval, comfort, security and recognition.

Yet, even if our classist amoralist is not quite so securely placed, it still is clearly the case that sometimes for some such people, with certain personality structures, it is in their rational self-interest, even their own long-term self-interest, to do something that they recognize is clearly wrong (immoral). Where individuals are concerned, it is not the case that morality is always the best policy. . . .

From the moral point of view moral reasons plainly override prudential reasons or any other kind of self-interested or purely class based reasons. Again, trivially, from an exclusively self-interested point of view or a purely class based point of view, self-interested or class grounded reasons override moral reasons. It is natural, in reflecting on this, to ask whether there is something called "the point of view of reason" which would show which kinds of reasons (form of life based reasons, if you will) are finally overriding? Taken from this very general point of view, abstracted from moral or class commitments or prudential commitments, can we show which of these particular types of reason, from the very point of reason itself (assuming for the nonce there is such a point of view), are finally overriding? I have been concerned to argue that reason (human intelligence and understanding) without the collaboration of *moral sentiment* does not require that moral reasons be taken as overriding. They are, of course, taken as overriding from the moral point of view. But that is a different matter. *Morality requires commitment here not still further understanding.* Though this is not at all to say or to suggest that the moral commitment must be blind or without understanding. That is an entirely different thing. And it is well to remember that there are many things we reasonably do that we do not do for a reason. But it also is true that nothing has been unearthed called the "point of view of reason" which would adjudicate matters here. We have not been able to show that reason requires the moral point of view or that all really rational persons, unhoodwinked by myth or ideology, not be individual egoists or classist amoralists. Reason doesn't decide here.

12

THE JUSTIFICATORY ARGUMENT FOR HUMAN RIGHTS

Alan Gewirth

I now wish to present my own answer to the justificatory or epistemological question of human rights. It will be recalled that the Justifying Basis or Ground of human rights must be a normative moral principle that serves to prove or establish that every person morally ought to have the necessary goods of action as something to which he or she is entitled. The epistemological question, hence, comes down to whether such a moral principle can be rationally justified.

It is important to note that not all moral principles will serve for this purpose. Utilitarian, organicist, and elitist moral principles either do not justify any moral rights at all, or justify them only as ancillary to and contingent upon various collective goals,[1] or do make rights primary but not as equally distributed among all humans. Hence, it will be necessary to show how the moral principle that justifies equal human rights is superior, in point of rational cogency, to these other kinds of moral principles.

Now, there are well-known difficulties in the attempt to provide a rational justification of any moral principle. Obviously, given some high-level moral principle, we can morally justify some specific moral rule or particular moral judgment or action by showing how its rightness follows from the principle. But how can we justify the basic principle itself? Here, by definition, there is no higher or more general moral principle to be appealed to as an independent variable. Is it the case, then, that justification comes to a stop here? This would mean that we cannot rationally adjudicate between *conflicting* moral principles and ways of life and society, such as those epitomized, for example, by Kant's categorical imperative, Bentham's utilitarianism, Kierkegaard's theological primacy, Stirner's egoism, Nietzsche's exaltation of the superman, Spencer's doctrine of the survival of the fittest, and so on.

From "The Epistemology of Human Rights," *Social Philosophy & Policy*, Vol. 1, No. 2 (1984),1–24. Reprinted by permission.

THE PROBLEM OF THE INDEPENDENT VARIABLE

One of the central problems here is that of the independent variable. Principles serve as independent variables for justifying lower-level rules and judgments; but what is the independent variable for justifying principles themselves? Another way to bring out this problem in relation to morality is to contrast particular empirical statements and particular moral judgments. Consider, on the one hand, such a statement as "Mrs. Jones *is* having an abortion," and, on the other hand, "Mrs. Jones *ought* to have an abortion." We know, at least in principle, how to go about checking the truth of the first statement, namely, by referring to certain empirical facts that serve as the independent variables for the statement to be checked against. But how do we go about checking the truth of the second statement, that Mrs. Jones *ought* to have an abortion? Indeed, what would it *mean* for the second statement to be true? What is the independent variable for *it* to be checked against? For the first statement to be true means that it corresponds to certain empirical facts. But with regard to a judgment like "Mrs. Jones *ought* to have an abortion," what facts would *it* have to correspond to in order to be true? Is there any moral *'ought'* in the world, in the way in which the factual *'is'* is in the world, serving as the independent variable for testing or confirming the relevant statements? If not, then is the moral judgment in no sense either true or false?

The problem we have reached, then, is whether there is any non-question-begging answer to the problem of the independent variable in morality. I now want to suggest that there is. To see this, we must recall that all moral precepts, regardless of their greatly varying contents, are concerned with how persons ought to *act* toward one another. Think, for example, of the Golden Rule: "*Do* unto others as you would have them do unto you." Think also of Kant's categorical imperative "*Act* in such a way that the maxim of your action can be a universal law." Similarly, Bentham tells us to *act* so as to maximize utility; Nietzsche tells us to *act* in accord with the ideals of the superman; Marx tells us to *act* in accord with the interests of the proletariat; Kierkegaard tells us to *act* as God commands, and so forth.

The independent variable of all morality, then, is human *action*. This independent variable cuts across the distinctions between secular and religious moralities, between egalitarian and elitist moralities, between deontological and teleological moralities, and so forth.

But how does this independent variable of action help us to resolve the difficulties of moral justification? Surely we can't take the various rival moral principles and justify one of them as against the others simply by checking it against the fact of human action. Moreover, since if action is to be genuinely the non-question-begging independent variable of morality, it must fit *all* moral principles, how does action enable us to justify *one* moral principle *as against* its rivals?

The answer to these questions is given by the fact that action has what I have called a *normative structure*, in that, logically implicit in action, there are certain evaluative and deontic judgments, certain judgments about goods and rights made by agents; and when these judgments are subjected to certain morally neutral rational requirements, they entail a certain supreme moral principle. Hence, if any agent denies the principle, he can be shown to have contradicted himself, so that his denial, and the actions stemming from it, cannot be rationally justifiable. Thus, together with action, the most basic kind of reason, deductive rationality, also serves as an independent variable for the justification of the supreme principle of morality.

WHY ACTION GIVES THE PRINCIPLE A RATIONALLY NECESSARY ACCEPTABILITY

It is important to note that because the principle is grounded in the generic features of action, it has a certain kind of *material necessity.* It will be recalled that some of the justificatory arguments for rights examined above failed because they did not satisfy the condition that they be acceptable to all rational persons as a matter of rational necessity. For example, why must any rational person accept Rawls's starting point in the "veil of ignorance"? Why, for that matter, is it rationally necessary for any rational person to accept the Golden Rule or any other moral principle that has hitherto been propounded?

The condition of rationally necessary acceptability is fulfilled, however, when the independent variable of the argument is placed in the generic features of action. For this involves that, simply by virtue of being an agent, one logically must accept the argument and its conclusion that all persons equally have certain moral rights. Now, being an actual or prospective agent is not an optional or variable condition for any person, except in the sense that he may choose to commit suicide or, perhaps, to sell himself into slavery; and even then the steps he intentionally takes toward these goals involve agency on his part. Hence, if there are moral rights and duties that logically accrue to every person simply by virtue of being an actual or prospective agent, the argument that traces this logical sequence will necessarily be rationally acceptable to every agent: he will have to accept the argument on pain of self-contradiction.

There is a sense in which this grounding of the moral principle in action involves a foundationalist conception of justification. For, as we shall see, the argument begins with a statement attributable to any agent, that he performs some purposive action. This statement is based on the agent's direct awareness of what he is doing, and it leads, in a unilinear sequence, to his statement that he and all other agents have certain rights and correlative duties. I need not be concerned, in the present context, with further epistemological issues about the certainty or trustworthiness of the rational agent's direct awareness or about any presumed "data" on which this awareness might be based. . . .

My argument, in contrast, begins not from variable moral judgments but from statements that must be accepted by every agent because they derive from the generic features of purposive action. Hence, my argument is not "foundationalist" in the sense that it begins from *moral* or *evaluative* statements that are taken to be self-justifying or self-evident. The present argument is one in which statements about actions, and not statements about values or duties, are taken as the basic starting point. And these statements entail, in a noncircular sense, certain judgments about the existence of human rights.

THE ARGUMENT FOR EQUAL HUMAN RIGHTS

I shall, now, give a brief outline of the rational line of argument that goes from action, through its normative structure, to the supreme principle of morality, and thence to equal human rights. In my book, *Reason and Morality*,[2] I have presented a full statement of the argument, so that for present purposes I shall stress only certain main points.

To begin with, we must note certain salient characteristics of action. In ordinary as well as scientific language, the word 'action' is used in many different senses: we talk, for example, about physical action at a distance, about the action of the liver, and so forth. But the meaning of 'action' that is relevant here is that which is the common object of all moral and other practical precepts, such as the examples I gave before. Moral and other practical precepts, as we have seen, tell persons to *act* in many different ways. But amid these differences, the precepts all assume that the persons addressed by them can control their behaviour by their unforced choice with a view to achieving whatever the precepts require. All actions as envisaged by moral and other practical precepts, then, have two *generic features*. One is *voluntariness* or *freedom,* in that the agents control or can control their behavior by their unforced choice while having knowledge of relevant circumstances. The other generic feature is *purposiveness* or *intentionality,* in that the agents aim to attain some end or goal which constitutes their reason for acting; this goal may consist either in the action itself or in something to be achieved by the action.

Now, let us take any agent A, defined as an actual or prospective performer of actions in the sense just indicated. When he performs an action, he can be described as saying or thinking:

(1) "I do X for end or purpose E."

Since E is something he unforcedly chooses to attain, he thinks E has sufficient value to merit his moving from quiescence to action in order to attain it. Hence, from his standpoint, (1) entails

(2) "E is good."

Note that (2) is here presented in quotation marks, as something said or thought by the agent A. The kind of goodness he here attributes to E need not be moral goodness; its criterion varies with whatever purpose E the agent may have in doing X. But what it shows already is that, in the context of action, the 'Fact-Value gap' is already bridged, for by the very *fact* of engaging in action, every agent must implicitly accept for himself a certain *value*-judgment about the value or goodness of the purposes for which he acts.

Now, in order to act for E, which he regards as good, the agent A must have the proximate necessary conditions of action. These conditions are closely related to the generic features of action that I mentioned before. You will recall that these generic features are voluntariness or freedom and purposiveness or intentionality. But when purposiveness is extended to the general conditions required for success in achieving one's purposes, it becomes a more extensive condition which I shall call *well-being.* Viewed from the standpoint of action, then, well-being consists in having the various substantive conditions and abilities, ranging from

life and physical integrity to self-esteem and education, that are required if a person is to act either at all or with general chances of success in achieving the purposes for which he acts. So freedom and well-being are the necessary conditions of action and of successful action in general. Hence, from the agent's standpoint, from (2) "E is good" there follows

(3) "My freedom and well-being are necessssary goods."

This may also be put as

(4) "I must have freedom and well-being,"

where this 'must' is a practical-prescriptive requirement, expressed by the agent, as to his having the necessary conditions of his action.

Now from (4) there follows

(5) "I have rights to freedom and well-being."

To show that (5) follows from (4), let us suppose that the agent were to deny (5). In that case, because of the correlativity of rights and strict 'oughts,' he would also have to deny

(6) "All other persons ought at least to refrain from removing or interfering with my freedom and well-being."

By denying (6), he must accept

(7) "It is not the case that all other persons ought at least to refrain from removing or interfering with my freedom and well-being."

By accepting (7), he must also accept

(8) "Other persons may (i.e. It is permissible that other persons) remove or interfere with my freedom and well-being."

And by accepting (8), he must accept

(9) "I may not (i.e. It is permissible that I not) have freedom and well-being."

But (9) contradicts (4), which said "I must have freedom and well-being." Since every agent must accept (4), he must reject (9). And since (9) follows from the denial of (5), "I have rights to freedom and well-being," every agent must also reject that denial. Hence, every agent logically must accept (5) "I have rights to freedom and well-being."

What I have shown so far, then, is that the concept of a right, as a justified claim or entitlement, is logically involved in all action as a concept that signifies for every agent his claim and requirement that he have, and at least not be prevented from having, the necesary conditions that enable him to act in pursuit of his purposes. I shall sometimes refer to these rights as *generic rights,* since they are rights that the generic features of action and of successful action characterize one's behavior.

It must be noted, however, that, so far, the criterion of these rights that every agent must claim for himself is only prudential, not moral, in that the criterion consists for each agent in his own needs of agency in pursuit of his own purposes. Even though the right-claim is addressed to all other persons as a correlative 'ought'-judgment, still its justifying criterion for each agent consists in the necessary conditions of his own action.

To see how this prudential right-claim also becomes a moral right, we must go through some further steps. Now, the sufficient as well as the necessary reason or justifying condition for which every agent must hold that he has rights to freedom and well-being is that he is a prospective purposive agent. Hence, he must accept

(10) "I have rights to freedom and well-being because I am a prospective purposive agent,"

where this "because" signifies a sufficient as well as a necessary justifying condition.

Suppose some agent were to reject (10), and were to insist, instead, that the only reason he has the generic rights is that he has some more restrictive characteristic R. Examples of R would include: being an

American, being a professor, being an *Übermensch,* being male, being a capitalist or a proletarian, being white, being named "Wordsworth Donisthorpe," and so forth. Thus, the agent would be saying

(11) "I have rights to freedom and well-being *only* because I am R,"

where "R" is something more restrictive than being a prospective purposive agent.

Such an agent, however, would contradict himself. For he would then be in the position of saying that if he did *not* have R, he would *not* have the generic rights, so that he would have to accept

(12) "I do not have rights to freedom and well-being."

But we saw before that, as an agent, he *must* hold that he has rights to freedom and well-being. Hence, he must drop his view that R alone is the sufficient justifying condition of his having the generic rights, so that he must accept that simply being a prospective purposive agent is a sufficient as well as a necessary justifying condition of his having rights to freedom and well-being. Hence, he must accept (10).

Now by virtue of accepting (10), the agent must also accept

(13) "All prospective purposive agents have rights to freedom and well-being."

(13) follows from (10) because of the principle of universalization. If some predicate P belongs to some subject S because that subject has some general quality Q (where this 'because' signifies a sufficient reason), then that predicate logically must belong to every subject that has Q. Hence, since the predicate of having the generic rights belongs to the original agent because he is a prospective purposive agent, he logically must admit that every purposive agent has the generic rights.

At this point the rights become moral ones, and not only prudential, on that meaning of "moral" where it has both the formal component of setting forth practical requirements that are categorically obligatory, and the material component that those requirements involve taking favorable account of the interests of persons other than or in addition to the agent or the speaker. When the original agent now says that *all* prospective purposive agents have rights to freedom and well-being, he is logically committed to respecting and hence taking favorable account of the interests of all other persons with regard to their also having the necessary goods or conditions of action.

Since all other persons are actual or potential recipients of his action, every agent is logically committed to accepting

(14) "I ought to act in accord with the generic rights of my recipients as well as of myself."

This requirement can also be expressed as the general moral principle:

(15) "Act in accord with the generic rights of your recipients as well as of yourself."

I shall call this the Principle of Generic Consistency (*PGC*), since it combines the formal consideration of consistency with the material consideration of the generic features and rights of action. As we have seen, every agent, on pain of contradiction and hence of irrationality, must accept this principle as governing all his interpersonal actions.

This, then, completes my argument for equal human rights. Its central point can be summarized in two main parts. In the first part (steps 1 to 9), I have argued that every agent logically must hold or accept that he has rights to freedom and well-being as the necessary conditions of his action, as conditions that he *must* have; for if he denies that he has these rights, then he must accept that other persons may remove or interfere with his freedom and well-being, so that he *may not* have them; but this would contradict his belief that he *must* have them. In the second part (steps 10 to 14), I have argued that the agent logically must accept that all other prospective purposive agents have the same rights to freedom and well-being as he claims for himself.

Since all humans are actual, prospective, or potential agents, the rights in question belong equally to all humans. Thus, the argument fulfills the specifications for human rights that I mentioned at the outset: that both the Subjects and the Respondents of the rights are all humans equally, that the Objects of the rights are the necessary goods of human action, and that the Justifying Basis of the rights is a valid moral principle.

NOTES

1. I have tried to show this elsewhere with regard to utilitarianism. See Alan Gewirth, "Can Utilitarianism Justify Any Moral Rights?" in *Nomos XXIV: Ethics, Economics, and the Law,* ed. J. Roland Pennock and John W. Chapman (New York: New York University Press, 1982), 158–178.

2. Alan Gewirth, *Reason and Morality* (Chicago: University of Chicago Press, 1978), chs. 1–3.

13

IMPARTIAL REASON

Stephen G. Darwall

Reasons to act are considerations that support rational choice and recommend or justify action. They have, then, a *normative aspect*. They ground judgments about what it would be best to do or what an agent ought (rationally) to do, all things considered.

To accept an internalist account of reasons is to accept that reasons also have a *motivational aspect*. Reasons are considerations about an act awareness of which can motivate, or lead an agent to favor, an action.

We may combine these two aspects and give a general internalist account of reasons to act:

p is a reason for S to do A if, and only if, *p* is a fact about A awareness of which by S, under conditions of *rational consideration*, would lead S to prefer his doing A to his not doing A, other things equal.

From *Impartial Reason*, copyright © 1983 by Cornell University Press, and "Reply to Turzis," *Canadian Journal of Philosophy*, Vol. 18 (1988). Editing done by the author. Reprinted by permission of the publishers.

The motivational aspect of reasons is clear on this account: a fact can only be a reason for someone to act if consideration of it, under certain conditions, would motivate him. But simply being moved by a consideration is not the same thing as judging it to be a reason. Even more clearly, the degree of motivation that a consideration provides is not identical with its weight as a reason. Reasons also have a normative aspect; they are ground for a person's judgment of what it would be best to do, all things considered, or of what he ought (rationally) to do.[1] The way in which this normative aspect is brought into the internalist account of reasons I shall propose is through the idea that what establishes some fact as a reason (and its weight) for a person is that his rational consideration of it would result in some motivation to prefer the act. The normativity of reasons, according to an internalist account of this sort, arises from a normative ideal of rational consideration and not through the externalist idea that there are simply some facts that have the intrinsic property of being action-guiding and some that do not. Because my proposal will be that the most fundamental sort of rational consideration must be from a standpoint that is impartial between rational agents, I call it *impartial reason,* or IR for short.

IR is more sensitive, I believe, to the normative character of reasons than internalist theories usually are. Internalist theories hold that something's being a reason depends somehow on its capacity to affect motivation. Unlike internalist theories that identify reasons with *de facto* motives, however, IR insists on the normative character of reasons as tending to *justify* conduct as rational. It does this by holding that a reason to act is something which motivates when *appropriately* (or *rationally*) considered. The normative or justificatory weight of reasons is thus held to derive from a normative ideal of rational reflection. Reasons inherit as justificatory weight the motivational force they would come to have in an ideally rational process of reflection.

I

Reasons to act, then, are facts that motivate us to prefer an act when we give consideration to them in a rational way. Rather than approach directly and all at once the question of what rational consideration itself consists in, I propose to build up an account indirectly and somewhat dialectically. We shall begin with what is uncontroversial—that rational consideration involves making oneself aware of relevant facts, putting oneself in mind of them in a way that allows one to appreciate their relevance. From this point we shall move to the question of how considerations that move us in conflicting ways can be evaluated, developing out of our initial account an enriched analysis of rational consideration. These preliminary accounts will then be linked to the agent's conception of the good life for him. The initial perspective of rational consideration, then, will be the *person's own* point of view, albeit as informed and dispassionate and as having a life that extends through time.

We begin very simply. Rational consideration of a fact requires, obviously enough, being aware of it on reflection—thinking about it in connection with the act in question. Let us call the sort of awareness one has when reflecting on or thinking about a fact in connection with whether to perform a given act *reflective awareness.* Since a reason is a fact that motivates when rationally considered, we may conclude that:

If p is a fact about A reflective awareness of which would move S to prefer his doing A (to his not doing A), then p is a (presumptive) reason for S to do A.

If reflective awareness of p is motivating, therefore, p is at least presumptively a reason.

Further reflection, say in the light of other facts, or perhaps from some other point of view from which we might rationally deliberate, may altogether cancel any initial motivation we had to prefer A. So any reason that p provides is only presumptive, and defeasible. Not only may a reason be overridden by other, weightier reasons (and still hold its weight as a reason), but further reflection may cancel any motivating power it had and convince us that what we took to be a reason was in fact no reason at all.

For example, when I consider the fact that it will give a child pleasure to have an object, I am moved to give it to him. When I consider the fact that the child's pleasure will itself consist in teasing his sister with the object, the motivation lapses. What seemed a reason for me to give the child the object turns out on further reflection not to be one after all. Its presumption as a reason is defeated by further considerations. That the object will give the child pleasure, I may think, is no reason at all if it is that kind of pleasure.

Nonetheless, if reflective awareness of a fact motivates, that does create the presumption that it is a reason for one to act. And that, at least, is a place to start. Let us call this the *initial account of rational consideration.* Within the class of facts that motivate an agent to prefer some act or state of affairs when reflectively considered, we may distinguish roughly between those that concern properties intrinsic to the preferred act or state and those that concern the act or state's relation to some further preferred state. Whenever something is preferred purely for its relation to some further state, the latter will itself also be the object of preference. We may distinguish, therefore, between acts or states preferred for their own sakes and those preferred for their relation to further preferred states.

Let us call the former preferences *intrinsic* and label *extrinsic* any preference whose object is preferred for the sake of something else. These categories are not mutually exclusive. For example, as Glaucon remarks in the *Republic,* we value knowledge and understanding both for their own sake and for their consequences.

Agents have, then, presumptive reasons to satisfy their intrinsic preferences: those reasons being whatever considerations regarding properties internal to the objects of intrinsic preference motivate the preferences.

To adjudicate rationally between conflicting intrinsic preferences we must adopt a standpoint from which we can reflectively and dispassionately consider the reasons for our individual intrinsic preferences, feel the force of these different reasons, and come to an all-things-considered preference. From this standpoint there is no reason to restrict our reflection to considerations that motivate our actual intrinsic preferences. There may be other considerations that would motivate yet other intrinsic preferences were we aware of them in a way that allowed us to feel their force. Since what gives us reason for our actual preferences are the facts that motivate them, and not the simple fact of preference itself, if further facts would motivate yet further preferences were we to consider them, then they give us reasons also.

Rational consideration involves in the limit, then, the ideal of reflection on all relevant considerations. According to our initial account, *relevant* considerations include whichever would provide an agent some motivation to prefer an act when she reflects on them in an imaginatively vivid way. At this point, however, we have no reason to suppose that rational consideration is limited to this sort of reflective awareness (from the agent's own standpoint), and I shall argue that it is not. Nonetheless, we may say on the basis of the argument so far that any consideration that would move an agent to prefer an act were she to "bring it to mind with full belief and maximal vividness" is a reason for her to act.

II

Some writers, following Sidgwick, have used the idea of a person's informed, all-things-considered preferences to define the notion of *a person's good,* on the whole, or of *a person's conception of the good.* Sidgwick held that "a man's future good on the whole is what he would now desire and seek on the whole if all the consequences of all the different lines of conduct open to him were accurately foreseen and adequately realized in imagination at the present point in time."[2] For example, Rawls takes an approach similar to Sidgwick's that highlights the way in which a rational person's preferences reflect not only a deliberate awareness of considerations as they arise in distinct situations but also an awareness of different *kinds of lives* that are available to him.

This latter is an important point. As beings who can reflect on ourselves as perduring through time, we form preferences with much wider scope than those that we are likely to be able to satisfy by specific actions in specific situations. In the limiting case, we may prefer, on the whole, to lead one kind of life rather than another. When such preferences are informed and all-things-considered preferences, they provide a rational framework within which we may pursue our lives in various situations as they arise. They are not, of course, absolute, inflexible, or unrevisable, and they do not always take precedence over what seems preferable in specific situations. They are usually sufficiently vague that significant choice is still left in individual situations, and whatever preferences we have for our lives considered on the whole will themselves likely change (and in a reason-supported way) when we reconsider them in the light of new developments or experience.

Rawls captures the idea of an informed, all-things-considered preference for one life rather than another with the notion of a *rational life plan* (p. 408). A life plan is some more or less determinate notion of what one prefers, on the whole, to do in one's life. Rawls counts a life plan *rational* if it meets two general conditions. First, since a plan will include not simply a preferential ordering of the ends one wants to achieve in life but also some notion of how those ends are to be achieved, it is necessary that the plan relate means to ends in a rational way. This involves satisfying a set of principles of means-end (or relative) rationality; such as, a plan is to be preferred if, other things equal, it achieves more ends, or is more likely to achieve ends, and so forth. But this is not sufficient, because the ends promoted may not themselves be rational. The second necessary condition of a rational life plan, therefore, is that the plan be one that one would choose "with full awareness of the relevant facts and after a careful consideration of the consequences" (ibid.). It follows from our initial account that a rational life plan gives a person presumptive reason to act on it. The actual reasons, more properly, are the considerations that would lead him, on reflection, to prefer the plan over others. Moreover, when an agent prefers a course of action considered in connection with such a plan, his preference has greater rational weight than any preference he might have with respect to the action considered independently of the plan, assuming this to be the only difference. This is simply because the former preference is more informed.

As Rawls points out, it may well not be rational for a person actually to reflect and deliberate to the point of discovering the plan that is most rational for him. Thinking about our lives, reconsidering our plans in the light of new experience and information, and seeking out more and more information and experience on which to base our plans, are all activities that themselves take time, energy, and attention. How much of our lives we have reason to devote to these activities cannot solely depend on whether the plan that results accords with our informed, all-things-considered preferences. It must depend on how much of our lives we would prefer to give over to such activities when we adequately consider both the results and what is involved in the activities themselves (together with what is forgone). There may, on the whole, be reasons for us to do things differently in our lives even if there is not, on the whole, reason for us to discover what those reasons are. Often we have reasons to leave well enough alone.

Rawls identifies the plan of life that is most rational for a person (in the sense of our initial account) with what he variously calls *the person's good* or *a rational conception of the person's good*. Now, our ordinary meaning of 'a person's own good' is perhaps related to what benefits the person *himself* in a way that makes the phrase to some degree inappropriate to express the notion that Rawls has in mind. Probably better would be *a rational conception of the good life for that person*.

We may now briefly rehearse the implications drawn thus far from the initial account of rational consideration. Our first conclusion was that facts that motivate an agent to prefer an act when he is reflectively aware of them are reasons for him to act. From that point we have moved, through various way stations, to the conclusion that facts that lead a person to prefer a plan for his life as a whole are reasons, weightier reasons, indeed, than those that support intrinsic preferences for acts taken one at a time.

To this juncture no challenge has yet arisen to a fundamentally self-centered view of practical reason. While the considerations that our initial account certifies as reasons need not be restricted to self-*regarding* ones, nonetheless, its standpoint of rational consideration is still the agent's own. According to it, we cannot judge whether a fact is a reason for someone to act unless we are somehow able to assume *his* point of view and see whether *he* would be motivated by reflective awareness of it.

In what follows I shall argue that an internalist theory of reasons that proceeds only this far would be seriously deficient. It would fail adequately to appreciate the normative character of reasons. A normatively adequate internalism, I shall argue, would require that there lie behind any genuine reason to act a sort of motivation that is available from a standpoint that is not any individual's as such, but one that is impartial between rational agents. This is not the same thing as holding that a reason for one person to act is always simultaneously a reason for anyone to want him to do so— that there are no agent-relative reasons. Rather, it is to hold that, if a consideration is a reason for one person to act, then it must be of a sort that anyone could be motivated, from an impartial standpoint, to prefer him to act on. Considerations that agents would themselves be motivated by on reflection from their own individual standpoints, it will turn out, are one such sort, but not the only one.

III

To this point we have focused primarily on the motivational aspect of reasons for acting: their capacity to motivate when they are rationally considered. Equally central to our notion of a reason is what I have called its *normative* aspect. Reasons for a person to do something are not simply facts about an action that motivate him to act. Rather, they are considerations that rationally *ought* to have force for a person and that do for a person who considers them as he rationally ought. Without the normative aspect of reasons there would be nothing to distinguish reasons *for* someone *to* do something from reasons *why* he did or will do it, reasons that justify or recommend action from those that explain it.

In order to illuminate the normative aspect of practical reasons we shall need the general notion of a *normative system,* or system of norms. Any normative system is comprised of a number of elements including, most obviously, *norms* themselves. Norms are the standards or principles that those to whom they apply, the *subjects* of the normative system, use to appraise and guide their conduct. This element is crucial. Norms are *guides* that subjects can themselves apply to regulate their own conduct.[3] The principle that 'ought' implies 'can' springs from this guiding aspect of norms. Subjects can be guided by their awareness of a norm to do only what it is possible for them to do.

If we think of rationality in the most general way, therefore, it involves a normative system. Regardless of what the specific norms are for appraising and guiding action as rational, they have a *minimal normative content:* they are principles or standards that are normative for all agents with rational capacity. This content is purely normative, since the capacity to be rational must itself be understood in terms of a capacity to guide behavior in accordance with the relevant norms. In claiming that some particular principle has the status of a principle of rationality, we claim that it is a principle that is normative for all rational agents: one they ought rationally to follow.

Two theses, first, that reasons have a normative aspect, and second, that the normative appraisal of acts as rational presupposes norms applying to all rational agents, together entail that if some fact is a reason for someone to act, then his or her acting on it is recommended as a consequence of a principle on which all agents ought rationally to act. The normative aspect of reasons consists in their being guides to what we ought rationally to do. And our judgment that some act ought rationally to be taken presupposes a general norm of rationality.

Now this may seem to conflict with our initial account of reasons. How can something's being a reason for a person require that her acting on that consideration be recommended by a universal principle of practical reason if something can be (even presumptively) a reason by virtue of whether *she* would be motivated by it, on reflection, from her own point of view? The answer is simply that while a fact's being a reason need not be grounded in universal *reason-specifying* principles, it still must be anchored in a universal principle: namely, that for any agent, if she would be motivated to prefer an act by rational consideration of a fact about it, then that fact is a reason for her to act. Moreover, when we assert that a particular process of consideration is a *rational* one, we are committed to the minimal normative content of all normative rationality claims. We affirm that the procedure determines for any person which acts are supported by reasons; consequently, we are committed to the judgment that any person ought (rationally) to act as she would be motivated to were she to consider matters in that way. To be normatively adequate, therefore, even our initial account is committed to holding that reasons are grounded in a principle on which all agents ought rationally to act.

Because rational appraisals are based on norms applying to all rational agents, they are fundamentally *impersonal*. When we appraise an act as rational, even if it is our own, we are committed to a fundament judgment from an impersonal standpoint—from the intersubjective standpoint available to subjects of the system of rational norms. Thus, when one judges that something is a reason for someone to act, even if that person is oneself, one makes a judgment that is impersonal and purports to be intersubjectively valid.

IV

Now, as I have said, IR aims to be an internalist theory of reasons, but one that respects their normative character. Like all internalist theories, it holds that to be a reason is to be capable of motivating when appropriately considered. And, like other internalist theories, it holds that garden variety reflective consideration is one sort of rational reflection, at least when it is more or less dispassionate, informed by knowledge and relevant experience, and so on. But, at the same time, IR insists that what makes facts that motivate on such reflection *reasons* is that they motivate on *rational* reflection, where the latter refers to a normative ideal. It agrees with other internalisms that being a reason is not a feature a fact can have independently of its capacity to motivate a rational agent, but at the same time accepts the thesis implicit in the distinction between motivating and justifyinng reasons that something's being a reason for someone to do something is not the same thing as its actually motivating him to do it. Unlike externalist accounts of this distinction, however, IR holds that the normative character of reasons is inherited from a normative ideal of something internal to the rational agent: an ideal of rational reflection. A reason to act is a fact *rational* consideration of which would motivate a preference for an act, other things equal.

Again, it is consistent with the internalist picture I have been presenting that a reason for Jones to act need not be a reason for Smith. A reason is that which motivates on rational reflection, and it may be that a consideration that motivates Jones on rational reflection would not motivate Smith. Nonetheless, IR holds that what would give the consideration a justificatory weight for Jones that it might not have for Smith is its relation to a normative ideal of rational reflection for rational agents as such.

But what is it for reflective consideration to be *rational*? If facts inherit their status as reasons, their justificatory weight, from their capacity to motivate on rational reflection, how does a sort of reflective consideration itself acquire normative status as rational? What does its normativity rest on?

Impartial reason holds that the same rationale that leads internalists to connect the reasonhood of a specific fact to its capacity to motivate is available at this level also. Just as the internalist holds that being a reason could not be completely independent of capacity to motivate, so should he also maintain that being a normative ideal of rational reflection could not be thoroughly independent of motivation to reflect in this way either. But because the normative ideal is universal, a pattern of reflection that all rational agents ought to engage in as such, IR holds that the movtivation to engage in it must be available from the standpoint of one rational agent among others, and that it must be motivation to prefer that all agents, and thus oneself *qua* rational agent, reflect in this way.

IR's central thesis does not follow directly from supposing that a normative ideal of reflection must itself be capable of engaging the will. It might be held, for instance, that the initial account itself enshrines a pattern of reflection that rational agents are motivated to engage in as such, but from their own distinct points of view and not impartially. But if this is so, why does IR suppose that a normative ideal of reflective practical guidance must depend on motivation from an impartial standpoint? Internalism as a general thesis, even applied at this second level, apparently does not require it.

The answer to this question has to do with the source and particular variety of IR's internalism. What lies behind IR is a Kantian "internalism of autonomy": an internalism that derives from thinking that rational conduct is autonomous conduct, and that whatever principles constrain rational agents as such must be fit to be critically endorsed by them in a way that enables guidance by such principles to be self-government. What IR takes to be fundamental is not any particular view about the ends rational activity should accomplish, nor even about what sort of conduct is rational, but a picture of the fully rational agent as one who is autonomous because he is guided by his own critical endorsement of principles as normative for rational agents.[4] In order for guidance by such an endorsement to realize self-governance critical endorsement must itself involve motivation; otherwise, guidance by critically endorsed principles will

depend on further motivation, external to the rational self. That is why IR's internalism is an "internalism of autonomy". Again, because the requisite normative ideal of reflective guidance is universal, connected to a principle that is normative for all rational agents as such, IR holds that candidates become normative in this way by virtue of being practically endorsable from a standpoint that is impartial between rational agents. Therefore, for IR, the question of what substantive rational norms there are, and thus what reasons there are for agents to act, depends ultimately on what principles can be practically endorsed from this standpoint.

We considered above the possibility of an agent who is motivated to guide conduct by the initial account, but motivated from his own point of view. As so far described, such guidance is not genuine autonomy. It will become autonomous only if reflective guidance by the initial account is itself critically endorsed by the agent in a way that explains his continued conformity to it. But what he must endorse here is a universal principle, any rational agent's guiding his conduct in this way. And unlike the endorsement *within* the initial account, an endorsement that is internal to his standpoint, this critical endorsement can only come from an intersubjective standpoint that is common to all rational agents. He must have impartial motivation to prefer that any person reflectively guide conduct in this way.

The constructive picture that IR offers is, then, the following. Beginning with the assumption that it is presumptively rational for agents to act as they would be motivated on dispassionate, informed reflection from their own individual standpoints, it then asks what can be willed from a standpoint that is impartial between them. IR is a theory of impartial reason, not of wholly impersonal reason. And so the standpoint it proposes as appropriate for assessing candidate normative ideals of reflective guidance is one that is impartial between individuals who have a presumptively rational interest in pursuing what they would informedly and dispassionately prefer from their own individual standpoints.

It then asks what principles it would be *instrumentally* rational to choose, from such an impartial standpoint, to inform the practical reflection and deliberation of all agents.[5] And it approaches this question via the Rawlsian device of a rational choice by an individual with the presumed rational interests, but behind a veil of ignorance regarding his specific characteristics. For situations in which no cooperation or conflict between agents is possible, it would apparently be rational to choose that individuals be guided by their own motivated preferences on informed and dispassionate reflection. For situations of possible cooperation or conflict, however, this is not necessarily so. For example, for Prisoner's Dilemma situations, it would obviously not be rational to want individuals to be guided simply by what would be good, on reflection, from their own individual points of view. If everyone's practical thinking conformed to our initial account in such situations their informed intrinsic preferences would be less well achieved than if they were to deliberate in a different way. For such situations, it would be rational to choose that individuals be guided by principles that appropriately constrain the pursuit of individual interest, so long as enough others are.

There is a tradition that seeks to understand moral obligation as resting on rules or principles the general following of which in Prisoner's Dilemma-like situations is in the interest of everyone, or that it would be rational to choose, from an impartial standpoint, that persons be guided by in such situations.[6] If this is so, and if impartial reason is correct in holding that the fact that it would be rational to choose, from an impartial standpoint, that agents' practical thinking be guided by principles of this sort in these situations, rather than by what they would informedly prefer from their own individual points of view, then it will follow that agents have good reason to do what they are morally obligated to do. Indeed, because it is rational to choose that agents constrain

their pursuit of their own informed preferences by such principles, it will follow according to impartial reason that the reasons provided by moral obligations outweigh the presumptive reasons anchored in the initial account. It does not, of course, follow that agents always have overriding reasons to do whatever they or anyone else might think they have a moral obligation to do. IR will only hold that moral obligations provide reasons that outweigh those that can motivate agents from their own individual standpoints if moral obligations themselves are embodied in principles that it would be rational to choose, from an impartial standpoint, to inform the practical thinking of agents in the situations contemplated.

It is frequently assumed that what is alternatively called the *authority* or *categoricality* of moral obligation, the idea that moral obligations provide reasons of overriding weight for anyone to whom they apply, can plausibly be defended only on an externalist theory of reasons. According to this line of thought, it is only if the existence of reasons to act, and their weight, is independent of what agents can be motivated to do, even in principle, that there is any hope of its being true that moral obligations are genuine categorical imperatives. If impartial reason is right, this assumption is mistaken. If one supposes that what reasons there are, as well as their rational weight, depends ultimately on what principles it would be instrumentally rational to prefer, from an impartial standpoint, to guide the conduct of all agents, then one is supposing that the existence of reasons for a person is linked to motivation, albeit from an impartial standpoint. What IR shows is that it is possible to be an internalist about reasons and still believe that there is always adequate reason not to do what is wrong.[7]

NOTES

1. Richard Brandt maintains that the normative aspect of rationality can be eliminated by analysis. Following his late colleague Charles

Stevenson, he proposes to use the method of "reforming definitions" to replace vague, unclear, and apparently mysterious language with definitions that lack these vices. Significantly, Brandt's own definition of 'rational' "does not import any substantive value judgments." But can we adequately characterize rationality in nonevaluative terms? What permits Brandt, for example, to speak of rational *criticism* when describing the way in which beliefs and desires are modified in the face of information and experience. Can there be criticism where there is not evaluative judgment? Must not the rational critic be capable of judging that beliefs or intentions are better or worse supported by reasons? See *A Theory of the Good and the Right* (Oxford: Oxford University Press, 1979), pp. 10–23, for this view.

Moreover, the reforming definition of 'rational' has the effect of not allowing certain issues even to arise. For example, we cannot sensibly ask whether it is rational for a person to do what is right if we know he does not want to do so on a full Brandtian reflection. For a criticism of Brandt's views along these lines see Nicholas Sturgeon, "Brandt's Moral Empiricism," *The Philosophical Review* 83 (1982), 389–422.

2. Henry Sidgwick, *The Methods of Ethics*, 7th ed. (London: Macmillan, 1967), pp.111–112; John Rawls, *A Theory of Justice* (Cambridge: Harvard University Press, 1971), pp.399–424; G. H. von Wright, *The Varieties of Goodness* (London: Routledge & Kegan Paul, 1963), pp. 86–113.

3. This is not necessarily so on externalist theories of conduct, whether of rational or of moral conduct, which hold that what agents ought to *do* is utterly independent of what considerations agents should be guided by in practical thinking.

4. This aspect of IR is discussed in "Rational Agent, Rational Act," *Philosophical Topics* 14 (1986), 33–57; and "How Nowhere Can You Get (And Do Ethics)?," *Ethics* 98 (1987), 152–157; and in *Impartial Reason*, pp.211–239.

5. There is no circularity here since the notion of instrumental rationality can be specified independently of any substantive principles of practical reason, and hence, any proposition about reasons to act.

6. Recent philosophers who have taken this position in one place or another would include Kurt Baier, *The Moral Point of View* (Ithaca: Cornell University Press, 1957); David Gauthier, *Morals By Agreement* (Oxford: Oxford University Press, 1986); John Rawls, *A Theory of Justice* (Cambridge: Harvard University Press, 1971), p. 111 [although Rawls usually advances this as a picture of justice, he suggests here that it may be held as a general theory of right, one he calls "rightness as fairness"]. T. M. Scanlon's proposal that "an act is wrong if its performance under the circumstances would be disallowed by any system of rules for the general regulation of behavior which no one could reasonably reject as a basis for informed, unforced general agreement" may also be considered to be in this same general tradition. See "Contractualism and Utilitarianism," in A. Sen and B. Williams, *Utilitarianism and Beyond* (Cambridge: Cambridge University Press, 1982), pp. 103–128.

7. If, of course, wrongdoing is understood in the suggested way.

14
MORALITY AS A SYSTEM OF HYPOTHETICAL IMPERATIVES
Philippa Foot

There are many difficulties and obscurities in Kant's moral philosophy, and few contemporary moralists will try to defend it all; many, for instance, agree in rejecting Kant's derivation of duties from the mere form of law expressed in terms of a universally legislative will. Nevertheless, it is generally supposed, even by those who would not dream of calling themselves his followers, that Kant established one thing beyond doubt—namely, the necessity of distinguishing moral judgments from hypothetical imperatives. That moral judgments cannot be hypothetical imperatives has come to seem an unquestionable truth. It will be argued here that it is not.

In discussing so thoroughly Kantian a notion as that of the hypothetical imperative, one naturally begins by asking what Kant himself meant by a hypothetical imperative, and it may be useful to say a little about the idea of an imperative as this

From *Philosophical Review* Vol. 8, No. 3 (1972): 305–316. Reprinted by permission of *Philosophical Review* and the author.

appears in Kant's works. In writing about imperatives Kant seems to be thinking at least as much of statements about what ought to be or should be done, as of injunctions expressed in the imperative mood. He even describes as an imperative the assertion that it would be "good to do or refrain from doing something"[1] and explains that for a will that "does not always do something simply because it is presented to it as a good thing to do" this has the force of a command of reason. We may therefore think of Kant's imperatives as statements to the effect that something ought to be done or that it would be good to do it.

The distinction between hypothetical imperatives and categorical imperatives, which plays so important a part in Kant's ethics, appears in characteristic form in the following passages from the *Foundations of the Metaphysics of Morals:*

All imperatives command either hypothetically or categorically. The former present the practical necessity of a possible action as a means to achieving something else which one desires (or which one may possibly desire). The categorical imperative would be one which presented an action as of itself objectively necessary, without regard to any other end.[2]

If the action is good only as a means to something else, the imperative is hypothetical; but if it is thought of as good in itself, and hence as necessary in a will which of itself conforms to reason as the principle of this will, the imperative is categorical.[3]

The hypothetical imperative, as Kant defines it, "says only that the action is good to some purpose" and the purpose, he explains, may be possible or actual. Among imperatives related to actual purposes Kant mentions rules of prudence, since he believes that all men necessarily desire their own happiness. Without committing ourselves to this view it will be useful to follow Kant in classing together as "hypothetical imperatives" those telling a man what he ought to do because (or if) he wants something and those telling him what he ought to do on grounds of self-interest. Common opinion agrees with Kant in insisting that a moral man must accept a rule of duty whatever his interests or desires.[4]

Having given a rough description of the class of Kantian hypothetical imperatives it may be useful to point to the heterogeneity within it. Sometimes what a man should do depends on his passing inclination, as when he wants his coffee hot and should warm the jug. Sometimes it depends on some long-term project, when the feelings and inclinations of the moment are irrelevant. If one wants to be a respectable philosopher one should get up in the mornings and do some work, though just at that moment when one should do it the thought of being a respectable philosopher leaves one cold. It is true nevertheless to say of one, at that moment, that one wants to be a respectable philosopher,[5] and this can be the foundation of a desire-dependent hypothetical imperative. The term "desire" as used in the original account of the hypothetical imperative was meant as a grammatically convenient substitute for "want," and was not meant to carry

any implication of inclination rather than long-term aim or project. Even the word "project," taken strictly, introduces undesirable restrictions. If someone is devoted to his family or his country or to any cause, there are certain things he wants, which may then be the basis of hypothetical imperatives, without either inclinations or projects being quite what is in question. Hypothetical imperatives should already be appearing as extremely diverse; a further important distinction is between those that concern an individual and those that concern a group. The desires on which a hypothetical imperative is dependent may be those of one man, or may be taken for granted as belonging to a number of people, engaged in some common project or sharing common aims.

Is Kant right to say that moral judgments are categorical, not hypothetical, imperatives? It may seem that he is, for we find in our language two different uses of words such as "should" and "ought," apparently corresponding to Kant's hypothetical and categorical imperatives, and we find moral judgments on the "categorical" side. Suppose, for instance, we have advised a traveler that he should take a certain train, believing him to be journeying to his home. If we find that he has decided to go elsewhere, we will most likely have to take back what we said: the "should" will now be unsupported and in need of support. Similarly, we must be prepared to withdraw our statement about what he should do if we find that the right relation does not hold between the action and the end—that it is either no way of getting what he wants (or doing what he wants to do) or not the most eligible among possible means. The use of "should" and "ought" in moral contexts is, however, quite different. When we say that a man should do something and intend a moral judgment we do not have to back up what we say by considerations about his interests or his desires; if no such connection can be found the "should" need not be withdrawn. It follows that the agent cannot rebut an assertion about what, morally speaking, he should do by showing that the action is not ancillary to his interests or desires. Without such a connection the "should" does not stand unsupported and in need of support; the support that *it* requires is of another kind.[6]

There is, then, one clear difference between moral judgments and the class of "hypothetical imperatives" so far discussed. In the latter "should" is used "hypothetically," in the sense defined, and if Kant were merely drawing attention to this piece of linguistic usage his point would be easily proved. But obviously Kant meant more than this; in describing moral judgments as non-hypothetical—that is, categorical imperatives—he is ascribing to them a special dignity and necessity which this usage cannot give. Modern philosophers follow Kant in talking, for example, about the "unconditional requirement" expressed in moral judgments. These tell us what we have to do whatever our interests or desires, and by their inescapability they are distinguished from hypothetical imperatives.

The problem is to find proof for this further feature of moral judgments. If anyone fails to see the gap that has to be filled it will be useful to point out to him that we find "should" used non-hypothetically in some non-moral statements to which no one attributes the special dignity and necessity conveyed by the description "categorical imperative." For instance, we find this non-hypothetical use of "should" in sentences enunciating rules of etiquette, as, for example, that an invitation in the third person should be answered in the third person, where the rule does not *fail to apply* to someone who has his own good reasons for ignoring this piece of nonsense, or who simply does not care about what, from the point of view of etiquette, he should do. Similarly, there is a non-hypothetical use of "should" in contexts where something like a club rule is in question. The club secretary who has told a member that he should not bring ladies into the smoking room does not say, "Sorry, I was mistaken" when informed that this member is resigning tomorrow and cares nothing about his reputation in the club. Lacking a connection with the agent's desires or interests, this "should" does not stand "unsupported and in need of support"; it requires only the backing of the rule. The use of "should" is therefore "non-hypothetical" in the sense defined.

It follows that if a hypothetical use of "should" gives a hypothetical imperative, and a non-hypothetical use of "should" a categorical imperative, then "should" statements based on rules of etiquette, or rules of a club, are categorical imperatives. Since this would not be accepted by defenders of the categorical imperative in ethics, who would insist that these other "should" statements give hypothetical imperatives, they must be using this expression in some other sense. We must therefore ask what they mean when they say that "You should answer . . . in the third person" is a hypothetical imperative. Very roughly the idea seems to be that one may reasonably ask why anyone should bother about what should$_e$ (should from the point of view of etiquette) be done, and that such considerations deserve no notice unless reason is shown. So although people give as their reason for doing something the fact that it is required by etiquette, we do not take this consideration as *in itself giving us reason to act*. Considerations of etiquette do not have any automatic reason-giving force, and a man might be right if he denied that he had reason to do "what's done."

This seems to take us to the heart of the matter, for, by contrast, it is supposed that moral considerations necessarily give reasons for acting to any man. The difficulty is, of course, to defend this proposition which is more often repeated than explained. Unless it is said, implausibly, that all "should" or "ought" statements give reasons for acting, which leaves the old problem of assigning a special categorical status to moral judgment, we must be told what it is that makes the moral "should" relevantly different from the "shoulds" appearing in normative statements of other kinds.[7] Attempts have sometimes been made to show that some kind of irrationality is involved in ignoring the "should" of morality: in saying

"Immoral—so what?" as one says "Not comme il faut—so what?" But as far as I can see these have all rested on some illegitimate assumption, as, for instance, of thinking that the amoral man, who agrees that some piece of conduct is immoral but takes no notice of that, is inconsistently disregarding a rule of conduct that he has accepted; or again of thinking it inconsistent to desire that others will not do to one what one proposes to do to them. The fact is that the man who rejects morality because he sees no reason to obey its rules can be convicted of villainy but not of inconsistency. Nor will his actions necessarily be irrational. Irrational actions are those in which a man in some way defeats his own purposes, doing what is calculated to be disadvantageous or to frustrate his ends. Immorality does not *necessarily* involve any such thing.

It is obvious that the normative character of moral judgment does not guarantee its reason-giving force. Moral judgments are normative, but so are judgments of manners, statements of club rules, and many others. Why should the first provide reasons for acting as the others do not? In every case it is because there is a background of teaching that the non-hypothetical "should" can be used. The behavior is required, not simply recommended, but the question remains as to why we should do what we are required to do. It is true that moral rules are often enforced much more strictly than the rules of etiquette, and our reluctance to press the non-hypothetical "should" of etiquette may be one reason why we think of the rules of etiquette as hypothetical imperatives. But are we then to say that there is nothing behind the idea that moral judgments are categorical imperatives but the relative stringency of our moral teaching? I believe that this may have more to do with the matter than the defenders of the categorical imperative would like to admit. For if we look at the kind of thing that is said in its defense we may find ourselves puzzled about what the words can even mean unless we connect them with the feelings that this stringent teaching implants. People talk, for instance, about the "binding force" of morality, but it is not clear what this means if not that we *feel* ourselves unable to escape. Indeed the "inescapability" of moral requirements is often cited when they are being contrasted with hypothetical imperatives. No one, it is said, escapes the requirements of ethics by having or not having particular interests or desires. Taken in one way this only reiterates the contrast between the "should" of morality and the hypothetical "should," and once more places morality alongside of etiquette. Both are inescapable in that behavior does not cease to offend against either morality or etiquette because the agent is indifferent to their purposes and to the disapproval he will incur by flouting them. But morality is supposed to be inescapable in some special way and this may turn out to be merely the reflection of the way morality is taught. Of course, we must try other ways of expressing the fugitive thought. It may be said, for instance, that moral judgments have a kind of necessity since they tell us what we "must do" or "have to do" whatever our interests and desires. The sense of this is, again, obscure. Sometimes when we use such expressions we are referring to physical or mental compulsion. (A man has to go along if he is pulled by strong men, and he has to give in if tortured beyond endurance.) But it is only in the absence of such conditions that moral judgments apply. Another and more common sense of the words is found in sentences such as "I caught a bad cold and had to stay in bed" where a penalty for acting otherwise is in the offing. The necessity of acting morally is not, however, supposed to depend on such penalties. Another range of examples, not necessarily having to do with penalties, is found where there is an unquestioned acceptance of some project or role, as when a nurse tells us that she has to make her rounds at a certain time, or we say that we have to run for a certain train.[8] But these too are irrelevant in the present context, since the acceptance condition can always be revoked.

No doubt it will be suggested that it is in

some other sense of the words "have to" or "must" that one has to or must do what morality demands. But why should one insist that there must be such a sense when it proves so difficult to say what it is? Suppose that what we take for a puzzling thought were really no thought at all but only the reflection of our *feelings* about morality? Perhaps it makes no sense to say that we "have to" submit to the moral law, or that morality is "inescapable" in some special way. For just as one may feel as if one is falling without believing that one is moving downward, so one may feel as if one has to do what is morally required without believing oneself to be under physical or psychological compulsion, or about to incur a penalty if one does not comply. No one thinks that if the word "falling" is used in a statement reporting one's sensations it must be used in a special sense. But this kind of mistake may be involved in looking for the special sense in which one "has to" do what morality demands. There is no difficulty about the idea that we feel we *have to* behave morally, and given the psychological conditions of the learning of moral behavior it is natural that we should have such feelings. What we cannot do is quote them in support of the doctrine of the categorical imperative. It seems, then, that in so far as it is backed up by statements to the effect that the moral *is* inescapable, or that we *do* have to do what is morally required of us, it is uncertain whether the doctrine of the categorical imperative even makes sense.

The conclusion we should draw is that moral judgments have no better claim to be categorical imperatives than do statements about matters of etiquette. People may indeed follow either morality or etiquette without asking why they should do so, but equally well they may not. They may ask for reasons and may reasonably refuse to follow either if reasons are not to be found.

It will be said that this way of viewing moral considerations must be totally destructive of morality, because no one could ever act morally unless he accepted such considerations as in themselves sufficient reason for action. Actions that are truly moral must be done "for their own sake," "because they are right," and not for some ulterior purpose. This argument we must examine with care, for the doctrine of the categorical imperative has owed much to its persuasion.

Is there anything to be said for the thesis that a truly moral man acts "out of respect for the moral law" or that he does what is morally right because it is morally right? That such propositions are not prima facie absurd depends on the fact that moral judgment concerns itself with a man's reasons for acting as well as with what he does. Law and etiquette require only that certain things are done or left undone, but no one is counted as charitable if he gives alms "for the praise of men," and one who is honest only because it pays him to be honest does not have the virtue of honesty. This kind of consideration was crucial in shaping Kant's moral philosophy. He many times contrasts acting out of respect for the moral law with acting from an ulterior motive, and what is more from one that is self-interested. In the early *Lectures on Ethics* he gave the principle of truth-telling under a system of hypothetical imperatives as that of not lying *if it harms one* to lie. In the *Metaphysics of Morals* he says that ethics cannot start from the ends which a man may propose to himself, since these are all "selfish."[9] In the *Critique of Practical Reason* he argues explicitly that when acting not out of respect for the moral law but "on a material maxim" men do what they do for the sake of pleasure or happiness.

All material practical principles are, as such, of one and the same kind and belong under the general principle of self love or one's own happiness.[10]

Kant, in fact, was a psychological hedonist in respect of all actions except those done for the sake of the moral law, and this faulty theory of human nature was one of the things preventing him from seeing that moral virtue might be compatible with the rejection of the categorical imperative.

If we put this theory of human action

aside, and allow as ends the things that seem to be ends, the picture changes. It will surely be allowed that quite apart from thoughts of duty a man may care about the suffering of others, having a sense of identification with them, and wanting to help if he can. Of course, he must want not the reputation of charity, nor even a gratifying role helping others, but, quite simply, their good. If this is what he does care about, then he will be attached to the end proper to the virtue of charity and a comparison with someone acting from an ulterior motive (even a respectable ulterior motive) is out of place. Nor will the conformity of his action to the rule of charity be merely contingent. Honest action may happen to further a man's career; charitable actions do not *happen* to further the good of others.

Can a man accepting only hypothetical imperatives possess other virtues besides that of charity? Could he be just or honest? This problem is more complex because there is no one end related to such virtues as the good of others is related to charity. But what reason could there be for refusing to call a man a just man if he acted justly because he loved truth and liberty, and wanted every man to be treated with a certain minimum respect? And why should the truly honest man not follow honesty for the sake of the good that honest dealing brings to men? Of course, the usual difficulties can be raised about the rare case in which no good is foreseen from an individual act of honesty. But it is not evident that a man's desires could not give him reason to act honestly even here. He wants to live openly and in good faith with his neighbors; it is not all the same to him to lie and conceal.

If one wants to know whether there could be a truly moral man who accepted moral principles as hypothetical rules of conduct, as many people accept rules of etiquette as hypothetical rules of conduct, one must consider the right kind of example. A man who demanded that morality should be brought under the heading of self-interest would not be a good candidate, nor would

anyone who was ready to be charitable or honest only so long as he felt inclined. A cause such as justice makes strenuous demands, but this is not peculiar to morality, and men are prepared to toil to achieve many ends not endorsed by morality. That they are prepared to fight so hard for moral ends—for example, for liberty and justice—depends on the fact that these are the kinds of ends that arouse devotion. To sacrifice a great deal for the sake of etiquette one would need to be under the spell of the emphatic "$ought_e$." One could hardly be devoted to behaving *comme il faut*.

In spite of all that has been urged in favor of the hypothetical imperative in ethics, I am sure that many people will be unconvinced and will argue that one element essential to moral virtue is still missing. This missing feature is the recognition of a *duty* to adopt those ends which we have attributed to the moral man. We have said that he *does* care about others, and about causes such as liberty and justice; that it is on this account that he will accept a system of morality. But what if he never cared about such things, or what if he ceased to care? Is is not the case that he *ought* to care? This is exactly what Kant would say, for though at times he sounds as if he thought that morality is not concerned with ends, at others he insists that the adoption of ends such as the happiness of others is itself dictated by morality.[11] How is this proposition to be regarded by one who rejects all talk about the binding force of the moral law? He will agree that a moral man has moral ends and cannot be indifferent to matters such as suffering and injustice. Further, he will recognize in the statement that one *ought* to care about these things a correct application of the non-hypothetical moral "ought" by which society is apt to voice its demands. He will not, however, take the fact that he $ought_m$ to have certain ends as in itself reason to adopt them. If he himself is a moral man then he cares about such things, but not "because he ought." If he is an amoral man he may deny that he has any reason to trouble his head over this or any other moral demand. Of course he may be mistaken, and his life as well as others' lives may be most sadly spoiled by his selfishness. But this is not what is urged by those who think they can close the matter by an emphatic use of "ought." My argument is that they are relying on an illusion, as if trying to give the moral "ought" a magic force.[12]

This conclusion may, as I said, appear dangerous and subversive of morality. We are apt to panic at the thought that we ourselves, or other people, might stop caring about the things we do care about, and we feel that the categorical imperative gives us some control over the situation. But it is interesting that the people of Leningrad were not similarly struck by the thought that only the *contingent* fact that other citizens shared their loyalty and devotion to the city stood between them and the Germans during the terrible years of the siege. Perhaps we should be less troubled than we are by fear of defection from the moral cause; perhaps we should even have less reason to fear it if people thought of themselves as volunteers banded together to fight for liberty and justice and against inhumanity and oppression. It is often felt, even if obscurely, that there is an element of deception in the official line about morality. And while some have been persuaded by talk about the authority of the moral law, others have turned away with a sense of distrust.[13]

NOTES

1. *Foundations of the Metaphysics of Morals,* Sec. II, trans. by L. W. Beck.
2. *Ibid.*
3. *Ibid.*
4. According to the position sketched here we have three forms of the hypothetical imperative: "If you want x you should do y," "Because you want x you should do y," and "Because x is in your interest you should do y." For Kant the third would automatically be covered by the second.
5. To say that at that moment one wants to be a respectable philosopher would be another matter. Such a statement requires a special connection between the desire and the moment.
6. I am here going back on something I said in an earlier article ("Moral Beliefs," *Proceedings of the Aristotelian Society, 1958–1959*) where I thought it necessary to show that virtue must benefit the agent. I believe the rest of the article can stand.
7. To say that moral considerations are *called* reasons is blatantly to ignore the problem.
8. I am grateful to Rogers Albritton for drawing my attention to this interesting use of expressions such as "have to" or "must."
9. Pt. II, Introduction, sec. II.
10. Immanuel Kant, *Critique of Practical Reason,* trans. by L. W. Beck, p. 133.
11. See, e.g., *The Metaphysics of Morals,* pt. II, sec. 30.
12. See G. E. M. Anscombe, "Modern Moral Philosophy," *Philosophy* (1958). My view is different from Miss Anscombe's, but I have learned from her.
13. So many people have made useful comments on drafts of this article that I despair of thanking them all. Derek Parfit's help has been sustained and invaluable, and special thanks are also due to Barry Stroud.

An earlier version of this paper was read at the Center for Philosophical Exchange, Brockport, N.Y., and published in *Philosophical Exchange* (Summer 1971).

15

MAXIMIZATION CONSTRAINED: THE RATIONALITY OF COOPERATION

David Gauthier

... Think of the state of nature as a condition in which each person seeks straightforwardly to maximize her individual utility. In interaction with her fellows, then, each chooses what she believes to be a utility-maximizing response to the choices she expects the other to make. Is it always possible for each person to be successful—that is, for each to act in a way that is utility-maximizing given the actions of the others? No—not if we take "action" in its ordinary sense. If you and I must choose between going to Toronto and going to Pittsburgh, and I want to go where you go, and you want to go where I do not go, then one of us will act in a way that is not utility-maximizing, given what the other does. But if we replace "action" by "strategy," where a

strategy is a probability distribution over possible actions, then it is always possible for each person to be successful—for each person's strategy to be utility-maximizing given the others' strategies. (There are some qualifications here; there must be only finitely many persons each with only finitely many actions. But they are not important.)

Suppose then that everyone is successful. We say that the outcome is in equilibrium—no one could do better for herself, given what the others do. No one could benefit from a unilateral change of strategy. But all may not be well. For although each is doing her best for herself, given what the others do, it may be possible for all to do better. The outcome may not be optimal (in the Pareto sense); some alternative might afford some persons greater utility and no person lesser utility.

In every (finite) situation, there is at least one outcome in equilibrium and at least one optimal outcome, but in some situations, no outcome is both in equilibrium and optimal. The Prisoner's Dilemma is the most familiar example of a situation with a unique equilibrium (mutual confession) which is not optimal (since mutual non-confession is better for both prisoners). If each person maximizes her utility given the strategies of others, then at least some person receives less utility than she might given each other person's utility. And if each person receives as much utility as she can, given each other person's utility, then at least some person does not maximize her utility given the strategies of others.

In the state of nature, each seeks to maximize her own utility. And so in some situations the outcome is not optimal. This provides a basis for society, considered (in Rawlsian terms) as "a cooperative venture for mutual advantage." Think of a cooperative venture as implementing a joint choice, without requiring each person's strategy to be utility-maximizing given the others. And think of mutual advantage as affording each person greater utility than she would expect otherwise—greater, then, than she would expect were each to maximize her utility given the others' choices.

The Foole then says, "Agree to a cooperative venture, but only if you expect agreement to pay." This is sound advice. But the Foole goes on to say, "And adhere to a cooperative venture, but only if you expect adherence to pay." This is not sound advice. In effect, the Foole advises you to adhere only if it proves utility-maximizing. But then no one does better than if each were to maximize her utility given the others' choices. The venture does not improve on the state of nature.

On the Foole's view, reason stands in the way of cooperation. What follows seeks to refute the Foole—to exhibit the rational basis, not merely for entering, but for adhering to, cooperative ventures.

In my discussion I refer to the preceding chapter five of the book, in which I argue that rational cooperation satisfies the principle of minimax relative concession. When straightforwardly maximizing behavior yields a sub-optimal outcome, there may be many different possible joint choices or cooperative ventures, each of which would afford mutual advantage. Not every such venture will be rationally acceptable to all concerned. Think of persons bargaining over possible cooperative ventures. Each considers her share of the benefits from cooperation, as compared with others' shares. Each begins by claiming as large a share as possible—the greatest utility for herself compatible with no one doing worse than in the absence of cooperation. To reach agreement on a particular venture from these claims, each must concede a part of her claim, but no one can be rationally expected to concede more, proportionately, than she recognizes some person must concede to reach agreement. Thus rational bargainers agree on that cooperative venture for which the maximum proportionate or relative concession made by any person is a minimum.

I refer also to condition A' for strategic rationality. The underlying condition A is that each person's choice must be a rational response to the choices he expects the others to make. The usual interpretation of this treats a rational response as a utility-maximizing response. But this leaves everyone in the state of nature. Condition A' states that each person's choice must be a fair optimizing response (where fairness is captured by the requirements of minimax concession) to the choices he expects the others to make, provided such a response is available to him; otherwise, his choice must be a utility-maximizing response. I defend condition A'.

2.1

The Foole, and those who share his conception of practical reason, must suppose that there are potentialities for cooperation to which each person would rationally agree, were he to expect the agreement to be carried out, but that remain unactualized, since each rationally expects that someone, perhaps himself, perhaps another, would not adhere to the agreement. In chapter five we argued that cooperation is rational if each cooperator may expect a utility nearly equal to what he would be assigned by the principle of minimax relative concession. The Foole does not dispute the necessity of this condition but denies its sufficiency. He insists that for it to be rational to comply with an agreement to cooperate, the utility an individual may expect from cooperation must also be no less than what he would expect were he to violate his agreement. And he then argues that for it to be rational to agree to cooperate, then, although one need not consider it rational to comply oneself, one must believe it rational for the others to comply. Given that everyone is rational, fully informed, and correct in his expectations, the Foole supposes that cooperation is actualized only if each person expects a utility from cooperation no less than his non-compliance utility. The benefits that could be realized through cooperative arrangements that do not afford each person at least his non-compliance utility remain forever beyond the reach of rational human beings—forever denied us because our very rationality would lead us to violate the agreements necessary to realize these benefits. Such agreements will not be made.

The Foole rejects what would seem to be the ordinary view that given neither unforeseen circumstances nor misrepresentation of terms, it is rational to comply with an agreement if it is rational to make it. He insists that holders of this view have failed to think out the full implications of the maximizing conception of practical rationality. In choosing, one takes one's stand in the present and looks to the expected utility that will result from each possible action. What has happened may affect this utility; that one has agreed may affect the utility one expects from doing, or not doing, what would keep the agreement. But what has happened provides in itself no reason for choice. That one had reason for making agreement can give one reason for keeping it only by affecting the utility of compliance. To think otherwise is to reject utility-maximization.

Let us begin our answer to the Foole with the distinction between an individual strategy and a joint strategy. An individual strategy is a lottery over the possible actions of a single actor. A joint strategy is a lottery over possible outcomes. Cooperators have joint strategies available to them.

We may think of participation in a cooperative activity, such as a hunt, in which each huntsman has his particular role coordinated with that of the others, as the implementation of a single joint strategy. We may also extend the notion to include participation in a practice, such as the making and keeping of promises, where each person's behavior is predicated on the conformity of others to the practice.

An individual is not able to ensure that he acts on a joint strategy since whether he does depends, not only on what he intends, but on what those with whom he interacts intend. But we may say that an individual bases his action on a joint strategy insofar as he intentionally chooses what the strategy requires of him. Normally, of course, one bases one's action on a joint strategy only if one expects those with whom one interacts to do so as well, so that one expects actually to act on that strategy. But we need not import such an expectation into the conception of basing one's action on a joint strategy.

A person cooperates with his fellows only if he bases his actions on a joint strategy; to agree to cooperate is to agree to employ a joint rather than an individual strategy. The Foole insists that it is rational to cooperate only if the utility one expects from acting on the cooperative joint strategy is at least equal to the utility one would expect were one to act instead on one's best individual strategy. This defeats the end of cooperation, which is in effect to substitute a joint strategy for individual strategies in situations in which this substitution is to everyone's benefit.

A joint strategy is fully rational only if it yields an optimal outcome or, in other words, only if it affords each person who acts on it the maximum utility compatible in the situation with the utility afforded each other person who acts on the strategy. Thus we may say that a person acting on a rational joint strategy maximizes his utility, subject to the constraint set by the utilities it affords to every other person. An individual strategy is rational if, and only if, it maximizes one's utility given the *strategies* adopted by the other persons; a joint strategy is rational only if (but not if, and only if) it maximizes one's utility given the *utilities* afforded to the other persons.

Let us say that a *straightforward* maximizer is a person who seeks to maximize his utility given the strategies of those with whom he interacts. A *constrained* maximizer, on the other hand, is a person who seeks in some situations to maximize her utility, given not the strategies but the utilities of those with whom she interacts. The Foole accepts the rationality of straightforward maximization. We, in defending condition A' for strategic rationality, accept the rationality of constrained maximization.

A constrained maximizer has a conditional disposition to base her actions on a joint strategy, without considering whether some individual strategy would yield her greater expected utility. But not all constraint could be rational; we must specify the characteristics of the conditional disposition. We shall therefore identify a constrained maximizer as someone (i) who is conditionally disposed to base her actions on a joint strategy or practice should the utility she expects were everyone so to base his action (a) be no less than what she would expect were everyone to employ individual strategies, and (b) approach what she would expect from the cooperative outcome determined by minimax relative concession, and (ii) who actually acts on this conditional disposition should her expected utility be greater than what she would expect were everyone to employ individual strategies. Or, in other words, a constrained maximizer is ready to cooperate in ways that, if followed by all, would yield outcomes that she would find beneficial and not unfair, and she does cooperate should she expect an actual practice or activity to be beneficial. In determining the latter, she must take into account the possibility that some persons will fail, or refuse, to act cooperatively. Henceforth, un-less we specifically state otherwise, we shall understand by a constrained maximizer one with this particular disposition.

There are three points in our character-ization of constrained maximization that should be noted. The first is that a con-strained maximizer is conditionally disposed to act not only on the unique joint strategy that would be prescribed by a rational bar-gain, but on any joint strategy that affords her a utility approaching what she would expect from fully rational cooperation. The range of acceptable joint strategies is, and must be left, unspecified. The idea is that in real interaction it is reasonable to accept cooperative arrangements that fall short of the ideal of full rationality and fairness provided they do not fall too far short. At some point, of course, one decides to ignore a joint strategy, even if acting on it would afford one an expected utility greater than one would expect were everyone to employ an individual strategy, because one hopes thereby to obtain agreement on, or acquies-cence in, another joint strategy which in being fairer is also more favorable to one-self. At precisely what point one decides this we make no attempt to say. We simply defend a conception of constrained maximi-zation that does not require that all accept-able joint strategies be ideal.

The second point is that a constrained maximizer does not base her actions on a joint strategy whenever a nearly fair and optimal outcome would result were every-one to do likewise. Her disposition to co-operate is conditional on her expectation that she will benefit in comparison with the utility she could expect were no one to cooperate. Thus she must estimate the likelihood that others involved in the pro-spective practice or interaction will act co-operatively and calculate not the utility she would expect were all to cooperate, but the utility she would expect if she cooperates, given her estimate of the degree to which others will cooperate. Only if this exceeds what she would expect from universal non-cooperation does her conditional disposi-tion to constraint actually manifest itself in a decision to base her actions on the co-operative joint strategy.

Thus, faced with persons whom she believes to be straightforward maximizers, a constrained maximizer does not play into their hands by basing her actions on the joint strategy she would like everyone to accept, but rather, to avoid being exploited, she behaves as a straightforward maximizer, acting on that individual strategy that maximizes her utility given the strategies she expects the others to employ. A constrained maximizer makes reasonably certain that she is among like-disposed persons before she actually constrains her direct pursuit of maximum utility.

But note that a constrained maximizer may find herself required to act in such a way that she would have been better off had she not entered into cooperation. She may be engaged in a cooperative activity that, given the willingness of her fellows to do their part, she expects to be fair and beneficial, but that, should chance so befall, requires her to act so that she incurs some loss greater than had she never engaged herself in the endeavor. Here she would still be disposed to comply, acting in a way that results in real disadvantage to herself, because given her *ex ante* beliefs about the dispositions of her fellows and the prospects of benefit, participation in the activity affords her greater expected utility than non-participation.

And this brings us to the third point, that constrained maximization is not straightforward maximization in its most effective disguise. The constrained maximizer is not merely the person who, taking a larger view than her fellows, serves her overall interest by sacrificing the immediate benefits of ignoring joint strategies and violating cooperative arrangements in order to obtain the long-term benefits of being trusted by others. Such a person exhibits no real constraint. The constrained maximizer does not reason more effectively about how to maximize her utility, but reasons in a different way. We may see this most clearly by considering how each faces the decision whether to base her action on a joint strategy. The constrained maximizer considers (i) whether the outcome, should everyone do so, be nearly fair and optimal, and (ii) whether the outcome she realistically expects should she do so affords her greater utility than universal non-cooperation. If both of these conditions are satisfied, she bases her action on the joint strategy. The straightforward maximizer considers simply whether the outcome he realistically expects, should he base his action on the joint strategy, affords him greater utility than the outcome he would expect were he to act on any alternative strategy—taking into account, of course, long-term as well as short-term effects. Only if this condition is satisfied, does he base his action on the joint strategy.

Consider a purely isolated interaction in which both parties know that how each chooses will have no bearing on how each fares in other interactions. Suppose that the situation has the familiar Prisoner's Dilemma structure; each benefits from mutual cooperation but each benefits from non-cooperation whatever the other does. In such a situation, a straightforward maximizer chooses not to cooperate. A constrained maximizer chooses to cooperate if given her estimate of whether or not her partner will choose to cooperate, her own expected utility is greater than the utility she would expect from the non-cooperative outcome.

Constrained maximizers can thus obtain cooperative benefits that are unavailable to straightforward maximizers, however far-sighted the latter may be. But straightforward maximizers can, on occasion, exploit unwary constrained maximizers. Each supposes her disposition to be rational. But who is right?

2.2

To demonstrate the rationality of suitably constrained maximization we solve a problem of rational choice. We consider what a rational individual would choose, given the alternatives of adopting straightforward maximization and of adopting constrained maximization, as his disposition for strategic behavior. Although this choice is about interaction, to make it is not to engage in interaction. Taking others' dispositions as fixed, the individual reasons parametrically to his own best disposition. Thus he compares the expected utility of disposing himself to maximize utility given others' expected strategy choices with the utility of disposing himself to cooperate with others in bringing about nearly fair and optimal outcomes.

To choose between these dispositions, a person needs to consider only those situations in which they would yield different behavior. If both would be expressed in a maximizing individual strategy or if both would lend one to base action on the joint strategy one expects from others, then their utility expectations are identical. But if the disposition to constraint would be expressed in basing action on a joint strategy whereas the disposition to maximize straightforwardly would be expressed in defecting from the joint strategy, then their utility expectations differ. Only situations giving rise to such differences need be considered. These situations must satisfy two conditions. First, they must afford the prospect of mutually beneficial and fair cooperation, since otherwise constraint would be pointless. And second, they must afford some prospect for individually beneficial defection, since otherwise no constraint would be needed to realize the mutual benefits.

We suppose, then, an individual, considering what disposition to adopt, for situations in which his expected utility is u should each person act on an individual strategy, u' should all act on a cooperative joint strategy, and u'' should he act on an individual strategy and the others base their actions on a cooperative joint strategy, and u is less than u' (so that he benefits from cooperation as required by the first condition) and u' in turn is less than u'' (so that he benefits from defection as required by the second condition).

Consider these two arguments which this person might put to himself:

Argument (1): Suppose I adopt straightforward maximization. Then if I expect the others to base their actions on a joint strategy, I defect to my best individual strategy and expect a utility, u''. If I expect the others to act on individual strategies, then so do I, and expect a utility, u. If the probability that others will base their actions on a joint strategy is p, then my overall expected utility is $(pu'' + (1 - p)u)$.

Suppose I adopt constrained maximization. Then if I expect the others to base their actions on a joint strategy, so do I, and expect a utility u'. If I expect the others to act on individual strategies, then so do I, and expect a utility, u. Thus my overall expected utility is $(pu' + (1 - p)u)$.

Since u'' is greater than u', $(pu'' + (1 - p)u)$ is greater than $(pu' + (1 - p)u)$, for any value of p other than 0 (and for $p = 0$, the two are equal). Therefore, to maximize my overall expectation of utility, I should adopt straightforward maximization.

Argument (2): Suppose I adopt straightforward maximization. Then I must expect the others to employ maximizing individual strategies in interacting with me; so do I, and expect a utility, u.

Suppose I adopt constrained maximization. Then if the others are conditionally disposed to constrained maximization, I may expect them to base their actions on a cooperative joint strategy in interacting with me; so do I, and expect a utility u'. If they are not so disposed, I employ a maximizing strategy and expect u as before. If the probability that others are disposed to constrained maximization is p, then my overall expected utility is $(pu' + (1 - p)u)$.

Since u' is greater than u, $(pu' + (1 - p)u)$ is greater than u for any value of p other than 0 (and for $p = 0$, the two are equal). Therefore, to maximize my overall expectation of utility, I should adopt constrained maximization.

Since these arguments yield opposed conclusions, they cannot both be sound. The first has the form of a dominance argument. In any situation in which others act noncooperatively, one may expect the same utility whether one is disposed to straightforward or to constrained maximization. In any situation in which others act cooperatively, one may expect a greater utility if one is disposed to straightforward maximization. Therefore, one should adopt straightforward maximization. But this argument would be valid only if the probability of others acting cooperatively were, as the argument assumes, independent of one's own disposition. And this is not the case. Since persons disposed to cooperation only act cooperatively with those whom they suppose to be similarly disposed, a straightforward maximizer does not have the opportunities to benefit which present themselves to the constrained maximizer. Thus argument (1) fails.

Argument (2) takes into account what argument (1) ignores—the difference between the way in which constrained maximizers interact with those similarly disposed and the way in which they interact with straightforward maximizers. Only those disposed to keep their agreements are rationally acceptable as parties to agreements. Constrained maximizers are able to make beneficial agreements with their fellows that the straightforward cannot, not because the latter would be unwilling to agree, but because they would not be admitted as parties to agreement given their disposition to violation. Straightforward maximizers are disposed to take advantage of their fellows should the opportunity arise; knowing this, their fellows would prevent such opportunity arising. With the same opportunities, straightforward maximizers would necessarily obtain greater benefits. A dominance argument establishes this. But because they differ in their dispositions, straightforward and constrained maximizers differ also in their opportunities, to the benefit of the latter.

But argument (2) unfortunately contains an undefended assumption. A person's expectations about how others will interact with him depend strictly on his own choice of disposition only if that choice is known by the others. What we have shown is that if the straightforward maximizer and the constrained maximizer appear in their true colors, then the constrained maximizer must do better. But need each so appear? The Foole may agree, under the pressure of our argument and its parallel in the second argument as we ascribed to Hobbes, that the question to be asked is not whether it is or is not rational to keep (particular) covenants, but whether it is or is not rational to be (generally) disposed to the keeping of covenants, and he may recognize that he cannot win by pleading the cause of straightforward maximization in a direct way. But may he not win by linking straightforward maximization to the appearance of constraint? Is not the Foole's ultimate argument that the truly prudent person, the fully rational utility-maximizer, must seek to appear trustworthy, an upholder of his agreements? For then he will not be excluded from the cooperative arrangements of his fellows, but will be welcomed as a partner, while he awaits opportunities to benefit at their expense—and, preferably, without their knowledge, so that he may retain the guise of constraint and trustworthiness.

There is a short way to defeat this maneuver. Since our argument is to be applied to ideally rational persons, we may simply add another idealizing assumption and take our persons to be *transparent*. Each is directly aware of the dispositions of his fellows and so aware whether he is interacting with straightforward or constrained maximizers. Deception is impossible; the Foole must appear as he is.

But to assume transparency may seem to rob our argument of much of its interest. We want to relate our idealizing assumptions to the real world. If constrained maximization defeats straightforward maximization only if all persons are transparent, then we shall have failed to show that under actual, or realistically possible, conditions, moral constraints are rational. We shall have refuted the Foole but at the price of robbing our refutation of all practical import.

However, transparency proves to be a stronger assumption than our argument requires. We may appeal instead to a more realistic *translucency,* supposing that persons are neither transparent nor opaque, so that their disposition to cooperate or not may be ascertained by others, not with certainty, but as more than mere guesswork. Opaque beings would be condemned to seek political solutions for those problems of natural interaction that could not be met by the market. But we shall show that for beings as translucent as we may reasonably consider ourselves to be, moral solutions are rationally available.

2.3

If persons are translucent, then constrained maximizers (CMs) will sometimes fail to recognize each other and will then interact non-cooperatively even if cooperation would have been mutually beneficial. CMs will sometimes fail to identify straightforward maximizers (SMs) and will then act cooperatively; if the SMs correctly identify the CMs, they will be able to take advantage of them. Translucent CMs must expect to do less well in interaction than would transparent CMs; translucent SMs must expect to do better than would transparent SMs. Although it would be rational to choose to be a CM were one transparent, it need not be rational if one is only translucent. Let us examine the conditions under which the decision to dispose oneself to constrained maximization is rational for translucent persons and ask if these are (or may be) the conditions in which we find ourselves.

As in the preceding subsection, we need consider only situations in which CMs and SMs may fare differently. These are situations that afford both the prospect of mutually beneficial cooperation (in relation to non-cooperation) and individually beneficial defection (in relation to cooperation). Let us simplify by supposing that the non-cooperative outcome results unless (1) those interacting are CMs who achieve mutual recognition, in which case the cooperative outcome results, or (2) those interacting

include CMs who fail to recognize SMs but are themselves recognized, in which case the outcome affords the SMs the benefits of individual defection and the CMs the costs of having advantage taken of mistakenly basing their actions on a cooperative strategy. We ignore the inadvertent taking of advantage when CMs mistake their fellows for SMs.

There are then four possible payoffs: non-cooperation, cooperation, defection, and exploitation (as we may call the outcome for the person whose supposed partner defects from the joint strategy on which he bases his action). For the typical situation, we assign defection the value one, cooperation u'' (less than one), non-cooperation u' (less than u''), and exploitation zero (less than u'). We now introduce three probabilities. The first, p, is the probability that CMs will achieve mutual recognition and so successfully cooperate. The second, q, is the probability that CMs will fail to recognize SMs but will themselves be recognized, so that defection and exploitation will result. The third, r, is the probability that a randomly selected member of the population is a CM. (We assume that everyone is a CM or a SM, so the probability that a randomly selected person is a SM is $(1 - r)$.) The values of p, q, and r must, of course, fall between zero and one.

Let us now calculate expected utilities for CMs and SMs in situations affording both the prospect of mutually beneficial cooperation and individually beneficial defection. A CM expects the utility u' unless (1) she succeeds in cooperating with other CMs or (2) she is exploited by a SM. The probability of (1) is the combined probability that she interacts with a CM, r, and that they achieve mutual recognition, p, or rp. In this case, she gains $(u'' - u')$ over her non-cooperative expectation u'. Thus the effect of (1) is to increase her utility expectation by a value $(rp(u'' - u'))$. The probability of (2) is the combined probability that she interacts with a SM, $1 - r$, and that she fails to recognize him but is recognized, q, or $(1 - r)q$. In this case she received zero, so she loses her non-cooperative expectation u'. Thus the effect of (2) is to reduce her utility expectation by a value $((1 - r)qu')$. Taking both (1) and (2) into account, a CM expects the utility $(u' + (rp(u'' - u'))) - (1 - r)qu')$.

A SM expects the utility u' unless he exploits a CM. The probability of this is the combined probability that he interacts with a CM, r, and that he recognizes her but is not recognized by her, q, or rq. In this case he gains $(1 - u')$ over his non-cooperative expectation u'. Thus the effect is to increase his utility expectation by a value $(rq(1 - u'))$. A SM thus expects the utility $(u' + (rq(1 - u')))$.

It is rational to dispose oneself to constrained maximization if, and only if, the utility expected by a CM is greater than the utility expected by a SM, which obtains if, and only if, p/q is greater than $((1 - u')/(u'' - u') + ((1 - r)u')/(r(u'' - u')))$.

The first term of this expression, $((1 - u')/(u'' - u'))$, relates the gain from defection to the gain through cooperation. The value of defection is of course greater than that of cooperation, so this term is greater than one. The second term, $(((1 - r)u')/(r(u'' - u')))$, depends for its value on r. If $r = 0$ (that is, if there are no CMs in the population), then its value is infinite. As r increases, the value of the expression decreases, until if $r = 1$ (that is, if there are only CMs in the population) its value is zero.

We may now draw two important conclusions. First, it is rational to dispose oneself to constrained maximization only if the ratio of p to q, that is, the ratio between the probability that an interaction involving CMs will result in cooperation and the probability that an interaction involving CMs and SMs will involve exploitation and defection, is greater than the ratio between the gain from defection and the gain through cooperation. If everyone in the population is a CM, then we may replace 'only if' by 'if, and only, if' in this statement, but in general it is only a necessary condition of the rationality of the disposition to constrained maximization.

Second, as the proportion of CMs in the population increases (so that the value of r increases), the value of the ratio of p to q that

is required for it to be rational to dispose oneself to constrained maximization decreases. The more constrained maximizers there are, the greater the risks a constrained maximizer may rationally accept of failing to achieve mutual recognition for cooperation with other CMs and failing to recognize SMs and so being exploited by them. However, these risks, and particularly the latter, must remain relatively small.

We may illustrate these conclusions by introducing typical numerical values for cooperation and non-cooperation and then considering different values for r. One may suppose that, on the whole, there is no reason that the typical gain from defection over cooperation would be either greater or smaller than the typical gain from cooperation over non-cooperation and, in turn, no reason that the latter gain would be greater or smaller than the typical loss from non-cooperation to exploitation. And so, since defection has the value one and exploitation zero, let us assign cooperation the value two-thirds and non-cooperation one-third.

The gain from defection, $(1 - u')$, thus is two-thirds; the gain through cooperation, $(u'' - u')$, is one-third. Since p/q must exceed $((1 - u')/(u'' - u') + ((1 - r)u')/(r(u'' - u')))$ for constrained maximization to be rational, in our typical case the probability p that CMs successfully cooperate must be more than twice the probability q that CMs are exploited by SMs, however great the probability r that a randomly selected person is a CM. In general, p/q must be greater than $(2 + (1 - r)/r)$ or, equivalently, greater than $(r + 1)/r$. If three persons out of four are CMs, so that $r = 3/4$, then p/q must be greater than 7/3; if one person out of two is a CM, then p/q must be greater than three; if one person in four is a CM, then p/q must be greater than five.

Suppose a population evenly divided between constrained and straightforward maximizers. If the constrained maximizers are able to cooperate successfully in two-thirds of their encounters and to avoid being exploited by straightforward maximizers in four-fifths of their encounters, then constrained maximizers may expect to do better than their fellows. Of course, the even distribution will not be stable; it will be rational for the straightforward maximizers to change their disposition. These persons are sufficiently translucent for them to find morality rational.

2.4

A constrained maximizer is conditionally disposed to cooperate in ways that, followed by all, would yield nearly optimal and fair outcomes and does cooperate in such ways when she may actually expect to benefit. In the two preceding sub-sections, we have argued that one is rationally so disposed if persons are transparent or persons are sufficiently translucent and enough are like-minded. But our argument has not appealed explicitly to the particular requirement that cooperative practices and activities be nearly optimal and fair. We have insisted that the cooperative outcome afford one a utility greater than non-cooperation, but this is much weaker than the insistence that it approach the outcome required by minimax relative concession.

But note that the larger the gain from cooperation, $(u'' - u')$, the smaller the minimum value of p/q that makes the disposition to constrained maximization rational. We may take p/q to be a measure of translucency; the more translucent constrained maximizers are, the better they are at achieving cooperation among themselves (increasing p) and avoiding exploitation by straightforward maximizers (decreasing q). Thus, as practices and activities fall short of optimality, the expected value of cooperation, u'', decreases, and so the degree of translucency required to make cooperation rational increases. And as practices and activities fall short of fairness, the expected value of cooperation for those with less than fair shares decreases, and so the degree of translucency required to make cooperation rational for them increases.

Thus our argument does appeal implicitly to the requirement that cooperation yield nearly fair and optimal outcomes.

But there is a further argument in support of our insistence that the conditional disposition to cooperate be restricted to practices and activities yielding nearly optimal and fair outcomes. And this argument turns, as does our general argument for constraint, on how one's dispositions affect the characteristics of the situations in which one may reasonably expect to find oneself. Let us call a person who is disposed to cooperate in ways that, followed by all, yield nearly optimal and fair outcomes, *narrowly compliant*. And let us call a person who is disposed to cooperate in ways that, followed by all, merely yield her some benefit in relation to universal non-cooperation, *broadly compliant*. We need not deny that a broadly compliant person would expect to benefit in some situations in which a narrowly compliant person would not. But in many other situations a broadly compliant person must expect to lose by her disposition. For insofar as she is known to be broadly compliant, others will have every reason to maximize their utilities at her expense, by offering "cooperation" on terms that offer her but little more than she could expect from non-cooperation. Since a broadly compliant person is disposed to seize whatever benefit a joint strategy may afford her, she finds herself with opportunities for but little benefit.

Since the narrowly compliant person is always prepared to accept cooperative arrangements based on the principle of minimax relative concession, she is prepared to cooperate whenever cooperation can be mutually beneficial on terms equally rational and fair to all. In refusing other terms, she does not diminish her prospects for cooperation with other rational persons, and she ensures that those not disposed to fair cooperation do not enjoy the benefits of any cooperation, thus making their unfairness costly to themselves, and so irrational. . . .

16

JUSTIFYING MORALITY: THE RIGHT AND THE WRONG WAYS

James P. Sterba

Contemporary philosophers offer three kinds of justification for morality. Some, following Plato, claim that morality is justified by self-interest.[1] Others, following Hume as he is frequently interpreted, claim that morality is justified in terms of other-regarding interests, wants or intentions that people happen to have.[2] And still others, following Kant, claim that morality is justified in terms of the requirements of practical reason.[3] . . . I argue that only a justification of this third sort can be fully adequate and then only when it is developed in a certain way.[4]

I begin by showing what is wrong or defective in the other justifications. Then I consider attempts by Kurt Baier and Alan Gewirth to elaborate the third sort of justification. Drawing upon their work, I present a justification based on the requirements of practical reason that succeeds in demonstrating that the rational egoist acts contrary to reason.

1. MORALITY AND SELF-INTEREST

Those who claim that morality is justified by self-interest tend to define morality as a system of rules and virtues that take into account the interests of everyone alike.[5] Whatever differences there are among proposed definitions, they are not relevant here, since proponents of this justification rarely try to argue for it by defining morality in a question-begging way.[6]

Yet obviously it is difficult to understand how a morality that takes into account the interests of everyone alike could be in the best interest of each and every person. For surely it would seem that morality so defined would require self-sacrifice from some, if not most, members of society. In particular, the rich and the powerful would seem to be required to sacrifice their interests, at least to some degree, for the sake of

From *Synthese* 72 (1987) 45–69. Copyright © 1987 by Reidel Publishing Company. Reprinted by permission of Kluwer Academic Publishers.

the poor and weak. However, philosophers justifying morality on the grounds of self-interest deny that such sacrifice is required. They contend that conflicts between morality and self-interest are only apparent and that closer examination reveals a complete harmony of interests.

One way philosophers defend this view is by distinguishing between people's "true" interests and their "false" interests (or people's "true" selves and their "false" selves) and then maintaining that the former but not the latter require people to be moral.[7] Unfortunately, this defense tends to either collapse the distinction between our first and second justifications or collapse the distinction between our first and third justifications. People's true interests are either taken to correspond to the other-regarding interests people happen to have, and then this defense would simply be maintaining, like our second justification, that morality is grounded in people's other-regarding interests, wants or intentions; or people's true interests are taken to be the interests they would have if they were acting in accord with practical reason. But, then, this defense would simply be maintaining, as does our third justification, that morality is grounded in the dictates of practical reason.

A more promising defense of the first justification is that apparent conflicts between morality and self-interest have their source in our failure to understand what is in our long-term self-interest. Some philosophers, for example, Robert Olson, claim that many violations of morality have their origin in impulsive action for which the remedy is deliberate and rational pursuit of long-term self-interest.[8] For others, like Michael Scriven, however, apparent conflicts between morality and self-interest come from institutional obstacles that make it difficult for people to realize what is in their best self-interest.[9] Marxists, in particular, hold that capitalism prevents both capitalists and proletarians from fully developing themselves.[10] They say that only with the advent of the final stage of communist society will complete and harmonious self-development be secured for all.[11] For still others, conflicts between morality and self-interest begin in people's failure to take into account an after-life in which virtue is rewarded and vice punished.[12]

Needless to say, to ground the justification for morality on the assumption of a justice-producing after-life is to give morality a foundation that is widely contested. In the end we may decide to rely on this assumption, as Henry Sidgwick did, but if we hope to rally as many as possible to the banner of morality we should consider endorsing such an assumption only if no less disputed alternative can be found.

By contrast, the other ways of arguing that morality is in our long-term self-interest clearly have a more general appeal. For many would frequently find it in their long-term self-interest to act morally if they only deliberated more or if their institutions were only better designed. At the same time, it seems that the world will always have its master criminals, and that occasions will arise for all of us in which it is in our self-interest to act immorally. Moreover, how could we suppose that moving from existing to ideal institutions could be done without self-sacrifice on the part of anyone?[13]

Yet even conceding that the dictates of morality and self-interest do not always coincide in the sense that "acting according to duty" (i.e., doing one's moral duty but not necessarily from the motive of doing one's duty) is not always in one's best interest, one still might argue that "acting from duty" (i.e., acting from the motive of doing one's moral duty but not necessarily doing one's duty) is still justified as the best way of achieving what is in one's overall self-interest.

Hoping to establish this conclusion, Peter Singer appeals to a widely recognized paradox: those who aim at their own happiness often fail to attain it, while others obtain happiness in the pursuit of other goals.[14] Singer argues that, given this paradox, to secure our own happiness, we must abandon self-interest for a broader goal, the obvious candidate being the goal of morality, i.e., acting from duty.

But Singer's conclusion goes beyond his premises. For although the paradox does suggest that steady attention to one's own happiness can be self-defeating, it does not follow that attending to quite different goals is the best way of securing one's happiness. All that follows is that we need to focus on activities that experience has shown us are closely connected with securing our own happiness, only checking from time to time whether these activities actually do make us happy. So, Singer has not shown that rejecting an overall goal of furthering one's self-interest and adopting the goal of acting from duty is required for our own happiness.

Thus, contemporary justifications for morality in terms of self-interest are inadequate in one or more of the following ways: (1) by confusing a justification in terms of self-interest with our other two types of justification for morality; (2) by failing to establish a sufficient correspondence between acting according to duty and what is in one's self-interest, without appealing to the widely disputed assumption of a justice-producing after-life; (3) by failing to establish that acting from duty is the best way to secure one's own happiness.[15]

2. MORALITY AND OTHER-REGARDING INTERESTS

Our second justification for morality, the view that morality is justified in terms of people's other-regarding interests, wants or intentions, has many prominent contemporary advocates. For example, it is common to Philippa Foot's account of morality as a system of hypothetical imperatives and Gilbert Harman's moral relativism.

Foot thinks moral judgments are hypothetical in that their reason-giving force depends upon the interests, wants or intentions people happen to have.[16] Thus, unless people have these other-regarding interests, wants or intentions, Foot claims, they will not have any reasons for acting morally.[17] It is this proclaimed relativity of the reason-giving force of moral judgments to the interests, wants and, particularly, the intentions people happen to have that Harman interprets to be a form of moral relativism.[18] Moral judgments so grounded Harman calls "inner judgments". They are said to imply reasons for acting and to apply to agents who are capable of being motivated by the relevant moral considerations. Nevertheless, Harman would probably agree with Foot that "an agent may fail to be moved by a reason (for acting) even when he is aware of it and he may be moved by something which is not a reason at all".[19]

Foot and Harman certainly do agree that there are other sorts of moral judgments that do not imply that an agent has the relevant moral reasons for acting.[20] I shall call these "outer judgments", and I shall use Harman's term "inner judgments" to refer to moral judgments, that, according to Foot and Harman, do imply reasons for acting. Outer judgments allow us to say that Hitler was an evil person or that cannibals ought not to eat their captives, or more generally, that someone is wicked or immoral, even when such agents lack the relevant reasons for acting morally.

Needless to say, there are differences between Foot's and Harman's views. For example, Foot would probably not characterize her view as a form of moral relativism, and Harman would probably reject Foot's account of moral virtues. But here I am only concerned with their shared account of moral judgments.

The basic difficulty with Foot and Harman's shared account of moral judgments is that their distinction between inner and outer judgments is irrelevant from the point of view of imputing moral responsibility. In imputing moral responsibility, it is not necessary to show that people have the relevant moral reasons for acting otherwise since we hold people morally responsible even when they lack such reasons, provided that they are morally responsible for the lack. For example, if political leaders had the capabilities and opportunities to become aware of their society's racist and sexist practices, but, in fact, failed to do so, with the consequence that they presently lack any moral reasons to oppose such practices, we would still hold them morally responsible because their lack of moral reasons in this regard is something for which they are morally responsible. Similarly, if people allow themselves to become so engrossed in advancing their own personal and family projects that they come to ignore the most basic needs of others even when they have a surplus of resources, and as a result, they come to lack any moral reasons to help people who are truly in need, we could still hold them morally responsible in this regard. As these examples indicate, having moral reasons to act otherwise is not necessary for imputing moral responsibility. Rather what is necessary is that people are or were able to acquire the relevant moral reasons. And clearly satisfaction of this condition is compatible not only with inner but also with many outer judgments as well.[21]

Now what this shows is that the justification for morality which Foot and Harman favor fails for a significant range of cases in which we hold people morally responsible. For in such cases the justification for those moral requirements that we hold people responsible for violating derives not from their having the relevant moral reasons but rather from their having the capacity and opportunity to acquire such reasons. It follows that possession of the relevant moral reasons is *not necessary* for justifying at least some of the requirements of morality.

Nor for that matter is possession of the relevant moral reasons *sufficient* for justifying the requirements of morality. For people typically possess or have possessed not only the capabilities and opportunities necessary to acquire the other-regarding interests, wants or intentions relevant to moral reasons for acting, but also possess (or have possessed) the capabilities and opportunities necessary to acquire the self-regarding interests, wants or intentions relevant to self-interested reasons for acting. Accordingly,

we would need to ask, given the capabilities and opportunities to develop in either direction, which sort of interests, wants or intentions should a person develop?[22]

Typically, of course, we have both moral and self-interested reasons to get others to become other-regarding. But at best this can provide an explanation not a justification for why people develop in one way rather than the other.[23] What we need to ask, assuming that people can develop either way, is why should they develop (or continue to develop) their other-regarding interests, wants or intentions rather than their self-regarding interests, wants or intentions? Or put another way, how do we show that developing into a morally good person is better than developing into a rationally self-interested person?

We may, of course, be able to provide self-interested reasons for acting according to duty, but, as we have already noted, it is implausible to think that we could always do so or that we could justify acting from duty in terms of self-interest.[24] Why then should one person develop so as to act from or according to duty rather than to act from or according to self-interest?

Now the justification for morality endorsed by Foot and Harman cannot answer this question. For the possession of the relevant moral reasons for acting is neither necessary nor sufficient to justify abiding by the requirements of morality. Only the third sort of justification for morality could conceivably answer this question by showing that the requirements of morality are in fact the requirements of practical reason.

3. MORALITY AND PRACTICAL REASON

I begin by considering two cases for this third sort of justification for morality—those offered by Kurt Baier and Alan Gewirth. Then I turn to my own defense.

In *The Moral Point of View* Baier attempts to justify morality by showing that moral reasons are superior to self-interested reasons.[25] Baier begins by assuming that the very purpose of following reason is "to maximize satisfaction and minimize frustration". He then argues that the recognition of moral reasons as superior by everyone would produce greater satisfaction and lesser frustration than the recognition of self-interested reasons as superior by everyone. From this he concludes that moral reasons should be recognized as superior to self-interested reasons by everyone.

However, Baier's initial assumption concerning the purpose of following reason is ambiguous between a utilitarian and an egoistic interpretation. Under the utilitarian interpretation,

reason requires the maximization of satisfaction and the minimization of frustration for everyone taken collectively.

Under the egoistic interpretation,

reason requires the maximization of satisfaction and the minimization of frustration for everyone taken individually.

Yet only when the assumption is given the utilitarian interpretation does the conclusion follow. Unfortunately, this interpretation begs the question against the egoist.

More recently, Baier has reformulated his justification for morality in terms of a number of requirements of practical reason, the most important of which are the following:

Universality
Since a fact F is a reason for someone to do A in virtue of her satisfying certain conditions D, F must be a reason to do A for anyone who satisfies D.

Empirical Substantiation
The soundness of the belief that C is the criterion that is to determine whether or not F is a reason of a certain strength for X to do A is to be determined by the way acceptance of this criterion affects the satisfactoriness of the relevant lives.

Universalizability
If F is a reason to do A for anyone who satisfies D, then F must also be capable of being a reason to do A for everyone who satisfies D.

Baier contends that only when moral reasons are taken to be supreme can these three requirements of practical reason be met, since only then would each person have the best reason grounded in the satisfactoriness of the person's own life that every person (not any person) can possibly have.[26]

To evaluate Baier's defense of morality, let us consider whether the standard opponent of morality, the rational egoist, can accept or reject all three of Baier's requirements without acting contrary to reason.[27] For a fully adequate defense of morality in terms of practical reason must show that the rational egoist acts contrary to reason. Accordingly, for Baier's defense of morality to go through, it must be the case that the rational egoist cannot accept or reject Baier's requirements without acting contrary to reason.

Now, at first glance, it would seem that the rational egoist would have no difficulty accepting at least the first two of Baier's three requirements. Certainly, the egoist could accept his Universality criterion. The egoist could grant, for example, that if the fact that it would make her very rich (fact F) is a reason for her to steal given that conditions are such that she could easily get away with the theft (condition D), then F must be a reason to steal for anyone who satisfies D. Baier's Empirical Substantiation criterion also seems equally acceptable. How could the egoist deny that the soundness of rational egoism depends on the effect of taking egoistic reasons to be overriding in the lives of rational egoists? Hence, at least initially, only acceptance of Universalizability would seem to present a problem for the rational egoist.

Part of the problem is that Baier gives different interpretations to this proposed requirement. Sometimes he interprets the requirement to imply (a) that it must be possible for everyone always to be perfectly rational.[28] At other times, he interprets the requirement to imply, or at least suggest, the stronger claim (b) that it must be a good thing for everyone always to be perfectly rational.[29]

Now the rational egoist would have little difficulty accepting Universalizability under interpretation (a). The rational egoist would simply argue that once the directives of rational egoism are plausibly interpreted,[30] it is surely possible for everyone always to be perfectly rational by following the directives of rational egoism.

Yet accepting Universalizability under interpretation (a) does raise a problem for the rational egoist's initial acceptance of Empirical Substantiation. For the negative effects on the satisfactoriness of the egoist's life arising from everyone following the directives of rational egoism appear to violate it. However, there are at least two reasons for thinking that the rational egoist can meet this requirement while accepting Universalizability under interpretation (a).

First of all, the effects on the satisfactoriness of the egoist's life from everyone following the directives of rational egoism may not be as disasterous as they are sometimes made out to be. For surely if we are to concede anything to the defenders of our first justification for morality it is that a world where everyone pursues long-term self-interest under ideal institutional arrangements may not be such a bad world to live in, although it would be different, as we have argued, from a world where everyone always acted from or according to duty. Thus, Hobbes's war of all against all may be a poor model for a state of affairs where rational egoism reigns.

Second, the impact on the satisfactoriness of the egoist's life when everyone follows rational egoism must be evaluated together with the effects on the satisfactoriness of the egoist's life when almost everyone, save the egoist, follows morality. Obviously, for good self-interested reasons the egoist opposes the taking of self-interested reasons to be supreme by others. The egoist admits that such behavior is fully rational but opposes it nonetheless. The egoist does not want others reaping the benefits of following self-interested reasons at his or her expense, and publicly endorses the following of moral reasons as strongly as anyone. The egoist observes that most people take a similar stand, and recognizes that many with the "proper upbringing" in fact come to care strongly for others and, as a result, follow moral reasons almost instinctively. Taking all this into account, the egoist is justified in concluding that it is improbable that circumstances will arise in which everyone followed the directives of rational egoism. Since the egoist can be assured that others will continue to follow the directives of morality even when the egoist follows those of self-interest, the egoist can reasonably expect that the overall effect on the satisfactoriness of his or her life from taking self-interested reasons to be supreme would be positive, and considerably better than the overall effect from taking moral reasons to be supreme.

Of course, someone might object to the introduction of probability assessments of other people's behavior into the calculation of the overall satisfactoriness of the egoist's life.[31] But what is the ground for this objection? The egoist grants that it is possible for everyone to follow rational egoism. The egoist simply judges that this is unlikely, and that accordingly the expected overall effect on the egoist's life from following rational egoism would be quite positive, and considerably better than the expected overall effect from following the directives of morality. Unlike the prisoner in the well-known Prisoner's Dilemma, the rational egoist justifiably believes that others are more likely to do the mutually beneficial action (not confessing in the Prisoner's Dilemma). Hence, the egoist has good reason to think that the overall satisfactoriness of his or her life would be furthered by taking self-interested reasons to be supreme (confessing in the Prisoner's Dilemma).[32]

Given then that the egoist can accept Baier's Universality, Empirical Substantiation, and Universalizability under interpretation (a), Baier's defense of morality must ultimately rest on the claim that it is contrary to reason for the egoist to reject Universalizability under interpretation (b). That the egoist has to reject Universalizability under this interpretation seems correct. The rational egoist has to deny that it is a good thing for everyone to be perfectly rational and take the directives of rational egoism to be supreme. But why is that rejection contrary to reason? Why is it contrary to reason to recognize that people ought to do what is in their best interest and yet not to think it is a good thing for them all to do what they ought?

Here the "oughts" found in most ordinary competitive games provide a useful analogy. For instance, tennis players can judge that their opponents ought to put maximum spin on their serves without being committed to thinking that it is a good thing for them if their opponents serve in this way and they counter with their best returns. For, if that occurred, it might be likely that they would lose the game. After all, not infrequently one side is victorious in a game only because the other side failed to execute its best moves.[33]

Of course, there is an important dissimilarity between these two types of "oughts." Since competitive games are governed by moral constraints when everyone does exactly what he or she ought to do, there is an accepted moral limit to what a person can lose. By contrast, when everyone takes self-interested reasons to be supreme, the only limit to what a person can lose is the point beyond which others would not benefit.[34]

But this dissimilarity does not destroy the analogy. For it is still the case that when judged from the individual player's or the egoist's point of view, it need not be a good thing for everyone to be perfectly rational. It follows, therefore, that the rational egoist cannot be convicted of acting contrary to reason for rejecting Baier's Universalizability criterion under interpretation (b). So if this third sort of justification for morality is to be successful, it will have to proceed from premises different from those Baier provides.

Nevertheless, Baier's general strategy for constructing such a justification is surely correct. What we are looking for is an argument supporting the requirements of morality which does not depend upon prem-ises that beg the question against the rational egoist. Only then will we have succeeded in showing that the rational egoist acts contrary to reason.

Using the same general strategy as Baier, Alan Gewirth has proposed a quite different argument to justify morality.[35] Gewirth's argument can be summarized as follows:

1. Every agent has to accept (a) "I must have freedom and well-being."
2. By virtue of accepting (a) every agent also has to accept (b) "I have a right to freedom and well-being."
3. Further, every agent has to accept (c) "I have a right to freedom and well-being because I am a prospective, purposive agent."
4. By virtue of accepting (c) every agent also has to accept (d) "All prospective, purposive agents have a right to freedom and well-being."

Now many of Gewirth's critics have focused on the inference from (1) to (2), contending that rational agents need not endorse *moral* rights to freedom and well-being simply because they accept (a).[36] In response, Gewirth has claimed that, as he interprets the argument, rational agents in accepting (b) do not commit themselves to moral rights but only to prudential rights. According to Gewirth, moral rights only appear in the argument in step (4) through the application of the principle of universalizability.

Obviously to many the notion of prudential rights is a strange notion, and Gewirth has attempted to elucidate the concept by pointing out that the grounds for the prudential right claim in (b) are simply the prudential purposes of the agent not the prudential purposes or interests of other persons to whom the right claim is directed. I take this to mean that in endorsing (b) agents are not assuming that other people have any reasons in terms of their prudential or moral purposes that would lead them to respect the right claims they, the agents, are making. Notice that in this respect Gewirth's notion of prudential rights is strikingly different from the standard understanding of moral rights because the grounds for moral rights are usually thought to include not only reasons or purposes the agent has but also reasons or purposes others have or should have as well. For example, if I say that I have a moral right based on a contractual agreement to lecture at a particular university, I not only imply that I have moral or prudential reasons for exercising this right, but I also imply that others have moral or prudential reasons for permitting me to do so. I point this out simply to indicate the special way that Gewirth is using the notion of rights in step (2) of his argument. Once one understands how Gewirth is using the notion of rights, it seems to me there is no problem with his inference from (1) to (2).

As I see it, the problematic inference in Gewirth's argument is the inference from (3) to (4). This is because the notion of rights that an agent endorses in (4) Gewirth contends is moral not prudential as it is in (2) and also in (3). According to Gewirth, it is by the process of universalizing that the prudential right claim in (3) is transformed into a moral right claim in (4). But why does Gewirth think that this inference is valid? What Gewirth says to justify the inference is the following:

Now the resulting generalization is a moral judgment, because it requires the agent to take favorable account of the interests of persons other than or in addition to himself. The agent logically must here recognize that other persons have the same rights he claims for himself because they fulfill the same justifying condition on which he has based his own right claim.[37]

Here again, a number of Gewirth's critics have not found this justification compelling, but although they have questioned this inference in Gewirth's argument, none of them, as far as I can tell, has attempted to show exactly what does follow from the application of the principle of universalizability to step (3) of the argument.[38] And it seems to me that this failure to justify an alternative inference may be what has kept Gewirth and his critics from reaching agreement concerning this important step of his argument.

Now in order to better see what inference can be drawn from step (3), it is useful to reformulate (3) as an ought claim rather than a right claim. This gives us

3') Every agent has to accept (c') "I ought (prudentially and prescriptively) to have freedom and well-being simply in virtue of being a prospective, purposive agent."

Since the right in (3) is said to be prudential, the qualifier "prudentially" in (3') is self-explanatory. The other qualifier "prescriptively" is included simply to indicate that the ought claims agents are committing themselves to are explicitly action-guiding ought claims—ones that require, other things being equal, an appropriate commitment to action. Now it seems to me that there are three possible inferences that might be claimed to follow from (3') by an application of the principle of universalizability.

One possibility is (4'):

4') By virtue of accepting (c') every agent also has to accept (d') "All prospective, purposive agents ought (morally and prescriptively) to have freedom and well-being."

This is, of course, the inference that Gewirth would want us to draw. Now by accepting the moral and prescriptive ought claim of (d') agents are not only committed to acting to secure their own freedom and well-being, they are also committed to making a contribution toward securing the freedom and well-being of others. But given that the freedom and well-being of people conflict, exactly what actions would be permissible or required would have to be determined by some moral weighing of the competing interests involved.

However, in addition to (4') as a possible inference from (3'), (4") and (4'") are also possibilities.

4") By virtue of accepting (c') every agent also has to accept (d") "All prospective, purposive agents ought (prudentially and prescriptively) to have freedom and well-being."

4'") By virtue of accepting (c') every agent has to

accept (d‴) "All prospective, purposive agents ought (prudentially but not necessarily prescriptively) to have freedom and well-being."

Now in his discussion of universal ethical egoism in his book *Morality and Reason* Gewirth considers the possibility of generalizations like (4″) and (4‴) and rejects them both, but, as far as I can tell, without good reason.[39]

Gewirth's reason for rejecting (4″) is that it will give rise to incompatible and self-defeating action-guiding directives. By endorsing (d″), the ought claim embedded in (4″), Gewirth thinks that agents will be committed to doing all that they can to secure their own freedom and well-being and also committed to doing all that they can to secure the freedom and well-being of others. Because these two courses of action are incompatible and self-defeating, Gewirth rejects (4″) as a possible inference from (3′). Yet one need not interpret (d″) in this way. Obviously, in the case of (d″) as in the case of (d′) the freedom and well-being of people conflict, and here too there is need to weigh the competing interests, but unlike in the case of (d′) the weighing required has to be prudential not moral because the ought claim involved is prudential not moral. However, it seems to me that there is a way of understanding how this weighing could take place without resulting in incompatible and self-defeating action-guiding directives, for we can imagine (d″) as requiring that agents take the interests of others into account except when they conflict with their own interests. This way of interpreting (d″) would require agents to do all that they can to secure their own freedom and well-being, and when there is no conflict they would also be required to do what they can to secure the freedom and well-being of others. This, of course, would not be an acceptable moral weighing of the competing interests involved, but it would be a weighing that, as promised, is prudential and prescriptive, and one that does not give rise to directives that are incompatible and self-defeating for agents.[40]

Turning to (4‴), Gewirth's reason for rejecting this possible inference is that, he claims, its use of "ought" equivocates between a use that is action-guiding or prescriptive, e.g., when the agent infers from (d‴) that she ought to have freedom and well-being, and a use that is not action-guiding or prescriptive, e.g., when the agent infers from (d‴) that others ought to have freedom and well-being.[41] Now although this use of "ought" in (d‴) is differentially action-guiding in just the way Gewirth suggests, nothing appears to be equivocal about this usage since it is analogous to the use of "ought" we employ in competitive games. Thus, to adapt an example of Jesse Kalin's, if you and I are playing chess, I may judge at a certain point in the game that you ought to move your bishop and put my king in check but this judgment is not appropriately action-guiding for me. What I, in fact, should do is sit there quietly hoping that you do not move as you ought. And if you fail to make the appropriate move and later in the game, I judge that I ought to move so as to put your king in check that judgment, by contrast, would be appropriately action-guiding for me.

As one might expect, Gewirth has considered the possibility that the use of "ought" in (d‴) is not equivocal because it is analogous to the use of "ought" employed in competitive games. In response, he claims that the differentially action-guiding "oughts" of competitive games follow conditionally from commitment to the principle that games ought to be played according to their rules and related objectives, and that our acceptance or advocacy of this principle is radically different from the acceptance or advocacy of (4‴).

But is this the case? Certainly we can grant that acceptance or advocacy of the first part of the principle of games that *everyone ought to play games according to their rules* supports judgments prohibiting various forms of cheating that are uniformly action-guiding. And in this respect the "oughts" of competitive games are disanalogous to the differentially action-guiding use of "ought" in (d‴).

However, acceptance or advocacy of the first part of the principle of games does not explain why we make judgments like "She ought to move her bishop and put my king in check" and "I ought to move my knight and take her queen" which are differentially action-guiding. What explains such judgments is our acceptance or advocacy of the second part of the principle of games that *everyone ought to play games according to their related objectives.* Since the most significant of these related objectives is *to win,* and winning typically requires making one's best moves, we have the derived principle that everyone ought to make his or her best moves when playing games. And it is our acceptance or advocacy of this derived principle that explains our acceptance or advocacy of the differentially action-guiding judgments we make with respect to competitive games. Since no one thinks that this differentially action-guiding use of "ought" in competitive games is equivocal, no one should think that the analogous differentially action-guiding use of "ought" in (d′′′) is equivocal either. Consequently, (4′′′) has not been excluded as a possible inference from step (3) of Gewirth's argument.

If I am right, three possible inferences—(4′), (4′′), and (4′′′)—might be claimed to follow from step (3) of Gewirth's argument. All three of these possible inferences allow the agent to favor her own freedom and well-being over the freedom and well-being of others, but to varying degrees: (4′) allows a limited preference in this regard, (4′′) a maximal preference, and (4′′′) an exclusive preference. As we have seen, Gewirth favors (4′), but I have argued that his reasons for rejecting (4′′) and (4′′′) are not sound. Moreover, in the absence of good reasons for ruling out (4′′) and (4′′′), it is important to see that they are the favored candidates for the appropriate inference to be drawn from (3′). This is because they both contain, in (d′′) and (d′′′), prudential rather than moral principles; and in the absence of good reasons to the contrary, it would seem that the appropriate generalization of the prudential claim (c′) should be another pruden-

tial claim such as (d′′) or (d′′′), rather than a moral claim such as (d′). But if this is the case, Gewirth's central argument for the justification of morality clearly fails, because the inference from (3) to (4) has not been established.

My own justification for morality employs the same general strategy as those offered by Baier and Gewirth. It primarily differs from them in that it draws upon and generalizes insights we have about holding people morally responsible to arrive at what purports to be a non-question-begging standard of reasonable conduct that succeeds in showing that the rational egoist acts contrary to reason.

As we have already noted, the reasons a person could have acquired can be relevant when assessing a person's conduct from a moral point of view. In such assessments, people are said to be morally responsible even when they presently lack any moral reasons to act otherwise, provided that they are morally responsible for the lack. For example, if I had the capacity and opportunity to become more sensitive to my child's needs, but, in fact, failed to do so, with the consequence that I presently lack the moral reasons to effectively respond to those needs, I would still be morally responsible because my lack of moral reasons in this regard is something for which I am morally responsible. What is not so generally recognized, however, is that the reasons a person could have acquired can also be relevant when assessing a person's conduct from a self-interest point of view.

Consider the following example. On the last day that it was being offered for sale an acquaintance of mine bought a house that turned out to be infested with termites to such an extent as to require several thousands of dollars to correct for structural damage. Apparently, the previous owners did not know about the termites, and my acquaintance, having inspected the house on her own, did not think that she needed to have the house professionally inspected. My acquaintance now admits, I think rightly, that she acted unreasonably in purchasing the house, but I think it is plausible to say that her action wasn't unreasonable in terms of any reasons she had at the time of purchase because at that time she didn't know or have reason to believe that the house had termites.[42] Rather her action is best seen as unreasonable in terms of the reasons she could have had at the time of purchase if only she had arranged to have the house professionally inspected.

What these examples taken together appear to support is the following general standard:

A Standard for Reasonable Conduct: Reasonable conduct accords with a rational weighing of all the relevant reasons that people are or were able to acquire.

Obviously not all the reasons people are or were able to acquire are *relevant* to an assessment of the reasonableness of their conduct. For some, reasons are not important enough to be relevant to such an assessment. For example, a reason for acting that I am able to acquire which would lead me to promote my own interests or that of a friend just slightly more than I am presently doing is hardly relevant to an assessment of the reasonableness of my conduct. Surely I could not be judged as unreasonable for failing to acquire such a reason. Rather, relevant reasons are those reasons which would lead one to avoid a *significant harm* to oneself (or others) or to secure a *significant benefit* to oneself (or others) at an acceptable cost to oneself (or others). Thus, the Standard for Reasonable Conduct is not concerned with the possibility of maximizing benefit or minimizing harm overall but only with the possibility of avoiding a significant harm or securing a significant benefit at an acceptable cost.[43]

Needless to say, a given individual may not actually reflect upon all of the reasons that are relevant to deciding what to do. In fact, one could only do so if one has already acquired all the relevant reasons. Nevertheless, reasonable conduct is ultimately determined by a rational weighing of all the

relevant reasons so that failing to accord with a rational weighing of all such reasons is to act contrary to reason.[44]

Of course, while defenders of rational egoism would certainly not want to deny the relevance of the self-interested reasons people are or were able to acquire to the rational assessment of conduct, they may want to deny that the moral reasons that people are or were able to acquire are similarly relevant. But what would be the basis for that denial? It could not be that rational egoists do not in fact act upon moral reasons. For that would no more show the irrelevance of moral reasons to the rational assessment of conduct than the fact that pure altruists do not act upon self-interested reasons would show the irrelevance of self-interested reasons to such an assessment. To argue on such grounds would simply beg the question against the opposing view, and most defenders of rational egoism have at least tried to support the view in a non-question-begging way.

In fact, most defenders of rational egoism have argued for egoism in its universal form, defending the following principle:

Every person ought to do what best serves her overall self-interest.

But defenders of rational egoism could no more support this principle by simply denying the relevance of moral reasons to a rational assessment of conduct than could defenders of pure altruism, by simply denying the relevance of self-interested reasons to a rational assessment of conduct, support their opposing principle:

Every person ought to do what best serves the overall interest of others.

Consequently, defenders of rational egoism seem to have no other alternative but to grant the relevance of moral reasons to the rational assessment of conduct and then try to show that such an assessment would never rationally require us to act upon moral reasons.

Unfortunately for the defenders of rational egoism, a rational assessment of the relevant reasons does not lead to this result. Quite the contrary, such an assessment shows that we are rationally required to act upon moral reasons. To see why this is so, two kinds of cases must be considered. First, there are cases in which there is conflict between the relevant moral reasons and self-interested reasons. Second, there are cases in which there is no such conflict.

Now it seems obvious that where there is no conflict, and both reasons are conclusive reasons of their kind, both reasons should be acted upon. In such contexts, we should do what is favored both by morality and by self-interest.

Consider the following example. Suppose that you accepted a job marketing a baby formula in under-developed countries, where the formula was improperly used, leading to increased infant mortality.[45] Imagine that you could just as well have accepted an equally attractive and rewarding job marketing a similar formula in developed countries, where the misuse does not occur, so that a rational weighing of the relevant self-interested reasons alone would not have favored your acceptance of one of these jobs over the other.[46] At the same time, there were obviously moral reasons that condemned your acceptance of the first job— reasons that you presumably are or were able to acquire. Moreover, by assumption in this case, the moral reasons do not clash with the relevant self-interested reasons; they simply made a recommendation where the relevant self-interested reasons are silent. Consequently, a rational weighing of all the relevant reasons in this case could not but favor acting in accord with the relevant moral reasons.[47]

Yet it might be objected that even in cases of this sort there would frequently be other reasons significantly opposed to these moral reasons—other reasons that you are or were able to acquire. Such reasons would be either *benevolent reasons* concerned to promote nonhuman welfare even at the cost of human lives or *malevolent reasons* seeking to bring about the suffering and death of other human beings or *aesthetic reasons* concerned to produce desirable results irrespective of the effects on human or nonhuman welfare. But presumably such benevolent reasons would normally be outweighed by reasons to promote nonhuman welfare by less costly means. And assuming malevolent reasons are ultimately rooted in a conception of the agent's good,[48] they would have already been taken into account, and presumably, for most people, outweighed in the calculation of self-interest in this case.[49] Only aesthetic reasons would not have been taken into account, but such reasons are not in fact relevant to justifying morality to the rational egoist.[50] Consequently, even with the presence of these three kinds of reasons, your acceptance of the first job can still be seen to violate the Standard for Reasonable Conduct.

Needless to say, defenders of rational egoism cannot but be disconcerted with this result, since it shows that actions that accord with rational egoism are contrary to reason at least when there are two equally good ways of pursuing one's self-interest, only one of which does not conflict with the basic requirements of morality. Notice also that in cases where there are two equally good ways of fulfilling the basic requirements of morality, only one of which does not conflict with what is in a person's best overall self-interest, it is not at all disconcerting for defenders of morality to admit that we are rationally required to choose the way that does not conflict with what is in our overall self-interest. Nevertheless, exposing this defect in rational egoism for cases where moral reasons and self-interested reasons do not conflict would be but a small victory for defenders of morality if it were not also possible to show that in cases where such reasons do conflict, moral reasons would have priority over self-interested reasons.

Now when rationally assessing the relevant reasons in such conflict cases, it is best to view the conflict not as a conflict between self-interested reasons and moral reasons but rather as a conflict between self-interested reasons and altruistic reasons. Viewed in this way, three solutions are possible. First, one could say that self-interested reasons always have priority over conflicting altruistic reasons. Second, one could say just the opposite: that altruistic reasons always have priority over conflicting self-interested reasons. Third, one could say that some kind of compromise is rationally required. In this compromise, sometimes self-interested reasons would have priority over altruistic reasons and sometimes altruistic reasons would have priority over self-interested reasons.

Once the conflict is described in this manner the third solution can be seen as to be the one that is rationally required. This is because the first and second solutions give exclusive priority to one class of relevant reasons over the other and no non-question-begging justification can be given for such an exclusive priority from the standpoint of the Standard for Reasonable Conduct. Only the third solution, by sometimes giving priority to self-interested reasons and sometimes giving priority to altruistic reasons, can provide a non-question-begging resolution from the standpoint of the Standard for Reasonable Conduct.

Consider the following example. Suppose you are in the waste disposal business and you decided to dispose of toxic wastes in a way that was cost efficient for you but predictably caused significant harm to future generations. Imagine that there were alternative methods available for disposing of the waste that were only slightly less cost efficient and which did not cause any significant harm to future generations.[51] In this case, the Standard for Reasonable Conduct required weighing of your self-interested reasons favoring the most cost efficient disposal of the toxic wastes against the relevant altruistic reasons favoring the avoidance of significant harm to future generations. If we suppose that the projected loss of benefit to yourself was ever so slight and the projected harm to future generations was ever so great, then any acceptable general compromise between

the relevant self-interested and altruistic reasons would have to favor the altruistic reasons in this case. Hence, as judged by the Standard for Reasonable Conduct, your method of waste disposal was contrary to the relevant reasons.

Now it is important to see how morality can be viewed as just such a compromise between self-interested and altruistic reasons. First of all, a certain amount of self-regard is morally required or at least morally acceptable. Where this is the case, the relevant self-interested reasons have priority over the relevant altruistic reasons. Secondly, morality obviously places limits on the extent to which people should pursue their own self-interest. Where this is the case, the relevant altruistic reasons have priority over the relevant self-interested reasons. In this way, morality can be seen as a compromise between self-interested and altruistic reasons, and the "moral reasons" which constitute that compromise can be seen as having an absolute priority over the self-interested or altruistic reasons which conflict with them.

Notice that this defense of morality succeeds not only against the view that rational egoism is rationally preferable to morality but also against the view that rational egoism is only rationally on a par with morality. The "weaker view" does not claim that we all ought to be egoists. Rather it claims that there is just as good reason for us to be egoists as to be pure altruists or anything in between. As Kai Nielson summarizes this view in a recent article:

We have not been able to show that reason requires the moral point of view or that all really rational persons not be individual egoists. Reason doesn't decide here.[52]

Yet since the above defense of morality shows morality to be the only non-question-begging resolution of the conflict between self-interested and altruistic reasons from the standpoint of the Standard of Reasonable Conduct, it is not the case that there are just as good reasons for us to endorse morality as to endorse rational egoism or pure altruism. Thus, the above defense of morality suceeds against the weaker as well as the stronger interpretation of rational egoism.

Unfortunately, my approach to defending morality has been generally neglected by previous moral theorists. The reason it has been neglected is that such theorists have tended to view the basic conflict with rational egoism as a conflict between morality and self-interest. For example, according to Baier,

The very *raison d'être* of a morality is to yield reasons which overrule the reasons of self-interest in those cases when everyone's following self-interest would be harmful to everyone.[53]

Viewed in this light, it did not seem possible for the defender of morality to be supporting a compromise view, for how could such a defender say that when morality and self-interest conflict, morality should sometimes be sacrificed for the sake of self-interest? But while previous theorists understood correctly that moral reasons could not be compromised in favor of self-interested reasons, they failed to recognize that this is because moral reasons are already the result of a compromise between self-interested and altruistic reasons. Thus, unable to see how morality could be represented as a compromise solution, previous theorists have generally failed to recognize this approach to defending morality.

Of course, exactly how this compromise solution is to be worked out is a matter of considerable debate. Utilitarians seem to favor one sort of a resolution, contractarians another, and libertarians still another—to mention just a few of the possibilities. My own view is that this debate can be adequately resolved at the practical level by showing how theoretically diverse views lead to the same practical requirements. For example, I have argued that libertarian, contractarian and socialist views all lead to the same practical requirements, which just happens to be those usually associated with the contractarian view.[54] Yet irrespective of how this debate is best resolved, it is clear that some sort of a compromise view or moral solution is rationally preferable to either rational egoism or pure altruism from the standpoint of the Standard of Reasonable Conduct.

What we have then is a sketch of a justification for morality in terms of the requirements of practical reason that succeeds in showing that the rational egoist acts contrary to reason. While this sketch needs to be completed in various ways, particularly by specifying the exact nature of the compromise that is rationally required between the relevant self-interested and altruistic reasons it already has certain advantages over the two other justifications we have considered. Unlike our first justification, which appeals to self-interest, this justification does not depend on a substantial correspondence between our interests and the interests of others, nor does it threaten those theoretical requirements of practical reason which place an intrinsic value on the well-being of other people. And unlike our second justification, which appeals to the other-regarding interests, wants, or intentions people happen to have, this justification correctly recognizes that people's having certain other-regarding interests, wants, or intentions is neither necessary nor sufficient to justify the requirements of morality. Of course, whether it is possible to link this justification up with an argument for the practical reconciliation of alternative moral and political ideals, so as to provide a completely adequate foundation for morality, remains to be seen.[55]

NOTES

1. Peter Singer: 1979, *Practical Ethics*, New York, Chapter 10; Robert Olson: 1965, *The Morality of Self-Interest*, New York; Neil Cooper: 1981, *The Diversity of Moral Thinking*, Oxford; Michael Scriven: 1966, *Primary Philosophy*, New York, Chapter VII; D. A. Lloyd Thomas: 1970, 'Why Should I Be Moral?', *Philosophy*, 128–39.

2. Philippa Foot: 1978, *Virtues and Vices*,

Berkeley; Gilbert Harman: 1975, 'Moral Relativism Defended', *Philosophical Review*, 75, 3–22; Bernard Williams: 1973, *Problems of the Self*, Cambridge, Chapter 15. Some, however, do not see this position as Humean, see W. D. Falk: 1975, 'Hume on Practical Reason', *Philosophical Studies*, 1–18.

3. Alan Gewirth: 1978, *Reason and Morality*, Chicago; Kurt Baier: 1978, 'The Social Source of Reason', *Proceedings and Addresses of the American Philosophical Association;* Alan Donagan: 1977, *The Theory of Morality*, Chicago; Stephen Darwall: 1983, *Impartial Reason*, Ithaca.

4. In my earlier work, I argued that rational egoism is a consistent view. (See 1979, 'Ethical Egoism and Beyond', *Canadian Journal of Philosophy* and 1980, *The Demands of Justice*, Notre Dame, Chapter 1.) I still think that this is the case, but I now think that it is possible to show that while consistent the view is contrary to reason.

5. Thomas, p. 130.

6. A question-begging definition would be one that obvious presupposed the truth of some form of egoism.

7. Milton Fisk: 1980, *Ethics and Society*, New York, pp. 139–40; Mary Gibson: 1977, 'Rationality', *Philosophy and Public Affairs*, 222. See also Isaiah Berlin: 1969, *Four Essays on Liberty*, New York, Chapter III.

8. Olson, p. 9.

9. Scriven, p. 251. Olson also holds this view.

10. Bertell Ollman: 1971, *Alienation*, New York, Part III.

11. Karl Marx: 1966, *Critique of the Gotha Program*, C. P. Dutt (ed.), New York. C. B. Macpherson also endorses the possibility of a harmonious development of people's interests. See 1973, *Democracy*, Oxford, p. 54.

12. Steven Evans: 'Could Divine Rewards Provide a Reason to be Moral?' in Harold Heie and David Wolfe (eds.): 1986. *Realities of Christian Learning*. Grand Rapids.

13. On this point, see Allen Buchanan: 1979, 'Revolutionary Motivation and Rationality', *Philosophy and Public Affairs*.

14. Peter Singer, Chapter 10. But see also Scriven, Chapter VII and Cooper, Chapters 15 and 16.

15. There is a further problem, as we shall see, with appealing to any kind of justification for morality in terms of self-interest in that such a justification involves rejecting theoretical requirements of practical reason which place an intrinsic value on the well-being of other people.

16. Philippa Foot: 'Morality As a System of Hypothetical Imperatives', in *Virtues and Vices*, 157–73.

17. Very few philosophers who use the expression "*X* has a reason for acting" are very clear about what they mean by it. However, I think the following conditions are common to Foot's and Harman's use of the expression as well as Kurt Baier's and Thomas Nagel's.

X has a reason (R) for acting if
(1) R is a consideration which is a reason to acting and
(2) X recognizes R to be a reason for acting and
(3) R is capable of motivating X to act, other things being equal.

See Kurt Baier: 'The Social Source of Reason', pp. 724–25. Thomas Nagel: 1970, *The Possibility of Altruism*, New York, pp. 110–11. E. J. Bond: 1974, 'Reasons, Wants and Values', *Canadian Journal of Philosophy*, pp. 333–47.

18. Gilbert Harman: 1977, 'Moral Relativism Defended', in *The Nature of Morality*, New York.

19. Philippa Foot: 'A Reply to Professor Frankena', in *Virtues and Vices*, p. 179.

20. Harman, pp. 4–5; Foot, 'Morality as a System of Hypothetical Imperatives', pp. 161–62.

21. In correspondence, Gilbert Harman says he rejects my proposed necessary condition for moral responsibility. He writes, "The thought that Hitler was so evil that he lacked such capabilities or opportunities does not seem to imply he was not morally responsible for his crimes". But I have trouble understanding what sense of moral responsibility Harman could be employing here. Clearly, an agent could be morally responsible in the sense of being strictly liable, but this sense of responsibility does not involve a judgment that the agent is evil. On the other hand, if an agent is morally responsible because she is evil, this does seem to at least imply that she possesses (or has possessed) the capabilities and opportunities to acquire reasons to act otherwise.

For an interesting discussion of some similar cases where we hold people morally responsible, see Holly Smith: 1983, 'Culpable Ignorance', *Philosophical Review*.

22. Obviously people do not find themselves with their capacities for acting morally or their capacities for acting self-interestedly totally undeveloped, but usually they do have a choice of whether to continue or to undercut the development that has already taken place.

23. Foot sometimes seems to confuse explanation with justification as when she accounts for the stringency of moral imperatives by the forcefulness of our teaching. See 'Morality as a System of Categorical Imperatives', in *Virtues and Vices*, p. 162.

24. See Section 1.

25. *The Moral Point of View*, pp. vi–vii.

26. See 1978, 'The Social Source of Reason,' *Proceedings and Addresses of the American Philosophical Association*; 1978, 'Moral Reasons and Reasons to be Moral', in A. I. Goldman and J. Kim (eds.), *Values and Morals*, Dordrecht, 1978, 'Moral Reason', in Peter French et al. (eds.), *Midwest Studies in Philosophy* III, Morris; 1982, 'The Conceptual Link Between Morality and Rationality', *Nous*,

27. The rational egoist is usually thought to be the opponent of morality under the assumption that the practical requirements of morality and those of self-interest conflict (On this point, see Section 1). But if one were to reject this assumption, the rational egoist would still be opposed to any theoretical requirements of practical reason which place an intrinsic value on the well-being of other people (See Section 4).

28. See, for example, 'Moral Reasons and Reasons to be Moral', p. 240.

29. See 'Moral Reasons', p. 69.

30. See *Demands of Justice*, Chapter 1.

31. Baier: 'Moral Reasons and Reasons to be Moral', pp. 249–50. R. M. Hare makes an analogous claim in *Freedom and Reason*, Oxford, p. 93. John Rawls also wants to impose a similar restriction on choice in his "original position". But Rawls realizes he is importing a moral constraint. See 1971, *A Theory of Justice*, Cambridge, pp. 11–22.

32. The egoist's response to the occurrence of genuine Prisoner's Dilemmas would be to transform them, if possible, into choice situations favoring the practice of rational egoism.

33. When players fail to execute their best moves it may simply be due to their own lack of skill or ability, *or* they may have been simply tricked into not executing their best moves.

34. Of course, defenders of our first justification for morality think this point comes fairly quickly.

35. Alan Gewirth, *Reason and Morality*, Chapters 2 and 3.

36. See, for example, the articles by R.M. Hare, D.D. Raphael, Kai Nielsen and W.D. Hudson in *Gewirth's Ethical Rationalism* edited by Edward Regis (Chicago, 1984).

37. *Gewirth's Ethical Rationalism*, p. 210.

38. *Ibid.* See, for example, the articles by R.M. Hare and Jesse Kalin.

39. Gewirth, *Reason and Morality*, pp. 82–89.

40. As we shall see later, accepting this interpretation does require a concession from the egoist. Nevertheless, it does not lead to anything resembling a moral perspective.

41. This way of putting Gewirth's objections and my response owes much to a symposium in which Gewirth's and I participated held at the University of Rochester and subsequent conversations that continued right up to the moment before his plane departed.

42. Notice that on the last day that the house was being offered for sale, it would not have been reasonable for my acquaintance to decide to have the house inspected since presumably the inspection and the sale could not have been completed in the same day.

43. Even utilitarians would find this interpretation of the Standard for Reasonable Conduct acceptable since they would not regard all failures to maximize benefits overall as unreasonable.

44. Of course, for individuals who neither possess nor have possessed the capabilities and opportunities to acquire such reasons for acting, the question of the reasonableness of their conduct simply does not arise. Likewise, the question does not arise for those who have lost the capabilities and opportunities to acquire such reasons for acting through no fault of their own.

45. For a discussion of the causal links involved here, see *Marketing and Promotion of Infant Formula in Developing Countries*. Hearing before the subcommittee of International Economic Policy and Trade of the Committee on Foreign Affairs, U.S. House of Representatives, 1980. See also Maggie McComas and others: 1983, *The Dilemma of Third World Nutrition*.

46. Assume that both jobs have the same beneficial effects on the interests of others.

47. I am assuming that acting contrary to reason is an important failing with respect to the requirements of reason, and that there are many ways of not acting in (perfect) accord with reason that do not constitute acting contrary to reason.

48. Otherwise, they would really fall under the classification of aesthetic reasons.

49. To deal with pure sadists (if any exist) for whom malevolent reasons or the reasons on which such reasons are grounded would not have been outweighed by other self-interested reasons, we might introduce an additional argument to show that pure sadists should team up with pure masochists (if any exist)!

50. Of course, such reasons would have to be taken into account at some point in a complete justification for morality.

51. Assume that all these methods of waste disposal have roughly the same amount of beneficial effect on the interests of others.

52. Kai Nielson: 1984, 'Why Should I be Moral? Revisited' (Selection 11).

53. *The Moral Point of View,* p. 150.

54. See 1982, 'A Marxist Dilemma for Social Contract Theory', *American Philosophical Quarterly* (Selection 18).

55. I attempt to establish such a link in *How to Make People Just* Rowman and Littlefield. (1988).

Suggested Readings

BAIER, KURT. *The Moral Point of View.* Ithaca: Cornell University Press, 1958.

BAIER, KURT. *"The Social Source of Reason."* Proceedings and Addresses of the American Philosophical Association. Lancaster: Lancaster Press, 1978.

BRANDT, RICHARD. *A Theory of the Good and the Right.* Oxford: Oxford University Press, 1979.

FOOT, PHILIPPA. *Virtues and Vices.* Berkeley: University of California Press, 1978.

GAUTHIER, DAVID, ED. *Morality and Rational Self-Interest.* Englewood Cliffs: Prentice-Hall, 1970.

GERT, BERNARD. *Moral Rules.* New York: Harper & Row, 1970.

GEWIRTH, ALAN. *Reason and Morality.* Chicago: University of Chicago Press, 1978.

MAY, BERNARD. *The Philosophy of Right and Wrong.* London: Routledge & Kegan Paul, 1986.

MONRO, D. H. *Empiricism & Ethics.* Cambridge: Cambridge University Press, 1967.

NAGEL, THOMAS. *The Possibility of Altruism.* Oxford: Clarendon Press, 1970.

NAGEL, THOMAS. *The View From Nowhere.* New York: Oxford University Press, 1986.

OLSON, ROBERT G. *The Morality of Self-Interest.* New York: Harcourt Brace & World, 1965.

RACHELS, JAMES. *The Elements of Moral Philosophy.* New York: Random House, 1986.

RAPHAEL, D. D. *Moral Philosophy.* Oxford: Oxford University Press, 1981.

REGIS, EDWARD, JR. *Gewirth's Ethical Rationalism.* Chicago: University of Chicago Press, 1984.

STERBA, JAMES P. *How To Make People Just.* Totowa: Rowman & Littlefield Publishers, 1988.

THOMAS, LAURENCE, ED. *Kurt Baier Festschrift, Synthese.* Vol. 72, No. 1 & 2 (1987).

WILLIAMS, BERNARD. *Ethics and the Limits of Philosophy.* Cambridge: Harvard University Press, 1985.

17
THE LIBERTARIAN MANIFESTO

John Hospers

The political philosophy that is called libertarianism (from the Latin *libertas,* liberty) is the doctrine that every person is the owner of his own life, and that no one is the owner of anyone else's life: and that consequently every human being has the right to act in accordance with his own choices, unless those actions infringe on the equal liberty of other human beings to act in accordance with their choices.

There are several other ways of stating the same libertarian thesis:

1. *No one is anyone else's master, and no one is anyone else's slave.* Since I am the one to decide how my life is to be conducted just as you decide about yours, I have no right (even if I had the power) to make you my slave and be your master, nor have you the right to become the master by enslaving me. Slavery is *forced* servitude, and since no one owns the life of anyone else, no one has the right to enslave

From "What Libertarianism Is," in *The Libertarian Alternative* edited by Tibor Machan (Nelson-Hall Inc., 1974). Reprinted by permission.

another. Political theories past and present have traditionally been concerned with who should be the master (usually the king, the dictator, or government bureaucracy) and who should be the slaves, and what the extent of the slavery should be. Libertarianism holds that no one has the right to use force to enslave the life of another, or any portion or aspect of that life.

2. *Other men's lives are not yours to dispose of.* I enjoy seeing operas; but operas are expensive to produce. Opera-lovers often say, "The state (or the city, etc.) should subsidize opera, so that we can all see it. Also it would be for people's betterment, cultural benefit, etc." But what they are advocating is nothing more or less than legalized plunder. They can't pay for the productions themselves, and yet they want to see opera, which involves a large number of people and their labor; so what they are saying in effect is, "Get the money through legalized force. Take a little bit more out of every worker's paycheck every week to pay for the operas we want to see." But I have no right to take by force from the workers' pockets to pay for what I want.

Perhaps it would be better if he *did* go to see opera—then I should try to convince him to go voluntarily. But to take the money from him forcibly, because in my opinion it would be good for *him,* is still seizure of his earnings, which is plunder.

Besides, if I have the right to force him to help pay for my pet projects, hasn't he equally the right to force me to help pay for his? Perhaps he in turn wants the government to subsidize rock-and-roll, or his new car, or a house in the country? If I have the right to milk him, why hasn't he the right to milk me? If I can be a moral cannibal, why can't he too?

We should beware of the inventors of utopias. They would remake the world according to their vision—with the lives and fruits of the labor of *other* human beings. Is it someone's utopian vision that others should build pyramids to beautify the landscape? Very well, then other men should provide the labor; and if he is in a position of political power, and he can't get men to do it voluntarily, then he must *compel* them to "cooperate"— i.e. he must enslave them.

A hundred men might gain great pleasure from beating up or killing just one insignificant human being; but other men's lives are not theirs to dispose of. "In order to achieve the worthy goals of the next five-year-plan, we must forcibly collectivize the peasants . . ."; but other men's lives are not theirs to dispose of. Do you want to occupy, rent-free, the mansion that another man has worked for twenty years to buy? But other men's lives are not yours to dispose of. Do you want operas so badly that everyone is forced to work harder to pay for their subsidization through taxes? But other men's lives are not yours to dispose of. Do you want to have free medical care at the expense of other people, whether they wish to provide it or not? But this would require them to work longer for you whether they want to or not, and other men's lives are not yours to dispose of. . . .

3. *No human being should be a nonvoluntary mortgage on the life of another.* I cannot claim your life, your work, or the products of your effort as mine. The fruit of one man's labor should not be fair game for every freeloader who comes along and demands it as his own. The orchard that has been carefully grown, nurtured, and harvested by its owner should not be ripe for the plucking for any bypasser who has a yen for the ripe fruit. The wealth that some men have produced should not be fair game for looting by government, to be used for whatever purposes its representatives determine, no matter what their motives in so doing may be. The theft of your money by a robber is not justified by the fact that he used it to help his injured mother.

It will already be evident that libertarian doctrine is embedded in a view of the rights of man. Each human being has the right to live his life as he chooses, compatibly with the equal right of all other human beings to live their lives as they choose.

All man's rights are implicit in the above statement. Each man has the right to life; any attempt by others to take it away from him, or even to injure him, violates this right, through the use of coercion against him. Each man has the right to liberty: to conduct his life in accordance with the alternatives open to him without coercive action by others. And every man has the right to property: to work to sustain his life (and the lives of whichever others he chooses to sustain, such as his family) and to retain the fruits of his labor.

People often defend the rights of life and liberty but denigrate property rights, and yet the right to property is as basic as the other two: indeed, without property rights no other rights are possible. Depriving you of property is depriving you of the means by which you live. . . .

I have no right to decide how *you* should spend your time or your money. I can make that decision for myself, but not for you, my neighbor. I may deplore your choice of lifestyle, and I may talk with you about it provided you are willing to listen to me. But I have no right to use force to change it. Nor have I the right to decide how you should spend the money you have earned. I may appeal to you to give it to the Red Cross, and you may prefer to go to prize-fights. But that is your decision, and however much I may chafe about it I do not have the right to interfere forcibly with it, for example by robbing you in order to use the money in accordance with *my* choices. (If I have the right to rob you, have you also the right to rob me?)

When I claim a right, I carve out a niche, as it were, in my life, saying in effect, "This activity I must be able to perform without interference from others. For you and everyone else, this is off limits." And so I put up a "no trespassing" sign, which marks off the area of my right. Each individual's right is his "no trespassing" sign in relation to me and others. I may not encroach upon his domain any more than he upon mine, without my consent. Every right entails a duty, true—but the duty is only that of *forbearance*—that is, of *refraining* from violating the other person's right. If you have a right to life, I have no right to take your life; if you have a right to the products of your labor (property), I have no right to take it from you without your consent. The nonviolation of these rights will not guarantee you protection against natural catastrophes such as floods and earthquakes, but it will protect you against the aggressive activities *of other men*. And rights, after all, have to do with one's relations to other human beings, not with one's relations to physical nature.

Nor were these rights created by government; governments—some governments, obviously not all—*recognize* and *protect* the rights that individuals already have. Governments regularly forbid homicide and theft; and, at a more advanced stage, protect individuals against such things as libel and breach of contract. . . .

The *right to property* is the most misunderstood and unappreciated of human rights, and it is one most constantly violated by governments. "Property" of course does not mean only real estate; it includes anything you can call your own—your clothing, your car, your jewelry, your books and papers.

The right of property is not the right to just *take* it from others, for this would interfere with *their* property rights. It is rather the right to work for it, to obtain noncoercively, the money or services which you can present in voluntary exchange.

The right to property is consistently underplayed by intellectuals today, sometimes even frowned upon, as if we should feel guilty for upholding such a right in view of all the poverty in the world. But the right to property is absolutely basic. It is your hedge against the future. It is your assurance that what you have worked to earn will still be there and be yours, when you wish or need to use it, especially when you are too old to work any longer.

Government has always been the chief enemy of the right to property. The officials of government, wishing to increase their power, and finding an increase of wealth an effective way to bring this about seize some or all of what a person has earned—and since government has a monopoly of physical force within the geographical area of the nation, it has the power (but not the right) to do this. When this happens, of course, every citizen of that country is insecure: he knows that no matter how hard he works the government can swoop down on him at any time and confiscate his earnings and possessions. A person sees his life savings wiped out in a moment when the tax-collectors descend to deprive him of the fruits of his work; or, an industry which has been fifty years in the making and cost millions of dollars and millions of hours of time and planning, is nationalized overnight. Or the government, via inflation, cheapens the currency, so that hard-won dollars aren't worth anything any more. The effect of such actions, of course, is that people lose hope and incentive: if no matter how hard they work the government agents can take it all away, why bother to work at all, for more than today's needs? Depriving people of property is *depriving them of the means by which they live*—the freedom of the individual citizen to do what he wishes with his own life and to plan for the future. Indeed only if property rights are respected is there any point to planning for the future and working to achieve one's goals. *Property rights are what makes long-range planning possible*—the kind of planning which is a distinctively human endeavor, as opposed to the day-byday activity of the lion who hunts, who depends on the supply of game tomorrow but has no real insurance against starvation in a day or a week. Without the right to property, the right to life itself amounts to little: how can you sustain your life if you cannot plan ahead? and how can you plan ahead if the fruits of your labor can at any moment be confiscated by government? . . .

Indeed, the right to property may well be considered second only to the right to life. Even the freedom of speech is limited by considerations of property. If a person visiting in your home behaves in a way undesired by you, you have every right to evict him; he can scream or agitate elsewhere if he wishes, but not in your home without your consent. Does a person have a right to shout obscenities in a cathedral? No, for the owners of the cathedral (presumably the Church) have not allowed others on their property for that purpose; one may go there to worship or to visit, but not just for any purpose one wishes. Their property right is prior to your or my wish to scream or expectorate or write graffiti on their building. Or, to take the stock example, does a person have a right to shout "Fire!" falsely in a crowded theater? No, for the theater owner has permitted others to enter and use his property only for a specific purpose, that of seeing a film or watching a stage show. If a person heckles or otherwise disturbs other members of the audience, he can be thrown out. (In fact, he can be removed for any reason the owner chooses, provided his admission money is returned.) And if he shouts "Fire!" when there is no fire, he may be endangering other lives by causing a panic or a stampede. The right to free speech doesn't give one the right to say anything anywhere; it is circumscribed by property rights.

Again, some people seem to assume that the right to free speech (including written speech) means that they can go to a newspaper publisher and demand that he print in his newspaper some propaganda or policy statement for their political party (or other group). But of course they have no right to the use of his newspaper. Ownership of the newspaper is the product of his labor, and he has a right to put into his newspaper whatever he wants, for whatever reason. If he excludes material which many readers would like to have in, perhaps they can find it in another newspaper or persuade him to print it himself (if there are enough of them, they will usually do just that). Perhaps they can even cause his newspaper to fail. But as long as he owns it, he has the right to put in it what he wishes; what would a property right be if he could not do this? They have no right to place their material in his newspaper without his consent—not for free, nor even for a fee. Perhaps other newspapers will include it, or perhaps they can start their own newspaper (in which case they have a right to put in it what they like). If not, an option open to them would be to mimeograph and distribute some handbills.

In exactly the same way, no one has a right to "free television time" unless the owner of the television station consents to give it; it is his station, he has the property rights over it, and it is for him to decide how to dispose of his time. He may not decide wisely, but it is his right to decide as he wishes. If he makes enough unwise decisions, and courts enough unpopularity with the viewing public or the sponsors, he may have to go out of business; but as he is free to make his own decisions, so is he free to face their consequences. (If the government owns the television station, then government officials will make the decisions, and there is no guarantee of *their* superior wisdom. The difference is that when "the government" owns the station, you are forced to help pay for its upkeep through your taxes, whether the bureaucrat in charge decides to give you television time or not.)

"But why have *individual* property rights? Why not have lands and houses owned by everybody together?" Yes, this involves no violation of individual rights, as long as everybody consents to this arrangement and no one is forced to join it. The parties to it may enjoy the communal living enough (at least for a time) to overcome certain inevitable problems: that some will work and some not, that some will achieve more in an hour than others can do in a day, and still they will all get the same income. The few who do the most will in the end consider themselves "workhorses" who do the work of two or three or twelve, while the others will be "freeloaders" on the efforts of these few. But as long as they can get out of the arrangement if they no longer like it, no violation of rights is involved. They got in voluntarily, and they can get out voluntarily; no one has used force.

"But why not say that everybody owns everything? That we *all* own everything there is?"

To some this may have a pleasant ring— but let us try to analyze what it means. If everybody owns everything, then everyone has an equal right to go everywhere, do what he pleases, take what he likes, destroy if he wishes, grow crops or burn them, trample them under, and so on. Consider what it would be like in practice. Suppose you have saved money to buy a house for yourself and your family. Now suppose that the principle, "everybody owns everything," becomes adopted. Well then, why shouldn't every itinerant hippie just come in and take over, sleeping in your beds and eating in your kitchen and not bothering to replace the food supply or clean up the mess? After all, it belongs to all of us, doesn't it? So we have just as much right to it as you, the buyer, have. What happens if we *all* want to sleep in the bedroom and there's not room for all of us? Is it the strongest who wins?

What would be the result? Since no one would be responsible for anything, the property would soon be destroyed, the food used up, the facilities nonfunctional. Beginning as a house that *one* family could use, it would end up as a house that *no one* could use. And if the principle continued to be adopted, no one would build houses any more—or anything else. What for? They would only be occupied and used by others, without remuneration.

Suppose two men are cast ashore on an island, and they agree that each will cultivate half of it. The first man is industrious and

grows crops and builds a shelter, making the most of the situation with which he is confronted. The second man, perhaps thinking that the warm days will last forever, lies in the sun, picks coconuts while they last, and does a minimum of work to sustain himself. At the time of harvest, the second man has nothing to harvest, nor does he assist the first man in his labors. But later when there is a dearth of food on the island, the second man comes to the first man and demands half of the harvest as his right. But of course he has no right to the product of the first man's labors. The first man may freely choose to give part of his harvest to the second out of charity rather than see him starve; but that is just what it is— charity, not the second man's right.

How can any of man's rights be violated? Ultimately, only by the use of force. I can make suggestions to you, I can reason with you, entreat you (if you are willing to listen), but I cannot *force* you without violating your rights, only by forcing you do I cut the cord between your free decisions and your actions. Voluntary relations between individuals involve no deprivation of rights, but murder, assault, and rape do, because in doing these things I make you the unwilling victim of my actions. A man's beating his wife involves no violation of rights if she *wanted* to be beaten. *Force is behavior that requires the unwilling involvement of other persons.*

Thus the use of force need not involve the use of physical violence. If I trespass on your property or dump garbage on it, I am violating your property rights, as indeed I am when I steal your watch; although this is not force in the sense of violence, it *is* a case of your being an unwilling victim of my action. Similarly, if you shout at me so that I cannot be heard when I try to speak, or blow a siren in my ear, or start a factory next door which pollutes my land, you are again violating my rights (to free speech, to property); I am, again, an unwilling victim of your actions. Similarly, if you steal a manuscript of mine and publish it as your own, you are confiscating a piece of my property and thus violating my right to keep what is the product of my labor. Of course, if I give you the manuscript with permission to sign your name to it and keep the proceeds, no violation of rights is involved—any more than if I give you permission to dump garbage on my yard.

According to libertarianism, the role of government should be limited to the retaliatory use of force against those who have initiated its use. It should not enter into any other areas, such as religion, social organization, and economics.

GOVERNMENT

Government is the most dangerous institution known to man. Throughout history it has violated the rights of men more than any individual or group of individuals could do: it has killed people, enslaved them, sent them to forced labor and concentration camps, and regularly robbed and pillaged them of the fruits of their expended labor. Unlike individual criminals, government has the power to arrest and try; unlike individual criminals, it can surround and encompass a person totally, dominating every aspect of one's life, so that one has no recourse from it but to leave the country (and in totalitarian nations even that is prohibited). Government throughout history has a much sorrier record than any individual, even that of a ruthless mass murderer. The signs we see on bumper stickers are chillingly accurate: "Beware: the Government Is Armed and Dangerous."

The only proper role of government, according to libertarians, is that of the protector of the citizen against aggression by other individuals. The government, of course, should never initiate aggression; its proper role is as the embodiment of the *retaliatory* use of force against anyone who initiates it use.

If each individual had constantly to defend himself against possible aggressors, he would have to spend a considerable portion of his life in target practice, karate exercises, and other means of self-defense, and even

so he would probably be helpless against groups of individuals who might try to kill, maim, or rob him. He would have little time for cultivating those qualities which are essential to civilized life, nor would improvements in science, medicine, and the arts be likely to occur. The function of government is to take this responsibility off his shoulders: the government undertakes to defend him against aggressors and to punish them if they attack him. When the government is effective in doing this, it enables the citizen to go about his business unmolested and without constant fear for his life. To do this, of course, government must have physical power—the police, to protect the citizen from aggression within its borders, and the armed forces, to protect him from aggressors outside. Beyond that, the government should not intrude upon his life, either to run his business, or adjust his daily activities, or prescribe his personal moral code.

Government, then, undertakes to be the individual's protector; but historically governments have gone far beyond this function. Since they already have the physical power, they have not hesitated to use it for purposes far beyond that which was entrusted to them in the first place. Undertaking initially to protect its citizens against aggression, it has often itself become an aggressor—a far greater aggressor, indeed, than the criminals against whom it was supposed to protect its citizens. Governments have done what no private citizen can do: arrest and imprison individuals without a trial and send them to slave labor camps. Government must have power in order to be effective—and yet the very means by which alone it can be effective make it vulnerable to the abuse of power, leading to managing the lives of individuals and even inflicting terror upon them.

What then should be the function of government? In a word, the *protection of human rights*.

1. *The right to life:* libertarians support all such legislation as will protect human beings against the use of force by others, for exam-

ple, laws against killing, attempting killing, maiming, beating, and all kinds of physical violence.

2. *The right to liberty:* there should be no laws compromising in any way freedom of speech, of the press, and peaceable assembly. There should be no censorship of ideas, books, films, or of anything else by government.

3. *The right to property:* libertarians support legislation that protects the property rights of individuals against confiscation, nationalization, eminent domain, robbery, trespass, fraud and misrepresentation, patent and copyright, libel and slander.

Someone has violently assaulted you. Should he be legally liable? Of course. He has violated one of your rights. He has knowingly injured you and since he has initiated aggression against you he should be made to expiate.

Someone has negligently left his bicycle on the sidewalk where you trip over it in the dark and injure yourself. He didn't do it intentionally; he didn't mean you any harm. Should he be legally liable? Of course; he has, however unwittingly, injured you, and since the injury is caused by him and you are the victim, he should pay.

Someone across the street is unemployed. Should you be taxed extra to pay for his expenses? Not at all. You have not injured him, you are not responsible for the fact that he is unemployed (unless you are a senator or bureaucrat who agitated for further curtailing of business, which legislation passed, with the result that your neighbor was laid off by the curtailed business). You may voluntarily wish to help him out, or better still, try to get him a job to put him on his feet again; but since you have initiated no aggressive act against him, and neither purposely nor accidentally injured him in any way, you should not be legally penalized for the fact of his unemployment. (Actually, it is just such penalties that increase unemployment.)

One man, A, works hard for years and finally earns a high salary as a professional man. A second man, B, prefers not to work at all, and to spend wastefully what money he has (through inheritance), so that after a

year or two he has nothing left. At the end of this time he has a long siege of illness and lots of medical bills to pay. He demands that the bills be paid by the government—that is, by the taxpayers of the land, including Mr. A.

But of course B has no such right. He chose to lead his life in a certain way—that was his voluntary decision. One consequence of that choice is that he must depend on charity in case of later need. Mr. A chose not to live that way. (And if everyone lived like Mr. B, on whom would he depend in case of later need?) Each has a right to live in the way he pleases, but each must live with the consequences of his own decision (which, as always, fall primarily on himself). He cannot, in time of need, claim A's beneficence as his right.

If a house-guest of yours starts to carve his initials in your walls and break up your furniture, you have a right to evict him, and call the police if he makes trouble. If someone starts to destroy the machinery in a factory, the factory-owner is also entitled to evict him and call the police. In both cases, persons other than the owner are permitted on the property only under certain conditions, at the pleasure of the owner. If those conditions are violated, the owner is entitled to use force to set things straight. The case is exactly the same on a college or university campus: if a campus demonstrator starts breaking windows, occupying the president's office, and setting fire to a dean, the college authorities are certainly within their rights to evict him forcibly; one is permitted on the college grounds only under specific conditions, set by the administration: study, peaceful student activity, even political activity if those in charge choose to permit it. If they do not choose to permit peaceful political activity on campus, they may be unwise, since a campus is after all a place where all sides of every issue should get discussed, and the college that doesn't permit this may soon lose its reputation and its students. All the same, the college official who does not permit it is quite within his rights; the students do not own the campus, nor do the hired troublemakers imported from elsewhere. In the case of a privately owned college, the owners, or whoever they have delegated to administer it, have the right to make the decisions as to who shall be permitted on the campus and under what conditions. In the case of a state university or college, the ownership problem is more complex: one could say that the "government" owns the campus or that "the people" do since they are the taxpayers who support it; but in either case, the university administration has the delegated task of keeping order, and until they are removed by the state administration or the taxpayers, it is theirs to decide who shall be permitted on campus, and what nonacademic activities will be permitted to their students on the premises.

Property rights can be violated by physical trespass, of course, or by anyone entering on your property for any reason without your consent. (If you *do* consent to having your neighbor dump garbage on your yard, there is no violation of your rights.) But the physical trespass of a person is only a special case of violation of property rights. Property rights can be violated by sound-waves, in the form of a loud noise, or the sounds of your neighbor's hi-fi set while you are trying to sleep. Such violations of property rights are of course the subject of action in the courts.

But there is another violation of property rights that has not thus far been honored by the courts; this has to do with the effects of *pollution* of the atmosphere.

From the beginnings of modern air pollution, the courts made a conscious decision not to protect, for example, the orchards of farmers from the smoke of nearby factories or locomotives. They said, in effect, to the farmers: yes, your private property is being invaded by this smoke, but we hold that "public policy" is more important than private property, and public policy holds factories and locomotives to be good things. These goods were allowed to override the defense of property rights—with our consequent headlong rush into pollution disaster. The remedy is both "radical" and crystal clear, and it has nothing to do with multibillion dollar palliative programs at the expense of the taxpayers which do not even

meet the real issue. The remedy is simply to enjoin anyone from injecting pollutants into the air, and thereby invading the rights of persons and property. Period. The argument that such an injunction prohibition would add to the costs of industrial production is as reprehensible as the pre-Civil War argument that the abolition of slavery would add to the costs of growing cotton, and therefore should not take place. For this means that the polluters are able to impose the high costs of pollution upon those whose property rights they are allowed to invade with impunity.[1]

What about automobiles, the chief polluters of the air? One can hardly sue every automobile owner. But one can sue the manufacturers of automobiles who do not install anti-smog devices on the cars which they distribute—and later (though this is more difficult), owners of individual automobiles if they discard the equipment or do not keep it functional.

The violation of rights does not apply only to air-pollution. If someone with a factory upstream on a river pollutes the river, anyone living downstream from him, finding his water polluted, should be able to sue the owner of the factory. In this way the price of adding the anti-pollutant devices will be the owner's responsibility, and will probably be added to the cost of the products which the factory produces and thus spread around among all consumers, rather than the entire cost being borne by the users of the river in the form of polluted water, with the consequent impossibility of fishing, swimming, and so on. In each case, pollution would be stopped at the source rather than having its ill effects spread around to numerous members of the population.

What about property which you do not work to earn, but which you *inherit* from someone else? Do you have a right to that? You have no right to it until someone decides to give it to you. Consider the man who willed it to you; it was his, he had the right to use and dispose of it as *he* saw fit; and if he decided to give it to you, this is a windfall for you, but it was only the exercise of *his* right. Had the property been seized by the government at the man's death, or distributed among numerous other people designated by the government, it *would* have been a violation of his rights: for he, who worked to earn and sustain it, would not have been able to dispose of it according to his own judgment. If he doesn't have the right to determine who shall have it, who does?

What about the property status of your intellectual activity, such as inventions you may devise and books you write? These, of course, are your property also; they are the products of your mind; you worked at them, you created them. Prior to that, they did not exist. If you worked five years to write a book, and someone stole it and published it as his own, receiving royalties from its sales, he would have stolen your property just as surely as if he had robbed your home. The same is true if someone used and sold without your permission an invention which was the product of your labor and ingenuity.

The role of government with respect to this issue, at least most governments of the Western world, is a proper one: government protects the products of your labor from the moment they materialize. Copyright law protects your writings from piracy. In the United States, one's writings are protected for a period of twenty-seven years, and another twenty-seven if one applies for renewal of the copyright. In most other countries, they are protected for a period of fifty years after the author's death, permitting both himself and his surviving heirs to reap the fruits of his labor. After that they enter the "public domain"—that is, anyone may reprint them without your or your heirs' permission. Patent law protects your inventions for a limited period, which varies according to the type of invention. In no case are you forced to avail yourself of this protection; you need not apply for patent or copyright coverage if you do not wish to do so. But the protection of your intellectual property is there, in case you wish to use it.

What about the property status of the airwaves? Here the government's position is far more questionable. The government now

claims ownership of the airwaves, leasing them to individuals and corporations. The government renews leases or refuses them depending on whether the programs satisfy authorities in the Federal Communications Commission. The official position is that "we all own the airwaves": but since only one party can broadcast on a certain frequency at a certain time without causing chaos, it is simply a fact of reality that "everyone" cannot use it. In fact the government decides who shall use the airwaves and one courts its displeasure only at the price of a revoked license. One can write without government approval, but one cannot use the airwaves without the approval of government.

What policy should have been observed with regard to the airwaves? Much the same as the policy that was followed in the case of the Homestead Act, when the lands of the American West were opening up for settlement. There was a policy of "first come, first served," with the government parcelling out a certain acreage for each individual who wanted to claim the land as his own. There was no charge for the land, but if a man had not used it and built a dwelling during the first two-year period, it was assumed that he was not homesteading and the land was given to the next man in line. The airwaves too could have been given out on a "first come, first served" basis. The first man who used a given frequency would be its owner, and the government would protect him in the use of it against trespassers. If others wanted to use the same frequency, they would have to buy it from the first man, if he was willing to sell, or try to buy another, just as one now does with the land.

Laws may be classified into three types: (1) laws protecting individuals against themselves, such as laws against fornication and other sexual behavior, alcohol, and drugs; (2) laws protecting individuals against aggressions by other individuals, such as laws against murder, robbery, and fraud; (3) laws requiring people to help one another; for example, all laws which rob Peter to pay Paul, such as welfare.

Libertarians reject the first class of laws

totally. Behavior which harms no one else is strictly the individual's own affair. Thus, there should be no laws against becoming intoxicated, since whether or not to become intoxicated is the individual's own decision: but there should be laws against driving while intoxicated, since the drunken driver is a threat to every other motorist on the highway (drunken driving falls into type 2). Similarly, there should be no laws against drugs (except the prohibition of sale of drugs to minors) as long as the taking of these drugs poses no threat to anyone else. Drug addiction is a psychological problem to which no present solution exists. Most of the social harm caused by addicts, other than to themselves, is the result of thefts which they perform in order to continue their habit—and then the *legal* crime is the theft, not the addiction. The actual cost of heroin is about ten cents a shot; if it were legalized, the enormous traffic in illegal sale and purchase of it would stop, as well as the accompanying proselytization to get new addicts (to make more money for the pusher) and the thefts performed by addicts who often require eighty dollars a day just to keep up the habit. Addiction would not stop, but the crimes would: it is estimated that 75 percent of the burglaries in New York City today are performed by addicts, and all these crimes could be wiped out at one stroke through the legalization of drugs. (Only when the taking of drugs could be shown to constitute a threat to *others*, should it be prohibited by law. It is only laws protecting people against *themselves* that libertarians oppose.)

Laws should be limited to the second class only: aggression by individuals against other individuals. These are laws whose function is to protect human beings against encroachment by others; and this, as we have seen, is (according to libertarianism) the sole function of government.

Libertarians also reject the third class of laws totally: no one should be forced by law to help others, not even to tell them the time of day if requested, and certainly not to give them a portion of one's weekly paycheck. Governments, in the guise of humanitarianism, have given to some by taking from others (charging a "handling fee" in the process, which, because of the government's waste and inefficiency, sometimes is several hundred percent). And in so doing they have decreased incentive, violated the rights of individuals and lowered the standard of living of almost everyone.

All such laws constitute what libertarians call *moral cannibalism*. A cannibal in the physical sense is a person who lives off the flesh of other human beings. A *moral* cannibal is one who believes he has a right to live off the "spirit" of other human beings—who believes that he has a moral claim on the productive capacity, time, and effort expended by others.

It has become fashionable to claim virtually everything that one needs or desires as one's *right*. Thus, many people claim that they have a right to a job, the right to free medical care, to free food and clothing, to a decent home, and so on. Now if one asks, apart from any specific context, whether it would be desirable if everyone had these things, one might well say yes. But there is a gimmick attached to each of them: *At whose expense?* Jobs, medical care, education, and so on, don't grow on trees. These are goods and services *produced only by men*. Who then is to provide them, and under what conditions?

If you have a right to a job, who is to supply it? Must an employer supply it even if he doesn't want to hire you? What if you are unemployable, or incurably lazy? (If you say "the government must supply it," does that mean that a job must be created for you which no employer needs done, and that you must be kept in it regardless of how much or little you work?) If the employer is forced to supply it at his expense even if he doesn't need you, then isn't *he* being enslaved to that extent? What ever happened to *his* right to conduct his life and his affairs in accordance with his choices?

If you have a right to free medical care, then, since medical care doesn't exist in nature as wild apples do, some people will have to supply it to you for free: that is, they will have to spend their time and money and energy taking care of you whether they want to or not. What ever happened to *their* right to conduct their lives as they see fit? Or do you have a right to violate theirs? Can there be a right to violate rights?

All those who demand this or that as a "free service" are consciously or unconsciously evading the fact that there is in reality no such thing as free services. All man-made goods and services are the result of human expenditure of time and effort. There is no such thing as "something for nothing" in this world. If you demand something free, you are demanding that other men give their time and effort to you without compensation. If they voluntarily choose to do this, there is no problem; but if you demand that they be *forced* to do it, you are interfering with their right not to do it if they so choose. "Swimming in this pool ought to be free!" says the indignant passerby. What he means is that others should build a pool, others should provide the material, and still others should run it and keep it in functioning order, so that *he* can use it without fee. But what right has he to the expenditure of *their* time and effort? To expect something "for free" is to expect it *to be paid for by others* whether they choose to or not.

Many questions, particularly about economic matters, will be generated by the libertarian account of human rights and the role of government. Should government have no role in assisting the needy, in providing social security, in legislating minimum wages, in fixing prices and putting a ceiling on rents, in curbing monopolies, in erecting tariffs, in guaranteeing jobs, in managing the money supply? To these and all similar questions the libertarian answers with an unequivocal no.

"But then you'd let people go hungry!" comes the rejoinder. This, the libertarian insists, is precisely what would not happen; with the restrictions removed, the economy would flourish as never before. With the controls taken off business, existing enterprises would expand and new ones would spring into existence satisfying more and more consumer needs; millions more people would be gainfully employed instead of subsisting on welfare, and all kinds of research and production, released from the stranglehold of government, would proliferate, fulfilling man's needs and desires as never before. It has always been so whenever government has permitted men to be free traders on a free market. But *why* this is so, and how the free market is the best solution to all problems relating to the material aspect of man's life, is another and far longer story.

NOTE

1. Murray Rothbard, "The Great Ecology Issue," *The Individualist*, 2, no. 2 (Feb. 1970), p. 5.

18

FROM LIBERTY TO WELFARE

James P. Sterba

Libertarians today are deeply divided over whether a night watchman state can be morally justified. Some, like Robert Nozick, hold that a night watchman state would tend to arise by an invisible-hand process if people generally respected each other's Lockean rights.[1] Others, like Murray Rothbard, hold that even the free and informed consent of all the members of a society would not justify such a state.[2] Despite this disagreement, libertarians are strongly united in opposition to welfare rights and the welfare state. According to Nozick, "the state may not use its coercive apparatus for the purpose of getting some citizens to aid others."[3] For Rothbard, "the libertarian position calls for the complete abolition of governmental welfare and reliance on private charitable aid."[4] Here I argue that this libertarian opposition to welfare rights and a welfare state is ill-founded. Welfare rights can be given a libertarian justification, and once this is recognized, a libertarian argument for a welfare state,

From *Social Theory and Practice*, Vol. 11, No. 3 (Fall 1985), 285–305. Reprinted by permission.

unlike libertarian arguments for the night watchman state, is both straightforward and compelling. . . .

Libertarians have defended their view in basically two different ways. Some libertarians, following Herbert Spencer, have 1) defined liberty as the absence of constraints, 2) taken a right to liberty to be the ultimate political ideal, and 3) derived all other rights from this right to liberty. Other libertarians, following John Locke, have 1) taken a set of rights, including, typically, a right to life or self-ownership and a right to property, to be the ultimate political ideal, 2) defined liberty as the absence of constraints in the exercise of these fundamental rights, and 3) derived all other rights, including a right to liberty, from these fundamental rights.

Each of these approaches has its difficulties. The principal difficulty with the first approach is that unless one arbitrarily restricts what is to count as an interference, conflicting liberties will abound, particularly in all areas of social life.[5] The principal difficulty with the second approach is that as long as a person's rights have not been violated, her liberty would not have been restricted either, even if she were kept in prison for the rest of her days.[6] I don't propose to try to decide between these two approaches. What I do want to show, however, is that on either approach welfare rights and a welfare state are morally required.

SPENCERIAN LIBERTARIANISM

Thus suppose we were to adopt the view of those libertarians who take a right to liberty to be the ultimate political ideal. According to this view, liberty is usually defined as follows:

The Want Conception of Liberty: Liberty is being unconstrained by other persons from doing what one wants.

This conception limits the scope of liberty in two ways. First, not all constraints whatever their source count as a restriction of liberty; the constraints must come from other persons. For example, people who are constrained by natural forces from getting to the top of Mount Everest do not lack liberty in this regard. Second, constraints that have their source in other persons, but that do not run counter to an individual's wants, constrain without restricting that individual's liberty. Thus, for people who do not want to hear Beethoven's Fifth Symphony, the fact that others have effectively proscribed its performance does not restrict their liberty, even though it does constrain what they are able to do.

Of course, libertarians may wish to argue that even such constraints can be seen to restrict a person's liberty once we take into account the fact that people normally want, or have a general desire, to be unconstrained by others. But other philosophers have thought that the possibility of such constraints points to a serious defect in this conception of liberty,[7] which can only be remedied by adopting the following broader conception of liberty:

The Ability Conception of Liberty: Liberty is being unconstrained by other persons from doing what one is able to do.

Applying this conception to the above example, we find that people's liberty to hear Beethoven's Fifth Symphony would be restricted even if they did not want to hear it (and even if, perchance, they did not want to be unconstrained by others) since other people would still be constraining them from doing what they are able to do. . . .

Of course, there will be numerous liberties determined by the Ability Conception that are not liberties according to the Want Conception. For example, there will be highly talented students who do not want to pursue careers in philosophy, even though no one constrains them from doing so. Accordingly, the Ability Conception but not the Want Conception would view them as possessing a liberty. And even though such liberties are generally not as valuable as those liberties that are common to both conceptions, they still are of some value, even when the manipulation of people's wants is not at issue.

Yet even if we accept all the liberties specified by the Ability Conception, problems of interpretation still remain. The major problem in this regard concerns what is to count as a constraint. On the one hand, libertarians would like to limit constraints to positive acts (that is, acts of commission) that prevent people from doing what they are otherwise able to do. On the other hand, welfare liberals and socialists interpret constraints to include, in addition, negative acts (that is, of omission) that prevent people from doing what they are otherwise able to do. In fact, this is one way to understand the debate between defenders of "negative liberty" and defenders of "positive liberty." For defenders of negative liberty would seem to interpret constraints to include only positive acts of others that prevent people from doing what they otherwise are able to do, while defenders of positive liberty would seem to interpret constraints to include both positive and negative acts of others that prevent people from doing what they are otherwise able to do.[8]

Suppose we interpret constraints in the manner favored by libertarians to include only positive acts by others that prevent people from doing what they are otherwise able to do, and let us consider a typical conflict situation between the rich and the poor.

In this conflict situation, the rich, of course, have more than enough resources to satisfy their basic needs. By contrast, the poor lack the resources to meet their most basic nutritional needs even though they have tried all the means available to them that libertarians regard as legitimate for acquiring such resources. Under circumstances like these, libertarians usually maintain that the rich should have the liberty to use their resources to satisfy their luxury needs if they so wish. Libertarians recognize that this liberty might well be enjoyed at the expense of the satisfaction of the most basic nutritional needs of the poor. Libertarians just think that a right to liberty always has priority over other political ideals, and since they assume that the liberty of the poor is not at stake in such conflict situations, it is easy for them to conclude that the rich should not be required to sacrifice their liberty so that the basic nutritional needs of the poor may be met.

From a consideration of the liberties involved, libertarians claim to derive a number of more specific requirements, in particular, a right to life, a right to freedom of speech, press and assembly, and a right to property.

Here it is important to observe that the libertarian's right to life is not a right to receive from others the goods and resources necessary for preserving one's life; it is simply a right not to be killed unjustly. Correspondingly, the libertarian's right to property is not a right to receive from others the goods and resources necessary for one's welfare, but rather a right to acquire goods and resources either by initial acquisition or by voluntary agreement.

Rights such as these, libertarians claim, can at best support only a limited role for government. That role is simply to prevent and punish initial acts of coercion—the only wrongful actions for libertarians. And, as we noted before, libertarians are deeply divided over whether a government with even such a limited role, that is, a night watchman state, can be morally justified.

Of course, libertarians would allow that it would be nice of the rich to share their surplus resources with the poor. Nevertheless, according to libertarians, such acts of charity should not be coercively required, because the liberty of the poor is not thought to be at stake in such conflict situations.

In fact, however, the liberty of the poor is at stake in such conflict situations. What is at stake is the liberty of the poor to take from the surplus possessions of the rich what is necessary to satisfy their basic nutritional needs. When libertarians are brought to see that this is the case, they are genuinely surprised, for they had not previously seen the conflict between the rich and the poor as a conflict of liberties.[9]

When the conflict between the rich and the poor is viewed as a conflict of liberties, we can either say that the rich should have the liberty to use their surplus resources for luxury purposes, or we can say that the poor should have the liberty to take from the rich what they require to meet their basic nutritional needs. If we choose one liberty, we must reject the other. What needs to be determined, therefore, is which liberty is morally preferable: the liberty of the rich or the liberty of the poor.

I submit that the liberty of the poor, which is the liberty to take from the surplus resources of others what is required to meet one's basic nutritional needs, is morally preferable to the liberty of the rich, which is the liberty to use one's surplus resources for luxury purposes. To see that this is the case we need only appeal to one of the most fundamental principles of morality, one that is common to all political perspectives, namely, the "ought" implies "can" principle. According to this principle, people are not morally required to do what they lack the power to do or what would involve so great a sacrifice that it would be unreasonable to ask them to perform such an action.[10] For example, suppose I promised to attend a departmental meeting on Friday, but on Thursday I am involved in a serious car accident which puts me into a coma. Surely it is no longer the case that I ought to attend the meeting now that I lack the power to do so. Or suppose instead that on Thursday I develop a severe case of pneumonia for which I am hospitalized. Surely I could claim that I no longer ought to attend the meeting on the grounds that the risk to my health involved in attending is a sacrifice that it would be unreasonable to ask me to bear.

Now applying the "ought" implies "can" principle to the case at hand, it seems clear that the poor have it within their power to willingly relinquish such an important liberty as the liberty to take from the rich what they require to meet their basic nutritional needs. Nevertheless, it would be unreasonable to ask them to make so great a sacrifice. In the extreme case, it would involve asking the poor to sit back and starve to death. Of course, the poor may have no real alternative to relinquishing this liberty. To do anything else may involve worse consequences for themselves and their loved ones and may invite a painful death. Accordingly, we may expect that the poor would acquiesce, albeit unwillingly, to a political system that denied them the welfare rights supported by such a liberty, at the same time that we recognize that such a system imposed an unreasonable sacrifice upon the poor—a sacrifice that we could not morally blame the poor for trying to evade.[11] Analogously, we might expect that a woman whose life was threatened would submit to a rapist's demands, at the same time that we recognize the utter unreasonableness of those demands.

By contrast, it would not be unreasonable to ask the rich to sacrifice the liberty to meet some of their luxury needs so that the poor can have the liberty to meet their basic nutritional needs. Of course, we might expect that the rich for reasons of self-interest and past contribution might be disinclined to make such a sacrifice. We might even suppose that the past contribution of the rich provides a good reason for not sacrificing their liberty to use their surplus for luxury purposes. Yet, unlike the poor, the rich could not claim that relinquishing such a liberty involved so great a sacrifice that it would be unreasonable to ask them to make it; unlike the poor, the rich could be morally blameworthy for failing to make such a sacrifice.

Consequently, if we assume that however else we specify the requirements of morality, they cannot violate the "ought" implies "can" principle, it follows that, despite what libertarians claim, the right to liberty endorsed by libertarians actually favors the liberty of the poor over the liberty of the rich.

Yet couldn't libertarians object to this conclusion, claiming that it would be unreasonable to ask the rich to sacrifice the liberty to meet some of their luxury needs so that the poor could have the liberty to meet their basic nutritional needs? As I have pointed out, libertarians don't usually see the situation as a conflict of liberties, but suppose they did. How plausible would such an objection be? Not very plausible at all, I think.

Consider this: what are libertarians going to say about the poor? Isn't it clearly unreasonable to ask the poor to sacrifice the liberty to meet their basic nutritional needs so that the rich can have the liberty to meet their luxury needs? Isn't it clearly unreasonable to ask the poor to sit back and starve to death? If it is, then there is no resolution of this conflict that would be reasonable to ask both the rich and the poor to accept. But that would mean that the libertarian ideal of liberty cannot be a moral ideal that resolves conflicts of interest in ways that it would be reasonable to ask everyone affected to accept. Therefore, as long as libertarians think of themselves as putting forth such a moral ideal, they cannot allow that it would be unreasonable both to ask the rich to sacrifice the liberty to meet some of their luxury needs in order to benefit the poor and to ask the poor to sacrifice the liberty to meet their basic nutritional needs in order to benefit the rich. But I submit that if one of these requests is to be judged reasonable, then, by any neutral assessment, it must be the request that the rich sacrifice the liberty to meet some of their luxury needs so that the poor can have the liberty to meet their basic nutritional needs; there is no other plausible resolution, if libertarians intend to be putting forth a moral ideal that reasonably resolves conflicts of interest.

But might not libertarians hold that putting forth a moral ideal means no more than being willing to universalize one's fundamental commitments? Surely we have no difficulty imagining the rich willing to universalize their commitments to relatively strong property rights. Yet, at the same time, we have no difficulty imagining the poor and their advocates willing to universalize their commitments to relatively weak property rights. Consequently, if the libertarian's moral ideal is interpreted in this fashion, it would not be able to provide a basis for reasonably resolving conflicts of interest between the rich and the poor. But without such a basis for conflict resolution, how could societies flourish, as libertarians claim they would, under a minimal state or with no state at all?[12] Surely, in order for societies to flourish in this fashion, the libertarian ideal must resolve conflicts of interest in ways that it would be reasonable to ask everyone affected to accept. But, as we have seen, that requirement can only be satisfied if the rich sacrifice the liberty to meet some of their luxury needs so that the poor can have the liberty to meet their basic nutritional needs.

It should also be noted that this case for restricting the liberty of the rich depends upon the willingness of the poor to take advantage of whatever opportunities are available to them for satisfying their basic needs by engaging in mutually beneficial work, so that failure of the poor to take advantage of such opportunities would normally either cancel or at least significantly reduce the obligation of the rich to restrict their own liberty for the benefit of the poor.[13] In addition, the poor would be required to return the equivalent of any surplus possessions they have taken from the rich once they are able to do so and still satisfy their basic needs. Nor would the poor be required to keep the liberty to which they are entitled. They could give up part of it, or all of it, or risk losing it on the chance of gaining a greater share of liberties or other social goods.[14] Consequently, the case for restricting the liberty of the rich for the benefit of the poor is neither unconditional, nor inalienable.

Even so, libertarians would have to be disconcerted about what turns out to be the practical upshot of taking a right to liberty to be the ultimate political ideal. For libertarians contend that their political ideal would support welfare rights only when constraints are "illegitimately" interpreted to include both positive and negative acts by others that prevent people from doing what they are otherwise able to do. By contrast, when constraints are interpreted to include only positive acts, libertarians contend, no such welfare rights can be justified.

Nevertheless, what the foregoing argument demonstrates is that this view is mistaken. For even when the interpretation of constraints favored by libertarians is employed, a moral assessment of the competing liberties still requires an allocation of liberties to the poor that will be generally sufficient to provide them with the goods and resources necessary for satisfying their basic nutritional needs.

One might think that once the rich realize that the poor should have the liberty not to be interfered with when taking from the surplus possessions of the rich what they require to satisfy their basic needs, it would be in the interest of the rich to stop producing any surplus whatsoever. Yet that would only be the case if first, the recognition of the rightful claims of the poor would exhaust the surplus of the rich and second, the poor would never be in a position to be obligated to repay what they appropriated from the rich. Fortunately for the poor both of these conditions are unlikely to obtain.

Of course, there will be cases where the poor fail to satisfy their basic nutritional needs, not because of any direct restriction of liberty on the part of the rich, but because the poor are in such dire need that they are unable even to attempt to take from the rich what they require to meet their basic nutritional needs. Accordingly, in such cases, the rich would not be performing any act of commission that prevents the poor from taking what they require. Yet, even in such cases, the rich would normally be performing acts of commission that prevent other persons from aiding the poor by taking from the surplus possessions of the rich. And when assessed from a moral point of view, restricting the liberty of these other persons would not be morally justified for the very same reason that restricting the liberty of the poor to meet their own basic nutritional needs would not be morally justified: it would not be reasonable to ask all of those affected to accept such a restriction of liberty. . . .

In brief, what this shows is that if a right to liberty is taken to be the ultimate political ideal, then, contrary to what libertarians claim, not only would a system of welfare rights be morally required, but also such a system would clearly benefit the poor.

LOCKEAN LIBERTARIANISM

Yet suppose we were to adopt the view of those libertarians who do not take a right to liberty to be the ultimate political ideal. According to this view, liberty is defined as follows:

The Rights Conception of Liberty. Liberty is being unconstrained by other persons from doing what one has a right to do.

The most important ultimate rights in terms of which liberty is specified are, according to

this view, a right to life understood as a right not to be killed unjustly and a right to property understood as a right to acquire goods and resources either by initial acquisition or voluntary agreement. In order to evaluate this view, we must determine what are the practical implications of these rights.

Presumably, a right to life understood as a right not to be killed unjustly would not be violated by defensive measures designed to protect one's person from life-threatening attacks. Yet would this right be violated when the rich prevent the poor from taking what they require to satisfy their basic nutritional needs? Obviously, as a consequence of such preventive actions poor people sometimes do starve to death. Have the rich, then, in contributing to this result, killed the poor, or simply let them die; and, if they have killed the poor, have they done so unjustly?

Sometimes the rich, in preventing the poor from taking what they require to meet their basic nutritional needs, would not in fact be killing the poor, but only causing them to be physically or mentally debilitated. Yet since such preventive acts involve resisting the life-preserving activities of the poor, when the poor do die as a consequence of such acts, it seems clear that the rich would be killing the poor, whether intentionally or unintentionally.

Of course, libertarians would want to argue that such killing is simply a consequence of the legitimate exercise of property rights, and hence, not unjust. But to understand why libertarians are mistaken in this regard, let us appeal again to that fundamental principle of morality, the "ought" implies "can" principle. In this context, the principle can be used to assess two opposing accounts of property rights. According to the first account, a right to property is not conditional upon whether other persons have sufficient opportunities and resources to satisfy their basic needs. This view holds that the initial acquisition and voluntary agreement of some can leave others, through no fault of their own, dependent upon charity for the satisfaction of their most basic needs. By contrast, according to the second account, initial acquisition and voluntary agreement can confer title of property on all goods and resources except those surplus goods and resources of the rich that are required to satisfy the basic needs of those poor who through no fault of their own lack opportunities and resources to satisfy their own basic needs.

Clearly, only the first of these two accounts of property rights would generally justify the killing of the poor as a legitimate exercise of the property rights of the rich. Yet it would be unreasonable to ask the poor to accept anything other than some version of the second account of property rights. Moreover, according to the second account, it does not matter whether the poor would actually die or are only physically or mentally debilitated as a result of such acts of prevention. Either result would preclude property rights from arising. Of course, the poor may have no real alternative to acquiescing to a political system modeled after the first account of property rights, even though such a system imposes an unreasonable sacrifice upon them—a sacrifice that we could not blame them for trying to evade. At the same time, although the rich would be disinclined to do so, it would not be unreasonable to ask them to accept a political system modeled after the second account of property rights—the account favored by the poor.

Consequently, if we assume that however else we specify the requirements of morality, they cannot violate the "ought" implies "can" principle, it follows that, despite what libertarians claim, the right to life and the right to property endorsed by libertarians actually support a system of welfare rights. . . .

Nevertheless, it might be objected that the welfare rights that have been established against the libertarian are not the same as the welfare rights endorsed by welfare liberals. We could mark this difference by referring to the welfare rights that have been established against the libertarian as "action welfare rights" and referring to the welfare rights endorsed by welfare liberals as both "action and recipient welfare rights." The significance of this difference is that a person's action welfare right can be violated only when other people through acts of commission interfere with a person's exercise of that right, whereas a person's action and recipient welfare right can be violated by such acts of commission and by acts of omission as well. However, this difference will have little practical import. For once libertarians come to recognize the legitimacy of action welfare rights, then in order not to be subject to the poor person's discretion in choosing when and how to exercise her action welfare right, libertarians will tend to favor two morally legitimate ways of preventing the exercise of such rights. First, libertarians can provide the poor with mutually beneficial job opportunities. Second, libertarians can institute adequate recipient welfare rights that would take precedence over the poor's action welfare rights. Accordingly, if libertarians adopt either or both of these ways of legitimately preventing the poor from exercising their action welfare rights, libertarians will end up endorsing the same sort of welfare institutions favored by welfare liberals.

Finally, once a system of welfare rights is seen to follow irrespective of whether one takes a right to liberty or rights to life and property as the ultimate political ideal, the justification for a welfare state become straightforward and compelling. For while it is at least conceivable that rights other than welfare rights could be adequately secured in a society without the enforcement agencies of a state, it is inconceivable that welfare rights themselves could be adequately secured without such enforcement agencies. Only a welfare state would be able to effectively solve the large-scale coordination problem necessitated by the provision of welfare. Consequently, once a system of welfare rights can be seen to have a libertarian justification, the argument for a welfare state hardly seems to need stating.[15]

NOTES

1. Robert Nozick, *Anarchy, State and Utopia* (New York: Basic Books, 1974), Part I.

2. Murray Rothbard, *The Ethics of Liberty* (Atlantic Highlands: Humanities Press, 1982), p. 230.

3. Nozick, *Anarchy, State and Utopia*, p. ix.

4. Murray Rothbard, *For a New Liberty* (New York: Collier Books, 1978), p. 148.

5. See, for example, James P. Sterba, "Neo-Libertarianism," *American Philosophical Quarterly* 15 (1978): 17–19; Ernest Loevinsohn, "Liberty and the Redistribution of Property," *Philosophy and Public Affairs* 6 (1977): 226–39; Zimmerman, "Coercive Wage Offers," *Philosophy and Public Affairs* 10 (1981): 121–45. To limit what is to count as coercive, Zimmerman claims that in order for P's offer to be coercive

(I)t must be the case that P does more than merely prevent Q *from taking from* P resources necessary for securing Q's strongly preferred preproposal situation; P must prevent Q *from acting on his own* (or with the help of others) *to produce or procure* the strongly preferred preproposal situation.

But this restriction seems arbitrary, and Zimmerman provides little justification for it. See David Zimmerman, "More on Coercive Wage Offers," *Philosophy and Public Affairs* 12 (1983): 67–68.

6. It might seem that this second approach could avoid this difficulty if a restriction of liberty is understood as the curtailment of one's prima facie rights. But in order to avoid the problem of a multitude of conflicting liberties, which plagues the first approach, the specification of prima facie rights must be such that they only can be overridden when one or more of them is violated. And this may involve too much precision for our notion of prima facie rights.

7. Isaiah Berlin, *Four Essays on Liberty* (New York: Oxford University Press, 1969), pp. XXXVIII–XL.

8. On this point, see Maurice Cranston, *Freedom* (New York: Basic Books, 1953), pp. 52–53; C. B. Macpherson, *Democratic Theory* (Oxford: Oxford University Press, 1973), p. 95; Joel Feinberg, *Rights, Justice and the Bounds of Liberty* (Princeton, Princeton University Press, 1980), Chapter 1.

9. See John Hospers, *Libertarianism*, (Los Angeles: Nash Publishing Co., 1971), Chapter 7.

10. Alvin Goldman, *A Theory of Human Action* (Englewood Cliffs: Prentice Hall, 1970), pp. 208–15; William Frankena, "Obligation and Ability," in *Philosophical Analysis* edited by Max Black (Ithaca, Cornell University Press, 1950), pp. 157–75.

Judging from some recent discussions of moral dilemmas by Bernard Williams and Ruth Marcus, one might think that the "ought" implies "can" principle would only be useful for illustrating moral conflicts rather than resolving them. (See Bernard Williams, *Problems of the Self* (Cambridge: Cambridge University Press, 1977), Chapters 11 and 12; Ruth Marcus, "Moral Dilemmas and Consistency" *The Journal of Philosophy* 80 (1980): 121–36. See also Terrance C. McConnell, "Moral Dilemmas and Consistency in Ethics," *Canadian Journal of Philosophy* 18 (1978): 269–87. But this is only true if one interprets the "can" in the principle to exclude only "what a person lacks the power to do." If one interprets the "can" to exclude in addition "what would involve so great a sacrifice that it would be unreasonable to ask the person to do it" then the principle can be used to resolve moral conflicts as well as state them. Nor would libertarians object to this broader interpretation of the "ought" implies "can" principle since they do not ground their claim to liberty on the existence of irresolvable moral conflicts.

11. See James P. Sterba, "Is There a Rationale for Punishment?" *The American Journal of Jurisprudence* 29 (1984): 29–44.

12. As further evidence, notice that those libertarians who justify a minimal state do so on the grounds that such a state would arise from reasonable disagreements concerning the application of libertarian rights. They do not justify the minimal state on the grounds that it would be needed to keep in submission large numbers of people who could not come to see the reasonableness of libertarian rights.

13. Obviously, the employment opportunities offered to the poor must be honorable and supportive of self-respect. To do otherwise would be to offer the poor the opportunity to meet some of their basic needs at the cost of denying some of their other basic needs.

14. The poor cannot, however, give up the liberty to which their children are entitled.

15. Of course, someone might still want to object to welfare states on the grounds that they "force workers to sell their labor" (see G. A. Cohen, "The Structure of Proletarian Unfreedom," *Philosophy and Public Affairs* 12 (1982): 3–33) and subject workers to "coercive wage offers." (See Zimmerman, "Coercive Wage Offers.") But for a defense of at least one form of welfare state against such an objection, see James P. Sterba, "A Marxist Dilemma for Social Contract Theory," *American Philosophical Quarterly* 21 (1981): 51–59.

19
A SOCIAL CONTRACT PERSPECTIVE

John Rawls

My aim is to present a conception of justice which generalizes and carries to a higher level of abstraction the familiar theory of the social contract as found, say in Locke, Rousseau, and Kant.[1] In order to do this we are not to think of the original contract as one to enter a particular society or to set up a particular form of government. Rather, the guiding idea is that the principles of justice for the basic structure of society are the object of the original agreement. They are the principles that free and rational persons concerned to further their own interests would accept in an initial position of equality as defining the fundamental terms of their association. These principles are to regulate all further agreements; they specify the kinds of social cooperation that can be entered into and the forms of government that can be established. This way of regarding the principles of justice I shall call justice as fairness.

Thus we are to imagine that those who engage in social cooperation choose together, in one joint act, the principles which are to assign basic rights and duties and to determine the division of social benefits. Men are to decide in advance how they are to regulate their claims against one another and what is to be the foundation charter of their society. Just as each person must decide by rational reflection what constitutes his good—that is, the system of ends which it is rational for him to pursue so a group of persons must decide once and for all what is to count among them as just and unjust. The choice which rational men would make in this hypothetical situation of equal liberty, assuming for the present that this choice problem has a solution, determines the principles of justice.

In justice as fairness the original position of equality corresponds to the state of nature in the traditional theory of the social contract. This original position is not, of course, thought of as an actual historical

Abridged from *A Theory of Justice* (1971), pp. 11–22, 60–65, 150–156, 302–303. Excerpted by permission of the publishers from *A Theory of Justice* by John Rawls. Cambridge, Mass.: Harvard University Press. Copyright © 1971 by the President and Fellows of Harvard College.

state of affairs, much less as a primitive condition of culture. It is understood as a purely hypothetical situation characterized so as to lead to a certain conception of justice.[2] Among the essential features of this situation is that no one knows his place in society, his class position or social status, nor does any one know his fortune in the distribution of natural assets and abilities, his intelligence, strength, and the like. I shall even assume that the parties do not know their conceptions of the good or their special psychological propensities. The principles of justice are chosen behind a veil of ignorance. This ensures that no one is advantaged or disadvantaged in the choice of principles by the outcome of natural chance or the contingency of social circumstances. Since all are similarly situated and no one is able to design principles to favor his particular condition, the principles of justice are the result of a fair agreement or bargain. For given the circumstances of the original position, the symmetry of everyone's relations to each other, this initial situation is fair between individuals as moral persons; that is, as rational beings with their own ends and capable, I shall assume, of a sense of justice. The original position is, one might say, the appropriate initial status quo, and thus the fundamental agreements reached in it are fair. This explains the propriety of the name "justice as fairness"; it conveys the idea that the principles of justice are agreed to in an initial situation that is fair. The name does not mean that the concepts of justice and fairness are the same, any more than the phrase "poetry as metaphor" means that the concepts of poetry and metaphor are the same.

Justice as fairness begins, as I have said, with one of the most general of all choices which persons might make together, namely with the choice of the first principles of a conception of justice which is to regulate all subsequent criticism and reform of institutions. Then, having chosen a conception of justice, we can suppose that they are to choose a constitution and a legislature to enact laws, and so on, all in accordance with the principles of justice initially agreed upon. Our social situation is just if it is such that by this sequence of hypothetical agreements we would have contracted into the general system of rules which defines it. Moreover, assuming that the original position does determine a set of principles (that is, that a particular conception of justice would be chosen), it will then be true that whenever social institutions satisfy these principles those engaged in them can say to one another that they are cooperating on terms to which they would agree if they were free and equal persons whose relations with respect to one another were fair. They could all view their arrangements as meeting the stipulations which they would acknowledge in an initial situation that embodies widely accepted and reasonable constraints on the choice of principles. The general recognition of this fact would provide the basis for a public acceptance of the corresponding principles of justice. No society can, of course, be a scheme of cooperation which men enter voluntarily in a literal sense; each person finds himself placed at birth in some particular position in some particular society, and the nature of this position materially affects his life prospects. Yet a society satisfying the principles of justice as fairness comes as close as a society can to being a voluntary scheme, for it meets the principles which free and equal persons would assent to under circumstances that are fair. In this sense its members are autonomous and the obligations they recognize self-imposed.

One feature of justice as fairness is to think of the parties in the initial situation as rational and mututally disinterested. This does not mean that the parties are egoists; that is, individuals with only certain kinds of interests, say in wealth, prestige, and domination. But they are conceived as not taking an interest in one another's interests. They are to presume that even their spiritual aims may be opposed, in the way that the aims of those of different religions may be opposed. Moreover, the concept of rationality must be interpreted as far as possible in the narrow sense, standard in economic theory, of taking the most effective means to given ends. I shall modify this concept to some extent . . . , but one must try to avoid introducing into it any controversial ethical elements. The initial situation must be characterized by stipulations that are widely accepted.

In working out the conception of justice as fairness one main task clearly is to determine which principles of justice would be chosen in the original position. To do this we must describe this situation in some detail and formulate with care the problem of choice which it presents. It may be observed, however, that once the principles of justice are thought of as arising from an original agreement in a situation of equality, it is an open question whether the principle of utility would be acknowledged. Offhand it hardly seems likely that persons who view themselves as equals, entitled to press their claims upon one another, would agree to a principle which may require lesser life prospects for some simply for the sake of a greater sum of advantages enjoyed by others. Since each desires to protect his interests, his capacity to advance his conception of the good, no one has a reason to acquiesce in an enduring loss for himself in order to bring about a greater net balance of satisfaction. In the absence of strong and lasting benevolent impulses, a rational man would not accept a basic structure merely because it maximized the algebraic sum of advantages irrespective of its permanent effects on his own basic rights and interests. Thus it seems that the principle of utility is incompatible with the conception of social cooperation among equals for mutual advantage. It appears to be inconsistent with the idea of reciprocity implicit in the notion of a well-ordered society. Or, at any rate, so I shall argue.

I shall maintain instead that the persons in the initial situation would choose two rather different principles: the first requires equality in the assignment of basic rights and duties, while the second holds that social and economic inequalities; for example, inequalities of wealth and authority; are just only if they result in compensating

benefits for everyone, and in particular for the least advantaged members of society. These principles rule out justifying institutions on the grounds that the hardships of some are offset by a greater good in the aggregate. It may be expedient but it is not just that some should have less in order that others may prosper. But there is no injustice in the greater benefits earned by a few provided that the situation of persons not so fortunate is thereby improved. The intuitive idea is that since everyone's well-being depends upon a scheme of cooperation without which no one could have a satisfactory life, the division of advantages should be such as to draw forth the willing cooperation of everyone taking part in it, including those less well situated. Yet this can be expected only if reasonable terms are proposed. The two principles mentioned seem to be a fair agreement on the basis of which those better endowed, or more fortunate in their social position, neither of which we can be said to deserve, could expect the willing cooperation of others when some workable scheme is a necessary condition of the welfare of all.[3] Once we decide to look for a conception of justice that nullifies the accidents of natural endowment and the contingencies of social circumstance as counters in quest for political and economic advantage, we are led to these principles. They express the result of leaving aside those aspects of the social world that seem arbitrary from a moral point of view.

The problem of the choice of principles, however, is extremely difficult. I do not expect the answer I shall suggest to be convincing to everyone. It is, therefore, worth noting from the outset that justice as fairness, like other contract views, consists of two parts: (1) an interpretation of the initial situation and of the problem of choice posed there, and (2) a set of principles which, it is argued, would be agreed to. One may accept the first part of the theory (or some variant thereof), but not the other, and conversely. The concept of the initial contractual situation may seem reasonable although the particular principles proposed are rejected. To be sure, I want to maintain that the most appropriate conception of this situation does lead to principles of justice contrary to utilitarianism and perfectionism, and therefore that the contract doctrine provides an alternative to these views. Still, one may dispute this contention even though one grants that the contractarian method is a useful way of studying ethical theories and of setting forth their underlying assumptions.

Justice as fairness is an example of what I have called a contract theory. Now there may be an objection to the term "contract" and related expressions, but I think it will serve reasonably well. Many words have misleading connotations which at first are likely to confuse. The terms "utility" and "utilitarianism" are surely no exception. They too have unfortunate suggestions which hostile critics have been willing to exploit; yet they are clear enough for those prepared to study utilitarian doctrine. The same should be true of the term "contract" applied to moral theories. As I have mentioned, to understand it one has to keep in mind that it implies a certain level of abstraction. In particular, the content of the relevant agreement is not to enter a given society or to adopt a given form of government, but to accept certain moral principles. Moreover, the undertakings referred to are purely hypothetical: a contract view holds that certain principles would be accepted in a well-defined initial situation.

The merit of the contract terminology is that it conveys the idea that principles of justice may be conceived as principles that would be chosen by rational persons, and that in this way conceptions of justice may be explained and justified. The theory of justice is apart, perhaps the most significant part, of the theory of rational choice. Furthermore, principles of justice deal with conflicting claims upon the advantages won by social cooperation; they apply to the relations among several persons or groups. The word "contract" suggests this plurality as well as the condition that the appropriate division of advantages must be in accordance with principles acceptable to all

parties. The condition of publicity for principles of justice is also connoted by the contract phraseology. Thus, if these principles are the outcome of an agreement, citizens have a knowledge of the principles that others follow. It is characteristic of contract theories to stress the public nature of political principles. Finally there is the long tradition of the contract doctrine. Expressing the tie with this line of thought helps to define ideas and accords with natural piety. There are then several advantages in the use of the term "contract." With due precautions taken, it should not be misleading.

A final remark. Justice as fairness is not a complete contract theory. For it is clear that the contractarian idea can be extended to the choice of more or less an entire ethical system; that is, to a system including principles for all the virtues and not only for justice. Now for the most part I shall consider only principles of justice and others closely related to them; I make no attempt to discuss the virtues in a systematic way. Obviously if justice as fairness succeeds reasonably well, a next step would be to study the more general view suggested by the name "rightness as fairness." But even this wider theory fails to embrace all moral relationships, since it would seem to include only our relations with other persons and to leave out of account how we are to conduct ourselves toward animals and the rest of nature. I do not contend that the contract notion offers a way to approach these questions, which are certainly of the first importance; and I shall have to put them aside. We must recognize the limited scope of justice as fairness and of the general type of view that it exemplifies. How far its conclusions must be revised once these other matters are understood cannot be decided in advance.

THE ORIGINAL POSITION AND JUSTIFICATION

I have said that the original position is the appropriate initial status quo which insures that the fundamental agreements reached in it are fair. This fact yields the name "justice as fairness." It is clear, then, that I want to say that one conception of justice is more reasonable than another, or justifiable with respect to it, if rational persons in the initial situation would choose its principles over those of the other for the role of justice. Conceptions of justice are to be ranked by their acceptability to persons so circumstanced. Understood in this way the question of justification is settled by working out a problem of deliberation: we have to ascertain which principles it would be rational to adopt given the contractual situation. This connects the theory of justice with the theory of rational choice.

If this view of the problem of justification is to succeed, we must, of course, describe in some detail the nature of this choice problem. A problem of rational decision has a definite answer only if we know the beliefs and interests of the parties, their relations with respect to one another, the alternatives between which they are to choose, the procedure whereby they make up their minds, and so on. As the circumstances are presented in different ways, correspondingly different principles are accepted. The concept of the original position, as I shall refer to it, is that of the most philosophically favored interpretation of this initial choice situation for the purposes of a theory of justice.

But how are we to decide what is the most favored interpretation? I assume, for one thing, that there is a broad measure of agreement that principles of justice should be chosen under certain conditions. To justify a particular description of the initial situation one shows that it incorporates these commonly shared presumptions. One argues from widely accepted but weak premises to more specific conclusions. Each of the presumptions should by itself be natural and plausible; some of them may seem innocuous or even trivial. The aim of the contract approach is to establish that taken together they impose significant bounds on acceptable principles of justice. The ideal outcome would be that these conditions determine a

unique set of principles; but I shall be satisfied if they suffice to rank the main traditional conceptions of social justice.

One should not be misled, then, by the somewhat unusual conditions which characterize the original position. The idea here is simply to make vivid to ourselves the restrictions that it seems reasonable to impose on arguments for principles of justice, and therefore on these principles themselves. Thus it seems reasonable and generally acceptable that no one should be advantaged or disadvantaged by natural fortune or social circumstances in the choice of principles. It also seems widely agreed that it should be impossible to tailor principles to the circumstances of one's own case. We should ensure further that particular inclinations and aspirations, and persons' conceptions of their good, do not affect the principles adopted. The aim is to rule out those principles that it would be rational to propose for acceptance, however little the chance of success, only if one knew certain things that are irrelevant from the standpoint of justice. For example, if a man knew that he was wealthy, he might find it rational to advance the principle that various taxes for welfare measures be counted unjust; if he knew that he was poor, he would most likely propose the contrary principle. To represent the desired restrictions one imagines a situation in which everyone is deprived of this sort of information. One excludes the knowledge of those contingencies which sets men at odds and allows them to be guided by their prejudices. In this manner the veil of ignorance is arrived at in a natural way. This concept should cause no difficulty if we keep in mind the constraints on arguments that it is meant to express. At any time we can enter the original position, so to speak, simply by following a certain procedure; namely, by arguing for principles of justice in accordance with these restrictions.

It seems reasonable to suppose that the parties in the original position are equal. That is, all have the same rights in the procedure for choosing principles; each can make proposals, submit reasons for their acceptance, and so on. Obviously the purpose of these conditions is to represent equality between human beings as moral persons, as creatures having a conception of their good and capable of a sense of justice. The basis of equality is taken to be similarity in these two respects. Systems of ends are not ranked in value; and each man is presumed to have the requisite ability to understand and to act upon whatever principles are adopted. Together with the veil of ignorance, these conditions define the principles of justice as those which rational persons concerned to advance their interests would consent to as equals when none are known to be advantaged or disadvantaged by social and natural contingencies.

There is, however, another side to justifying a particular description of the original position. This is to see if the principles which would be chosen match our considered convictions of justice or extend them in an acceptable way. We can note whether applying these principles would lead us to make the same judgments about the basic structure of society which we now make intuitively and in which we have the greatest confidence; or whether, in cases where our present judgments are in doubt and given with hesitation, these principles offer a resolution which we can affirm on reflection. There are questions which we feel sure must be answered in a certain way. For example, we are confident that religious intolerance and racial discrimination are unjust. We think that we have examined these things with care and have reached what we believe is an impartial judgment not likely to be distorted by an excessive attention to our own interests. These convictions are provisional fixed points which we presume any conception of justice must fit. But we have much less assurance as to what is the correct distribution of wealth and authority. Here we may be looking for a way to remove our doubts. We can check an interpretation of the initial situation, then, by the capacity of its principles to accommodate our firmest convictions and to provide guidance where guidance is needed.

In searching for the most favored description of this situation we work from both ends. We begin by describing it so that it represents generally shared and preferably weak conditions. We then see if these conditions are strong enough to yield a significant set of principles. If not, we look for future premises equally reasonable. But if so, and these principles match our considered convictions of justice, then so far well and good. But presumably there will be discrepancies. In this case we have a choice. We can either modify the account of the initial situation or we can revise our existing judgments, for even the judgments we take provisionally as fixed points are liable to revision. By going back and forth, sometimes altering the conditions of the contractual circumstances, at others withdrawing our judgments and conforming them to principle, I assume that eventually we shall find a description of the initial situation that both expresses reasonable conditions and yields principles which match our considered judgments duly pruned and adjusted. This state of affairs I refer to as reflective equilibrium.[4] It is an equilibrium because at last our principles and judgments coincide; and it is reflective since we know to what principles our judgments conform and the premises of their derivation. At the moment everything is in order. But this equilibrium is not necessarily stable. It is liable to be upset by further examination of the conditions which should be imposed on the contractual situation and by particular cases which may lead us to revise our judgments. Yet for the time being we have done what we can to render coherent and to justify our convictions of social justice. We have reached a conception of the original position.

I shall not, of course, actually work through this process. Still, we may think of the interpretation of the original position that I shall present as the result of such a hypothetical course of reflection. It represents the attempt to accommodate within one scheme both reasonable philosophical conditions on principles as well as our considered judgments of justice. In arriving at the favored interpretation of the initial situation there is no point at which an appeal is made to self-evidence in the traditional sense either of general conceptions or particular convictions. I do not claim for the principles of justice proposed that they are necessary truths or derivable from such truths. A conception of justice cannot be deduced from self-evident premises or conditions on principles; instead, its justification is a matter of the mutual support of many considerations, of everything fitting together into one coherent view.

A final comment. We shall want to say that certain principles of justice are justified because they would be agreed to in an initial situation of equality. I have emphasized that this original position is purely hypothetical. It is natural to ask why, if this agreement is never actually entered into, we should take any interest in these principles, moral or otherwise. The answer is that the conditions embodied in the description of the original position are ones that we do in fact accept. Or if we do not, then perhaps we can be persuaded to do so by philosophical reflection. Each aspect of the contractual situation can be given supporting grounds. Thus what we shall do is to collect together into one conception a number of conditions on principles that we are ready upon due consideration to recognize as reasonable. These constraints express what we are prepared to regard as limits on fair terms of social cooperation. One way to look at the idea of the original position, therefore, is to see it as an expository device which sums up the meaning of these conditions and helps us to extract their consequences. On the other hand, this conception is also an intuitive notion that suggests its own elaboration, so that led on by it we are drawn to define more clearly the standpoint from which we can best interpret moral relationships. We need a conception that enables us to envision our objective from afar: the intuitive notion of the original position is to do this for us. . . .

TWO PRINCIPLES OF JUSTICE

I shall now state in a provisional form the two principles of justice that I believe would be chosen in the original position. In this section I wish to make only the most general comments, and therefore the first formulation of these principles is tentative. As we go on I shall run through several formulations and approximate step by step the final statement to be given much later. I believe that doing this allows the exposition to proceed in a natural way.

The first statement of the two principles reads as follows:

First: each person is to have an equal right to the most extensive basic liberty compatible with a similar liberty for others.

Second: social and economic inequalities are to be arranged so that they are both (a) reasonably expected to be to everyone's advantage, and (b) attached to positions and offices open to all.

There are two ambiguous phrases in the second principle, namely "everyone's advantage" and "open to all." Determining their sense more exactly will lead to a second formulation of the principle. . . .

By way of general comment, these principles primarily apply, as I have said, to the basic structure of society. They are to govern the assignment of rights and duties and to regulate the distribution of social and economic advantages. As their formulation suggests, these principles presuppose that the social structure can be divided into two more or less distinct parts, the first principle applying to the one, the second to the other. They distinguish between those aspects of the social system that define and secure the equal liberties of citizenship and those that specify and establish social and economic inequalities. The basic liberties of citizens are, roughly speaking, political liberty (the right to vote and to be eligible for public office) together with freedom of speech and assembly; liberty of conscience and freedom of thought; freedom of the person along with the right to hold personal property;

and freedom from arbitrary arrest and seizure as defined by the concept of the rule of
law. These liberties are all required to be
equal by the first principle, since citizens of a
just society are to have the same basic rights.

The second principle applies, in the first
approximation, to the distribution of income and wealth and to the design of
organizations that make use of differences
in authority and responsibility, or chains of
command. While the distribution of wealth
and income need not be equal, it must be to
everyone's advantage, and at the same time,
positions of authority and offices of command must be accessible to all. One applies
the second principle by holding positions
open, and then, subject to this constraint,
arranges social and economic inequalities so
that everyone benefits.

These principles are to be arranged in a
serial order with the first principle prior to
the second. This ordering means that a
departure from the institutions of equal
liberty required by the first principle cannot
be justified by, or compensated for, by
greater social and economic advantages.
The distribution of wealth and income, and
the hierarchies of authority, must be consistent with both the liberties of equal citizenship and equality of opportunity.

It is clear that these principles are rather
specific in their content, and their acceptance rests on certain assumptions that I
must eventually try to explain and justify. A
theory of justice depends upon a theory of
society in ways that will become evident as
we proceed. For the present, it should be
observed that the two principles (and this
holds for all formulations) are a special case
of a more general conception of justice that
can be expressed as follows:

All social values—liberty and opportunity, income and wealth, and the bases of self-respect—
are to be distributed equally unless an unequal
distribution of any, or all, of these values is to
everyone's advantage.

Injustice, then, is simply inequalities that are
not to the benefit of all. Of course, this
conception is extremely vague and requires
interpretation.

As a first step, suppose that the basic
structure of society distributes certain primary goods, that is, things that every rational man is presumed to want. These
goods normally have a use whatever a person's rational plan of life. For simplicity,
assume that the chief primary goods at the
disposition of society are rights and liberties,
powers and opportunities, income and
wealth. (Later on . . . the primary good of
self-respect has a central place.) These are
the social primary goods. Other primary
goods such as health and vigor, intelligence
and imagination, are natural goods; although their possession is influenced by the
basic structure, they are not so directly
under its control. Imagine, then, a hypothetical initial arrangement in which all the social
primary goods are equally distributed: everyone has similar rights and duties, and income and wealth are evenly shared. This
state of affairs provides a benchmark for
judging improvements. If certain inequalities of wealth and organizational powers
would make everyone better off than in this
hypothetical starting situation, then they
accord with the general conception.

Now it is possible, at least theoretically,
that by giving up some of their fundamental
liberties men are sufficiently compensated
by the resulting social and economic gains.
The general conception of justice imposes
no restrictions on what sort of inequalities
are permissible; it only requires that everyone's position be improved. We need not
suppose anything so drastic as consenting to
a condition of slavery. Imagine instead that
men forgo certain political rights when the
economic returns are significant and their
capacity to influence the course of policy by
the exercise of these rights would be marginal in any case. It is this kind of exchange
which the two principles as stated rule out;
being arranged in serial order they do not
permit exchanges between basic liberties
and economic and social gains. The serial
ordering of principles expresses an underlying preference among primary social goods.

When this preference is rational so likewise is the choice of these principles in this order.

In developing justice as fairness I shall, for the most part, leave aside the general conception of justice and examine instead the special case of the two principles in serial order. The advantage of this procedure is that from the first the matter of priorities is recognized and an effort made to find principles to deal with it. One is led to attend throughout to the conditions under which the acknowledgment of the absolute weight of liberty with respect to social and economic advantages, as defined by the lexical order of the two principles, would be reasonable. Offhand, this ranking appears extreme and too special a case to be of much interest; but there is more justification for it than would appear at first sight. Or at any rate, so I shall maintain. . . . Furthermore, the distinction between fundamental rights and liberties and economic and social benefits marks a difference among primary social goods that one should try to exploit. It suggests an important division in the social system. Of course, the distinctions drawn and the ordering proposed are bound to be at best only approximations. There are surely circumstances in which they fail. But it is essential to depict clearly the main lines of a reasonable conception of justice; and under many conditions, anyway, the two principles in serial order may serve well enough. When necessary we can fall back on the more general conception.

The fact that the two principles apply to institutions has certain consequences. Several points illustrate this. First of all, the rights and liberties referred to by these principles are those that are defined by the public rules of the basic structure. Whether men are free is determined by the rights and duties established by the major institutions of society. Liberty is a certain pattern of social forms. The first principle simply requires that certain sorts of rules, those defining basic liberties, apply to everyone equally and that they allow the most extensive liberty compatible with a like liberty for all. The only reason for circumscribing the rights defining liberty and making men's freedom less extensive than it might otherwise be is that these equal rights as institutionally defined would interfere with one another.

Another thing to bear in mind is that when principles mention persons, or require that everyone gain from an inequality, the reference is to representative persons holding the various social positions, or offices, or whatever, established by the basic structure. Thus in applying the second principle I assume that it is possible to assign an expectation of well-being to representative individuals holding these positions. This expectation indicates their life prospects as viewed from their social station. In general, the expectations of representative persons depend upon the distribution of rights and duties throughout the basic structure. When this changes, expectations change. I assume, then, that expectations are connected: by raising the prospects of the representative man in one position we presumably increase or decrease the prospects of representative men in other positions. Since it applies to institutional forms, the second principle (or rather the first part of it) refers to the expectations of representative individuals. As I shall discuss below, neither principle applies to distributions of particular goods to particular individuals who may be identified by their proper names. The situation where someone is considering how to allocate certain commodities to needy persons who are known to him is not within the scope of the principles. They are meant to regulate basic institutional arrangements. We must not assume that there is much similarity from the standpoint of justice between an administrative allotment of goods to specific persons and the appropriate design of society. Our common sense intuitions for the former may be a poor guide to the latter.

Now the second principle insists that each person benefit from permissible inequalities in the basic structure. This means that it must be reasonable for each relevant representative man defined by this structure, when he views it as a going concern, to prefer his prospects with the inequality, to his prospects without it. One is not allowed to justify differences in income or organizational powers on the ground that the disadvantages of those in one position are outweighed by the greater advantages of those in another. Much less can infringements of liberty be counterbalanced in this way. Applied to the basic structure, the principle of utility would have us maximize the sum of expectations of representative men (weighted by the number of persons they represent, on the classical view); and this would permit us to compensate for the losses of some by the gains of others. Instead, the two principles require that everyone benefit from economic and social inequalities.

THE REASONING LEADING TO THE TWO PRINCIPLES OF JUSTICE

It will be recalled that the general conception of justice as fairness requires that all primary social goods be distributed equally unless an unequal distribution would be to everyone's advantage. No restrictions are placed on exchanges of these goods and therefore a lesser liberty can be compensated for by greater social and economic benefits. Now looking at the situation from the standpoint of one person selected arbitrarily, there is no way for him to win special advantages for himself. Nor, on the other hand, are there grounds for his acquiescing in special disadvantages. Since it is not reasonable for him to expect more than an equal share in the division of social goods, and since it is not rational for him to agree to less, the sensible thing for him to do is to acknowledge as the first principle of justice one requiring an equal distribution. Indeed, this principle is so obvious that we would expect it to occur to anyone immediately.

Thus, the parties start with a principle establishing equal liberty for all, including equality of opportunity, as well as an equal distribution of income and wealth. But there is no reason why this acknowledgment should be final. If there are inequalities in the basic structure that work to make everyone better off in comparison with the benchmark of initial equality, why not permit them? The immediate gain which a greater equality might allow can be regarded as intelligently invested in view of its future return. If, for example, these inequalities set up various incentives which succeed in eliciting more productive efforts, a person in the original position may look upon them as necessary to cover the costs of training and to encourage effective performance. One might think that ideally individuals should want to serve one another. But since the parties are assumed not to take an interest in one another's interests, their acceptance of these inequalities is only the acceptance of the relations in which men stand in the circumstances of justice. They have no grounds for complaining of one another's motives. A person in the original position would, therefore, concede the justice of these inequalities. Indeed, it would be short-sighted of him not to do so. He would hesitate to agree to these regularities only if he would be dejected by the bare knowledge or perception that others were better situated; and I have assumed that the parties decide as if they are not moved by envy. In order to make the principle regulating inequalities determinate, one looks at the system from the standpoint of the least advantaged representative man. Inequalities are permissible when they maximize, or at least all contribute to, the long-term expectations of the least fortunate group in society.

Now this general conception imposes no constraints on what sorts of inequalities are allowed, whereas the special conception, by putting the two principles in serial order (with the necessary adjustments in meaning), forbids exchanges between basic liberties and economic and social benefits. I shall not try to justify this ordering here. . . . But roughly, the idea underlying this ordering is that if the parties assume that their basic liberties can be effectively exercised, they will not exchange a lesser liberty for an improvement in economic well-being. It is only when social conditions do not allow the effective establishment of these rights that one can concede their limitation; and these restrictions can be granted only to the extent that they are necessary to prepare the way for a free society. The denial of equal liberty can be defended only if it is necessary to raise the level of civilization so that in due course these freedoms can be enjoyed. Thus in adopting a serial order we are in effect making a special assumption in the original position, namely, that the parties know that the conditions of their society, whatever they are, admit the effective realization of the equal liberties. The serial ordering of the two principles of justice eventually comes to be reasonable if the general conception is consistently followed. This lexical ranking is the long-run tendency of the general view. For the most part I shall assume that the requisite circumstances for the serial order obtain.

It seems clear from these remarks that the two principles are at least a plausible conception of justice. The question, though, is how one is to argue for them more systematically. Now there are several things to do. One can work out their consequences for institutions and note their implications for fundamental social policy. In this way they are tested by a comparison with our considered judgments of justice. . . . But one can also try to find arguments in their favor that are decisive from the standpoint of the original position. In order to see how this might be done, it is useful as a heuristic device to think of the two principles as the maximin solution to the problem of social justice. There is an analogy between the two principles and the maximin rule for choice under uncertainty.[5] This is evident from the fact that the two principles are those a person would choose for the design of a society in which his enemy is to assign him his place. The maximin rule tells us to rank alternatives by their worst possible outcomes: we are to adopt the alternative the worst outcome of which is superior to the worst outcomes of the others. The persons in the original position do not, of course, as-sume that their initial place in society is decided by a malevolent opponent. As I note below, they should not reason from false premises. The veil of ignorance does not violate this idea, since an absence of information is not misinformation. But that the two principles of justice would be chosen if the parties were forced to protect themselves against such a contingency explains the sense in which this conception is the maximin solution. And this analogy suggests that if the original position has been described so that it is rational for the parties to adopt the conser-vative attitude expressed by this rule, a conclusive argument can indeed be con-structed for these principles. Clearly the maximin rule is not, in general, a suitable guide for choices under uncertainty. But it is attractive in situations marked by certain special features. My aim, then, is to show that a good case can be made for the two princi-ples based on the fact that the original position manifests these features to the full-est possible degree, carrying them to the limit, so to speak.

Consider the gain-and-loss table below. It represents the gains and losses for a situa-tion which is not a game of strategy. There is no one playing against the person making the decision; instead he is faced with several possible circumstances which may or may not obtain. Which circumstances happen to exist does not depend upon what the person choosing decides or whether he announced his moves in advance. The numbers in the table are monetary values (in hundreds of dollars) in comparison with some initial situation. The gain (g) depends upon the individual's decision (d) and the circum-stances (c). Thus $g = f(d,c)$. Assuming that there are three possible decisions and three possible circumstances, we might have this gain-and-loss table.

Decisions	Circumstances		
	c_1	c_2	c_3
d_1	−7	8	12
d_2	−8	7	14
d_3	5	6	8

The maximin rule requires that we make the third decision. For in this case the worse that can happen is that one gains five hundred dollars, which is better than the worst for the other actions. If we adopt one of these we may lose either eight or seven hundred dollars. Thus, the choice of d_3 maximizes $f(d,c)$ for that value of c which for a given d, minimizes f. The term "maximin" means the *maximum minimorum;* and the rule directs our attention to the worst that can happen under any proposed course of action, and to decide in the light of that.

Now there appear to be three chief features of situations that give plausibility to this unusual rule.[6] First, since the rule takes no account of the likelihoods of the possible circumstances, there must be some reason for sharply discounting estimates of these probabilities. Offhand, the most natural rule of choice would seem to be to compute the expectation of monetary gain for each decision and then to adopt the course of action with the highest prospect. (This expectation is defined as follows: let us suppose that g_{ij} represent the numbers in the gain-and-loss table, where i is the row index and j is the column index; and let $p_i, j = 1, 2, 3$, be the likelihoods of the circumstances, with $\Sigma p_j = 1$. Then the expectation for the ith decision is equal to $\Sigma p_i g_{ij}$.) Thus it must be, for example, that the situation is one in which a knowledge of likelihoods is impossible, or at best extremely insecure. In this case it is unreasonable not to be skeptical of probabilistic calculations unless there is no other way out, particularly if the decision is a fundamental one that needs to be justified to others.

The second feature that suggests the maximin rule is the following: the person choosing has a conception of the good such that he cares very little, if anything, for what he might gain above the minimum stipend that he can, in fact, be sure of by following the maximin rule. It is not worthwhile for him to take a chance for the sake of a further advantage, especially when it may turn out that he loses much that is important to him. This last provision brings in the third feature; namely, that the rejected alternatives have outcomes that one can hardly accept. The situation involves grave risks. Of course these features work most effectively in combination. The paradigm situation for following the maximin rule is when all three features are realized to the highest degree. This rule does not, then, generally apply, nor of course is it self-evident. Rather, it is a maxim, a rule of thumb, that comes into its own in special circumstances. Its application depends upon the qualitative structure of the possible gains and losses in relation to one's conception of the good, all this against a background in which it is reasonable to discount conjectural estimates of likelihoods.

It should be noted, as the comments on the gain-and-loss table say, that the entries in the table represent monetary values and not utilities. This difference is significant since for one thing computing expectations on the basis of such objective values is not the same thing as computing expected utility and may lead to different results. The essential point, though, is that in justice as fairness the parties do not know their conception of the good and cannot estimate their utility in the ordinary sense. In any case, we want to go behind de facto preferences generated by given conditions. Therefore expectations are based upon an index of primary goods and the parties make their choice accordingly. The entries in the example are in terms of money and not utility to indicate this aspect of the contract doctrine.

Now, as I have suggested, the original position has been defined so that it is a situation in which the maximin rule applies. In order to see this, let us review briefly the nature of this situation with these three special features in mind. To begin with, the veil of ignorance excludes all but the vaguest knowledge of likelihoods. The parties have no basis for determining the probable nature of their society, or their place in it. Thus they have strong reasons for being wary of probability calculations if any other course is open to them. They must also take into account the fact that their choice of principles should seem reasonable to others, in particular their descendants, whose rights will be deeply affected by it. There are further grounds for discounting that I shall mention as we go along. For the present it suffices to note that these considerations are strengthened by the fact that the parties know very little about the gain-and-loss table. Not only are they unable to conjecture the likelihoods of the various possible circumstances, they cannot say much about what the possible circumstances are, much less enumerate them and foresee the outcome of each alternative available. Those deciding are much more in the dark than the illustration by a numerical table suggests. It is for this reason that I have spoken of an analogy with the maximin rule.

Several kinds of arguments for the two principles of justice illustrate the second feature. Thus, if we can maintain that these principles provide a workable theory of social justice, and that they are compatible with reasonable demands of efficiency, then this conception guarantees a satisfactory minimum. There may be, on reflection, little reason for trying to do better. Thus much of the argument . . . is to show, by their application to the main questions of social justice, that the two principles are a satisfactory conception. These details have a philosophical purpose. Moreover, this line of thought is practically decisive if we can establish the priority of liberty, the lexical ordering of the two principles. For this priority implies that the persons in the original position have no desire to try for greater gains at the expense of the equal liberties. The minimum assured by the two principles in lexical order is not one that the parties wish to jeopardize for the sake of greater economic and social advantages. . . .

Finally, the third feature holds if we can assume that other conceptions of justice may lead to institutions that the parties would find intolerable. For example, it has some-times been held that under some conditions the utility principle (in either form) justifies, if not slavery or serfdom, at any rate serious infractions of liberty for the sake of greater social benefits. We need not consider here the truth of this claim, or the likelihood that the requisite conditions obtain. For the moment, this contention is only to illustrate the way in which conceptions of justice may allow for outcomes which the parties may not be able to accept. And having the ready alternative of the two principles of justice which secure a satisfactory minimum, it seems unwise, if not irrational, for them to take a chance that these outcomes are not realized.

So much, then, for a brief sketch of the features of situations in which the maximin rule comes into its own and the way in which the arguments for the two principles of justice can be subsumed under them. . . .

THE FINAL FORMULATION OF THE PRINCIPLES OF JUSTICE

. . . I now wish to give the final statement of the two principles of justice for institutions. For the sake of completeness, I shall give a full statement including earlier formulations.

First Principle
Each person is to have an equal right to the most extensive total system of equal basic liberties compatible with a similar system of liberty for all.

Second Principle
Social and economic inequalities are to be arranged so that they are both:
(a) to the greatest benefit of the least advantaged, consistent with the just savings principle, and
(b) attached to offices and positions open to all under conditions of fair equality of opportunity.

First Priority Rule (The Priority of Liberty)
The principles of justice are to be ranked in lexical order and therefore liberty can be

restricted only for the sake of liberty. There are two cases:

> (a) a less extensive liberty must strengthen the total system of liberty shared by all;
> (b) a less than equal liberty must be acceptable to those with the lesser liberty.

Second Priority Rule (The Priority of Justice over Efficiency and Welfare)

The second principle of justice is lexically prior to the principle of efficiency and to that of maximizing the sum of advantages; and fair opportunity is prior to the difference principle. There are two cases:

> (a) an inequality of opportunity must enhance the opportunities of those with the lesser opportunity;
> (b) an excessive rate of saving must on balance mitigate the burden of those bearing this hardship.

General Conception

All social primary goods—liberty and opportunity, income and wealth, and the bases of self-respect—are to be distributed equally unless an unequal distribution of any or all of these goods is to the advantage of the least favored.

By way of comment, these principles and priority rules are no doubt incomplete. Other modifications will surely have to be made, but I shall not further complicate the statement of the principles. It suffices to observe that when we come to nonideal theory, we do not fall back straightway upon the general conception of justice. The lexical ordering of the two principles, and the valuations that this ordering implies, suggest priority rules which seem to be reasonable enough in many cases. By various examples I have tried to illustrate how these rules can be used and to indicate their plausibility. Thus the ranking of the principles of justice in ideal theory reflects back and guides the application of these principles to nonideal situations. It identifies which limitations need to be dealt with first. The drawback of the general conception of justice is that it lacks the definite structure of the two principles in serial order. In more extreme and tangled instances of nonideal theory there may be no alternative to it. At

some point the priority of rules for nonideal cases will fail; and indeed, we may be able to find no satisfactory answer at all. But we must try to postpone the day of reckoning as long as possible, and try to arrange society so that it never comes. . . .

NOTES

1. As the text suggests, I shall regard Locke's *Second Treatise of Government,* Rousseau's *The Social Contract,* and Kant's ethical works beginning with *The Foundations of the Metaphysics of Morals* as definitive of the contract tradition. For all of its greatness, Hobbes's *Leviathan* raises special problems. A general historical survey is provided by J. W. Gough, *The Social Contract,* 2nd ed. (Oxford, The Clarendon Press, 1957), and Otto Gierke, *Natural Law and the Theory of Society,* trans. with an introduction by Ernest Barker (Cambridge, The University Press, 1934). A presentation of the contract view as primarily an ethical theory is to be found in G. R. Grice, *The Grounds of Moral Judgment* (Cambridge: The University Press, 1967).

2. Kant is clear that the original agreement is hypothetical. See *The Metaphysics of Morals,* pt. I (*Rechtslehre*), especially §§ 47, 52; and pt. II of the essay "Concerning the Common Saying: This May Be True in Theory but It Does Not Apply in Practice," in *Kant's Political Writings,* ed. Hans Reiss and trans. by H. B. Nisbet (Cambridge, The University Press, 1970), pp. 73–87. See Georges Vlachos, *Le Pensée politique de Kant* (Paris, Presses Universitaires de France, 1962), pp. 326–335; and J. G. Murphy, *Kant: The Philosophy of Right* (London, Macmillan, 1970), pp. 109–112, 133–136, for a further discussion.

3. For the formulation of this intuitive idea I am indebted to Allan Gibbard.

4. The process of mutual adjustment of principles and considered judgments is not peculiar to moral philosophy. See Nelson Goodman, *Fact, Fiction, and Forecast* (Cambridge, Mass., Harvard University Press, 1965), pp. 65–68, for parallel remarks concerning the justification of the principles of deductive and inductive inference.

5. An accessible discussion of this and other rules of choice under uncertainty can be found in W. J. Baumol, *Economic Theory and Operations*

Analysis, 2nd ed. (Englewood Cliffs, N.J., Prentice-Hall, 1965), ch. 24. Baumol gives a geometric interpretation of these rules, including the diagram used . . . to illustrate the difference principle. See pp. 558–562. See also R. D. Luce and Howard Raiffa, *Games and Decisions* (New York, John Wiley and Sons, Inc., 1957, ch. XIII, for a fuller account.

6. Here I borrow from William Fellner, *Probability and Profit* (Homewood, Ill., Richard D. Irwin, 1965), pp. 140–142, where these features are noted.

20
ETHICAL THEORY AND UTILITARIANISM

R. M. Hare

Contemporary moral philosophy (and the British is no exception) is in a phase which must seem curious to anybody who has observed its course since, say, the 1940s. During all that time moral philosophers of the analytic tradition have devoted most of their work to fundamental questions about the analysis or the meaning of the moral words and the types of reasoning that are valid on moral questions. It may be that some of them were attracted by the intrinsic theoretical interest of this branch of philosophical logic; and indeed it is interesting. But it may surely be said that the greater part, like myself, studied these questions with an ulterior motive: they saw this study as the philosopher's main contribution to the solution of practical moral problems such as trouble most of us. For if we do not understand the very terms in which the problems are posed, how shall we ever get to the root of them? I, at least, gave evidence of

this motive in my writings and am publishing many papers on practical questions.[1] But, now that philosophers in greater numbers have woken up to the need for such a contribution, and whole new journals are devoted to the practical applications of philosophy, what do we find the philosophers doing? In the main they proceed as if nothing had been learnt in the course of all that analytical enquiry—as if we had become no clearer now than in, say, 1936, or even 1903, how good moral arguments are to be distinguished from bad.

I cannot believe that we need be so pessimistic; nor that I am alone in thinking that logic can help with moral argument. But surprisingly many philosophers, as soon as they turn their hands to a practical question, forget all about their peculiar art, and think that the questions of the market place can be solved only by the methods of the market place—i.e. by a combination of prejudice (called intuition) and rhetoric. The philosopher's special contribution to such discussions lies in the ability that he ought to possess to clarify the concepts that

From *Contemporary British Philosophy*, edited by H. D. Lewis, London: Allen and Unwin, 1976. Reprinted by permission of the author.

are being employed (above all the moral concepts themselves) and thus, by revealing their logical properties, to expose fallacies and put valid arguments in their stead. This he cannot do unless he has an understanding (dare I say a theory?) of the moral concepts; and that is what we have been looking for all these years. And yet we find philosophers writing in such a way that it is entirely unclear what understanding they have of the moral concepts or of the rules of moral reasoning.[2] It is often hard to tell whether they are naturalists, relying on supposed equivalences between moral and non-moral concepts, or intuitionists, whose only appeal is to whatever moral sentiments they can get their readers to share with them. Most of them seem to be some sort of descriptivists; but as they retreat through an ever vaguer naturalism into a hardly avowed intuitionism, it becomes more and more obscure what, in their view, moral statements say, and therefore how we could decide whether to accept them or not. Philosophy, as a rational discipline, has been left behind.

It is the object of this paper to show how a theory about the meanings of the moral words can be the foundation for a theory of normative moral reasoning. The conceptual theory is of a nondescriptivist but nevertheless rationalist sort.[3] That this sort of theory could claim to provide the basis of an account of moral reasoning will seem paradoxical only to the prejudiced and to those who have not read Kant. It is precisely that sort of prejudice which has led to the troubles I have been complaining of: the belief that only a descriptivist theory can provide a rational basis for morality, and that therefore it is better to explore any blind alley than expose oneself to the imputation of irrationalism and subjectivism by becoming a non-descriptivist.

The normative theory that I shall advocate has close analogies with utilitarianism, and I should not hesitate to call it utilitarian, were it not that this name covers a wide variety of views, all of which have been the victims of prejudices rightly excited by the cruder among them. In calling my own normative theory utilitarian, I beg the reader to look at the theory itself, and ask whether it cannot avoid the objections that have been made against other kinds of utilitarianism. I hope to show in this paper that it can avoid at least some of them. But if I escape calumny while remaining both a non-descriptivist and a utilitarian, it will be a marvel.

In my review of Professor Rawls's book[4] I said that there were close formal similarities between rational contractor theories such as Rawls's, ideal observer theories such as have been advocated by many writers[5] and my own universal prescriptivist theory. I also said that theories of this form can be made to lead very naturally to a kind of utilitarianism, and that Rawls avoided this outcome only by a very liberal use of intuitions to make his rational contractors come to a non-utilitarian contract. Rawls advocates his theory as an alternative to utilitarianism. Whether the system which I shall sketch is to be regarded as utilitarian or not is largely a matter of terminology. The form of argument which it employs is, as I have already said, formally extremely similar to Rawls's; the substantive conclusions are, however, markedly different. I should like to think of my view as, in Professor Brandt's expression, 'a credible form of utilitarianism';[6] no doubt Rawls would classify it as an incredible form of utilitarianism; others might say that it is a compromise between his views and more ordinary kinds of utilitarianism. This does not much matter.

I try to base myself, unlike Rawls, entirely on the formal properties of the moral concepts as revealed by the logical study of moral language; and in particular on the features of prescriptivity and universalisability which I think moral judgements, in the central uses which we shall be considering, all have. These two features provide a framework for moral reasoning which is formally similar to Rawls's own more dramatic machinery. But, rather than put the argument in his way, I will do overtly what he does covertly—that is to say, I do not speculate about what some fictitious rational contractors *would* judge if they were put in a certain position subject to certain restrictions; rather, I subject myself to certain (formally analogous) restrictions and put myself (imaginatively) in this position, as Rawls in effect does,[7] and *do* some judging. Since the position and the restrictions are formally analogous, this ought to make no difference.

In this position, I am prescribing universally for all situations just like the one I am considering; and thus for all such situations, *whatever* role, among those in the situations, I might myself occupy. I shall therefore give equal weight to the equal interests of the occupants of all the roles in the situation; and, since any of these occupants might be myself, this weight will be positive. Thus the impartiality which is the purpose of Rawls's 'veil of ignorance' is achieved by purely formal means; and so is the purpose of his insistence that his contractors be rational, i.e. prudent. We have therefore, by consideration of the logic of the moral concepts alone, put ourselves in as strong a position as Rawls hopes to put himself by his more elaborate, but at the same time, as I have claimed, less firmly based apparatus.

Let us now use these tools. Rawls himself says that an ideal observer theory leads to utilitarianism; and the same ought to be true of the formal apparatus which I have just sketched. How does giving equal weight to the equal interests of all the parties lead to utilitarianism? And to what kind of utilitarianism does it lead? If I am trying to give equal weight to the equal interests of all the parties in a situation, I must, it seems, regard a benefit or harm done to one party as of equal value or disvalue to an equal benefit or harm done to any other party. This seems to mean that I shall promote the interests of the parties most, while giving equal weight to them all, if I maximise the total benefits over the entire population; and this is the classical principle of utility. For fixed populations it is practically equivalent to the average utility principle which bids us maximise not total but average utility; when the size of the population is itself affected by a decision, the two princi-

ples diverge, and I have given reasons in my review of Rawls's book for preferring the classical or total utility principle. In these calculations, benefits are to be taken to include the reduction of harms.

I am not, however, going to put my theory in terms of benefits and the reduction of harms, because this leads to difficulties that I wish to avoid. Let us say, rather, that what the principle of utility requires of me is to do for each man affected by my actions what I wish were done for me in the hypothetical circumstances that I were in precisely his situation; and, if my actions affect more than one man (as they nearly always will) to do what I wish, all in all, to be done for me in the hypothetical circumstances that I occupied all their situations (not of course at the same time but, shall we say?, in random order). This way of putting the matter, which is due to C. I. Lewis,[8] emphasises that I have to give the same weight to everybody's equal interests; and we must remember that, in so far as I am one of the people affected (as in nearly all cases I am) my own interests have to be given the same, and no more, weight—that is to say, my own actual situation is one of those that I have to suppose myself occupying in this random order.

Some further notes on this suggestion will be in place here. First, it is sometimes alleged that justice has to be at odds with utility. But if we ask how we are to be just between the competing interests of different people, it seems hard to give any other answer than that it is by giving equal weight, impartially, to the equal interests of everybody. And this is precisely what yields the utility principle. It does not necessarily yield equality in the resulting distribution. There are, certainly, very good utilitarian reasons for seeking equality in distribution too; but justice is something distinct. The utilitarian is sometimes said to be indifferent between equal and unequal distributions, provided that total utility is equal. This is so; but it conceals two important utilitarian grounds for a fairly high degree of equality of actual goods (tempered, of course, as in most systems including Rawls's, by various advantages that are secured by moderate inequalities). The first is the diminishing marginal utility of all commodities and of money, which means that approaches towards equality will tend to increase total utility. The second is that inequalities tend to produce, at any rate in educated societies, envy, hatred and malice, whose disutility needs no emphasising. I am convinced that when these two factors are taken into account, utilitarians have no need to fear the accusation that they could favour extreme inequalities of distribution in actual modern societies. Fantastic hypothetical cases can no doubt be invented in which they would have to favour them; but, as we shall see, this is an illegitimate form of argument.

Secondly, the transition from a formulation in terms of interests to one in terms of desires or prescriptions, or vice versa, is far from plain sailing. Both formulations raise problems which are beyond the scope of this paper. If we formulate utilitarianism in terms of interests, we have the problem of determining what are someone's true interests. Even if we do not confuse the issue, as some do, by introducing moral considerations into this prudential question (i.e. by alleging that becoming morally better, or worse, in itself affects a man's interests),[9] we still have to find a way of cashing statements about interests in terms of such states of mind as likings, desires, etc., both actual and hypothetical. For this reason a formulation directly in terms of these states of mind ought to be more perspicuous. But two different problems remain: the first is that of how present desires and likings are to be balanced against future, and actual desires and likings against those which would be experienced if certain alternative actions were taken; the second is whether desires need to be mentioned at all in a formulation of utilitarianism, or whether likings by themselves will do. It would seem that if we arrive at utilitarianism via universal prescriptivism, as I am trying to do, we shall favour the former of the last pair of alternatives; for desires, in the required sense, are assents to

prescriptions. All these are questions within the theory of prudence, with which, although it is an essential adjunct to normative moral theory, I do not hope to deal in this paper.[10]

I must mention, however, that when I said above that I have to do for each man affected by my actions what I wish were done for me, etc., I was speaking inaccurately. When I do the judging referred to on pages 191–2, I have to do it as rationally as possible. This, if I am making a moral judgement, involves prescribing universally; but in prescribing (albeit universally) I cannot, if rational, ignore prudence altogether, but have to universalise this prudence. Put more clearly, this means that, whether I am prescribing in my own interest or in someone else's (see the next paragraph), I must ask, not what I or he does actually at present wish, but what, prudentially speaking, we should wish. It is from this rational point of view (in the prudential sense of 'rational') that I have to give my universal prescriptions. In other words, it is *qua* rational that I have to judge; and this involves at least judging with a clear and unconfused idea of what I am saying and what the actual consequences of the prescription that I am issuing would be, for myself and others. It also involves, when I am considering the desires of others, considering what they would be if those others were perfectly prudent—i.e. desired what they would desire if they were fully informed and unconfused. Thus morality, at least for the utilitarian, can only be founded on prudence, which has then to be universalised. All this we shall have to leave undiscussed, remembering, however, that when, in what follows, I say 'desire', 'prescribe', etc., I mean 'desire, prescribe, etc., from the point of view of one who is prudent so far as his own interest goes'. It is important always to supply this qualification whether I am speaking of our own desires or those of others; but I shall omit it from now on because it would make my sentences intolerably cumbrous, and signalise the omission, in the next paragraph only, by adding the subscript '$_p$' to the words 'desire', etc., as required, omitting even this subscript thereafter. I hope that one paragraph will suffice to familiarise the reader with this point.

Thirdly, when we speak of the 'situations' of the various parties, we have to include in the situations all the $desires_p$, $likings_p$, etc., that the people have in them—that is to say, I am to do for the others what I wish to be done for me were I to have their $likings_p$, etc., and not those which I now have. And, similarly, I am not to take into account (when I ask what I $wish_p$ should be done to me in a certain situation) my own present $desires_p$, $likings_p$, etc. There is one exception to this: I have said that one of the situations that I have to consider is my own present situation; I have to $love_p$ my neighbour *as*, but *no more than* and *no less than*, myself, and likewise to do to others *as* I $wish_p$ them to do to me. Therefore just as, when I am considering what I $wish_p$ to be done to me were I in X's situation, where X is somebody else, I have to think of the situation as including *his* $desires_p$, $likings_p$, etc., and discount my own, so, in the single case where X is myself, I have to take into account *my* $desires_p$, $likings_p$, etc. In other words, *qua* author of the moral decision I have to discount my own $desires_p$, etc., and consider only the $desires_p$, etc., of the affected party; but where (as normally) I am one of the affected parties, I have to consider my own $desires_p$, etc., *qua* affected party, on equal terms with those of all the other affected parties.[11]

It will be asked: if we strip me, *qua* author of the moral decision, of all desires and likings, how is it determined what decision I shall come to? The answer is that it is determined by the desires and likings of those whom I take into account as affected parties (including, as I said, myself, but only *qua* affected party and not *qua* author). I am to ask, indeed, what I *do* wish should be done for me, were I in their situations; but were I in their situations, I should have their desires, etc., so I must forget about my own present desires (with the exception just made) and consider only the desires which

they have; and if I do this, what I *do* wish for will be the satisfaction of *those* desires; that, therefore, is what I shall prescribe, so far as is possible.

I wish to point out that my present formulation enables me to deal in an agreeably clear way with the problem of the fanatic, who has given me so much trouble in the past.[12] In so far as, in order to prescribe universally, I have to strip away (*qua* author of the moral decision) all my present desires, etc., I shall have to strip away, among them, all the ideals that I have; for an ideal is a kind of desire or liking (in the generic sense in which I am using those terms); it is, to use Aristotle's word, an *orexis*.[13] This does not mean that I have to give up having ideals, nor even that I must stop giving any consideration to my ideals when I make my moral decisions; it means only that I am not allowed to take them into account *qua* author of the moral decision. I am, however, allowed to take them into account, along with the ideals of all the other parties affected, when I consider my own position, among others, as an affected party. This means that for the purposes of the moral decision it makes no difference *who has* the ideal. It means that we have to give impartial consideration to the ideals of ourselves and others. In cases, however, where the pursuit of our own ideals does not affect the ideals or the interests of others, we are allowed and indeed encouraged to pursue them.

All this being so, the only sort of fanatic that is going to bother us is the person whose ideals are so intensely pursued that the weight that has to be given to them, considered impartially, outbalances the combined weights of all the ideals, desires, likings, etc., that have to be frustrated in order to achieve them. For example, if the Nazi's desire not to have Jews around is intense enough to outweigh all the sufferings caused to Jews by arranging not to have them around, then, on this version of utilitarianism, as on any theory with the same formal structure, it ought to be satisfied. The problem is to be overcome by, first, pointing out that fanatics of this heroic stature are never likely to be encountered (that no *actual* Nazis had such intense desires is, I think, obvious); secondly, by remembering that, as I shall be showing in a moment, cases that are never likely to be actually encountered do not have to be squared with the thinking of the ordinary man, whose principles are not designed to cope with such cases. It is therefore illegitimate to attack such a theory as I have sketched by saying 'You can't ask us to believe that it would be right to give this fantastic fanatical Nazi what he wanted'; this argument depends on appealing to the ordinary man's judgement about a case with which, as we shall see, his intuitions were not designed to deal.

A similar move enables us to deal with another alleged difficulty (even if we do not, as we legitimately might, make use of the fact that all desires that come into our reasoning are desires$_p$, i.e. desires that a man will have after he has become perfectly prudent). It is sometimes said to be a fault in utilitarianism that it makes us give weight to bad desires (such as the desire of a sadist to torture his victim) solely in proportion to their intensity; received opinion, it is claimed, gives no weight at all, or even a negative weight, to such desires. But received opinion has grown up to deal with cases likely to be encountered; and we are most *un*likely, even if we give sadistic desires weight in accordance with their intensity, to encounter a case in which utility will be maximised by letting the sadist have his way. For first, the suffering of the victim will normally be more intense than the pleasure of the sadist. And, secondly, sadists can often be given substitute pleasures or even actually cured. And, thirdly, the side-effects of allowing the sadist to have what he wants are enormous. So it will be clear, when I have explained in more detail why fantastic cases in which these disutilities do not occur cannot legitimately be used in this kind of argument, why it is perfectly all right to allow weight to bad desires.

We have now, therefore, to make an important distinction between two kinds or 'levels' of moral thinking. It has some affinities with a distinction made by Rawls in his article 'Two Concepts of Rules'[14] (in which he was by way of defending utilitarianism), though it is not the same; it also owes something to Sir David Ross,[15] and indeed to others. I call it the difference between level-1 and level-2 thinking, or between the principles employed at these two levels.[16] Level-1 principles are for use in practical moral thinking, especially under conditions of stress. They have to be general enough to be impartable by education (including self-education), and to be 'of ready application in the emergency',[17] but are not to be confused with rules of thumb (whose breach excites no compunction). Level-2 principles are what would be arrived at by leisured moral thought in completely adequate knowledge of the facts, as the right answer in a specific case. They are universal but can be as specific (the opposite of 'general', not of 'universal'[18]) as needs be. Level-1 principles are inculcated in moral education; but the selection of the level-1 principles for this purpose should be guided by leisured thought, resulting in level-2 principles for specific considered situations, the object being to have those level-1 principles whose general acceptance will lead to actions in accord with the best level-2 principles in most situations that are actually encountered. Fantastic and highly unusual situations, therefore, need not be considered for this purpose.

I have set out this distinction in detail elsewhere;[19] here we only need to go into some particular points which are relevant. The thinking that I have been talking about so far in this paper, until the preceding paragraph, and indeed in most of my philosophical writings until recently, is level-2. It results in a kind of act-utilitarianism which, because of the universalisability of moral judgements, is practically equivalent to a rule-utilitarianism whose rules are allowed to be of any required degree of specificity. Such thinking is appropriate only to 'a cool hour', in which there is time for unlimited investigation of the facts, and there is no temptation to special pleading. It can use hypothetical cases, even fantastic ones. In principle it can, given superhuman knowledge of the facts, yield answers as to what should be done in any cases one cares to describe.

The commonest trick of the opponents of utilitarianism is to take examples of such thinking, usually addressed to fantastic cases, and confront them with what the ordinary man would think. It makes the utilitarian look like a moral monster. The anti-utilitarians have usually confined their own thought about moral reasoning (with fairly infrequent lapses which often go unnoticed) to what I am calling level 1, the level of everyday moral thinking on ordinary, often stressful, occasions in which information is sparse. So they find it natural to take the side of the ordinary man in a supposed fight with the utilitarian whose views lead him to say, if put at the disconcertingly unfamiliar standpoint of the archangel Gabriel, such extraordinary things about these carefully contrived examples.

To argue in this way is entirely to neglect the importance for moral philosophy of a study of moral education. Let us suppose that a fully-informed archangelic act-utilitarian is thinking about how to bring up his children. He will obviously not bring them up to practise on every occasion on which they are confronted with a moral question the kind of archangelic thinking that he himself is capable of; if they are ordinary children, he knows that they will get it wrong. They will not have the time, or the information, or the self-mastery to avoid self-deception prompted by self-interest; this is the real, as opposed to the imagined, veil of ignorance which determines our moral principles.

So he will do two things. First, he will try to implant in them a set of good general principles. I advisedly use the word 'implant'; these are not rules of thumb, but principles which they will not be able to break without the greatest repugnance, and whose breach by others will arouse in them the highest indignation. These will be the principles they will use in their ordinary level-1 moral thinking, especially in situations of stress. Secondly, since he is not always going to be with them, and since they will have to educate *their* children, and indeed continue to educate themselves, he will teach them, as far as they are able, to do the kind of thinking that he has been doing himself. This thinking will have three functions. First of all, it will be used when the good general principles conflict in particular cases. If the principles have been well chosen, this will happen rarely; but it will happen. Secondly, there will be cases (even rarer) in which, though there is no conflict between general principles, there is something highly unusual about the case which prompts the question whether the general principles are really fitted to deal with it. But thirdly, and much the most important, this level-2 thinking will be used to *select* the general principles to be taught both to this and to succeeding generations. The general principles may change, and should change (because the environment changes). And note that, if the educator were not (as we have supposed him to be) archangelic, we could not even assume that the best level-1 principles were imparted in the first place; perhaps they might be improved.

How will the selection be done? By using level-2 thinking to consider cases, both actual and hypothetical, which crucially illustrate, and help to adjudicate, disputes between rival general principles. But, because the general principles are being selected for use in actual situations, there will have to be a careful proportioning of the weight to be put upon a particular case to the probability of its actually occurring in the lives of the people who are to use the principles. So the fantastic cases that are so beloved of anti-utilitarians will have very little employment in this kind of thinking (except as a diversion for philosophers or to illustrate purely logical points, which is sometimes necessary). Fantastic unlikely cases will never be used to turn the scales as between rival general principles for practical use. The result will be a set of general principles, constantly evolving, but on the whole stable, such that their use in moral education, including self-education, and their consequent acceptance by the society at large, will lead to the nearest possible approximation to the prescriptions of archangelic thinking. They will be the set of principles with the highest acceptance-utility. They are likely to include principles of justice.

It is now necessary to introduce some further distinctions, all of which, fortunately, have already been made elsewhere, and can therefore be merely summarised. The first, alluded to already, is that between specific rule-utilitarianism (which is practically equivalent to universalistic act-utilitarianism) and general rule-utilitarianism.[20] Both are compatible with act-utilitarianism if their roles are carefully distinguished. Specific rule-utilitarianism is appropriate to level-2 thinking, general rule-utilitarianism to level-1 thinking; and therefore the rules of specific rule-utilitarianism can be of unlimited specificity, but those of general rule-utilitarianism have to be general enough for their role. The thinking of our archangel will thus be of a specific rule-utilitarian sort; and the thinking of the ordinary people whom he has educated will be for the most part of a general rule-utilitarian sort, though they will supplement this, when they have to and when they dare, with such archangelic thinking as they are capable of.

The second distinction is that between what Professor Smart[21] calls (morally) 'right' actions and (morally) 'rational' actions. Although Smart's way of putting the distinction is not quite adequate, as he himself recognises, I shall, as he does, adopt it for the sake of brevity. Both here, and in connexion with the 'acceptance-utility' mentioned above, somewhat more sophisticated calculations of probability are required than might at first be thought. But for simplicity let us say that an action is rational if it is the action most likely to be right, even if, when all the facts are known, as they were not when it was done, it turns out not to have been right. In such a society as we have described, the (morally) rational action will nearly always be that in accordance with the good general principles of level 1, because they have been selected precisely in order to make this the case. Such actions may not always turn out to have been (morally) right in Smart's sense when the cards are turned face upwards; but the agent is not to be blamed for this.

It is a difficult question, just how simple and general these level-1 principles ought to be. If we are speaking of the principles to be inculcated throughout the society, the answer will obviously vary with the extent to which the members of it are sophisticated and morally self-disciplined enough to grasp and apply relatively complex principles without running into the dangers we have mentioned. We might distinguish sub-groups within the society, and individuals within these sub-groups, and even the same individual at different stages, according to their ability to handle complex principles. Most people's level-1 principles become somewhat more complex as they gain experience of handling different situations, and they may well become so complex as to defy verbal formulation; but the value of the old simple maxims may also come to be appreciated. In any case, level-1 principles can never, because of the exigencies of their role, become as complex as level-2 principles are allowed to be.

A third distinction is that between good actions and the right action.[22] The latter is the action in accordance with level-2 principles arrived at by exhaustive, fully-informed and clear thinking about specific cases. A good action is what a good man would do, even if not right. In general this is the same as the morally rational action, but there may be complications, in that the motivation of the man has to be taken into account. The good (i.e. the morally well-educated) man, while he is sometimes able and willing to question and even to amend the principles he has been taught, will have acquired in his upbringing a set of motives and dispositions such that breaking these principles goes very much against the grain for him. The very goodness of his character will make him sometimes do actions which do not conform to archangelic prescriptions. This may be for one of at least two reasons. The first is that when he did them he was not fully informed and perhaps knew it, and knew also his own moral and intellectual weaknesses, and therefore (humbly and correctly) thought it morally rational to abide by his level-1 principles, and thus did something which turned out in the event not to be morally right. The second is that, although he could have known that the morally rational action was on this unusual occasion one in breach of his ingrained principles (it required him, say, to let down his closest friend), he found it so much against the grain that he just could not bring himself to do it. In the first case what he did was both rational and a morally good action. In the second case it was morally good but misguided—a wrong and indeed irrational act done from the best of motives. And no doubt there are other possibilities.

The situation I have been describing is a somewhat stylised model of our own, except that we had no archangel to educate us, but rely on the deliverances, not even of philosopher kings, but of Aristotelian *phronimoi* of very varying degrees of excellence. What will happen if a lot of moral philosophers are let loose on this situation? Level-1 thinking forms the greater part of the moral thinking of good men, and perhaps the whole of the moral thinking of good men who have nothing of the philosopher in them, including some of our philosophical colleagues. Such are the intuitionists, to whom their good ingrained principles seem to be sources of unquestionable knowledge. Others of a more enquiring bent will ask why they should accept these intuitions, and, getting no satisfactory answer, will come to the conclusion that the received principles have no ground at all and that the only way to decide what you ought to do is to reason it out on each occasion. Such people will at best become a crude kind of act-utilitarians. Between these two sets of philosophers there will be the sort of ludicrous battles that we have been witnessing so

much of. The philosopher who understands the situation better will see that both are right about a great deal and that they really ought to make up their quarrel. They are talking about different levels of thought, both of which are necessary on appropriate occasions.

What kind of philosopher will this understanding person be? Will he be any kind of utilitarian? I see no reason why he should not be. For, first of all, level-2 thinking, which is necessary, is not only utilitarian but act-utilitarian (for, as we have seen, the specific rule-utilitarian thinking of this level and universalistic act-utilitarianism are practically equivalent). And there are excellent act-utilitarian reasons for an educator to bring up his charges to follow, on most occasions, level-1 thinking on the basis of a set of principles selected by high-quality level-2 thinking. This applies equally to self-education. So at any rate all acts that could be called educative or self-educative can have a solid act-utilitarian foundation. To educate oneself and other men in level-1 principles *is* for the best, and only the crudest of act-utilitarians fails to see this. There will also be good act-utilitarian reasons for *following* the good general principles in nearly all cases; for to do so will be rational, or most likely to be right; and even an act-utilitarian, when he comes to tell us how we should proceed when choosing what to do, can tell us to do what is *most probably* right, because we do not know, when choosing, what *is* right.

There will be occasions, as I have said, when a man brought up (on good general principles) by a consistent act-utilitarian will do a rational act which turns out not to be right; and there will even be occasions on which he will do a good action which is neither rational nor right, because, although he could have known that it would be right on this unusual occasion to do an act contrary to the good general principles, he could not bring himself to contemplate it, because it went so much against the grain. And since one cannot pre-tune human nature all that finely, it may well be that the act-utilitarian educator will have to put up with the possibility of such cases, in the assurance that, if his principles are well chosen, they will be rare. For if he attempted to educate people so that they would do the rational thing in these cases, it could only be by incorporating into their principles clauses which might lead them, in other more numerous cases, to do acts most likely to be wrong. Moral upbringing is a compromise imposed by the coarseness of the pupil's discrimination and the inability of his human educators to predict with any accuracy the scrapes he will get into.

The exclusion from the argument of highly unusual cases, which I hope I have now achieved, is the main move in my defence of this sort of utilitarianism. There are also some subsidiary moves, some of which I have already mentioned, and all of which will be familiar. It is no argument against act-utilitarianism that in some unusual cases it would take a bad man to do what according to the utilitarian is the morally right or even the morally rational thing; good men are those who are firmly wedded to the principles which *on nearly all actual occasions* will lead them to do the right thing, and it is inescapable that on unusual occasions moderately good men will do the wrong thing. The nearer they approach archangelic status, the more, on unusual occasions, they will be able to chance their arm and do what they think will be the right act in defiance of their principles; but most of us ordinary mortals will be wise to be fairly cautious. As Aristotle said, we have to incline towards the vice which is the lesser danger for *us*, and away from that extreme which is to *us* the greater temptation.[23] For some, in the present context, the greater danger may be too much rigidity in the application of level-1 principles; but perhaps for more (and I think that I am one of them) it is a too great readiness to let them slip. It is a matter of temperament; we have to know ourselves (empirically); the philosopher cannot tell each of us which is the greater danger for him.

The moves that I have already made will, I think, deal with some other cases which are well known from the literature. Such are the case of the man who is tempted, on utilitarian grounds, to use electricity during a power crisis, contrary to the government's instructions; and the case of the voter who abstains in the belief that enough others will vote. In both these cases it is alleged that some utility would be gained, and none lost, by these dastardly actions. These are not, on the face of it, fantastic or unusual cases, although the degree of knowledge stipulated as to what others will do is perhaps unusual. Yet it would be impolitic, in moral education, to bring up people to behave like this, if we were seeking level-1 principles with the highest acceptance-utility; if we tried, the result would be that nearly everyone would consume electricity under those conditions, and hardly anybody would vote. However, the chief answer to these cases is that which I have used elsewhere[24] to deal with the car-pushing and death-bed promise cases which are also well canvassed. It is best approached by going back to the logical beginning and asking whether I am prepared to prescribe, or even permit, that others should (*a*) use electricity, thus taking advantage of my law-abidingness, when I am going without it; (*b*) abstain from voting when I do so at inconvenience to myself, thereby taking advantage of my public spirit; (*c*) only pretend to push the car when I am rupturing myself in the effort to get it started; (*d*) make death-bed promises to me (for example to look after my children) and then treat them as of no weight. I unhesitatingly answer 'No' to all these questions; and I think that I should give the same answer even if I were perfectly prudent and were universalising my prescription to cover other perfectly prudent affected parties. For it is not imprudent, but prudent rather, to seek the satisfaction of desires which are important to me, even if I am not going to know whether they have been satisfied or not. There is nothing in principle to prevent a fully informed and clear-headed person wanting above all that his children should not starve after his death; and if that is what he wants above all, it is prudent for him to seek what will achieve it, and therefore prescribe this.

Since the logical machinery on which my brand of utilitarianism is based yields these answers, so should the utilitarianism that is based on it; and it is worth while to ask, How? The clue lies in the observation that to frustrate a desire of mine is against my interest even if I do not know that it is being frustrated, or if I am dead. If anybody does not agree, I ask him to apply the logical apparatus direct and forget about interests. Here is a point at which, perhaps, some people will want to say that my Kantian or Christian variety of utilitarianism, based on giving equal weight to the prudent prescriptions or desires of all, diverges from the usual varieties so much that it does not deserve to be called a kind of utilitarianism at all. I am not much interested in that terminological question; but for what it is worth I will record my opinion that the dying man's interests *are* harmed if promises are made to him and then broken, and even more that mine are harmed if people are cheating me without my knowing it. In the latter case, they are harmed because I very much want this not to happen; and my desire that it should not happen is boosted by my level-1 sense of justice, which the utilitarian educators who brought me up wisely inculcated in me.

Whichever way we put it, whether in terms of what I am prepared to prescribe or permit universally (and therefore also for when I am the victim) or in terms of how to be fair as between the interests of all the affected parties, I conclude that the acts I have listed will come out wrong on the act-utilitarian calculation, because of the harms done to the interests of those who are cheated, or the non-fulfilment of prescriptions to which, we may assume, they attach high importance. If we add to this move the preceding one which rules out fantastic cases, and are clear about the distinction between judgements about the character of the agent, judgements about the moral rationality of the action, and judgements about its moral rightness as shown by the

outcome, I think that this form of utilitarianism can answer the objections I have mentioned. Much more needs to be said; the present paper is only a beginning, and is not very original.[25] I publish it only to give some indication of the way in which ethical theory can help with normative moral questions, and to try to get the discussion of utilitarianism centred round credible forms of it, rather than forms which we all know will not do.

NOTES

1. See, for example, my *Freedom and Reason* (*FR*) (Oxford, 1963), ch. 11; *Applications of Moral Philosophy* (London, 1972); 'Rules of War and Moral Reasoning', *Ph. and Public Affairs*, 1 (1972); 'Language and Moral Education', *New Essays in the Philosophy of Education,* G. Langford and D. J. O'Connor (eds) (London, 1973); 'Abortion and the Golden Rule', *Ph. and Public Affairs*, 4 (1975); 'Political Obligation', *Social Ends and Political Means,* T. Honderich (ed.) (forthcoming); and 'Contrasting Methods of Environmental Planning', *Nature and Conduct,* R. S. Peters (ed.) (London, 1975).

2. See the beginning of my paper 'Abortion and the Golden Rule', cited in note 1.

3. It is substantially that set out in *FR*. For the distinction between nondescriptivism and subjectivism, see my 'Some Confusions about Subjectivity', Lindley Lecture, 1974, University of Kansas.

4. *Ph.Q.,* 23 (1973); cf. my paper 'Rules of War and Moral Reasoning', cited in note 1, and B. Barry, *The Liberal Theory of Justice* (Oxford, 1973), pp. 12–13.

5. See, for example, the discussion between R. Firth and R. B. Brandt in *Ph. and Phen. Res.,* 12 (1952) and 15 (1955); also D. Haslett, *Moral Rightness* (The Hague, 1974).

6. R. B. Brandt, 'Towards a Credible Form of Utilitarianism', *Morality and the Language of Conduct,* H.-N. Castaneda and G. Nakhnikian (eds) (Detroit, 1963).

7. See my review of Rawls, *Ph.Q.,* 23 (1973), p. 249.

8. *An Analysis of Knowledge and Valuation* (La Salle, 1946), p. 547; see also Haslett, op. cit., ch. 3.

9. Cf. Plato, *Republic,* 335.

10. The theory of prudence is ably handled in D. A. J. Richards, *A Theory of Reasons for Action* (Oxford, 1971); Haslett, op. cit.; and R. B. Brandt, John Locke Lectures (Oxford, forthcoming).

11. Professor Bernard Williams says, 'It is absurd to demand of such a man, when the sums come in from the utility network which the projects of others have in part determined, that he should just step aside from his own project and decision and acknowledge the decision which utilitarian calculation requires.' (J. J. C. Smart and B. A. O. Williams, *Utilitarianism: For and Against* (Cambridge, 1973), p. 116, and cf. p. 117n.) Christian humility and *agape* and their humanist counterparts are, then, according to Williams's standards, an absurd demand (which is hardly remarkable). What is more remarkable is the boldness of the persuasive definition by which he labels the self-centred pursuit of one's own projects 'integrity' and accounts it a fault in utilitarianism that it could conflict with this.

12. *FR*, ch. 9; 'Wrongness and Harm', in my *Essays on the Moral Concepts* (London, 1972).

13. *De Anima*, 433a 9ff.

14. *Ph. Rev.*, 64 (1955).

15. *The Right and the Good* (Oxford, 1930), pp. 19ff.

16. See my review of Rawls, cited in note 4, p. 153; 'Principles', *Proc. Arist. Soc.*, 72 (1972–3); 'Rules of War and Moral Reasoning', cited in note 1; *FR*, pp. 43–5.

17. Burke; see *FR*, p. 45.

18. See 'Principles', cited in note 16.

19. See note 16.

20. See 'Principles', cited in note 16.

21. Smart and Williams, op. cit., pp. 46f.

22. See my *The Language of Morals*, p. 186.

23. *Nicomachean Ethics*, 1109 b 1.

24. See my paper 'The Argument from Received Opinion' in my *Essays on Philosophical Method* (London, 1971), pp. 128ff.; *FR*, pp. 132ff.

25. Among many others from whose ideas I have learnt, I should like in particular to mention Dr. Lynda Sharp (Mrs Lynda Paine), in whose thesis *Forms and Criticisms of Utilitarianism* (deposited in the Bodleian Library at Oxford) some of the above topics are discussed in greater detail.

21

RADICAL EGALITARIANISM

Kai Nielson

I

I have talked of equality as a right and of equality as a goal. And I have taken, as the principal thing, to be able to state what goal we are seeking when we say equality is a goal. When we are in a position actually to achieve that goal, then that same equality becomes a right. The goal we are seeking is an equality of basic condition for everyone. Let me say a bit what this is: everyone, as far as possible, should have equal life prospects, short of genetic engineering and the like and the rooting out any form of the family and the undermining of our basic freedoms. There should, where this is possible, be an equality of access to equal resources over each person's life as a whole, though this should be qualified by people's varying needs. Where psychiatrists are in short supply only people who are in need of psychiatric help should

From *Equality and Liberty,* Rowman and Littlefield (1985) pp. 283–292, 302–306, 309. Reprinted by permission.

have equal access to such help. This equal access to resources should be such that it stands as a barrier to their being the sort of differences between people that allow some to be in a position to control and to exploit others; such equal access to resources should also stand as a barrier to one adult person having power over other adult persons that does not rest on the revokable consent on the part of the persons over whom he comes to have power. Where, because of some remaining scarcity in a society of considerable productive abundance, we cannot reasonably distribute resources equally, we should first, where considerations of desert are not at issue, distribute according to stringency of need, second according to the strength of unmanipulated preferences and third, and finally, by lottery. We should, in trying to attain equality of condition, aim at a condition of autonomy (the fuller and the more rational the better) for everyone and at a condition where everyone alike, to the fullest extent possible, has his or her needs and wants satisfied. The limitations on the satisfaction of people's wants should be only where that satisfaction is incompatible with everyone getting the same treatment. Where we have conflicting wants, such as where two persons want to marry the same person, the fair thing to do will vary with the circumstances. In the marriage case, freedom of choice is obviously the fair thing. But generally, what should be aimed at is having everyone have their wants satisfied as far as possible. To achieve equality of condition would be, as well, to achieve a condition where the necessary burdens of the society are equally shared, where to do so is reasonable, and where each person has an equal voice in deciding what these burdens shall be. Moreover, everyone, as much as possible, should be in a position—and should be equally in that position—to control his own life. The goals of egalitarianism are to achieve such equalities.

Minimally, classlessness is something we should all aim at if we are egalitarians. It is necessary for the stable achievement of equalities of the type discussed in the previous paragraph. Beyond that, we should also aim at a statusless society, though not at an undifferentiated society or a society which does not recognize merit. It is only in such a classless, statusless society that the ideals of equality (the conception of equality as a very general goal to be achieved) can be realized. In aiming for a statusless society, we are aiming for a society which, while remaining a society of material abundance, is a society in which there are to be no extensive differences in life prospects between people because some have far greater income, power, authority or prestige than others. This is the *via negativia* of the egalitarian way. The *via postiva* is to produce social conditions, where there is generally material abundance, where well-being and satisfaction are not only maximized (the utilitarian thing) but, as well, a society where this condition, as far as it is achievable, is sought equally for all (the egalitarian thing). This is the underlying conception of the egalitarian commitment to equality of condition.

II

Robert Nozick asks "How do we decide how much equality is enough?"[1] In the preceding section we gestured in the direction of an answer. I should now like to be somewhat more explicit. Too much equality, as we have been at pains to point out, would be to treat everyone identically, completely ignoring their differing needs. Various forms of "barracks equality" approximating that would also be too much. Too little equality would be to limit equality of condition, as did the old egalitarianism, to achieving equal legal and political rights, equal civil liberties, to equality of opportunity and to a redistribution of gross disparities in wealth sufficient to keep social peace, the rationale for the latter being that such gross inequalities if allowed to stand would threaten social stability. This Hobbesist stance indicates that the old egalitarianism proceeds in a very pragmatic manner. Against the old egalitarianism I would argue that we must at least aim at an equality of whole life prospects, where that is not read simply as the right to compete for scarce positions of advantage, but where there is to be brought into being the kind of equality of condition that would provide everyone equally, as far as possible, with the resources and the social conditions to satisfy their needs as fully as possible compatible with everyone else doing likewise. (Note that between people these needs will be partly the same but will still often be importantly different as well.) Ideally, as a kind of ideal limit for a society of wondrous abundance, a radical egalitarianism would go beyond that to a similar thing for wants. We should, that is, provide all people equally, as far as possible, with the resources and social conditions to satisfy their wants, as fully as possible compatible with everyone else doing likewise. (I recognize that there is a slide between wants and needs. As the wealth of a society increases and its structure changes, things that started out as wants tend to become needs, e.g. someone in the Falkland Islands might merely reasonably want an auto while someone in Los Angeles might not only want it but need it as well. But this does not collapse the distinction between wants and needs. There are things in any society people need, if they are to survive at all in anything like a commodious condition, whether they want them or not, e.g., they need food, shelter, security, companionship and the like. An egalitarian starts with basic needs, or at least with what are taken in the cultural environment in which a given person lives to be basic needs, and moves out to other needs and finally to wants as the productive power of the society increases.)

I qualified my above formulations with "as far as possible" and with "as fully as possible compatible with everyone else doing likewise." These are essential qualifications. Where, as in societies that we know, there are scarcities, even rather minimal scarcities, not everyone can have the resources or at least all the resources necessary to have their needs satisfied. Here we must first ensure that, again as far as possible, their basic needs are all satisfied and then we move on to other needs and finally to wants. But sometimes, to understate it, even in very affluent societies, everyone's needs cannot be met, or at least they cannot be equally met. In such circumstances we have to make some hard choices. I am thinking of a situation where there are not enough dialysis machines to go around so that everyone who needs one can have one. What then should we do? The thing to aim at, to try as far as possible to approximate, if only as a heuristic ideal, is the full and equal meeting of needs and wants of everyone. It is when we have that much equality that we have enough equality. But, of course, "ought implies can," and where we can't achieve it we can't achieve it. But where we reasonably can, we ought to do it. It is something that fairness requires.

The "reasonably can" is also an essential modification: we need situations of sufficient abundance so that we do not, in going for such an equality of condition, simply spread the misery around or spread very Spartan conditions around. Before we can rightly aim for the equality of condition I mentioned, we must first have the productive capacity and resource conditions to support the institutional means that would make possible the equal satisfaction of basic needs and the equal satisfaction of other needs and wants as well.

Such achievements will often not be possible; perhaps they will never be fully possible, for, no doubt, the physically handicapped will always be with us. Consider, for example, situations where our scarcities are such that we cannot, without causing considerable misery, create the institutions and mechanisms that would work to satisfy all needs, even all basic needs. Suppose we have the technology in place to develop all sorts of complicated life-sustaining machines all of which would predictably provide people with a quality of life that they, viewing the matter clearly, would rationally choose if they were simply choosing for themselves. But suppose, if we put such technologies in place, we will then not have the wherewithal to provide basic health care in outlying regions in the country or adequate educational services in such places. We should not, under those circumstances, put those technologies in place. But we should also recognize that where it becomes possible to put these technologies in place without sacrificing other more pressing needs, we should do so. The underlying egalitarian rationale is evident enough: produce the conditions for the most extensive satisfaction of needs for everyone. Where A's need and B's need are equally important (equally stringent) but cannot both be satisfied, satisfy A's need rather than B's if the satisfaction of A's need would be more fecund for the satisfaction of the needs of others than B's, or less undermining of the satisfaction of the needs of others than B's. (I do not mean to say that that is our only criterion of choice but it is the criterion most relevant for us here.) We should seek the satisfaction of the greatest compossible set of needs where the conditions for compossibility are (a) that everyone's needs be considered, (b) that everyone's needs be *equally* considered and where two sets of needs cannot both be satisfied, the more stringent set of needs shall first be satisfied. (Do not say we have no working criteria for what they are. If you need food to keep you from starvation or debilitating malnutrition and I need a vacation to relax after a spate of hard work, your need is plainly more stringent than mine. There would, of course, be all sorts of disputable cases, but there are also a host of perfectly determinate cases indicating that we have working criteria.) The underlying rationale is to seek compossible sets of needs so that we approach as far as possible as great a satisfaction of needs as possible for everyone.

This might, it could be said, produce a situation in which very few people got those things that they needed the most, or at least wanted the most. Remember Nozick with his need for the resources of Widner Library in an annex to his house. People, some might argue, with expensive tastes and extravagant needs, say a need for really good wine, would never, with a stress on such compossibilia, get things they are really keen about.[2] Is that the kind of world we would reflectively want? Well, *if* their not getting them is the price we have to pay for everyone having their basic needs met, then it is a price we ought to pay. I am very fond of very good wines as well as fresh ripe mangos, but if the price of my having them is that people starve or suffer malnutrition in the Sahel, or indeed anywhere else, then plainly fairness, if not just plain human decency, requires that I forego them.

In talking about how much equality is enough, I have so far talked of the benefits that equality is meant to provide. But egalitarians also speak of an equal sharing of the necessary burdens of the society as well. Fairness requires a sharing of the burdens, and for a radical egalitarian this comes to an equal sharing of the burdens where people are equally capable of sharing them. Translated into the concrete this does *not* mean that a child or an old man or a pregnant woman are to be required to work in the mines or that they be required to collect garbage, but it would involve something like

requiring every able-bodied person, say from nineteen to twenty, to take his or her turn at a fair portion of the necessary unpleasant jobs in the world. In that way we all, where we are able to do it, would share equally in these burdens—in doing the things that none of us want to do but that we, if we are at all reasonable, recognize the necessity of having done. (There are all kinds of variations and complications concerning this—what do we do with the youthful wonder at the violin? But, that notwithstanding, the general idea is clear enough.) And, where we think this is reasonably feasible, it squares with our considered judgments about fairness.

I have given you, in effect appealing to my considered judgments but considered judgments I do not think are at all eccentric, a picture of what I would take to be enough equality, too little equality and not enough equality. But how can we know that my proportions are right? I do not think we can avoid or should indeed try to avoid an appeal to considered judgments here. But working with them there are some arguments we can appeal to to get them in wide reflective equilibrium. Suppose we go back to the formal principle of justice, namely that we must treat like cases alike. Because it does not tell us *what* are like cases, we cannot derive substantive criteria from it. But it may, indirectly, be of some help here. We all, if we are not utterly zany, want a life in which our needs are satisfied and in which we can live as we wish and do what we want to do. Though we differ in many ways, in our abilities, capacities for pleasure, determination to keep on with a job, we do not differ about wanting our needs satisfied or being able to live as we wish. Thus, *ceterus paribus*, where questions of desert, entitlement and the like do not enter, it is only fair that all of us should have our needs equally considered and that we should, again *ceterus paribus*, all be able to do as we wish in a way that is compatible with others doing likewise. From the formal principle of justice and a few key facts about us, we can get to the claim that *ceterus paribus* we should go for this much equality. But this is the core content of a radical egalitarianism.

However, how do we know that *ceterus* is *paribus* here? What about our entitlements and deserts? Suppose I have built my house with my own hands, from materials I have purchased and on land that I have purchased and that I have lived in it for years and have carefully cared for it. The house is mine and I am entitled to keep it even if by dividing the house into two apartments greater and more equal satisfaction of need would obtain for everyone. Justice requires that such an entitlement be respected here. (Again, there is an implicit *ceterus paribus* clause. In extreme situations, say after a war with housing in extremely short supply, that entitlement could be rightly overridden.)

There is a response on the egalitarian's part similar to a response utilitarians made to criticisms of a similar logical type made of utilitarianism by pluralistic deontologists. One of the things that people in fact need, or at least reflectively firmly want, is to have such entitlements respected. Where they are routinely overridden to satisfy other needs or wants, we would *not* in fact have a society in which the needs of everyone are being maximally met. To the reply, but what if more needs for everyone were met by ignoring or overriding such entitlements, the radical egalitarian should respond that that is, given the way we are, a thoroughly hypothetical situation and that theories of morality cannot be expected to give guidance for all logically possible worlds but only for worlds which are reasonably like what our actual world is or plausibly could come to be. Setting this argument aside for the moment, even if it did turn out that the need satisfaction linked with having other things—things that involved the overriding of those entitlements—was sufficient to make it the case that more need satisfaction all around for *everyone* would be achieved by overriding those entitlements, then, for reasonable people who clearly saw that, these entitlements would not have the weight presently given to them. They either would not have the importance presently attached to them or the need for

the additional living space would be so great that their being overridden would seem, everything considered, the lesser of two evils (as in the example of the postwar housing situation).

There are without doubt genuine entitlements and a theory of justice must take them seriously, but they are not absolute. If the need is great enough we can see the merit in overriding them, just as in law as well as morality the right of eminent domain is recognized. Finally, while I have talked of entitlements here, parallel arguments will go through for desert.

III

I want now to relate this articulation of what equality comes to to my radically egalitarian principles of justice. My articulation of justice is a certain spelling out of the slogan proclaimed by Marx "From each according to his ability, to each according to his needs." The egalitarian conception of society argues for the desirability of bringing into existence a world, once the springs of social wealth flow freely, in which everyone's needs are as fully satisfied as possible and in which everyone gives according to his ability. Which means, among other things, that everyone, according to his ability, shares the burdens of society. There is an equal giving and equal responsibility here according to ability. It is here, with respect to giving according to ability and with respect to receiving according to need, that a complex equality of result, i.e., equality of condition, is being advocated by the radical egalitarian. What it comes to is this: each of us, where each is to count for one and none to count for more than one, is to give according to ability and receive according to need.

My radical egalitarian principles of justice, read as follows:

1. Each person is to have an equal right to the most expensive total system of equal basic liberties and opportunities (including equal opportunities for meaningful work, for self-

determination and political and economic participation) compatible with a similar treatment of all. (This principle gives expression to a commitment to attain and/or sustain equal moral autonomy and equal self-respect.)

2. After provisions are made for common social (community) values, for capital overhead to preserve the society's productive capacity, allowances made for differing unmanipulated needs and preferences, and due weight is given to the just entitlements of individuals, the income and wealth (the common stock of means) is to be so divided that each person will have a right to an equal share. The necessary burdens requisite to enhance human well-being are also to be equally shared, subject, of course, to limitations by differing abilities and differing situations. (Here I refer to different natural environments and the like and not to class position and the like.)

Here we are talking about equality as a right rather than about equality as a goal as has previously been the subject matter of equality in this chapter. These principles of egalitarianism spell out rights people have and duties they have under *conditions of very considerable productive abundance.* We have a right to certain basic liberties and opportunities and we have, subject to certain limitations spelled out in the second principle, a right to an equal share of the income and wealth in the world. We also have a duty, again subject to the qualifications mentioned in the principle, to do our equal share in shouldering the burdens necessary to protect us from ills and to enhance our well-being.

What is the relation between these rights and the ideal of equality of condition discussed earlier? That is a goal for which we can struggle now to bring about conditions which will some day make its achievement possible, while these rights only become rights when the goal is actually achievable. We have no such rights in slave, feudal or capitalist societies or such duties in those societies. In that important way they are not natural rights for they depend on certain social conditions and certain social structures (socialist ones) to be realizable. What

we can say is that it is always desirable that socio-economic conditions come into being which would make it possible to achieve the goal of equality of condition so that these rights and duties I speak of could obtain. But that is a far cry from saying we have such rights and duties now.

It is a corollary of this, if these radical egalitarian principles of justice are correct, that capitalist societies (even capitalist welfare state societies such as Sweden) and statist societies such as the Soviet Union or the People's Republic of China cannot be just societies or at least they must be societies, structured as they are, which are defective in justice. (This is not to say that some of these societies are not juster than others. Sweden is juster than South Africa, Canada than the United States and Cuba and Nicaragua than Honduras and Guatemala.) But none of these statist or capitalist societies can satisfy these radical egalitarian principles of justice, for equal liberty, equal opportunity, equal wealth or equal sharing of burdens are not at all possible in societies having their social structure. So we do not have such rights now but we can take it as a goal that we bring such a society into being with a commitment to an equality of condition in which we would have these rights and duties. Here we require first the massive development of productive power.

The connection between equality as a goal and equality as a right spelled out in these principles of justice is this. The equality of condition appealed to in equality as a goal would, if it were actually to obtain, have to contain the rights and duties enunciated in those principles. There could be no equal life prospects between all people or anything approximating an equal satisfaction of needs if there were not in place something like the system of equal basic liberties referred to in the first principle. Furthermore, without the rough equality of wealth referred to in the second principle, there would be disparities in power and self-direction in society which would render impossible an equality of life prospects or the social conditions required for an equal satisfaction of needs. And plainly, without a roughly equal sharing of burdens, there cannot be a situation where everyone has equal life prospects or has the chance equally to satisfy his needs. The principles of radical egalitarian justice are implicated in its conception of an ideally adequate equality of condition.

IV

The principles of radical egalitarian justice I have articulated are meant to apply globally and not just to particular societies. But it is certainly fair to say that not a few would worry that such principles of radical egalitarian justice, if applied globally, would force the people in wealthier sections of the world to a kind of financial hari-kari. There are millions of desperately impoverished people. Indeed millions are starving or malnourished and things are not getting any better. People in the affluent societies cannot but worry about whether they face a bottomless pit. Many believe that meeting, even in the most minimal way, the needs of the impoverished is going to put an incredible burden on people—people of all classes—in the affluent societies. Indeed it will, if acted on non-evasively, bring about their impoverishment, and this is just too much to ask. Radical egalitarianism is forgetting Rawls' admonitions about "the strains of commitment"— the recognition that in any rational account of what is required of us, we must at least give a minimal healthy self-interest its due. We must construct our moral philosophy for human beings and not for saints. Human nature is less fixed than conservatives are wont to assume, but it is not so elastic that we can reasonably expect people to impoverish themselves to make the massive transfers between North and South—the industrialized world and the Third World—required to begin to approach a situation where even Rawls' principles would be in place on a global level, to say nothing of my radical egalitarian principles of justice.[3]

The first thing to say in response to this is that my radical egalitarian principles are meant actually to guide practice, to directly determine what we are to do, only in a world of extensive abundance where, as Marx put it, the springs of social wealth flow freely. If such a world cannot be attained with the undermining of capitalism and the full putting into place, stabilizing, and developing of socialist relations of production, then such radical egalitarian principles can only remain as heuristic ideals against which to measure the distance of our travel in the direction of what would be a perfectly just society.

Aside from a small capitalist class, along with those elites most directly and profitably beholden to it (together a group constituting not more than 5 percent of the world's population), there would, in taking my radical egalitarian principles as heuristic guides, be no impoverishment of people in the affluent societies, if we moved in a radically more egalitarian way to start to achieve a global fairness. There would be massive transfers of wealth between North and South, but this could be done in stages so that, for the people in the affluent societies (capitalist elites apart), there need be no undermining of the quality of their lives. Even what were once capitalist elites would not be impoverished or reduced to some kind of bleak life though they would, the incidental Spartan types aside, find their life styles altered. But their health and general well being, including their opportunities to do significant and innovative work, would, if anything, be enhanced. And while some of the sources of their enjoyment would be a thing of the past, there would still be a considerable range of enjoyments available to them sufficient to afford anyone a rich life that could be lived with verve and zest.

A fraction of what the United States spends on defense spending would take care of immediate problems of starvation and malnutrition for most of the world. For longer range problems such as bringing conditions of life in the Third World more in line with conditions of life in Sweden and Switzerland, what is necessary is the dismantling of the capitalist system and the creation of a socio-economic system with an underlying rationale directing it toward producing for needs—everyone's needs. With this altered productive mode, the irrationalities and waste of capitalist production would be cut. There would be no more built-in obsolescence, no more merely cosmetic changes in consumer durables, no more fashion roulette, no more useless products and the like. Moreover, the enormous expenditures that go into the war industry would be a thing of the past. There would be great transfers from North to South, but it would be from the North's capitalist fat and not from things people in the North really need. (There would, in other words, be no self-pauperization of people in the capitalist world.) . . .

VIII

It has been repeatedly argued that equality undermines liberty. Some would say that a society in which principles like my radical egalitarian principles were adopted, or even the liberal egalitarian principles of Rawls or Dworkin were adopted, would not be a free society. My arguments have been just the reverse. I have argued that it is only in an egalitarian society that full and extensive liberty is possible.

Perhaps the egalitarian and the anti-egalitarian are arguing at cross purposes? What we need to recognize, it has been argued, is that we have two kinds of rights both of which are important to freedom but to rather different freedoms and which are freedoms which not infrequently conflict.[4] We have rights to *fair terms of cooperation* but we also have rights to *non-interference*. If a right of either kind is overridden our freedom is diminished. The reason why it might be thought that the egalitarian and the anti-egalitarian may be arguing at cross purposes is that the egalitarian is pointing to the fact that rights to fair terms of cooperation and their associated liberties require equality while the anti-egalitarian is pointing to the

fact that rights to non-interference and their associated liberties conflict with equality. They focus on different liberties.

What I have said above may not be crystal clear, so let me explain. People have a right to fair terms of cooperation. In political terms this comes to the equal right to all to effective participation in government and, in more broadly social terms, and for a society of economic wealth, it means people having a right to a roughly equal distribution of the benefits and burdens of the basic social arrangements that effect their lives and for them to stand in such relations to each other such that no one has the power to dominate the life of another. By contrast, rights to non-interference come to the equal right of all to be left alone by the government and more broadly to live in a society in which people have a right peacefully to pursue their interests without interference.

The conflict between equality and liberty comes down to, very essentially, the conflicts we get in modern societies between rights to fair terms of cooperation and rights to non-interference. As Joseph Schumpeter saw and J. S. Mill before him, one could have a thoroughly democratic society (at least in conventional terms) in which rights to non-interference might still be extensively violated. A central anti-egalitarian claim is that we cannot have an egalitarian society in which the very precious liberties that go with the rights to non-interference would not be violated.

Socialism and egalitarianism plainly protect rights to fair terms of cooperation. Without the social (collective) ownership and control of the means of production, involving with this, in the initial stages of socialism at least, a workers' state, economic power will be concentrated in the hands of a few who will in turn, as a result, dominate effective participation in government. Some right-wing libertarians blind themselves to that reality, but it is about as evident as can be. Only an utter turning away from the facts of social life could lead to any doubts about this at all. But then this means that in a workers' state, if some people have capitalistic impulses, that they would have their rights peacefully to pursue their own interests interfered with. They might wish to invest, retain and bequeath in economic domains. In a workers' state these capitalist acts in many circumstances would have to be forbidden, but that would be a violation of an individual's right to non-interference and the fact, if it was a fact, that we by democratic vote, even with vast majorities, had made such capitalist acts illegal would still not make any difference because individuals' rights to non-interference would still be violated.

We are indeed driven, by egalitarian impulses, of a perfectly understandable sort, to accept interference with laissez-faire capitalism to protect non-subordination and non-domination of people by protecting the egalitarian right to fair terms of cooperation and the enhanced liberty that that brings. Still, as things stand, this leads inevitably to violations of the right to non-interference and this brings with it a diminution of liberty. There will be people with capitalist impulses and they will be interfered with. It is no good denying, it will be said, that egalitarianism and particularly socialism will not lead to interference with very precious individual liberties, namely with our right peacefully to pursue our interests without interference.[5]

The proper response to this, as should be apparent from what I have argued throughout, is that to live in any society at all, capitalist, socialist or whatever, is to live in a world in which there will be some restriction or other on our rights peacefully to pursue our interests without interference. I can't lecture in Albanian or even in French in a standard philosophy class at the University of Calgary, I can't jog naked on most beaches, borrow a book from your library without your permission, fish in your trout pond without your permission, take your dog for a walk without your say so and the like. At least some of these things have been thought to be things which I might peacefully pursue in my own interests. Stopping me from doing them is plainly interfering

with my peaceful pursuit of my own interests. And indeed it is an infringement on liberty, an interference with my doing what I may want to do.

However, for at least many of these activities, and particularly the ones having to do with property, even right-wing libertarians think that such interference is perfectly justified. But, justified or not, they still plainly constitute a restriction on our individual freedom. However, what we must also recognize is that there will always be some such restrictions on freedom in any society whatsoever, just in virtue of the fact that a normless society, without the restrictions that having norms imply, is a contradiction in terms.[6] Many restrictions are hardly felt as restrictions, as in the attitudes of many people toward seat-belt legislation, but they are, all the same, plainly restrictions on our liberty. It is just that they are thought to be unproblematically justified.

To the question would a socialism with a radical egalitarianism restrict some liberties, including some liberties rooted in rights to noninterference, the answer is that it indeed would; but so would laissez-faire capitalism, aristocratic conceptions of justice, liberal conceptions or any social formations at all, with their associated conceptions of justice. The relevant question is which of these restrictions are justified.

The restrictions on liberty proferred by radical egalitarianism and socialism, I have argued, are justified for they, of the various alternatives, give us both the most extensive and the most abundant system of liberty possible in modern conditions with their thorough protection of the right to fair terms of cooperation. Radical egalitarianism will also, and this is central for us, protect our civil liberties and these liberties are, of course, our most basic liberties. These are the liberties which are the most vital for us to protect. What it will not do is to protect our unrestricted liberties to invest, retain and bequeath in the economic realm and it will not protect our unrestricted freedom to buy and sell. There is, however, no good reason to think that these restrictions are restrictions of anything like a basic liberty. Moreover, we are justified in restricting our freedom to buy and sell if such restrictions strengthen, rather than weaken, our total system of liberty. This is in this way justified, for only by such market restrictions can the rights of the vast majority of people to effective participation in government and an equal role in the control of their social lives be protected. I say this because if we let the market run free in this way, power will pass into the hands of a few who will control the lives of the many and determine the fundamental design of the society. The actual liberties that are curtailed in a radically egalitarian social order are inessential liberties whose restriction in contemporary circumstances enhances human well-being and indeed makes for a firmer entrenchment of basic liberties and for their greater extension globally. That is to say, we here restrict some liberty in order to attain more liberty and a more equally distributed pattern of liberty. More people will be able to do what they want and have a greater control over their own lives than in a capitalist world order with its at least implicit inegalitarian commitments.

However, some might say I still have not faced the most central objection to radical egalitarianism, namely its statism. (I would prefer to say its putative statism.) The picture is this. The egalitarian state must be in the redistribution business. It has to make, or make sure there is made, an equal relative contribution to the welfare of every citizen. But this in effect means that the socialist state or, for that matter, the welfare state, will be deeply interventionist in our personal lives. It will be in the business, as one right-winger emotively put it, of cutting one person down to size in order to bring about that person's equality with another person who was in a previously disadvantageous position.[7] That is said to be morally objectionable and it would indeed be deeply morally objectionable in many circumstances. But it isn't in the circumstances in which the radical egalitarian presses for redistribution. (I am not speaking of what might be mere equalizing

upwards.) The circumstances are these: Capitalist A gets his productive property confiscated so that he could no longer dominate and control the lives of proletarians B, C, D, E, F, and G. But what is wrong with it where this "cutting down to size"—in reality the confiscation of productive property or the taxation of the capitalist—involves no violation of A's civil liberties or the harming of his actual well-being (health, ability to work, to cultivate the arts, to have fruitful personal relations, to live in comfort and the like) and where B, C, D, E, F, and G will have their freedom and their well-being thoroughly enhanced if such confiscation or taxation occurs? Far from being morally objectional, it is precisely the sort of state of affairs that people ought to favor. It certainly protects more liberties and more significant liberties than it undermines.

There is another familiar anti-egalitarian argument designed to establish the liberty-undermining qualities of egalitarianism. It is an argument we have touched upon in discussing meritocracy. It turns on the fact that in any society there will be both talents and handicaps. Where they exist, what do we want to do about maintaining equal distribution? Egalitarians, radical or otherwise, certainly do not want to penalize people for talent. That being so, then surely people should be allowed to retain the benefits of superior talent. But this in some circumstances will lead to significant inequalities in resources and in the meeting of needs. To sustain equality there will have to be an ongoing redistribution in the direction of the less talented and less fortunate. But this redistribution from the more to the less talented does plainly penalize the talented for their talent. That, it will be said, is something which is both unfair and an undermining of liberty.

The following, it has been argued, makes the above evident enough.[8] If people have talents they will tend to want to use them. And if they use them they are very likely to come out ahead. Must not egalitarians say they ought not to be able to come out ahead no matter how well they use their talents and no matter how considerable these talents are? But that is intolerably restrictive and unfair.

The answer to the above anti-egalitarian argument is implicit in a number of things I have already said. But here let me confront this familiar argument directly. Part of the answer comes out in probing some of the ambiguities of "coming out ahead." Note, incidentally, that (1) not all reflective, morally sensitive people will be so concerned with that, and (2) that being very concerned with that is a mentality that capitalism inculcates. Be that as it may, to turn to the ambiguities, note that some take "coming out ahead" principally to mean "being paid well for the use of those talents" where "being paid well" is being paid sufficiently well so that it creates inequalities sufficient to disturb the preferred egalitarian patterns. (Without that, being paid well would give one no relative advantage.) But, as we have seen, "coming out ahead" need not take that form at all. Talents can be recognized and acknowledged in many ways. First, in just the respect and admiration of a fine employment of talents that would naturally come from people seeing them so displayed where these people were not twisted by envy; second, by having, because of these talents, interesting and secure work that their talents fit them for and they merit in virtue of those talents. Moreover, having more money is not going to matter much—for familiar marginal utility reasons—where what in capitalist societies would be called the welfare floors are already very high, this being made feasible by the great productive wealth of the society. Recall that in such a society of abundance everyone will be well off and secure. In such a society people are not going to be very concerned about being a little better off than someone else. The talented are in no way, in such a

situation, robbed to help the untalented and handicapped or penalized for their talents. They are only prevented from amassing wealth (most particularly productive wealth), which would enable them to dominate the untalented and the handicapped and to control the social life of the world of which they are both a part. . . .

NOTES

1. See the debate between Robert Nozick, Daniel Bell and James Tobin, "If Inequality Is Inevitable What Can Be Done About It?" *The New York Times,* January 3, 1982, p. E5. The exchange between Bell and Nozick reveals the differences between the old egalitarianism and right-wing libertarianism. It is not only that the right and left clash but sometimes right clashes with right.

2. Amartya Sen, "Equality of What?" *The Tanner Lectures on Human Values,* vol. 1 (1980), ed. Sterling M. McMurrin (Cambridge, England: Cambridge University Press, 1980), pp. 198–220.

3. Henry Shue, "The Burdens of Justice," *The Journal of Philosophy* 80, no. 10 (October 1983): 600–601; 606–8.

4. Richard W. Miller, "Marx and Morality," in *Marxism,* eds. J. R. Pennock and J. W. Chapman, Nomos 26 (New York: New York University Press, 1983), pp. 9–11.

5. Ibid., p. 10.

6. This has been argued from both the liberal center and the left. Ralf Dahrendorf, *Essays in the Theory of Society* (Stanford, Cal.: Stanford University Press, 1968), pp. 151–78; and G. A. Cohen, "Capitalism, Freedom and the Proletariat" in *The Idea of Freedom: Essays in Honour of Isaiah Berlin,* ed. Alan Ryan (Oxford: Oxford University Press, 1979).

7. The graphic language should be duly noted. Jan Narveson, "On Dworkinian Equality," *Social Philosophy and Policy* 1, no. 1 (autumn 1983): 4.

8. Ibid., p. 1 24.

22
THE BASIC REQUIREMENTS OF PRACTICAL REASONABLENESS

John Finnis

1 THE GOOD OF PRACTICAL REASONABLENESS STRUCTURES OUR PURSUIT OF GOODS

There is no reason to doubt that each of the basic aspects of human well-being is worth seeking to realize. But there are many such basic forms of human good; I identified seven.* And each of them can be participated in, and promoted, in an inexhaustible variety of ways and with an inexhaustible variety of combinations of emphasis, concentration, and specialization. To participate thoroughly in any basic value calls for skill, or at least a thoroughgoing commitment. But our life is short.

By disclosing a horizon of attractive possibilities for us, our grasp of the basic values thus creates, not answers, the problem for intelligent decision: What is to be done? What may be left undone? What is not to be

done? We have, in the abstract, no reason to leave any of the basic goods out of account. But we do have good reason to choose commitments, projects, and actions, knowing that choice effectively rules out many alternative reasonable or possible commitment(s), project(s), and action(s).

To have this choice between commitment to concentration upon one value (say, speculative truth) and commitment to others, and between one intelligent and reasonable project (say, understanding this book) and other eligible projects for giving definite shape to one's participation in one's selected value, and between one way of carrying out that project and other appropriate ways, is the primary respect in which we can call ourselves both free and responsible.

For amongst the basic forms of good that we have no good reason to leave out of account is the good of practical reasonableness, which is participated in precisely by shaping one's participation in the other basic goods, by guiding one's commitments, one's selection of projects, and what one does in carrying them out.

The principles that express the general ends of human life do not acquire what would nowadays be called a 'moral' force until they are brought to bear upon definite ranges of project, disposition, or action, or upon particular projects, dispositions, or actions. How they are thus to be brought to bear *is* the problem for practical reasonableness. 'Ethics', as classically conceived, is simply a recollectively and/or prospectively reflective expression of this problem and of the general lines of solutions which have been thought reasonable.

How does one tell that a decision is practically reasonable? This question is the subject-matter of the present chapter. The classical exponents of ethics (and of theories of natural law) were well aware of this problem of criteria and standards of judgment. They emphasize that an adequate response to that problem can be made only by one who has experience (both of human wants and passions and of the conditions of human life) and intelligence and a desire for reasonableness stronger than the desires that might overwhelm it. Even when, later, Thomas Aquinas clearly distinguished a class of practical principles which he considered self-evident to anyone with enough experience and intelligence to understand the words by which they are formulated, he emphasized that moral principles such as those in the Ten Commandments are *conclusions from* the primary self-evident principles, that reasoning to such conclusions requires good judgment, and that there are many other more complex and particular moral norms to be followed and moral judgments and decisions to be made, all requiring a degree of practical wisdom which (he says) few men in fact possess.

Now, you may say, it is all very well for Aristotle to assert that ethics can be satisfactorily expounded only by and to those who are experienced and wise and indeed of good habits,[1] and that these characteristics are only likely to be found in societies that already have sufficiently sound standards of conduct,[2] and that the popular morality of such societies (as crystallized and detectable in their language of praise and blame, and their lore) is a generally sound pointer in the elaboration of ethics.[3] He may assert that what is right and morally good is simply *seen* by the man (the *phronimos*, or again the *spoudaios*) who is right-minded and morally good,[4] and that what such a man thinks and does *is* the criterion of sound terminology and correct conclusions in ethics (and politics).[5] Such assertions can scarcely be denied. But they are scarcely helpful to those who are wondering whether their own view of what is to be done is a reasonable view *or not*. The notion of 'the mean', for which Aristotle is perhaps too well known, seems likewise to be accurate but not very helpful (though its classification of value-words doubtless serves as a reminder of the dimensions of the moral problem). For what is 'the mean and best, that is characteristic of virtue'? It is 'to feel [anger, pity, appetite, etc.] when one ought to, and in relation to the objects and persons that one ought to, and with the motives and in the manner that one ought to . . .'.[6] Have we no more determinate guide than this?

In the two millennia since Plato and Aristotle initiated formal inquiry into the content of practical reasonableness, philosophical reflection has identified a considerable number of requirements of *method* in practical reasoning. Each of these requirements has, indeed, been treated by some philosopher with exaggerated respect, as if it were the exclusive controlling and shaping requirement. For, as with each of the basic forms of good, each of these requirements is fundamental, underived, irreducible, and hence is capable when focused upon of seeming the most important.

Each of these requirements concerns what one *must* do, or think, or be if one is to participate in the basic value of practical reasonableness. Someone who lives up to these requirements is thus Aristotle's *phronimos*; he has Aquinas's *prudentia*; they are requirements of reasonableness or practical wisdom, and to fail to live up to them is irrational. But, secondly, reasonableness both *is* a basic aspect of human well-being and *concerns* one's participation in all the (other) basic aspects of human well-being. Hence its requirements concern fullness of well-being (in the measure in which any one person can enjoy such fullness of well-being in the circumstances of his lifetime). So someone who lives up to these requirements is also Aristotle's *spoudaios* (mature man), his life is *eu zen* (well-living) and, unless circumstances are quite against him, we can say that he has Aristotle's *eudaimonia* (the inclusive all-round flourishing or well-being—not safely translated as 'happiness'). But, thirdly, the basic forms of good are opportunities of *being;* the more fully a man participates in them the more he is what he can be. And for this state of being fully what one can be, Aristotle appropriated the word *physis,* which was translated into Latin as *natura.* So Aquinas will say that these requirements are requirements not only of reason, and of goodness, but also (by entailment) of (human) nature.

Thus, speaking very summarily, we could say that the requirements to which we now turn express the 'natural law method' of working out the (moral) 'natural law' from the first (pre-moral) 'principles of natural law'. Using only the modern terminology (itself of uncertain import) of 'morality', we can say that the following sections of this chapter concern the sorts of reasons why (and thus the ways in which) there are things that morally ought (not) to be done.

2 A COHERENT PLAN OF LIFE

First, then, we should recall that, though they correspond to urges and inclinations which can make themselves felt prior to any intelligent consideration of what is worth pursuing, the basic aspects of human well-being are discernible only to one who thinks about his opportunities, and thus are realizable only by one who intelligently directs, focuses, and controls his urges, inclinations, and impulses. In its fullest form, therefore, the first requirement of practical reasonableness is what John Rawls calls a rational plan of life.[7] Implicitly or explicitly one must have a harmonious set of purposes and orientations, not as the 'plans' or 'blueprints' of a pipe-dream, but as effective commitments. (Do not confuse the adoption of a set of basic personal or social commitments with the process, imagined by some contemporary philosophers, of 'choosing basic values'!) It is unreasonable to live merely from moment to moment, following immediate cravings, or just drifting. It is also irrational to devote one's attention exclusively to specific projects which can be carried out completely by simply deploying defined means to defined objectives. Commitment to the practice of medicine (for the sake of human life), or to scholarship (for the sake of truth), or to any profession, or to a marriage (for the sake of friendship and children) . . . all require both direction and control of impulses, and the undertaking of specific projects; but they also require the redirection of inclinations, the reformation of habits, the abandonment of old and adoption of new projects, as circumstances require, and, overall, the harmonization of all one's deep commitments—for which there is no recipe or blueprint, since basic aspects of human good are not like the definite objectives of particular projects, but are *participated in.* . . .

The content and significance of this first requirement will be better understood in the light of the other requirements. For indeed, all the requirements are interrelated and capable of being regarded as aspects one of another.

3 NO ARBITRARY PREFERENCES AMONGST VALUES

Next, there must be no leaving out of account, or arbitrary discounting or exaggeration, of any of the basic human values. Any commitment to a coherent plan of life is going to involve some degree of concentration on one or some of the basic forms of good, at the expense, temporarily or permanently, of other forms of good. But the commitment will be rational only if it is on the basis of one's assessment of one's capacities, circumstances, and even of one's tastes. It will be unreasonable if it is on the basis of a devaluation of any of the basic forms of human excellence, or if it is on the basis of an overvaluation of such merely derivative and supporting or instrumental goods as wealth or 'opportunity' or of such merely secondary and conditionally valuable goods as reputation or (in a different sense of secondariness) pleasure.

A certain scholar may have little taste or capacity for friendship, and may feel that life for him would have no savour if he were prevented from pursuing his commitment to knowledge. None the less, it would be unreasonable for him to deny that, objectively, human life (quite apart from truth-seeking and knowledge) and friendship are good in themselves. It is one thing to have little capacity and even no 'taste' for scholarship, or friendship, or physical heroism, or sanctity; it is quite another thing, and stupid or arbitrary, to think or speak or act as if these were not real forms of good.

So, in committing oneself to a rational plan of life, and in interacting with other people (with their own plans of life), one must not use Rawls's 'thin theory of the good'. For the sake of a 'democratic'[8] impartiality between differing conceptions of human good, Rawls insists that, in selecting principles of justice, one must treat as primary goods only liberty, opportunity, wealth, and self-respect, and that one must not attribute intrinsic value to such basic forms of good as truth, or play, or art, or friendship. Rawls gives no satisfactory reason for this radical emaciation of human good, and no satisfactory reason is available: the 'thin theory' is arbitrary. It is quite reasonable for many men to choose not to commit themselves to any real pursuit of knowledge, and it is quite unreasonable for a scholar-statesman or scholar-father to demand that all his subjects or children should conform themselves willy-nilly to the modes and standards of excellence that he chooses and sets for himself. But it is even more unreasonable for anyone to deny that knowl-

edge *is* (and is to be treated as) a form of excellence, and that error, illusion, muddle, superstition, and ignorance are evils that no one should wish for, or plan for, or encourage in himself or in others. If a statesman or father or any self-directing individual treats truth or friendship or play or any of the other basic forms of good as of no account, and never asks himself whether his life-plan(s) makes reasonable allowance for participation in those intrinsic human values (and for avoidance of their opposites), then he can be properly accused both of irrationality and of stunting or mutilating himself and those in his care.

4 NO ARBITRARY PREFERENCES AMONGST PERSONS

Next, the basic goods are human goods, and can in principle be pursued, realized, and participated in by any human being. Another person's survival, his coming to know, his creativity, his all-round flourishing, may not interest me, may not concern me, may in any event be beyond my power to affect. But have I any *reason* to deny that they are really good, or that they are fit matters of interest, concern, and favour by that man and by all those who have to do with him? The questions of friendship, collaboration, mutual assistance, and justice are the subject of the next chapters. Here we need not ask just who is responsible for whose well-being. But we can add, to the second requirement of fundamental impartiality of recognition of each of the basic forms of good, a third requirement: of fundamental impartiality among the human subjects who are or may be partakers of those goods.

My own well-being (which, as we shall see, includes a concern for the well-being of others, my friends; but ignore this for the moment) is reasonably the first claim on my interest, concern, and effort. Why can I so regard it? Not because it is of more value than the well-being of others, simply because it is mine: intelligence and reasonableness can find no basis in the mere fact that A is A and is not B (that I am I and am not you) for evaluating his (our) well-being differentially. No: the only *reason* for me to prefer my well-being is that it is through *my* self-determined and self-realizing participation in the basic goods that I can do what reasonableness suggests and requires, viz. favour and realize the forms of human good indicated in the first principles of practical reason.

There is, therefore, reasonable scope for self-preference. But when all allowance is made for that, this third requirement remains, a pungent critique of selfishness, special pleading, double standards, hypocrisy, indifference to the good of others whom one could easily help ('passing by on the other side'), and all the other manifold forms of egoistic and group bias. So much so that many have sought to found ethics virtually entirely on this principle of impartiality between persons. In the modern philosophical discussion, the principle regularly is expressed as a requirement that one's moral judgments and preferences be *universalizable*.

The classical non-philosophical expression of the requirement is, of course, the so-called Golden Rule formulated not only in the Christian gospel but also in the sacred books of the Jews, and not only in didactic formulae but also in the moral appeal of sacred history and parable. It needed no drawing of the moral, no special traditions of moral education, for King David (and every reader of the story of his confrontation with Nathan the prophet) to feel the rational conclusiveness of Nathan's analogy between the rich man's appropriation of the poor man's ewe and the King's appropriation of Uriah the Hittite's wife, and thus the rational necessity for the King to extend his condemnation of the rich man to himself. 'You are the man' (2 Samuel 12:7).

'Do to (or for) others what you would have them do to (or for) you.' Put yourself in your neighbour's shoes. Do not condemn others for what you are willing to do yourself. Do not (without special reason) prevent others getting for themselves what you are trying to get for yourself. These are requirements of reason, because to ignore them is to be arbitrary as between individuals.

But what are the bounds of reasonable self-preference, of reasonable discrimination in favour of myself, my family, my group(s)? In the Greek, Roman, and Christian traditions of reflection, this question was approached via the heuristic device of adopting the viewpoint, the standards, the principles of justice, of one who sees the whole arena of human affairs and who has the interests of each participant in those affairs equally at heart and equally in mind—the 'ideal observer'. Such an impartially benevolent 'spectator' would condemn some but not all forms of self-preference, and some but not all forms of competition. The heuristic device helps one to attain impartiality as between the possible subjects of human well-being (persons) and to exclude mere bias in one's practical reasoning. It permits one to be impartial, too, among inexhaustibly many of the life-plans that differing individuals may choose. But, of course, it does not suggest 'impartiality' about the basic aspects of human good. It does not authorize one to set aside the second requirement of practical reason by indifference to death and disease, by preferring trash to art, by favouring the comforts of ignorance and illusion, by repressing all play as unworthy of man, by praising the ideal of self-aggrandizement and condemning the ideal of friendship, or by treating the search for the ultimate source and destiny of things as of no account or as an instrument of statecraft or a plaything reserved for leisured folk . . .

Therein lies the contrast between the classical heuristic device of the benevolently divine viewpoint and the equivalent modern devices for eliminating mere bias, notably the heuristic concept of the social contract. Consider Rawls's elaboration of the social contract strategy, an elaboration which most readily discloses the purpose of that strategy as a measure and instrument of practical reason's requirement of interpersonal impartiality. Every feature of Rawls's construction is designed to guarantee that if a supposed principle of justice is one that would be unanimously agreed on, behind the 'veil of ignorance', in the 'Original Position', then it must be a principle that is fair and unbiased as between persons. Rawls's heuristic device is thus of some use to anyone who is concerned for the third requirement of practical reasonableness, and in testing its implications. Unfortunately, Rawls disregards the second requirement of practical reasonableness, viz. that each basic or intrinsic human good be treated as a basic and intrinsic good. The conditions of the Original Position are designed by Rawls to guarantee that no principle of justice will systematically favour any life-plan simply because that life-plan participates more fully in human well-being in any or all of its basic aspects (e.g. by favouring knowledge over ignorance and illusion, art over trash, etc.).

And it simply does not follow, from the fact that a principle chosen in the Original Position would be unbiased and fair as between individuals, that a principle which would *not* be chosen in the Original Position must be unfair or not a proper principle of justice in the real world. For in the real world, as Rawls himself admits, intelligence can discern intrinsic basic values and their contraries.[9] Provided we make the distinctions mentioned in the previous section, between basic practical principles and mere matters of taste, inclination, ability, etc., we are able (and are required in reason) to favour the basic forms of good and to avoid and discourage their contraries. In doing so we are showing no improper favour to individuals as such, no unreasonable 're-spect of persons', no egoistic or group bias, no partiality opposed to the Golden Rule or to any other aspect of this third requirement of practical reason.

5 DETACHMENT AND COMMITMENT

The fourth and fifth requirements of practical reasonableness are closely complementary both to each other and to the first requirement of adopting a coherent plan of life, order of priorities, set of basic commitments.

In order to be sufficiently open to all the basic forms of good in all the changing circumstances of a lifetime, and in all one's relations, often unforeseeable, with other persons, and in all one's opportunities of effecting their well-being or relieving hardship, one must have a certain detachment from all the specific and limited projects which one undertakes. There is no good reason to take up an attitude to any of one's particular objectives, such that if one's project failed and one's objective eluded one, one would consider one's life drained of meaning. Such an attitude irrationally devalues and treats as meaningless the basic human good of authentic and reasonable self-determination, a good in which one meaningfully participates simply by trying to do something sensible and worthwhile, whether or not that sensible and worthwhile project comes to nothing. Moreover, there are often straightforward and evil consequences of succumbing to the temptation to give one's particular project the overriding and unconditional significance which only a basic value and a general commitment can claim: they are the evil consequences that we call to mind when we think of fanaticism. So the fourth requirement of practical reasonableness can be called detachment.

The fifth requirement establishes the balance between fanaticism and dropping out, apathy, unreasonable failure or refusal to 'get involved' with anything. It is simply the requirement that having made one's general commitments one must not abandon them lightly (for to do so would mean, in the extreme case, that one would fail ever to really participate in any of the basic values). And this requirement of fidelity has a positive aspect. One should be looking creatively for new and better ways of carrying out one's commitments, rather than restricting one's horizon and one's effort to the projects, methods, and routines with which one is familiar. Such creativity and development shows that a person, or a society, is really living on the level of practical *principle,* not merely on the level of conventional rules of conduct, rules of thumb, rules of method, etc., whose real appeal is not to reason (which would show up their inadequacies) but to the sub-rational complacency of habit, mere urge to conformity, etc.

6 THE (LIMITED) RELEVANCE OF CONSEQUENCES: EFFICIENCY, WITHIN REASON

The sixth requirement has obvious connections with the fifth, but introduces a new range of problems for practical reason, problems which go to the heart of 'morality'. For this is the requirement that one bring about good in the world (in one's own life and the lives of others) by actions that are efficient for their (reasonable) purpose(s). One must not waste one's opportunities by using inefficient methods. One's actions should be judged by their effectiveness, by their fitness for their purpose, by their utility, their consequences . . .

There is a wide range of contexts in which it is possible and only reasonable to calculate, measure, compare, weigh, and assess the consequences of alternative decisions. Where a choice must be made it is reasonable to prefer human good to the good of animals. Where a choice must be made it is reasonable to prefer basic human goods (such as life) to merely instrumental goods (such as property). Where damage is inevitable, it is reasonable to prefer stunning to wounding, wounding to maiming, maiming to death: i.e. lesser rather than greater damage to one-and-the-same basic good in one-and-the-same instantiation. Where one way of participating in a human good includes *both* all the good aspects and effects of its alternative, *and* more, it is reasonable to prefer that way: a remedy that both relieves pain and heals is to be preferred to the one that merely relieves pain. Where a person or a society has created a personal or social hierarchy of practical norms and orientations, through reasonable choice of commit-

ments, one can in many cases reasonably measure the benefits and disadvantages of alternatives. (Consider a man who has decided to become a scholar, or a society that has decided to go to war.) Where one is considering objects or activities in which there is reasonably a market, the market provides a common denominator (currency) and enables a comparison to be made of prices, costs, and profits. Where there are alternative techniques or facilities for achieving definite objectives, cost–benefit analysis will make possible a certain range of reasonable comparisons between techniques or facilities. Over a wide range of preferences and wants, it is reasonable for an individual or society to seek to maximize the satisfaction of those preferences or wants.

But this sixth requirement is only one requirement among a number. The first, second, and third requirements require that in seeking to maximize the satisfaction of preferences one should discount the preferences of, for example, sadists (who follow the impulses of the moment, and/or do not respect the value of life, and/or do not universalize their principles of action with impartiality). The first, third, and (as we shall see) seventh and eighth requirements require that cost–benefit analysis be contained within a framework that excludes any project involving certain intentional killings, frauds, manipulations of personality, etc. And the second requirement requires that one recognize that each of the basic aspects of human well-being is equally basic, that none is objectively more important than any of the others, and thus that none can provide a common denominator or single yardstick for assessing the utility of all projects: they are incommensurable, and any calculus of consequences that pretends to commensurate them is irrational.

As a general strategy of moral reasoning, utilitarianism or consequentialism is irrational. The utilitarian or (more generally) the consequentialist claims that (i) one should always choose the act that, so far as one can see, will yield the greatest net good on the whole and in the long run ('act-utilitarianism'), or that (ii) one should always choose according to a principle or rule the adoption of which will yield the greatest net good on the whole and in the long run ('rule-utilitarianism'). Each of these claims is not so much false as senseless (in a sense of 'senseless' that will shortly be explained). For no plausible sense can be given, here, to the notion of a 'greatest net good', or to any analogous alternative notions such as 'best consequences', 'lesser evil', 'smallest net harm', or 'greater balance of good over bad than could be expected from any available alternative action'. . . .

The sixth requirement—of efficiency in pursuing the definite goals which we adopt for ourselves and in avoiding the definite harms which we choose to regard as unacceptable—is a real requirement, with indefinitely many applications in 'moral' (and hence in legal) thinking. But its sphere of proper application has limits, and every attempt to make it the exclusive or supreme or even the central principle of practical thinking is irrational and hence immoral. Still, we ought not to disguise from ourselves the *ultimate* (and hence inexplicable, even 'strange'[10]) character of the basic principles and requirements of reasonableness (like the basic aspects of the world . . .) once we go beyond the intellectual routines of calculating cost–benefit and efficiency.

7 RESPECT FOR EVERY BASIC VALUE IN EVERY ACT

The seventh requirement of practical reasonableness can be formulated in several ways. A first formulation is that one should not choose to do any act which *of itself does nothing but* damage or impede a realization or participation of any one or more of the basic forms of human good. For the only 'reason' for doing such an act, other than the non-reason of some impelling desire, could be that the good *consequences* of the act *outweigh* the damage done in and through the act itself. But, outside merely technical contexts, consequentialist 'weighing' is al-

ways and necessarily arbitrary and delusive for the reasons indicated in the preceding section. . . .

The basic values, and the practical principles expressing them, are the only guides we have. Each is objectively basic, primary, incommensurable with the others in point of objective importance. If one is to act intelligently at all one must choose to realize and participate in some basic value or values rather than others, and this inevitable concentration of effort will indirectly impoverish, inhibit, or interfere with the realization of those other values. If I commit myself to truthful scholarship, then I fail to save the lives I could save as a doctor, I inhibit the growth of the production of material goods, I limit my opportunities for serving the community through politics, entertainment, art, or preaching. And within the field of science and scholarship, my research into K means that L and M go as yet undiscovered. These unsought but unavoidable side-effects accompany every human choice, and their consequences are incalculable. But it is always reasonable to leave some of them, and often reasonable to leave all of them, out of account. Let us for brevity use the word 'damage' to signify also impoverishment, inhibition, or interference, and the word 'promote' to signify also pursuit or protection. Then we can say this: to indirectly damage any basic good (by choosing an act that directly and immediately promotes either that basic good in some other aspect or participation, or some other basic good or goods) is obviously quite different, rationally and thus morally, from directly and immediately damaging a basic good in some aspect or participation by choosing an act which in and of itself simply (or, we should now add, primarily) damages that good in some aspect or participation but which indirectly, *via* the mediation of expected consequences, is to promote either that good in some other aspect or participation, or some other basic good(s).

To choose an act which in itself simply (or primarily) damages a basic good is thereby to engage oneself willy-nilly (but directly) in an act of opposition to an incommensurable value (an aspect of human personality) which one treats as if it were an object of measurable worth that could be outweighed by commensurable objects of greater (or cumulatively greater) worth. To do this will often accord with our feelings, our generosity, our sympathy, and with our commitments and projects in the forms in which we undertook them. But it can never be justified in reason. We must choose rationally (and this rational judgment can often promote a shift in our perspective and consequently a realignment of initial feelings and thus of our commitments and projects). Reason requires that every basic value be at least respected in each and every action. If one could ever rightly choose a single act which *itself* damages and *itself* does not promote some basic good, then one could rightly choose whole programmes and institutions and enterprises that themselves damage and do not promote basic aspects of human well-being, for the sake of their 'net beneficial consequences'. Now we have already seen that consequences, even to the extent that they can be 'foreseen as certain', cannot be commensurably *evaluated,* which means that 'net beneficial consequences' is a literally absurd general objective or criterion. It only remains to note that a man who thinks that his rational responsibility to be always doing and pursuing good is satisfied by a commitment to act always for best consequences is a man who treats every aspect of human personality (and indeed, therefore, treats himself) as a utensil. He holds himself ready to do *anything* (and thus makes himself a tool for all those willing to threaten sufficiently bad consequences if he does not cooperate with them).

But the objection I am making to such choices is not that programmes of mass killing, mass deception, etc. would then be more eligible (though they would) and indeed morally required (though they would), but that no sufficient reason can be found for treating any act as immune from the only direction which we have, viz. the direc-tion afforded by the basic practical principles. These each direct that a form of good is to be pursued and done; and each of them bears not only on all our large-scale choices of general orientations and commitments, and on all our medium-scale choices of projects (in which attainment of the objective will indeed be the good consequence of successful deployment of effective means), but also on each and every choice of an act which itself is a complete act (whether or not it is also a step in a plan or phase in a project). The incommensurable value of an aspect of personal full-being (and its corresponding primary principle) can never be rightly subordinated to any project or commitment. But such an act of subordination inescapably occurs at least whenever a distinct choice-of-act has in *itself* no meaning save that of damaging that basic value (thus violating that primary principle).

Such, in highly abstract terms, is the seventh requirement, the principle on which alone rests . . . the strict inviolability of basic human rights. There is no human right that will not be overridden if feelings (whether generous and unselfish, or mean and self-centred) are allowed to govern choice, or if cost–benefit considerations are taken outside their appropriate technical sphere and allowed to govern one's direct engagement (whether at the level of commitment, project, or individual act) with basic goods. And the perhaps unfamiliar formulation which we have been considering should not obscure the fact that this 'seventh requirement' is well recognized, in other formulations: most loosely, as 'the end does not justify the means'; more precisely, though still ambiguously, as 'evil may not be done that good might follow therefrom'; and with a special Enlightenment flavour, as Kant's 'categorical imperative': 'Act so that you treat humanity, whether in your own person or in that of another, always as an end and never as a means only'.[11]

Obviously, the principal problem in considering the implications of this requirement is the problem of individuating and characterizing actions, to determine what is one complete act-that-itself-does-nothing-but-damage-a-basic-good. Human acts are to be individuated primarily in terms of those factors which we gesture towards with the word 'intention'. Fundamentally, a human act is a that-which-is-decided-upon (or -chosen) and its primary proper description is as what-is-chosen. A human action, to be humanly regarded, is to be characterized in the way it was characterized in the conclusion to the relevant train of practical reasoning of the man who chose to do it. On the other hand, the world with its material (including our bodily selves) and its structures of physical and psycho-physical causality is not indefinitely malleable by human intention. The man who is deciding what to do cannot reasonably shut his eyes to the causal structure of his project; he cannot characterize his plans *ad lib.* One can be engaged willy-nilly but directly, in act, with a basic good, such as human life.

Perhaps the consequences of one's act seem likely to be very good and would themselves directly promote further basic human good. Still, these expected goods will be realized (if at all) not as aspects of one-and-the-same act, but as aspects or consequences of other acts (by another person, at another time and place, as the upshot of another free decision . . .). So, however 'certainly foreseeable' they may be, they cannot be used to characterize the act itself as, *in and of itself,* anything other than an intentional act of, say, man-killing. This is especially obvious when a blackmailer's price for sparing his hostages is 'killing that man'; the person who complies with the demand, in order to save the lives of the many, cannot deny that he is choosing an act which of itself does nothing but kill.

Sometimes, however, the 'good effects' are really aspects of one-and-the-same act, and can form part of the description of what it is in and of itself. Then we cannot characterize the act as in and of itself *nothing but* damaging to human good. But is it rationally justifiable? Not necessarily; the seventh requirement is not an isolated requirement, and

such a choice may flout the second, third, fourth, and fifth requirements. The choice a man makes may be one he would not make if he were sufficiently detached from his impulses and his peculiar project to avoid treating a particular act or project as if it were itself a basic aspect of human well-being; or if he were *creatively* open to all the basic goods and thus careful to adjust his projects so as to minimize their damaging 'side-effects' and to avoid substantial and irreparable harms to persons. The third requirement here provides a convenient test of respect for good: would the person acting have thought the act reasonable had *he* been the person harmed? Considerations such as these are woven into the notion of *directly* choosing against a basic value. And for most practical purposes this seventh requirement can be summarized as: Do not choose directly against a basic value. . . .

8 THE REQUIREMENTS OF THE COMMON GOOD

Very many, perhaps even most, of our concrete moral responsibilities, obligations, and duties have their basis in the eighth requirement. We can label this the requirement of favouring and fostering the common good of one's communities. The sense and implications of this requirement are complex and manifold.

9 FOLLOWING ONE'S CONSCIENCE

The ninth requirement might be regarded as a particular aspect of the seventh (that no basic good may be directly attacked in any act), or even as a summary of all the requirements. But it is quite distinctive. It is the requirement that one should not do what one judges or thinks or 'feels'-all-in-all should not be done. That is to say one must act 'in accordance with one's conscience'.

This chapter has been in effect a reflection on the workings of conscience. If one were by inclination generous, open, fair, and steady in one's love of human good, or if one's milieu happened to have settled on reasonable *mores,* then one would be able, without solemnity, rigmarole, abstract reasoning, or casuistry, to make the particular practical judgments (i.e. judgments of conscience) that reason requires. If one is not so fortunate in one's inclinations or upbringing, then one's conscience will mislead one, unless one strives to be reasonable and is blessed with a pertinacious intelligence alert to the forms of human good yet undeflected by the sophistries which intelligence so readily generates to rationalize indulgence, time-serving, and self-love. (The stringency of these conditions is the permanent ground for the possibility of authority in morals, i.e. of authoritative guidance, by one who meets those conditions, acknowledged willingly by persons of conscience.)

The first theorist to formulate this ninth requirement in all its unconditional strictness seems to have been Thomas Aquinas: if one chooses to do what one judges to be in the last analysis unreasonable, or if one chooses not to do what one judges to be in the last analysis required by reason, then one's choice is unreasonable (wrongful), however erroneous one's judgments of conscience may happen to be. (A *logically* necessary feature of such a situation is, of course, that one is ignorant of one's mistake.)

This dignity of even the mistaken conscience is what is expressed in the ninth requirement. It flows from the fact that practical reasonableness is not simply a mechanism for producing correct judgments, but an aspect of personal full-being, to be respected (like all the other aspects) in every act as well as 'over-all'—whatever the consequences.

10 THE PRODUCT OF THESE REQUIREMENTS: MORALITY

Now we can see why some philosophers have located the essence of 'morality' in the reduction of harm, others in the increase of well-being, some in social harmony, some in universalizability of practical judgment, some in the all-round flourishing of the individual, others in the preservation of freedom and personal authenticity. Each of these has a place in rational choice of commitments, projects, and particular actions. Each, moreover, contributes to the sense, significance, and force of terms such as 'moral', '[morally] ought', and 'right'; not every one of the nine requirements has a direct role in every moral judgment, but some moral judgments do sum up the bearing of each and all of the nine on the questions in hand, and every moral judgment sums up the bearing of one or more of the requirements. . . .

If, finally, we look back over the complex of basic principles and basic requirements of practical reasonableness, we can see how 'natural' is that diversity of moral opinion which the sceptic makes such play of. It is a diversity which has its source in too exclusive attention to some of the basic value(s) and/or some basic requirement(s), and inattention to others. Sometimes, no doubt, the distortion or deflection is most immediately explicable by reference to an uncritical, unintelligent spontaneity; sometimes, by reference to the bias and oversight induced by conventions of language, social structure, and social practice; and sometimes (and always, perhaps, most radically) by the bias of self-love or of other emotions and inclinations that resist the concern to be simply reasonable.

NOTES

*Editor's Note: The seven basic forms of human good are life, knowledge, play, aesthetic experience, friendship, religion, and practical reasonableness.

1. *Nic. Eth.* I, 3: 1095a7–11; 4: 1095b5–13; X, 9: 1179b27–30.

2. *Nic. Eth.* X, 9: 1179b27–1180a5.

3. See *Nic. Eth.* VI, 5: 1140a24–25; II, 5: 1105b30–31; III, 6: 1115a20; III, 10: 1117b32; cf. X, 2: 1173a1.

4. *Nic. Eth.* VI, 11: 1143a35–1143b17.

5. *Nic. Eth.* X, 10: 1176a17–18; cf. III, 6: 1113a33; IX, 4: 1166a12–13: see also I.4, above.

6. *Nic. Eth.* II, 6: 1106b21–24.

7. *Theory of Justice,* pp. 408–23, adopting the terminology of W. F. R. Hardie, 'The Final Good in Aristotle's Ethics' (1965) 60 *Philosophy* 277.

8. Cf. *Theory of Justice,* p. 527.

9. *Theory of Justice,* p. 328.

10. Thus Brian Barry rightly begins his 'Justice Between Generations', *Essays,* pp. 269–84, by asking (quoting Wilfred Beckerman) 'Suppose that, as a result of using up all the world's resources, human life did come to an end. So what?' and concludes a thorough analysis of the issues for practical reasonableness by saying '. . .

the continuation of human life into the future is something to be sought (or at least not sabotaged) even if it does not make for the maximum total happiness. Certainly, if I try to analyse the source of my own strong conviction that we should be wrong to take risks with the continuation of human life, I find that it does not lie in any sense of injury to the interests of people who will not get born but rather in a sense of its cosmic impertinence—that we should be grossly abusing our position by taking it upon ourselves to put a term on human life and its possibilities' (p. 284).

11. Kant, *Foundations of the Metaphysics of Morals* (1785; trans. Beck, Indianapolis: 1959), p. 47.

23
WHAT DO WOMEN WANT IN A MORAL THEORY?

Annette C. Baier

When I finished reading Carol Gilligan's "In Another Voice", I asked myself the obvious question for a philosopher reader, namely what differences one should expect in the moral philosophy done by women, supposing Gilligan's sample of women representative, and supposing her analysis of their moral attitudes and moral development to be correct. Should one expect them to want to produce moral theories, and if so, what sort of moral theories? How will any moral theories they produce differ from those produced by men?

Obviously one does not have to make this an entirely *a priori* and hypothetical question. One can look and see what sort of contributions women have made to moral philosophy. Such a look confirms, I think, Gilligan's findings. What one finds *is* a bit different in tone and approach from the standard sort of moral philosophy as done by men following in the footsteps of the great moral philosophers (all men). Generalizations are ex-

Reprinted by permission of the author and of the editor of *Noûs*, Vol. 19 (1985): 53–63.

tremely rash, but when I think of Philippa Foot's work on the moral virtues, of Elizabeth Anscombe's work on intention and on modern moral philosophy, of Iris Murdoch's philosophical writings, of Ruth Barcan Marcus' work on moral dilemmas, of the work of the radical feminist moral philosophers who are not content with orthodox Marxist lines of thought, of Jenny Teichman's book on Illegitimacy, of Susan Wolf's recent articles, of Claudia Card's essay on mercy, Sabina Lovilbond's recent book, Gabriele Taylor's work on pride, love and on integrity, Cora Diamond's and Mary Midgeley's work on our attitude to animals, Sissela Bok's work on lying and on secrecy, Virginia Held's work, the work of Alison Jaggar, Marilyn Frye, and many others, I seem to hear a different voice from the standard moral philosopher's voice. I hear the voice Gilligan heard, made reflective and philosophical. What women want in moral philosophy is what they are providing. And what they are providing seems to me to confirm Gilligan's theses about women. One has to be careful here, of course, for not all important contributions to moral philosophy by women fall easily into the Gilligan stereotype, nor its philosophical extension. Nor has it been only women who recently have been proclaiming discontent with the standard approach in moral philosophy, and trying new approaches. Michael Stocker, Alasdair MacIntyre, Ian Hacking when he assesses the game theoretic approach to morality,[1] all should be given the status of honorary women, if we accept the hypothesis that there are some moral insights which for whatever reason women seem to attain more easily or more reliably than men do. Still, exceptions confirm the rule, so I shall proceed undaunted by these important exceptions to my generalizations.

If Hacking is right, preoccupation with prisoner's and prisoners' dilemma is a big boys' game, and a pretty silly one too. It is, I think, significant that women have not rushed into the field of game-theoretic moral philosophy, and that those who have dared enter that male locker room have said distinctive things there. Edna Ullman Margalit's book *The Emergence of Norms* put prisoners' dilemma in its limited moral place. Supposing that at least part of the explanation for the relatively few women in this field is disinclination rather than disability, one might ask if this disinclination also extends to a disinclination for the construction of moral theories. For although we find out what sort of moral philosophy women want by looking to see what they have provided, if we do that for moral theory, the answer we get seems to be "none". For none of the contributions to moral philosophy by women really count as moral theories, nor are seen as such by their authors.

Is it that reflective women, when they become philosophers, want to do without moral theory, want no part in the construction of such theories? To conclude this at this early stage, when we have only a few generations of women moral philosophers to judge from, would be rash indeed. The term "theory" can be used in wider and narrower ways, and in its widest sense a moral theory is simply an internally consistent fairly comprehensive account of what morality is and when and why it merits our acceptance and support. In that wide sense, a moral theory is something it would take a sceptic, or one who believes that our intellectual vision is necessarily blurred or distorted when we let it try to take in too much, to be an anti-theorist. Even if there were some truth in the latter claim, one might compatibly with it still hope to build up a coherent total account by a mosaic method, assembling a lot of smaller scale works until one had built up a complete account—say taking the virtues or purported virtues one by one until one had a more or less complete account. But would that sort of comprehensiveness in one's moral philosophy entitle one to call the finished work a moral theory? If it does, then many women moral philosophers today can be seen as engaged in moral theory construction. In the weakest sense of "theory", namely coherent near-comprehensive account, then there are plenty incomplete theories to be found in the works of women moral philosophers. And in *that* sense of theory, most of what are recognized as the current moral theories are also incomplete, since they do not purport to be yet really comprehensive. Wrongs to animals and wrongful destruction of our physical environment are put to one side by Rawls, and in most "liberal" theories there are only hand waves concerning our proper attitude to our children, to the ill, to our relatives, friends and lovers.

Is comprehensiveness too much to ask of a moral theory? The paradigm examples of moral theories—those that are called by their authors "moral theories", are distinguished not by the comprehensiveness of their internally coherent account, but by the *sort* of coherence which is aimed at over a fairly broad area. Their method is not the mosaic method, but the broad brushstroke method. Moral theories, as we know them, are, to change the art form, vaults rather than walls—they are not built by assembling painstakingly-made brick after brick. In *this* sense of theory, namely fairly tightly systematic account of a fairly large area of morality, with a key stone supporting all the rest, women moral philosophers have not yet, to my knowledge, produced moral theories, nor claimed that they have.

Leaving to one side the question of what good purpose (other than good clean intellectual fun) is served by such moral theories, and supposing for the sake of argument that women can, if they wish, systematize as well as the next man, and if need be systematize in a mathematical fashion as well as the next mathematically minded moral philosopher, then what key concept, or guiding *motif*, might hold together the structure of a moral theory hypothetically produced by a reflective woman, Gilligan-style, who has taken up moral theorizing as a calling? What would be a suitable central question, principle, or concept, to structure a moral theory which might accommodate those moral insights women tend to have more readily than men, and to answer those moral questions which, it seems, worry women more than men? I hypothesized that the women's theory, expressive mainly of women's insights and concerns, would be an ethics of love, and this hypothesis seems to be Gilligan's too, since she has gone on from "In a Different Voice" to write about the limitations of Freud's understanding of love as women know it.[2] But presumably women theorists will be like enough to men to want their moral theory to be acceptable to all, so acceptable both to reflective women and to reflective men. Like any good theory, it will need not to ignore the partial truth of previous theories. So it must accommodate both the insights men have more easily than women, and those women have more easily than men. It should swallow up its predecessor theories. Women moral theorists, if any, will have this very great advantage over the men whose theories theirs supplant, that they can stand on the shoulders of men moral theorists, as no man has yet been able to stand on the shoulders of any woman moral theorist. There can be advantages, as well as handicaps, in being latecomers. So women theorists will need to connect their ethics of love with what has been the men theorists' preoccupation, namely obligation.

The great and influential moral theorists have in the modern era taken *obligation* as the key and the problematic concept, and have asked what justifies treating a person as morally bound or obliged to do a particular thing. Since to be bound is to be unfree, by making obligation central one at the same time makes central the question of the justification of coercion, of forcing or trying to force someone to act in a particular way. The concept of obligation as justified limitation of freedom does just what one wants a good theoretical concept to do—to divide up the field (as one looks at different ways one's freedom may be limited, freedom in different spheres, different sorts and versions and levels of justification) and at the same time hold the subfields together. There must in a theory be some generalization and some specification or diversification, and a good rich key concept guides on both in recognizing the diversity and in recognizing the unity in it. The concept of obligation has served this function very well for the area of morality it covers, and so we have some fine theories about that area. But as Aristotelians and Christians, as well as women, know, there is a lot of morality *not* covered by that concept, a lot of very great importance even for the area where there are obligations.

[In the next section, omitted here, I discuss responsibility for forming new members of the moral community to be capable of taking obligations seriously, and also discuss military duties. I attempt to show that current theories of obligation, especially contractarian ones, fail to yield conclusions compatible with their own principles on who is to do the ruthless human destruction and the loving human reproduction we depend on having done, so these theories are at best incomplete and at worst incoherent or in bad faith.]

Granted that the men's theories of obligation need supplementation, to have much chance of integrity and coherence, and that the women's hypothetical theories will want to cover obligation as well as love, then what concept brings them together? My tentative answer is—the concept of appropriate trust, oddly neglected in moral theory. This concept also nicely mediates between reason and feeling, those tired old candidates for moral authority, since to trust is neither quite to believe something about the trusted, nor necessarily to feel any emotion towards them—but to have a belief-informed and action-influencing attitude. To make it plausible that the neglected concept of appropriate trust is a good one for the enlightened moral theorist to make central, I need to show, or begin to show, how it could include obligation, indeed shed light on obligations and their justification, as well as include love and the other moral concerns of Gilligan's women, and many of the topics women moral philosophers have chosen to address, mosaic fashion. I would also need to show that it could connect all of these in a way which holds out promise both of synthesis and of comprehensive moral coverage. A moral theory which looked at the conditions for proper trust of all the various sorts we show, and at what sorts of reasons justify inviting such trust, giving it, and meeting it, would, I believe, not have to avoid turning its gaze on the conditions for the survival of the practices it endorses, so it could avoid that unpleasant choice many current liberal theories seem to have—between incoherence and bad faith. I do not pretend that we will easily agree once we raise the questions I think we should raise, but at least we may have a language adequate to the expression of both men's and women's moral viewpoints.

My trust in the concept of trust is based in part on my own attempts to restate and consider what was right and what was wrong with men's theories, especially Hume's, which I consider the best of the lot. There I found myself reconstructing his account of the artifices of justice as an account of the progressive enlargement of a climate of trust, and found that a helpful way to see it. It has some textual basis, but is nevertheless a reconstruction, and one I found, immodestly, an improvement. So it is because I have tried the concept, and explored its dimensions a bit—the variety of goods we may trust others not to take from us, the variety of sort of security or insurance we have when we do, the sorts of defences or potential defences we lay down when we trust, the various conditions for reasonable trust of various types— that I am hopeful about its power as a theoretical not just an exegetical tool. I also found myself needing to use it, when I made a brief rash attempt at that women's topic, caring (invited in by a man philosopher,[3] I should say). That it does generalize some central moral features both of the recognition of binding obligations and moral virtues, and of loving, as well as of other important relations between persons, such as teacher-pupil, confider-confidante, worker to co-worker in the same cause, professional to client, I am reasonably sure. Indeed it is fairly obvious that love, the main moral phenomenon women want attended to, involves trust, so I anticipate little quarrel when I claim that, if we had a moral theory spelling out the conditions for appropriate trust and distrust, that would include a morality of love in all its variants—parental love, love of children for their parents, love of family members, love of friends, of lovers in the strict sense, of co-workers, of one's country, and its figureheads, of exemplary heroines and heros, of goddesses and gods.

Love and loyalty demand maximal trust of one sort, and maximal trustworthiness, and in investigating the conditions for maximal trust and maximal risk we must think about the ethics of love. More controversial may be my claim that the ethics of obligation will also be covered. I see it as covered since to recognize a set of obligations is to trust some group of persons to instill them, to demand that they be met, possibly to levy sanctions if they are not, and this is to trust persons with very significant coercive power over others. Less coercive but still significant power is possessed by those shaping our conception of the virtues, and expecting us to display them, approving when we do, disapproving and perhaps shunning us when we do not. Such coercive and manipulative power over others requires justification, and is justified only if we have reason to trust those who have it to use it properly, and to use the discretion which is always given when trust is given in a way which serves the purpose of the whole system of moral control, and not merely self serving or morally improper purposes. Since the question of the justification of coercion becomes, at least in part, the question of the wisdom of trusting the coercers to do their job properly, the morality of obligation, in as far as it reduces to the morality of coercion, is covered by the morality of proper trust. Other forms of trust may also be involved, but trusting enforcers with the use of force is the most problematic form of trust involved.

The coercers and manipulators are, to some extent, all of us, so to ask what our obligations are and what virtues we should exhibit is to ask what it is reasonable to trust us to demand, expect, and contrive to get, from one another. It becomes, in part, a question of what powers we can in reason trust ourselves to exercise properly. But self-trust is a dubious or limit case of trust, so I prefer to postpone the examination of the concept of proper self-trust at least until proper trust of others is more clearly understood. Nor do we distort matters too much if we concentrate on those cases where moral sanctions and moral pressure and moral manipulation is not self applied but applied to others, particularly by older persons to younger persons. Most moral pressuring that has any effects goes on in childhood and early youth. Moral sanctions may continue to be applied, formally and informally, to adults, but unless the criminal courts apply them it is easy enough for adults to ignore them, to brush them aside. It is not difficult to become a sensible knave, and to harden one's heart so that one is insensible to the moral condemnation of one's victims and those who sympathize with them. Only if the pressures applied in the morally formative stage have given one a heart that rebels against the thought of such ruthless independence of what others think will one see any reason *not* to ignore moral condemnation, not to treat it as mere powerless words and breath. Condemning sensible

knaves is as much a waste of breath as arguing with them—all we can sensibly do is to try to protect their children against their influence, and ourselves against their knavery. Adding to the criminal law will not be the way to do the latter, since such moves will merely challenge sensible knaves to find new knavish exceptions and loopholes, not protect us from sensible knavery. Sensible knaves are precisely those who exploit us without breaking the law. So the whole question of when moral pressure of various sorts, formative, reformative, and punitive, ought to be brought to bear by whom is subsumed under the question of whom to trust when and with what, and for what good reasons.

In concentrating on obligations, rather than virtues, modern moral theorists have chosen to look at the cases where more trust is placed in enforcers of obligations than is placed in ordinary moral agents, the bearers of the obligations. In taking, as contractarians do, contractual obligations as the model of obligations, they concentrate on a case where the very minimal trust is put in the obligated person, and considerable punitive power entrusted to the one to whom the obligation is owed (I assume here that Hume is right in saying that when we promise or contract, we formally subject ourselves to the penalty, in case of failure, of never being trusted as a promisor again). This is an interesting case of the allocation of trust of various sorts, but it surely distorts our moral vision to suppose that *all* obligations, let alone all morally pressured expectations we impose on others, conform to that abnormally coercive model. It takes very special conditions for it to be safe to trust persons to inflict penalties on other persons, conditions in which either we can trust the penalizers to have the virtues necessary to penalize wisely and fairly, or else we can rely on effective threats to keep unvirtuous penalizers from abusing their power—that is to say, rely on others to coerce the first coercers into proper behaviour. But that reliance too will either be trust, or will have to rely on threats from coercers of the coercers of coercers, and so on. Morality on this model becomes a nasty, if intellectually intriguing, game of mutual mutually corrective threats. The central question of who should deprive whom of what freedom soon becomes the question of whose anger should be dreaded by whom (the theory of obligation) supplemented perhaps by an afterthought on whose favor should be courted by whom (the theory of the virtues).

Undoubtedly some important part of morality does depend in part on a system of threats and bribes, at least for its survival in difficult conditions when normal goodwill and normally virtuous dispositions may be insufficient to motivate the conduct required for the preservation and justice of the moral network of relationships. But equally undoubtedly life will be nasty, emotionally poor, and worse than brutish (even if longer), if that is all morality is, or even if that coercive structure of morality is regarded as the backbone, rather than as an available crutch, should the main support fail. For the main support has to come from those we entrust with the job of rearing and training persons so that they can be trusted in various ways, some trusted with extraordinary coercive powers, some with public decision-making powers, all trusted as parties to promise, most trusted by some who love them and by one or more willing to become co-parents with them, most trusted by dependent children, dependent elderly relatives, sick friends, and so on. A very complex network of a great variety of sorts of trust structures our moral relationships with our fellows, and if there is a *main* support to this network it is the trust we place in those who respond to the trust of new members of the moral community, namely to children, and prepare them for new forms of trust.

A theory which took as its central question "Who should trust whom with what, and why?" would not have to forego the intellectual fun and games previous theorists have had with the various paradoxes of morality—curbing freedom to increase freedom, curbing self interest the better to satisfy self interest, not aiming at happiness in order to become happier. For it is easy enough to get a paradox of trust, to accompany or, if I am right, to generalize the paradoxes of freedom, self interest and hedonism. To trust is to make oneself or let oneself be more vulnerable than one might have been to harm from others—to give them an opportunity to harm one, in the confidence that they will not take it, because they have no good reason to.[4] Why would one take such a risk? For risk it always is, given the partial opaqueness to us of the reasoning and motivation of those we trust and with whom we cooperate. Our confidence may be, and quite often is, misplaced. That is what we risk when we trust. If the best reason to take such a risk is the expected gain in security which comes from a climate of trust, then in trusting we are always giving up security to get greater security, exposing our throats so that others become accustomed to not biting. A moral theory which made proper trust its central concern could have its own categorical imperative, could replace obedience to self made laws and freely chosen restraint on freedom with security-increasing sacrifice of security, distrust in the promoters of a climate of distrust, and so on.

Such reflexive use of one's central concept, negative or affirmative, is an intellectually satisfying activity which is bound to have appeal to those system-lovers who want to construct moral theories, and it may help them design their theory in an intellectually pleasing manner. But we should beware of becoming hypnotized by our slogans, or of sacrificing truth to intellectual elegance. Any theory of proper trust should not *prejudge* the questions of when distrust is proper. We might find more objects of proper distrust than just the contributors to a climate of reasonable distrust, just as freedom should be restricted not just to increase human freedom but to protect human life from poisoners and other killers. I suspect, however, that all the objects of reasonable distrust are more reasonably seen as falling into the category of ones who contribute to a decrease in the scope of proper trust, than can all who are reasonably coerced be seen as themselves guilty of wrongful coercion. Still, even if all proper trust turns out to be for such persons and on such matters as will increase the scope or stability of a climate of reasonable trust, and all proper distrust for such persons and on such matters as increase the scope of reasonable distrust, overreliance on such nice reflexive formulae can distract us from asking all the questions about trust which need to be asked, if an adequate moral theory is to be constructed around that concept. These questions should include when to *respond* to trust with *un*trustworthiness, when and when not to invite trust, as well as when to give and refuse trust. We should not assume that promiscuous trustworthiness is any more a virtue than is undiscriminating distrust. It is appropriate trustworthiness, appropriate trustingness, appropriate encouragement to trust, which will be virtues, as will be judicious untrustworthiness, selective refusal to trust, discriminating discouragement of trust.

Women are particularly well placed to appreciate these last virtues, since they have sometimes needed them to get into a position to even consider becoming moral theorizers. The long exploitation and domination of women by men depended on men's trust in women and women's trustworthiness to play their allotted role and so to perpetuate their own and their daughters' servitude. However keen women now are to end the lovelessness of modern moral philosophy, they are unlikely to lose sight of the cautious virtue of appropriate distrust, or of the tough virtue of principled betrayal of the exploiters' trust.

Gilligan's girls and women saw morality as a matter of preserving valued ties to others, of preserving the conditions for that care and mutual care without which human life becomes bleak, lonely, and after a while, as the mature men in her study found, not self affirming, however successful in achieving the egoistic goals which had been set. The boys and men saw morality as a matter of finding workable traffic rules for self assertors, so that they not needlessly frustrate one another, and so that they could, should they so choose, cooperate in more positive ways to mutual advantage. Both for the women's sometimes unchosen and valued ties with others, and for the men's mutual respect as sovereigns and subjects of the same minimal moral traffic rules (and for their more voluntary and more selective associations of profiteers) trust is important. Both men and women are concerned with cooperation, and the dimensions of trust-distrust structure the different cooperative relations each emphasize. The various considerations which arise when we try to defend an answer to any question about the appropriateness of a particular form of cooperation with its distinctive form of trust or distrust, that is when we look into the terms of all sorts of cooperation, at the terms of trust in different cases of trust, at what are fair terms and what are trust-enhancing and trust-preserving terms, are suitably many and richly interconnected. A moral theory (or family of theories) that made trust its central problem could do better justice to men's and women's moral intuitions than do the going men's theories. Even if we don't easily agree on the answer to the question of who should trust whom with what, who should accept and who should meet various sorts of trust, and why, these questions might enable us better to morally reason together than we can when the central moral questions are reduced to those of whose favor one must court and whose anger one must dread. But such programmatic claims as I am making will be tested only when women standing on the shoulders of men, or men on the shoulders of women, or some theorizing Tiresias, actually work out such a theory. I am no Tiresias, and have not foresuffered all the labor pains of such a theory. I aim here only to fertilize.

NOTES

1. Ian Hacking, "Winner Take Less," a review of *The Evolution of Cooperation* by Robert Axelrod, *New York Review of Books,* vol. XXX, no. 11, June 28, 1984.

2. Carol Gilligan, "The Conquisador and the Dark Continent: Reflections on the Psychology of Love," *Daedalus,* Summer, 1984.

3. "Caring About Caring," a response to Harry Frankfurt's "What We Care About," both in *Matters of the Mind, Synthese,* vol. 53, no. 2, November, 1982, pp. 257–290. My paper will also be included in *Postures of the Mind,* University of Minnesota Press, (1985).

4. I defend this claim about trust in "Trust and Antitrust," *Ethics* (1986).

Suggested Readings

ACKERMAN, BRUCE A. *Social Justice in the Liberal State*. New Haven: Yale University Press, 1980.

ARTHUR, JOHN, AND SHAW, WILLIAM, EDS. *Justice and Economic Distribution*. Englewood Cliffs: Prentice-Hall, 1978.

BEAUCHAMP, TOM L., ED. *Philosophical Ethics*. Englewood Cliffs: Prentice-Hall, 1982.

DONAGAN, ALAN. *The Theory of Morality*. Chicago: University of Chicago Press, 1977.

FISK, MILTON. *Ethics and Society: A Marxist Interpretation of Value*. New York: New York University Press, 1980.

GILLIGAN, CAROL. *In A Different Voice*. Cambridge: Harvard University Press, 1982.

HARE, R. M. *Moral Thinking*. Oxford: Clarendon Press, 1981.

HARRINGTON, MICHAEL. *Socialism*. New York: Bantam Books, 1970.

HOSPERS, JOHN. *Libertarianism*. Los Angeles: Nash Publishing, 1971.

JAGGAR, ALISON. *Feminist Politics and Human Nature*. Totowa: Rowman & Allanheld, 1983.

KITTAY, EVA FEDER, AND MEYERS, DIANA T., EDS. *Women and Moral Theory*. Totowa: Rowman and Littlefield, 1987.

MACINTYRE, ALASDAIR. *After Virtue*. Notre Dame: University of Notre Dame Press, 1981.

NOZICK, ROBERT. *Anarchy, State and Utopia*. New York: Basic Books, 1974.

OLDENQUIST, ANDREW. *The Nonsuicidal Society*. Bloomington: University of Indiana Press, 1986.

PARFIT, DEREK. *Reasons and Persons*. Oxford: Clarendon Press, 1984.

ROTHBARD, MURRAY N. *For a New Liberty*. London: Collier Macmillan, 1973.

STERBA, JAMES P., ED. *Justice: Alternative Political Perspectives*. Belmont: Wadsworth Publishing Co., 1980.

STERBA, JAMES P. *How To Make People Just*. Totowa: Rowman & Littlefield Publishers, 1988.

WALZER, MICHAEL. *The Spheres of Justice*. New York: Basic Books, 1983.

24
MORAL DILEMMAS AND CONSISTENCY

Ruth Barcan Marcus

I WANT to argue that the existence of moral dilemmas, even where the dilemmas arise from a categorical principle or principles, need not and usually does not signify that there is some inconsistency (in a sense to be explained) in the set of principles, duties, and other moral directives under which we define our obligations either individually or socially. I want also to argue that, on the given interpretation, consistency of moral principles or rules does not entail that moral dilemmas are resolvable in the sense that acting with good reasons in accordance with one horn of the dilemma erases the original obligation with respect to the other. The force of this latter claim is not simply to indicate an intractable fact about the human condition and the inevitability of guilt. The point to be made is that, although dilemmas are not settled without residue, the recognition of their reality has a dynamic force. It motivates us to arrange our lives and institutions with a view to avoiding such conflicts. It is the underpinning for a second-order regulative principle: that as rational agents with some control of our lives and institutions, we ought to conduct our lives and arrange our institutions so as to minimize predicaments of moral conflict.

I

Moral dilemmas have usually been presented as predicaments for individuals. Plato, for example, describes a case in which the return of a cache of arms has been promised to a man who, intent on mayhem, comes to claim them. Principles of promise keeping and benevolence generate conflict. One does not lack for examples. It is safe to say that most individuals for whom moral principles figure in practical reasoning have confronted di-

From *Journal of Philosophy*, Vol. LXXVII, No. 3, March 1980, pp. 121–136. © 1980 The Journal of Philosophy, Inc. Reprinted by permission.

This paper was written during my tenure as a Fellow at the Center for the Advanced Study of the Behavioral Sciences. I am grateful to Robert Stalnaker for his illuminating comments. A version of the paper was delivered on January 17, 1980, at Wayne State University as the Gail Stine Memorial Lecture.

lemmas, even though these more common-place dilemmas may lack the poignancy and tragic proportions of those featured in biblical, mythological, and dramatic literature. In the one-person case there are principles in accordance with which one ought to do x and one ought to do y, where doing y requires that one refrain from doing x; i.e., one ought to do not-x. For the present rough-grained discussion, the one-person case may be seen as an instance of the n-person case under the assumption of shared principles. Antigone's sororal (and religious) obligations conflict with Creon's obligations to keep his word and preserve the peace. Antigone is obliged to arrange for the burial of Polyneices; Creon is obliged to prevent it. Under generality of principles they are each obliged to respect the obligations of the other.

It has been suggested that moral dilemmas, on their face, seem to reflect some kind of inconsistency in the principles from which they derive. It has also been supposed that such conflicts are products of a plurality of principles and that a single-principled moral system does not generate dilemmas.

In the introduction to the *Metaphysics of Morals* Kant[1] says, "Because however duty and obligation are in general concepts that express the objective practical necessity of certain actions . . . it follows . . . that a conflict of duties and obligations is inconceivable (*obligationes non colliduntor*)." More recently John Lemmon,[2] citing a familiar instance of dilemma, says, "It may be argued that our being faced with this moral situation merely reflects an implicit inconsistency in our existing moral code; we are forced, if we are to remain both moral and logical, by the situation to restore consistency to our code by adding exception clauses to our present principles or by giving priority to one principle over another, or by some such device. The situation is as it is in mathematics: there, if an inconsistency is revealed by derivation, we are compelled to modify our axioms; here, if an inconsistency is revealed in application, we are forced to revise our principles." Donald Davidson,[3] also citing examples of conflict, says, "But then unless we take the line that moral principles *cannot* conflict in application to a case, we must give up the concept of the nature of practical reason we have so far been assuming. For how can premises, all of which are true (or acceptable) entail a contradiction? It is astonishing that in contemporary moral philosophy this problem has received little attention and no satisfactory treatment."

The notion of inconsistency which views dilemmas as evidence for inconsistency seems to be something like the following. We have to begin with a set of one or more moral principles which we will call a *moral code*. To count as a principle in such a code, a precept must be of a certain generality; that is, it cannot be tied to specific individuals at particular times or places, except that on any occasion of use it takes the time of that occasion as a zero coordinate. The present rough-grained discussion does not require that a point be made of the distinction between categorical moral principles and conditional moral principles, which impose obligations upon persons in virtue of some condition, such as that of being a parent, or a promise-maker or contractee. For our purposes we may think of categorical principles as imposing obligations in virtue of one's being a person and a member of a moral community.

In the conduct of our lives, actual circumstances may arise in which a code mandates a course of action. Sometimes, as in dilemmas, incompatible actions x and y are mandated; that is, the doing of x precludes the doing of y; y may in fact be the action of refraining from doing x. The underlying view that takes dilemmas as evidence of inconsistency is that a code is consistent if it applies without conflict to all actual—or, more strongly—to all possible cases. Those who see a code as the foundation of moral reasoning and adopt such a view of consistency argue that the puzzle of dilemmas can be resolved by elaboration of the code: by hedging principles with exception clauses, or establishing a rank ordering of principles, or both, or a procedure of assigning weights, or some combination of these. We need not go into the question of whether exception clauses can be assimilated to priority rankings, or priority rankings to weight assignments. In any case, there is some credibility in such solutions, since they fit some of the moral facts. In the question of whether to return the cache of arms, it is clear (except perhaps to an unregenerate Kantian) that the principle requiring that the promise be kept is overridden by the principle requiring that we protect human lives. Dilemmas, it is concluded, are merely apparent and not real. For, with a complete set of rules and priorities or a complete set of riders laying out circumstances in which a principle does not apply, in each case one of the obligations will be vitiated. What is incredible in such solutions is the supposition that we could arrive at a complete set of rules, priorities, or qualifications which would, in every possible case, unequivocally mandate a single course of action; that where, on any occasion, doing x conflicts with doing y, the rules with qualifications or priorities will yield better clear reasons for doing one than for doing the other.

The foregoing approach to the problem of moral conflict—ethical formalism—attempts to dispel the reality of dilemmas by expanding or elaborating on the code. An alternative solution, that of moral intuitionism, denies that it is possible to arrive at an elaboration of a set of principles which will apply to all particular circumstances. W. D. Ross,[4] for example, recognizes that estimates of the stringency of different prima facie principles can sometimes be made, but argues that no general universally applicable rules for such rankings can be laid down. However, the moral intuitionists *also* dispute the reality of moral dilemmas. Their claim is that moral codes are only guides; they are not the only and ultimate ground of decision making. Prima facie principles play an important heuristic role in our deliberations, but not as a set of principles that can tell us how we ought to act in all particular circumstances. That ultimate determination is a matter of intuition, albeit rational intuition. Moral dilemmas are prima facie, not real

conflicts. In apparent dilemmas there *is* always a correct choice among the conflicting options; it is only that, and here Ross quotes Aristotle, "the decision rests with perception." For Ross, those who are puzzled by moral dilemmas have failed to see that the problem is epistemological and not ontological, or real. Faced with a dilemma generated by prima facie principles, *uncertainty* is increased as to whether, in choosing x over y, we have in fact done the right thing. As Ross puts it, "Our judgments about our actual duty in concrete situations, have none of the certainty that attaches to our recognition of general principles of duty. . . . Where a possible act is seen to have two characteristics in virtue of one of which it is prima facie right and in virtue of the other prima facie wrong we are well aware that we are not certain whether we ought or ought not to do it. Whether we do it or not we are taking a moral risk" (30). For Ross, as well as the formalist, it is only that we may be uncertain of the right way. To say that dilemma is evidence of inconsistency is to confuse inconsistency with uncertainty. There *is* only one right way to go, and hence no problem of inconsistency.

There are, as we see, points of agreement between the formalist and the intuitionist as here described. Both claim that the appearance of dilemma and inconsistency flows from prima facie principles and that dilemmas can be resolved by supplementation. They differ in the nature of the supplementation.[5] They further agree that it is the multiplicity of principles which generates the prima facie conflicts; that if there were one rule or principle or maxim, there would be no conflicts. Quite apart from the unreasonableness of the belief that we can arrive ultimately at a single moral principle, such proposed single principles have played a major role in moral philosophy, Kant's categorical imperative and various versions of the principle of utility being primary examples. Setting aside the casuistic logical claim that a single principle can always be derived by conjunction from a multiplicity, it can be seen that the single-principle solution is mistaken. There is always the analogue of

Buridan's ass. Under the single principle of promise keeping, I might make two promises in all good faith and reason that they will not conflict, but then they do, as a result of circumstances that were unpredictable and beyond my control. All other considerations may balance out. The lives of identical twins are in jeopardy, and, through force of circumstances, I am in a position to save only one. Make the situation as symmetrical as you please. A single-principled framework is not necessarily unlike the code with qualifications or priority rule, in that it would appear that, however strong our wills and complete our knowledge, we might be faced with a moral choice in which there are no moral grounds for favoring doing x over y.

Kant imagined that he had provided a single-principled framework from which all maxims flowed. But Kantian ethics is notably deficient in coping with dilemmas. Kant seems to claim that they don't really arise, and we are provided with no moral grounds for their resolution.

It is true that unregenerate act utilitarianism is a plausible candidate for dilemma-free principle or conjunction of principles, but not because it can be framed as a single principle. It is rather that attribution of rightness or wrongness to certain kinds of acts *per se* is ruled out whether they be acts of promise keeping or promise breaking, acts of trust or betrayal, of respect or contempt. One might, following Moore, call such attributes "non-natural kinds," and they enter into all examples of moral dilemmas. The attribute of having maximal utility as usually understood is not such an attribute. For to the unregenerate utilitarian it is not features of an act *per se* which make it right. The only thing to be counted is certain consequences, and, for any given action, one can imagine possible circumstances, possible worlds if you like, in each of which the action will be assigned different values—depending on different outcomes in those worlds. In the unlikely cases where in fact two conflicting courses of action have the same utility, it is open to the act utilitarian to adopt a procedure for deciding, such as tossing a coin.

In suggesting that, in all examples of dilemma, we are dealing with attributions of rightness *per se* independent of consequences is not to say that principles of utility do not enter into moral dilemmas. It is only that such conflicts will emerge in conjunction with non-utilitarian principles. Indeed, such conflicts are perhaps the most frequently debated examples, but not, as we have seen, the only ones. I would like to claim that it is a better fit with the moral facts that all dilemmas are real, even where the reasons for doing x outweigh, and in whatever degree, the reasons for doing y. That is, wherever circumstances are such that an obligation to do x and an obligation to do y cannot as a matter of circumstance be fulfilled, the obligations to do each are not erased, even though they are unfulfillable. Mitigating circumstances may provide an explanation, an excuse, or a defense, but I want to claim that this is not the same as denying one of the obligations altogether.

We have seen that one of the motives for denying the reality of moral dilemmas is to preserve, on some notion of consistency, the consistency of our moral reasoning. But other not unrelated reasons have been advanced for denying their reality which have to do with the notion of guilt. If an agent ought to do x, then he is guilty if he fails to do it. But if, however strong his character and however good his will and intentions, meeting other equally weighted or overriding obligations precludes his doing x, then we cannot assign guilt, and, if we cannot, then it is incoherent to suppose that there is an obligation. Attendant feelings of the agent are seen as mistaken or misplaced.

That argument has been rejected by Bas van Fraassen[6] on the ground that normative claims about when we ought to assign guilt are not part of the analysis of the concept of guilt, for if it were, such doctrines as that of "original sin" would be rendered incoherent. The Old Testament assigns guilt to three or four generations of descendants of those who worship false gods. Or consider the burden of guilt borne by all the descendants of the house of Atreus, or, more recently, the readiness of many Germans to assume a burden of guilt for the past actions of others. There are analogous converse cases, as in the assumption of guilt by parents for actions of adult children. Having presented the argument, I am not wholly persuaded that a strong case can be made for the coherence of such doctrines. However, the situation faced by agents in moral dilemmas is not parallel. Where moral conflict occurs, there is a genuine sense in which both what is done and what fails to be done are, before the actual choice among irreconcilable alternatives, within the agent's range of options. But, as the saying goes—and it is not incoherent—you are damned if you do and you are damned if you don't.

I will return to the question of the reality of moral dilemmas, but first let me propose a definition of consistency for a moral code which is compatible with that claim.

II

Consistency, as defined for a set of meaningful sentences or propositions, is a property that such a set has if it is possible for all of the members of the set to be true, in the sense that contradiction would not be a logical consequence of supposing that each member of the set is true. On that definition 'grass is white' and 'snow is green' compose a consistent set although false to the facts. There is a possible set of circumstances in which those sentences are true, i.e., where snow is green and grass is white. Analogously we can define a set of rules as consistent if there is some possible world in which they are all obeyable in all circumstances in *that* world. (Note that I have said "obeyable" rather than "obeyed" for I want to allow for the partition of cases where a rule-governed action fails to be done between those cases where the failure is a personal failure of the agent—an imperfect will in Kant's terms—and those cases where "external" circumstances prevent the agent from meeting conflicting obligations. To

define consistency relative to a kingdom of ends, a deontically perfect world in which all actions that ought to be done are done, would be too strong; for that would require both perfection of will *and* the absence of circumstances that generate moral conflict.) In such a world, where all rules are obeyable, persons intent on mayhem have not been promised or do not simultaneously seek the return of a cache of arms. Sororal obligations such as those of Antigone do not conflict with obligations to preserve peace, and so on. Agents may still fail to fulfill obligations.

Consider, for example, a silly two-person card game. (This is the partial analogue of a two-person dilemma. One can contrive silly games of solitaire for the one-person dilemma.) In the two-person game the deck is shuffled and divided equally, face down between two players. Players turn up top cards on each play until the cards are played out. Two rules are in force: black cards trump red cards, and high cards (ace high) trump lower-valued cards without attention to color. Where no rule applies, e.g., two red deuces, there is indifference and the players proceed. We could define the winner as the player with the largest number of tricks when the cards are played out. There is an inclination to call such a set of rules inconsistent. For suppose the pair turned up is a red ace and a black deuce; who trumps? This is not a case of rule indifference as in a pair of red deuces. Rather, two rules apply, and both cannot be satisfied. But, on the definition here proposed, the rules are consistent in that there are possible circumstances where, in the course of playing the game, the dilemma would not arise and the game would proceed to a conclusion. It is possible that the cards be so distributed that, when a black card is paired with a red card, the black card happens to be of equal or higher value. Of course, with shuffling, the likelihood of dilemma-free circumstances is small. But we could have invented a similar game where the likelihood of proceeding to a conclusion without dilemma is greater.

Indeed a game might be so complex that its being dilemmatic under any circumstances is very small and may not even be known to the players.[7] On the proposed definition, rules are consistent if there are possible circumstances in which no conflict will emerge. By extension, a set of rules is inconsistent if there are *no* circumstances, no possible world, in which all the rules are satisfiable.[8]

A pair of offending rules which generates inconsistency as *here* defined provides *no* guide to action under any circumstance. Choices are thwarted whatever the contingencies. Well, a critic might say, you have made a trivial logical point. What pragmatic difference is there between the inconsistent set of rules and a set, like those of the game described above, where there is a likelihood of irresolvable dilemma? A code is, after all, supposed to guide action. If it allows for conflicts without resolution, if it tells us in some circumstances that we ought to do x and we ought to do y even though x and y are incompatible in those circumstances, that is tantamount to telling us that we ought to do x and we ought to refrain from doing x and similarly for y. The code has failed us as a guide. If it is not inconsistent, then it is surely deficient, and, like the dilemma-provoking game, in need of repair.

But the logical point is not trivial, for there are crucial disanalogies between games and the conduct of our lives. It is part of the canon of the family of games of chance like the game described, that the cards must be shuffled. The distribution of the cards must be "left to chance." To stack the deck, like loading the dice, is to cheat. But, presumably, the moral principles we subscribe to are, whatever their justification, not justified merely in terms of some canon for games. Granted, they must be guides to action and hence not totally defeasible. But consistency in our sense is surely only a necessary but not a sufficient condition for a set of moral rules. Presumably, moral principles have some ground; we adopt principles when we have reasons to believe that they serve to guide us in right action. Our interest is not merely in having a playable game whatever the accidental circumstances, but in doing the right thing to the extent that it is possible. We want to maximize the likelihood that in all circumstances we can act in accordance with each of our rules. To that end, our alternative as moral agents, individually and collectively, as contrasted with the card-game players, is to try to stack the deck so that dilemmas do not arise.

Given the complexity of our lives and the imperfection of our knowledge, the occasions of dilemma cannot always be foreseen or predicted. In playing games, when we are faced with a conflict of rules we abandon the game or invent new playable rules; dissimilarly, in the conduct of our lives we do not abandon action, and there may be no justification for making new rules to fit. We proceed with choices as best we can. Priority rules and the like assist us in those choices and in making the best of predicaments. But, if we do make the best of a predicament, and make a choice, to claim that one of the conflicting obligations has thereby been erased is to claim that it would be mistaken to feel guilt or remorse about having failed to act according to that obligation. So the agent would be said to believe falsely that he is guilty, since his obligation was vitiated and his feelings are inappropriate. But that is false to the facts. Even where priorities are clear and overriding and even though the burden of guilt may be appropriately small, explanations and excuses are in order. But in such tragic cases as that described by Jean-Paul Sartre[9] where the choice to be made by the agent is between abandoning a wholly dependent mother and not becoming a freedom fighter, it is inadequate to insist that feelings of guilt about the rejected alternative are mistaken and that assumption of guilt is inappropriate. Nor is it puritanical zeal which insists on the reality of dilemmas and the appropriateness of the attendant feelings. For dilemmas, when they occur, are data of a kind. They are to be taken into account in the future conduct of our lives. If we are to avoid dilemmas we must be motivated to do so. In the absence of associated feelings, motivation to stack the deck, to arrange our lives and institutions so as to minimize or avoid dilemma is tempered or blunted.

Consider, for example, the controversies surrounding nonspontaneous abortion. Philosophers are often criticized for inventing bizarre examples and counterexamples to make a philosophical point. But no contrived example can equal the complexity and the puzzles generated by the actual circumstances of foetal conception, parturation, and ultimate birth of a human being. We have an organism, internal to and parasitic upon a human being, hidden from view but relentlessly developing into a human being, which at some stage of development can live, with nurture, outside of its host. There are arguments that recognize competing claims: the right to life of the foetus (at some stage) versus the right of someone to determine what happens to his body. Arguments that justify choosing the mother over the foetus (or vice-versa) where their survival is in competition. Arguments in which foetuses that are defective are balanced against the welfare of others. Arguments in which the claims to survival of others will be said to override survival of the foetus under conditions of great scarcity. There are even arguments that deny prima facie conflicts altogether on some metaphysical grounds, such as that the foetus is not a human being or a person until quickening, or until it has recognizable human features, or until its life can be sustained external to its host, or until birth, or until after birth when it has interacted with other persons. Various combinations of such arguments are proposed in which the resolution of a dilemma is seen as more uncertain, the more proximate the foetus is to whatever is defined as being human or being a person. What all the arguments seem to share is the assumption that there is, despite uncertainty, a resolution without residue; that there is a correct set of metaphysical claims, principles, and priority rankings of principles which will justify the choice. Then, given the belief that one choice is justified, assignment of guilt relative to the overridden alternative is seen as inappropriate, and feelings of guilt or pangs of conscience are viewed as, at best, sentimental. But as one tries to unravel the tangle of arguments, it is clear that to insist that there is in every case a solution without residue is false to the moral facts.

John Rawls,[10] in his analysis of moral sentiments, says that it is an essential characteristic of a moral feeling that an agent, in explaining the feeling, "invokes a moral concept and its associated principle. His (the agent's) account of his feeling makes reference to an acknowledged right or wrong." Where those ingredients are absent, as, for example, in the case of someone of stern religious background who claims to feel guilty when attending the theater although he no longer believes it is wrong, Rawls wants to say that such a person has certain sensations of uneasiness and the like which resemble those he has when he feels guilty, but, since he is not apologetic for his behavior, does not resolve to absent himself from the theater, does not agree that negative sanctions are deserved, he experiences not a feeling of guilt, but only something like it. Indeed, it is the feeling which needs to be explained; it is not the action which needs to be excused. For, says Rawls, in his discussion of moral feelings and sentiments, "When plagued by feelings of guilt . . . a person wishes to act properly in the future and strives to modify his conduct accordingly. He is inclined to admit what he has done, to acknowledge and accept reproofs and penalties." Guilt qua feeling is here defined not only in terms of sensations but also in terms of the agent's disposition to acknowledge, to have wishes and make resolutions about future actions, to accept certain outcomes, and the like. Where an agent acknowledges conflicting obligations, unlike the theatergoer who acknowledges no obligation, there is sufficient overlap with dilemma-free cases of moral failure to warrant describing the associated feelings where present as guilt, and where absent as appropriate to an agent with moral sensibility. Granted that, unlike agents who fail to meet their obligations simpliciter, the agent who was confronted with a dilemma may finally act on the best available reasons. Still, with respect to the rejected alternative he acknowledges a wrong in that he recognizes that it was within his power to do otherwise. He may be apologetic and inclined to explain and make excuses. He may sometimes be inclined to accept external reproofs and penalties. Not perhaps those which would be a consequence of a simple failure to meet an obligation but rather like the legal cases in which mitigating circumstances evoke a lesser penalty—or reproof.[11]

Even if, as Rawls supposes, or hopes (but as seems to me most unlikely), a complete set of rules and priorities were possible which on rational grounds would provide a basis for choosing among competing claims in all cases of moral conflict that actually arise, it is incorrect to suppose that the feeling evoked on such occasions, if it is evoked, only resembles guilt, and that it is inappropriate on such occasions to ascribe guilt. *Legal* ascriptions of guilt require sanctions beyond the pangs of conscience and self-imposed reproofs. In the absence of clear external sanctions, legal guilt is normally not ascribable. But that is one of the many distinctions between the legal and the moral.

Most important, an agent in a predicament of conflict will also "wish to act properly in the future and strive to modify his actions accordingly." He will strive to arrange his own life and encourage social arrangements that would prevent, to the extent that it is possible, future conflicts from arising. To deny the appropriateness or correctness of ascriptions of guilt is to weaken the impulse to make such arrangements.[12]

III

I have argued that the consistency of a set of moral rules, even in the absence of a complete set of priority rules, is not incompatible with the reality of moral dilemmas. It would appear, however, that at least some versions of the principle "'ought' implies 'can'" are

being denied; for dilemmas are circumstances where, for a pair of obligations, if one is satisfied then the other cannot be. There is, of course, a range of interpretations of the precept resulting from the various interpretations of 'ought', 'can', and 'implies'. Some philosophers who recognize the reality of dilemmas have rejected the precept that "'ought' implies 'can'"; some have accepted it.[13] If we interpret the 'can' of the precept as "having the ability in this world to bring about," then, as indicated above, in a moral dilemma, 'ought' *does* imply 'can' for *each* of the conflicting obligations, *before* either one is met. And after an agent has chosen one of the alternatives, there is still something which he ought to have done and could have done and which he did not do. 'Can', like 'possible', designates a modality that cannot always be factored out of a conjunction. Just as 'possible P and possible Q' does not imply 'possible both P and Q', so 'A can do x and A can do y' does not imply 'A can do both x and y'. If the precept "'ought' implies 'can'" is to be preserved, it must also be maintained that 'ought' designates a modality that cannot be factored out of a conjunction. From 'A ought to do x' and 'A ought to do y' it does not follow that 'A ought to do x and y'. Such a claim is of course a departure from familiar systems of deontic logic.

The analysis of consistency and dilemmas advanced in this paper suggests a second-order principle which relates 'ought' and 'can' and which provides a plausible gloss of the Kantian principle "Act so that thou canst will they maxim to become a universal law of nature." As Kant understood laws of nature, they are, taken together, universally and jointly applicable in all particular circumstances. It is such a second-order principle that has been violated when we knowingly make conflicting promises. It is such a second-order principle that has, for example, been violated when someone knowingly and avoidably conducts himself in such a way that he is confronted with a choice between the life of a foetus, the right to determine what happens to one's body, and benefits to others. To will maxims to become universal laws we must will the means, and among those means are the conditions for their compatibility. One ought to act in such a way that, if one ought to do x and one ought to do y, then one can do both x and y. But the second-order principle is regulative. This second-order 'ought' does *not* imply 'can'.[14] There is no reason to suppose, this being the actual world, that we can, individually or collectively, however holy our wills or rational our strategies, succeed in foreseeing and wholly avoiding such conflict. It is not merely failure of will, or failure of reason, which thwarts moral maxims from becoming universal laws. It is the contingencies of this world.

IV

Where does that leave us? I have argued that all dilemmas are real in a sense I hope has been made explicit. Also that there is no reason to suppose on considerations of consistency that there *must* be principles which, on moral grounds, will provide a sufficient ordering for deciding all cases. But, it may be argued, when confronted with what are *apparently* symmetrical choices undecidable on moral grounds, agents do, finally, choose. That is sometimes understood as a way in which, given good will, an agent makes explicit the rules under which he acts. It is the way an agent discovers a priority principle under which he orders his actions. I should like to question that claim.

A frequently quoted remark of E. M. Forster[15] is "if I had to choose between betraying my country and betraying my friend, I hope I should have the courage to betray my country." One could of course read that as if Forster had made manifest some priority rule: that certain obligations to friends override obligations to nation. But consider a remark of A. B. Worster, "if I had to choose between betraying my country and betraying my friend, I hope I should have the courage to betray my friend." Both recognize a dilemma, and one can read Worster as subscribing to a different prior-

ity rule and, to that extent, a different set of rules from Forster's. But is that the only alternative? Suppose Forster had said that, morally, Worster's position is as valid as his own. That there was no moral reason for generalizing his own choice to all. That there was disagreement between them not about moral principles but rather about the kind of persons they wished to be and the kind of lives they wished to lead. Forster may not want Worster for a friend; a certain possibility of intimacy may be closed to them which perhaps Forster requires in a friend. Worster may see in Forster a sensibility that he does not admire. But there is no reason to suppose that such appraisals are or must be moral appraisals. Not all questions of value are moral questions, and it may be that not all moral dilemmas are resolvable by principles for which moral justification can be given.

NOTES

1. Immanuel Kant, *The Metaphysical Elements of Justice:* Part I of the *Metaphysics of Morals*, translated by John Ladd (Indianapolis: Bobbs-Merrill, 1965), p. 24.

2. "Deontic Logic and the Logic of Imperatives," *Logique et Analyse*, VIII, 29 (April 1965): 39–61. Lemmon originally presented his paper at a symposium of the Western Division meeting of the American Philosophical Association in May 1964. My unpublished comments on that occasion contain some of the ideas here presented.

3. "How Is Weakness of the Will Possible?", in Joel Feinberg, ed., *Moral Concepts* (New York: Oxford, 1970), p. 105.

4. *The Right and the Good* (New York: Oxford, 1930), p. 41.

5. For the formalist, priority rankings (like Rawls's lexical ordering), or weights permitting some computation, or qualifications of principles to take care of all problematic cases, are supposed possible. For the intuitionist it is intuitive "seeing" in each case which supplements prima facie principles.

6. "Values and the Heart's Command," *Journal of Philosophy*, LXX, 1 (Jan. 11, 1973): 5–19. Van Fraassen makes the point that such a claim would make *the* doctrine of "original sin" incoher-

ent. As I see it, there are at least three interesting doctrines, two of them very likely true, which could qualify as doctrines of original sin. One of them, which I call "inherited guilt," is the doctrine that some of the wrongful actions of some persons are such that other persons, usually those with some special connection to the original sinners, are also judged to be sinners; their feelings of guilt are appropriate, their punishment "deserved," and so on. Such is the case described in Exodus and Deuteronomy here mentioned. A second notion of original sin is to be found in the account of the Fall. Here it is suggested that, however happy our living arrangements, however maximal the welfare state, we will each of us succumb to some temptation. There is universality of sin because of universality of weakness of will, but specific sins are neither inherited by nor bequeathed to others.

A third candidate supposes the reality and inevitability, for each of us, of moral dilemma. Here we do not inherit the sins of others, nor need we be weak of will. The circumstances of the world conspire against us. However perfect our will, the contingencies are such that situations arise where, if we are to follow one right course of action, we will be unable to follow another.

7. There is a question whether, given such rules, the "game" is properly described as a game. Wittgenstein says "Let us suppose that the game [which I have invented] is such that whoever begins can always win by a particular simple trick. But this has not been realized;—so it is a game. Now someone draws our attention to it—and it stops being a game." *Remarks on the Foundations of Mathematics*, ed., G. H. von Wright *et al.*, translated by G. E. M. Anscombe (Oxford: Blackwell, 1956), II 78, p. 100e. Wittgenstein is pointing to that canon of a game which requires that both players have some opportunity to win. The canon that rules out dilemmatic rules is that the game must be playable to a conclusion. (I am beholden to Robert Fogelin for reminding me of this quotation.)

8. Bernard Williams, in *Problems of the Self* (New York: Cambridge, 1977), chs. 11 and 12, also recognizes that the source of some apparent inconsistencies in imperatives and rules is to be located in the contingency of their simultaneous inapplicability on a given occasion.

9. Sartre in "Existentialism Is a Humanism" describes a case where a student is faced with a decision between joining the Free French forces and remaining with his mother. He is her only surviving son and her only consolation. Sartre's advice was that "No rule of general morality can show you what you ought to do." His claim is that in such circumstances "nothing remains but to trust our instincts." But what is "trust" here? Does our action reveal to us that we subscribe to a priority principle or that in the absence of some resolving principles we may just as well follow our inclination? In any case to describe our feelings about the rejected alternative as "regret" seems inadequate. See Walter Kaufmann, ed., *Existentialism from Dostoevsky to Sartre* (New York: Meridian, 1956), pp. 295–298.

10. *A Theory of Justice* (Cambridge, Mass.: Harvard, 1971), pp. 481–483. Rawls's claim is that such sensations, to be properly describable as "guilt feelings" and not something resembling such feelings, must occur in the broader context of beliefs, strivings, acknowledgements, and readiness to accept outcomes, and cannot be detached from that context. He rejects the possibility that there are such "pure" sensations that can occur independent of the broader context. This is partially, perhaps, an empirical claim about identifying sameness of feeling. The theater-goer might claim that he does feel guilty because he has the same feeling he has when he acknowledges that he is guilty, that what remains is to give an account of when such feelings of guilt are justified. Still, Rawls's analysis seems to me to be a better account.

11. To insist that "regret" is appropriate rather than "guilt" or "remorse" is false to the facts. It seems inappropriate, for example, to describe as "regret" the common feelings of guilt that women have in cases of abortion even where they believe (perhaps mistakenly) that there was moral justification in such an undertaking.

12. Bernard Williams ["Politics and Moral Character," in Stuart Hampshire, ed., *Public and Private Morality* (New York: Cambridge, 1978), pp. 54–74] discusses the question in the context of politics and the predicament of "dirty hands." He argues that, where moral ends of politics justify someone in public life lying, or misleading, or using others, "the moral disagreeableness of these acts is not merely cancelled." In particular, we would not want, as our politicians, those "practical politicians" for whom the disagreeableness does not arise.

13. For example, John Lemmon, in "Moral Dilemmas," *Philosophical Review*, LXXI, 2 (April 1962): 139–158, p. 150, rejects the principle that 'ought' implies 'can'. Van Fraassen, *op. cit.*, pp. 12/3, accepts it, as does Bernard Williams seem-

ingly in *Problems of the Self, op. cit.,* pp. 179–184. Van Fraassen and Williams see that such acceptance requires modification of the principle of factoring for the deontic "ought." There are other received principles of deontic logic which will have to be rejected, but they will be discussed in a subsequent paper. It should also be noted that, in "Ethical Consistency" and "Consistency and Realism" in *Problems of the Self,* Williams also articulates the contingent source of dilemmas and argues for their "reality."

14. See fn 13. The reader is reminded that, on the present analysis, 'ought' is indexical in the sense that applications of principles on given occasions project into the future. They concern bringing something about.

15. *Two Cheers for Democracy* (London: E. Arnold, 1939).

25
AGAINST MORAL DILEMMAS

Earl Conee

Call an agent's predicament a "moral dilemma" just when the agent cannot do everything that it is morally obligatory for him to do in the situation, though he can carry out each obligation. A typical putative example of the phenomenon is a case where someone can keep each of two solemn trusted promises, but not both. Here I defend the view that no moral dilemma is possible. There is no fact of moral life that cannot be accounted for at least as well without moral dilemmas, and their possibility would cast a shroud of impenetrable obscurity over the concept of moral obligation.

In several recent discussions, philosophers have been indulgent of moral dilemmas. E. J. Lemmon[1] and Ruth Marcus[2] have asserted their existence, Bernard Williams[3] has said that they are required to make sense of certain moral sentiments and considerations, and Bas van Fraassen[4] has held that their existence is sufficiently tenable to mandate revising deontic logic to allow for

them. I believe that none of this tolerance is justified. I will examine their principal reasons for it below, to see how well we can do without any moral dilemmas.

First, why do I think we should deny the very possibility of a moral dilemma? The basis for my principal objection was supplied by van Fraassen as he argued for making room in deontic logic for dilemmas.[5] If we accept the alleged cases as genuine, then we must reconcile ourselves to this result: actions are possible that are *both* absolutely, unconditionally, and not merely prima facie morally obligatory, *and* absolutely, unconditionally, and not merely prima facie morally impermissible. That, I submit, is absolutely, unconditionally, and not merely prima facie incredible. Yet the reasoning to that consequence is simple and secure. If there are moral dilemmas, then some truths have this form:

(1) $O(A)$ & $O(-A)$

For example, many an agent has made equally firm commitments to do something

From *The Philosophical Review* XCI, No. 1 (January 1982):87–97. Reprinted by permission.

and to refrain from doing it. Obligation is related to permission as follows:

(2) $O(A) \equiv -P(-A)$

From (1) and (2) by propositional logic alone we can infer:

(3) $O(-A) \ \& \ -P(-A)$

Again I emphasize that the topic is unconditional, non-prima facie moral obligation. On that interpretation of "O" in (3), (3) cannot be true.

Fortunately, all available defenses of (1) and its ilk are objectionable. Let us begin to consider them. E. J. Lemmon asserts principles that would land us in many moral dilemmas. He writes:

[A] man ought to do something if it is his duty to do that thing. Equally, he ought to do it if he is under an obligation to do it, and he ought to do it if it is right, in view of some moral principle to which he subscribes, that he should do it.[6]

Lemmon tells us that the relevant duties include those incurred in virtue of one's job; e.g., duties as policeman, as headmaster, or as garbage collector.[7] We are "under an obligation" in the relevant sense when we make a specific commitment, e.g., by signing an agreement.[8]

Moral obligations are not that easily incurred, however. An extreme example makes the point most vividly. Consider the executioner in some horrendous death camp. He has duties in virtue of being executioner. But they are not moral duties; they are merely part of the job. Nor do they become moral obligations if he has committed himself to killing his victims, nor if he subscribes to the moral necessity of his work.[9] So we should not accept moral dilemmas on the basis of these principles that Lemmon offers. They are false.

Williams, Marcus, and van Fraassen all find support for moral dilemmas in cases where moral sentiments play a prominent role. Williams' defense depends upon the legitimacy of regret in some cases where the agent has acted for the best. He appeals to the example of Agamemnon at Aulis. Agamemnon is told by a seer that he must sacrifice his daughter to satisfy a goddess who is delaying at Aulis his expedition against Troy. Agamemnon accepts that his duty to carry out his mission takes priority over sparing his daughter, and he sacrifices her. As they bear on his example, Williams' observations tell us that Agamemnon may well have regretted his terrible deed in part because of his belief that he ought not to have done it, even though it was morally best.[10] Williams points out that it can be admirable, and far from irrational, to feel such regret.[11] And he maintains that it does not account for those things to hold that the duty to spare the daughter was merely prima facie. His reason for this last contention is that a prima facie duty makes a claim for consideration as "the only thing that matters" in the case,

. . . and if a course of action has failed to make good this claim in a situation of conflict, how can it maintain in that situation some residual influence on . . . moral thought?[12]

This objection to appealing to the notion of prima facie duty clearly fails. A prima facie duty does not make a claim to be the only thing that matters in a situation. Its claim is to be something that matters. What yields a prima facie duty is, in W. D. Ross's words, "a definite circumstance which cannot seriously be held to be without moral significance."[13] So such an act can have moral importance when something else matters more and is obligatory. Thus, foregoing a prima facie duty *can* be a source of reasonable regret.

There is another dilemma-free way in which we can account for the sort of regret that Williams discusses. We can suppose that Agamemnon subscribed to a moral code that he had no reason to question, on which both sacrificing and sparing his daughter were obligatory. That would be a flaw in the code, but nothing that would place it beyond reasonable belief. If we like, we can say that we thereby acknowledge moral dilemmas as "facts of rational moral psychology." That gives very little to advocates of the real possibility of moral dilemmas. What they need is reason to think that some rationally acceptable dilemma-prone moral code might possibly be true. In analogous terms, the best of the semantic paradoxes show that inconsistent beliefs are "facts of rational doxastic psychology." Reasonable thinkers have on occasion accepted all the premises of a paradox. That scarcely shows that an inconsistency is possibly true. Returning to the moral case, if Agamemnon's regret were partly prompted by a reasonably believed failure of obligation, it would have been rational and admirable. No actual dilemma is required.

There is another salient ground for regret in Agamemnon's case—the dreadful fact of his having killed his innocent, beloved daughter. No need for him even to *think* that he was obligated *not* to do that. It is regrettable enough that he *was* obligated to do something that bad, and that he could do nothing better. In fact, the story does not have Agamemnon recognize any obligation not to sacrifice his daughter. It does have him lament, "Which of these courses is without evil?"[14] as he weighs his alternatives. The basis for that lament is sufficient justification for regret.

Williams claims that a dilemma-free morality "eliminates from the scene the 'ought' not acted on."[15] That is true on the reading where "ought" expresses absolute moral obligation. When such an "ought" is obeyed, no alternative one is neglected. But Williams is wrong in claiming that dilemma-free moralities must have it that obedience in cases like Agamemnon's occasions only feelings of "relief (at escaping mistake), or self-congratulation (for having got the right answer), or possibly self-criticism (for having so nearly been misled)."[16] One who believes in a dilemma-free morality can reasonably feel regret in cases where adhering to it had harmful results. I conclude that Williams' assertions about regret offer no substantial support for moral dilemmas.

Marcus and van Fraassen acknowledge that dilemma-free moralities permit justification for regret.[17] But they contend that some instances where the moral sentiment of guilt is appropriate do supply evidence for moral dilemmas. Marcus holds that even when the act chosen is clearly superior, it is

... inadequate to insist that the feelings of guilt about the rejected alternatives are mistaken, and that the assumption of guilt is inappropriate.[18]

Marcus claims that those who deny moral dilemmas do hold that such guilt is mistaken and inappropriate, and that she calls "false to the facts."[19] Making a similar point, van Fraassen asserts, "it is appropriate to feel guilty if and only if one is guilty."[20] Thus we are to infer that those who feel appropriate guilt while having acted for the moral best must *be* guilty of having violated another moral duty.

What goes into this emotion of moral guilt? It at least includes believing that one has somehow failed morally, and feeling sorry about a supposed bad feature of the believed lapse. That belief and feeling are appropriate *to the facts* only if one has not done all that morality requires.[21] But another sort of appropriateness is also relevant here. Feeling guilty is *subjectively* appropriate when the belief that one has failed which prompts the feeling fits one's moral principles. If your convictions include that every debt morally must be repaid, it is appropriate to your morality for you to feel guilty about defaulting. When someone does what is morally best while neglecting something his morality requires, his feeling guilty is therefore appropriate only because it is called for by morality as he sees it. It does not fit the facts. This sort of appropriate guilt does not imply that a moral mistake has been made. So an opponent of moral dilemmas can consistently hold that feeling guilty about a morally superior act is clearly appropriate at times—but in this subjective way, not in light of any omitted actual moral obligation.

Another sort of case mentioned by both

Marcus and van Fraassen is that in which equally strong moral claims demand incompatible actions. Marcus suggests that we consider an example where equally worthy identical twins are in jeopardy, and either, but not both, can be saved.[22] Van Fraassen turns our attention to the character Nora in Ibsen's *A Doll's House*.[23] Near the end of the play, Nora must choose between a duty to her family and a duty to herself that she recognizes to be equally compelling.

We must grant that there are cases where competing moral considerations have exactly the same force. And we must grant that Nora is faced with conflicting duties. So if each of Nora's duties is morally mandatory, or there is an absolute moral obligation to each twin, then the possibility of moral dilemmas has been established. But there is no need to count each of these alternatives as morally required. We have the familiar option of holding that when moral factors are equal, each act is permitted and none is absolutely obligatory. The sense in which these alternatives are clearly "duties" is not that of being all things considered moral requirements. Not every duty given by one's role in a family is morally mandated. Rather, each is required to carry out a role that has considerable moral significance. Similarly, duties to oneself are requirements for self-fulfillment, which gives them moral importance. We can go so far as to count all such requirements as prima facie moral duties. The crucial point is that such requirements have a moral bearing that permits there to be rival conduct having equal moral worth. Thus it is possible consistently to acknowledge that there are conflicts between things properly called "duties," while maintaining that ties for first place between competing moral considerations never generate moral dilemmas.

Van Fraassen considers and rejects this sort of account.[24] He attributes it to the axiologist, that is, one who affirms:

"It ought to be the case that *A*" is true exactly if some value attaching to some outcome of the alternatives making *A* true is higher than any attaching to any outcome of the alternatives making not-*A* true.[25]

Van Fraassen contends that denying conflicting moral demands in Nora's case amounts to taking it to be

fundamentally the same as that of the philanthropist who regrets that he has but one fortune to give to mankind and agonizes over the choice between endowing the arts and furthering birth control (or as the case of the revolutionary who agonizes over the question where he should risk his life against oppression—in Bolivia or in Guatemala).[26]

It is important to realize that the axiologist is not alone in denying all moral dilemmas. Ross's avowedly deontological theory excludes dilemmas.[27] And there is no need to appeal to Ross's special technical concept of a prima facie duty in order to state a believable morality which is both nonaxiological and dilemma-free. We can do this with permissibility as the only deontic primitive. To illustrate with a simple view, here is a miniscule morality that forbids harming people, and counts promise-keeping and returning borrowed items on time as equal positive qualities of acts:

(M) An act is permissible if, and only if, it harms no one unless harm is unavoidable and it satisfies at least one of the following:
   (i)   it is an act of promise-keeping,
   (ii)   it is an act of returning a borrowed item on time, or
   (iii) no alternative to it is either an act of promise-keeping or an act of returning a borrowed item on time unless each such act harms someone.

The idea behind a theory of this form is that some features of acts, like being of harm to someone, render an act impermissible when an alternative without such a feature exists. Other qualities of acts, like being a timely return of a loan, render an act obligatory (i.e., not permissibly not done) if the act does not have a forbidding feature and nothing else of the same merit can be done instead. When an equally worthy alternative is available, each of them is permitted. When no choice has a morally significant quality, any choice is permitted. Clearly, (M) is not axiological. It permits and forbids in sheer independence of the values of alternative outcomes. Yet (M) never yields a moral dilemma.

This theory's form poses a noteworthy pedagogical problem. Consider how best to teach a child what is moral. (M) purports to state a necessary and sufficient condition for permissibility. To do that in the manner of (M), we would have to list every morally important quality of acts so that permission could be given to do other things when nothing with such a quality was available. Obviously (M) does not actually do that. But suppose that the truth about moral permissibility is a much lengthier version of (M). Think of how difficult it would be to teach a counterpart of (M) that contains all the relevant conditions. It would be ineffective merely to recommend simple implications of the doctrine like this one: promise-keeping is permitted when no one is thereby harmed. That is easy to convey, but weak. It forbids nothing. It is much more effective to say that promises are not permissibly broken, and loans must be repaid on time. Those simple dicta make the same moral evaluations as (M) except when more than one alternative has a morally significant quality. Even then, if some such maxim is followed, an (M)-like theory permits the act unless it has a forbidding feature as well. Thus even if our best moral insights favor something like (M), it is no wonder that in most moral training such simple (though dilemma-prone) maxims are taught. In any event, we see that consistent theory-based opposition to moral dilemmas is not restricted to axiologists.

We turn now to the analogies that van Fraassen offers to cast doubt on the dilemma-free interpretation of Nora's predicament. He claims that Nora's case is parallel to those of the philanthropist and the revolutionary only if a feeling of guilt is appropriate exactly when regret is.[28] It

seems that we are to see that guilt is the emotion appropriate for Nora, while regret is all that fits foregoing one charity or revolution for another. In reply, first it should be repeated that when we do see things that way we may be discerning appropriateness to certain presumed moral convictions. By assuming their belief in any of a variety of common moral codes, we can find Nora appropriately guilty and the other two appropriately regretful. But again, this subjective appropriateness leaves us free to deny all actual conflict of absolute moral obligations. Another weakness in the case for dilemmas based upon these analogies is that they break down on a misleading contrast. In the example of Nora's predicament (and Marcus' example of the twins in jeopardy), known harm will come to known appreciated individuals whichever alternative is taken. Thus sorrow is clearly justified there. In the examples of the philanthropist and the revolutionary, the choices have unknown effects, difficult even to guess. Perhaps misgivings fit such evidence about consequences, but not sorrow. This difference can mislead us into thinking that the more troubling emotion of guilt fits the facts in Nora's case (and the twins' case), but not the other two. But this difference in the strength of warranted discomfort, unlike that between factual warrant for feelings of guilt and for regret only, does not imply a difference in moral status. There is no disanalogy here that supports the possibility of a moral dilemma.

The last claim on behalf of moral dilemmas for us to consider was made by Marcus. It concerns a salubrious effect of appropriate ascriptions of guilt:

[A]n agent in a predicament of conflict . . . will strive to arrange his own life and encourage social arrangements that would prevent, to the extent that it is possible, future conflicts from arising. To deny the appropriateness or correctness of ascriptions of guilt is to weaken the impulse to make such arrangements.[29]

Marcus advocates a principle according to which it is invariably morally obligatory to make such arrangements:

One ought to act in such a way that, if one ought to do x and one ought to do y, then one can do both x and y.[30]

This principle is inescapably obeyed if there can be no moral dilemmas. But if they can arise, then the principle has it that morality counsels us always to prevent them. So motivation to arrange for their prevention would always incline us toward actions we ought to perform.

It is not inevitably morally best to avoid the sorts of situations where proponents of moral dilemmas find them, however. To take a dramatic example, the spy whose information deters a nuclear conflict may have had to cheat, to betray family and friends, and to abuse innocent strangers in order to get that information. If so, then given that the prevention of nuclear war was at stake, he was morally required to do those things despite the fact that the moral defects of those acts are of sorts that are supposed to create obligations not to perform them. So the proponent of dilemmas would say that the spy faced several of them on that assignment. Yet if the mission was the sole means of averting the disaster and the spy could have arranged to cancel it, then it was morally mandatory that he not do so. Thus not all motivation for preventing circumstances that would be alleged to contain dilemmas works for the best.

Nonetheless, it is usually a good thing to prevent such situations from coming about. And being troubled about a believed moral failing does motivate such prevention. But there is no need to attribute moral dilemmas in order to justify powerful negative sentiments in these cases. In our examples of Nora and Agamemnon, evils ensue whatever is done. To say that guilt is not in fact appropriate is not to imply that only weaker negative feelings are suitable. Abhorrence of the ensuing evils is fitting. And that emotion equally inclines us to prevent circumstances

from arising in which something so harmful must be done. So without presupposing any conflict among absolute obligations we can still ascribe and justify feelings that help to keep us out of these predicaments.

We have seen no instance in which attributing a moral dilemma improves our understanding of the case. Moral dilemmas are of no special assistance in accounting for moral sentiments or in promoting good behavior. And as we saw at the outset, their existence would confound us with the prospect of impermissible obligations. The reasonable conclusion is that they are impossible.[31]

NOTES

1. E. J. Lemmon, "Moral Dilemmas," *Philosophical Review,* 71 (1962), 148.

2. Ruth Marcus, "Moral Dilemmas and Consistency," *Journal of Philosophy,* 77 (1980), 126.

3. Bernard Williams, "Ethical Consistency," *Problems of the Self* (Cambridge: Cambridge University Press, 1973), pp. 173–76.

4. Bas van Fraassen, "Values and the Heart's Command," *Journal of Philosophy,* 70 (1973), 15.

5. Van Fraassen, p. 12.

6. Lemmon, p. 140.

7. Lemmon, p. 140.

8. Lemmon, p. 141.

9. Indeed, we can use this kind of case to see that the feature of being required in one's line of work has no moral force at all by itself.

10. Williams, p. 174.

11. Williams, p. 173.

12. Williams, p. 176.

13. W. D. Ross, "What Makes Right Acts Right?" *The Right and the Good* (Oxford: Clarendon Press, 1930), p. 21.

14. Aeschylus, *Agamemnon,* tr. Eduard Fraenkel (Oxford: Clarendon Press, 1950), line 211.

15. Williams, p. 175.

16. Williams, p. 176.

17. Marcus, pp. 131–33; van Fraassen, p. 14.

18. Marcus, p. 131.

19. Marcus, p. 130.

20. Van Fraassen, p. 13.

21. It has been suggested that omitting a prima facie duty may be sufficient to make a feeling of guilt objectively appropriate. I am inclined to believe rather that feeling guilty fits

the facts only if one really is guilty of wrongdoing, while regret is the appropriate emotive response to failing to carry out what is just a prima facie duty. But if the suggestion is correct, then we have another way in which guilt feelings can be appropriate while no absolute moral duty is left undone.

22. Marcus, p. 125.
23. Van Fraassen, p. 9.
24. Van Fraassen, p. 14.
25. Van Fraassen, p. 7.
26. Van Fraassen, p. 14.
27. Ross counts each most stringent prima facie duty as something that it is morally right to fulfill (Ross, p. 41).
28. Van Fraassen, p. 14.
29. Marcus, p. 133.
30. Marcus, p. 135.

31. I am grateful for comments on a previous version of this paper from Eva Bodanszky, Herbert Heidelberger, and the editors and a referee for the *Philosophical Review*.

26
CONSISTENCY IN RATIONALIST MORAL SYSTEMS

Alan Donagan

In one of the most valuable of his *Essays on Actions and Events*, Donald Davidson[1] has remarked that "life is crowded with examples" of the following sort: "I ought to do it because it will save a life, I ought not because it will be a lie; if I do it, I will break my word to Lavinia, if I don't I will break my word to Lolita; and so on" (34). And of such examples he went on to say this:

Anyone may find himself in this fix, whether he be upright or temporizing, weak-willed or strong. But then unless we take the line that moral principles cannot conflict in application to a case, we must give up the concept of the nature of practical reason we have so far been assuming. For how can premises, all of which are true (or acceptable), entail a contradiction? It is astonishing that in contemporary moral philosophy this problem has received little attention, and no satisfactory treatment (*loc. cit.*).

Of course, in making these remarks, Davidson had not forgotten the solution of his problem that may be found in the neointuitionist theory of W. D. Ross, C. D. Broad, and their numerous followers.[2] According to that theory, which remains popular in an underground way, Davidson's contradiction-entailing premises only appear to be so: correctly understood, they are covertly qualified as *"prima facie"* only. The full sense of "I ought to do it because it will save a life, I ought not because it will be a lie" is *"Prima facie* I ought to do it because it will save a life, and *prima facie* I ought not, because it will be a lie." And that is equivalent to: "There is a (moral) reason for doing it, namely that it would save a life, but conceivably it may be overridden by a stronger reason; and likewise there is a (moral) reason for not doing it, namely that it would be a lie, but conceivably that too may be overridden by a stronger reason." Plainly, there is no contradiction here. What appeared to be contradictory premises are now revealed as no more than statements of

From *The Journal of Philosophy*, Vol. LXXXI, No. 6, (June 1984): 291–309. © 1984 The Journal of Philosophy, Inc. Reprinted by permission.

defeasible reasons, one for the action in question, and one against it. According to neointuitionist theory, a moralist's task is to determine which reason or set of reasons bearing on the question whether or not something proposed is to be done outweighs and so overrides those on the other side. There are no formal procedures by which such tasks can be performed: they call for good judgement, not for reasoning. Moral reflection is not a matter of practical reasoning, as it is commonly understood, but of surveying considerations intuitively perceived to be relevant, in the hope that none will be overlooked, and then of intuitively gauging their relative weight.

This theoretical strategy, however, is suicidal. No theory of moral reasoning can dispose of the objection that contradictions follow from premises it recognizes as true by denying that those premises are really premises. Nor is it easy to accept that reaching conclusions about what one is morally obliged to do is not a matter of reasoning—that, as Davidson has satirically put it, the sum of our moral wisdom concerning what to do in a given situation has the form: there is something to be said for doing so and so, and something to be said against—and also for and against not doing it (35).[3] It is true that from the fact that moral wisdom is reasoned and hence has an analyzable structure, it does not follow that it is usefully formalizable. Legal reasoning is not usually formalizable, and yet its structure can be analyzed. Judges are perhaps not unknown whose findings consist of listing considerations pro and con followed by announcing the result of an intuitive weighing, but their reputations are not high.

There is a class of moral theories in which moral reasoning is taken to resemble legal reasoning. Members of that class are sometimes described as "rationalist," in my opinion happily. Historically, the best known rationalist theories of morality are the theory of natural law that can be extracted from St. Thomas Aquinas's theological writings, and the theory expounded by Kant in the two volumes of his *Metaphysik der Sitten,* for which his *Grundlegung* broke the ground. Most rationalist theories of the present day are deeply indebted to Aquinas or Kant or both. The chief formal characteristics of such theories are five: (1) they rest on a few fundamental principles, sometimes one, which are advanced as true without exception; (2) each of those principles lays down some condition upon all human action as being required by practical reason; (3) those principles do not constitute a set of axioms, from which all the remaining moral precepts of the theory can be deduced; but, rather, (4) the remaining moral precepts are deduced from the fundamental principles by way of additional premises specifying further the conditions those principles lay down as required of all human action; and (5) both principles and additional premises are adopted on the basis of informal dialectical reasoning.

No set of formal characteristics, however, can capture what gives life to the rationalist approach to morality. When, as sometimes happens, a particular rationalist theory turns out to have implications that fall foul of dialectical considerations at least as strong as those on which it rests, either its principles or its additional premises must be revised. The fundamental methodological idea of rationalism is the nonformal idea that no revision of a premise may be ad hoc, merely intended to obviate an obnoxious implication; each must also turn out either to accord better with the dialectical considerations on the basis of which the unrevised premise was accepted, or to follow from a line of dialectical reasoning that is intrinsically superior.

A simple illustration may be found in Kant's *Lectures on Ethics.*[4] From the principle that no rational being is to be treated merely as a means, it is tempting to argue that, since giving to another information you believe to be false so far reduces him to a mere means to your purposes, it must be wrong to make any utterance to another that is contrary to your mind. Most moralists agree that an ancient example shows this to be a simple-minded error: namely, that of an armed would-be murderer who threatens an un-armed bystander with death unless he is informed of the whereabouts of his innocent quarry. How could it be wrong to give false information in such a case? But the new precept to which the example leads, namely that falsehood is wrong only in conditions of free communication where violence is neither done nor threatened to anybody concerned, is not ad hoc. It is derivable from the same principle as the unrevised one, but by way of an additional premise for which the dialectical grounds are stronger than those for the premise by which the rejected precept was derived. For the latter premise, that all falsehoods reduce those to whom they are told to mere means, is plainly indefensible when those to whom they are told have resorted to violence. It is, after all, a main theme in Kantian moral theory that not even the use of force to restrain those who use or threaten violence reduces them to mere means.

The problem of moral conflict is dismissed by rationalists as spurious, root and branch. In the following passage from the Introduction to his *Metaphysik der Sitten*, often quoted, but as a rule with astonishment or even incredulity, Kant gave classical expression to what is common to all of them:

Because, however, duty and obligation are in general concepts that express the objective practical necessity of certain actions and because two mutually opposing rules cannot be necessary at the same time, then, if it is a duty to act according to one of them, it is not only not a duty but contrary to duty to act according to the other. It follows, therefore, that a collision of duties and obligations is inconceivable (*obligationes non colliduntur*). It may, however, happen that two grounds of obligation, one or the other of which is inadequate to bind as a duty (*rationes obligandi non obligantes*), are conjoined in a subject and in the rule that he prescribes to himself, and then one of the grounds is not a duty. When two such grounds are in conflict, practical philosophy does not say that the stronger obligation holds the upper hand (*fortior obligatio vincit*), but that the stronger ground binding to a duty holds the field (*fortior obligandi ratio vincit*).[5]

This passage is sometimes interpreted as anticipating neointuitionism by resolving some alleged conflicts of obligations into conflicts of grounds of obligation. But that is textually indefensible. In describing conflict between grounds of obligation, Kant avoided the metaphor for victorious struggle, namely, "holding the upper hand," which he employed in depicting what a putative conflict of obligations would be, and instead represented it as a conflict in which one ground 'holds the field', while the other, a mere *ratio obligandi non obligans*, simply vacates it, as being inadequate to bind as a duty.

What specifically has Kant in mind here? The distinction between perfect and imperfect duties in the *Grundlegung*, which is elaborated in *Metaphysik der Sitten*, supplies the answer.[6] Grounds of obligation of two kinds: those binding to perfect duties—duties to perform certain kinds of action other than those by which one executes the rational policies of self-culture or beneficence it is one's duty to form for oneself; and those binding to imperfect duties—or duties to execute such policies. Kant considered it obviously impossible that perfect duties or their grounds could ever be in collision. And he also held it to be impossible that imperfect duties could be in collision either with one another or with perfect duties: not obviously, but because of a condition on rational policies of self-culture or beneficence, namely that such policies must themselves be consistent and must not entail violating other duties, whether perfect or imperfect. In themselves, apart from this condition on rational policies, grounds of self-culture and beneficence can of course be in conflict with themselves, with one another, and with perfect duties; but so taken, they are for that very reason *rationes obligandi non obligantes* and, hence, inadequate to bind as duties.

Neither the rationalist nor the neointuitionist denial of the possibility of a genuine conflict of duties has been prominent in philosophical discussions of moral conflict in the past twenty years or so. Two innovations have captured most attention. One has been the elaboration, by John Rawls, of a contractarian version of Kant, according to which a system of morality is to be constructed by considering what precepts rational persons would agree to accept as binding, if the agreement were reached under conditions designed to secure a morally sound result. Consistency is obtained by providing that the precepts agreed upon be assigned a lexical order and that observance of those later in the order be conditional upon observance of those earlier in it. In his *Theory of Reasons for Action*, David A. J. Richards offers a specimen of such a system of lexically ordered precepts.[7] But it would be out of place, in a study of consistency in rationalist moral systems, to investigate this contractarian device; for if the rationalist approach to morality is sound, lexical ordering is either superfluous, because any morally necessary restriction on the scope of a precept must be deducible from the principles of an adequate system, or ad hoc, because it would exclude possible conflicts of precepts by imposing restrictions that are not thus deducible. The second innovation, however, is another matter. It is the acceptance, by a number of original and influential philosophers, of moral conflict as being with us much as the poor have been believed to be: either necessarily and always, or at least for a very long time.

Bernard Williams has succinctly expressed the idea underlying this innovation. Neointutionist and rationalist moral theories, he contends, "do not do justice to the facts of regret and related considerations; basically because they eliminate from the scene the ought that is not acted on."[8] It simply is not the case that, when one ground for acting is held to be stronger than another, the rejected ground is annihilated. "A man may feel regret because he has broken a promise in the course of acting (as he sincerely supposes) for the best; and his regret at having broken a promise must surely arise *via* a moral thought . . . A tendency to feel regrets, particularly creative regrets, at having broken a promise even in

the course of acting for the best might well be considered a reassuring sign that an agent took his promises seriously (175).

There is a familiar objection to this. Is it not simply inconsistent on the one hand to decide that it is for the best to act contrary to a certain ought and on the other to refuse to eliminate that ought from the scene? However, if that is inconsistent, it should be possible to show it.

In examples like Williams's, the conflict that compels the agent to act contrary to a certain ought is generated by his acceptance of three propositions:

1. I ought to save this life.
2. I ought to keep this promise.
3. I cannot both save this life and keep this promise.

Yet, although accepting this triad, together with the belief that it is better to save this life than to keep this promise, leaves the agent no rational option but to break this promise, it does not follow that the triad, taken as it stands, is inconsistent. A contradiction is a proposition to the effect that something both is and is not the case. But that (1) an agent ought to act in a certain way, and that (2) he ought to act in a certain other way, do not together with the fact that (3) he cannot act in both ways, entail either that it is and is not the case that he ought to act in a certain way, or that it is and is not the case that he cannot act in both ways; and there is no other contradiction they can plausibly be supposed to entail. The fact that the triad generates a conflict does not show that it is inconsistent.

Why then do most moral philosophers reject as inconsistent any moral position that contains such triads? Because, as Williams has pointed out, they take moral positions generally to be committed to two presuppositions, one logical and one ethical (*ibid.*). The logical presupposition, which Williams calls "the agglomeration principle," is the generalization of the proposition that if it is the case that I ought to save this life and also the case that I ought to keep this promise, then it is the case that I ought both to save this life and to keep this promise. The ethical presupposition is expressed in the Kantian slogan "Ought implies can," and can be formulated as "If you ought to do an action of a certain kind then you can do an action of that kind." Asserting the triad together with these presuppositions is certainly inconsistent; for from (1) and (2), together with the agglomeration principle, it follows that it is the case that I ought both to save this life and to keep this promise, whereas from (3) and the contrapositive of the Kantian slogan as I have formulated it, it follows that this is not the case.

Hence, if they are to avoid inconsistency, those who accept triads like the one we have been investigating because they agree with Williams that the moral ought that is not acted on cannot be eliminated from the scene, have no choice but to abandon either the agglomeration principle or the principle expressed in the slogan "Ought implies can." Neither course is inviting.

Williams himself, followed by Bas C. van Fraassen, opts for the former. Because, as the facts of regret show, the ought that is not acted on is not eliminated even when it is for the best not to act on it, he argues that the picture of moral thinking according to which "there can be two things, each of which I ought to do and each of which I can do, but of which I cannot do both" is "more realistic" than one according to which there cannot, and that we should have no qualms at abandoning the less realistic of the two pictures (182).

The contribution of van Fraassen has been to equip Williams's conclusion with a semantical interpretation. In standard systems of deontic logic, the "ought" operator is taken to be analogous to the necessity operator of modal logic; and in all standard systems of modal logic, if it is necessary that p and necessary that q, it is necessary that p and q. But van Fraassen has pointed out that there are command theories of morality according to which ought-statements of the form "It ought to be the case that p" are true if and only if some authority compe-

tent to issue moral commands has issued one (e.g. "Let it be brought about that p") that would not be fulfilled if it were not the case that p.[9] Such a command theory may exclude as ill-formed any putative command to do what cannot be done, so that "Let it be brought about that p and q," where it cannot be brought about that both are true, would not be a genuine command. Yet it would remain possible, on such a theory, that the competent authority should issue conflicting commands—commands each of which can be carried out, although all cannot be carried out together. "Let it be brought about that p' and 'Let it be brought about that q'" may each be genuine commands, even though "Let it be brought about that p and q" is not. Some divine-command theories of morality appear to be of this kind, for example, that of St. Gregory the Great, who held that human beings could be trapped by the devil into situations in which they were confronted with conflicting divine commands.[10]

Although most deontic logicians resist van Fraassen's proposal for amending the orthodox semantic foundations of their subject, the fundamental objection to adopting a semantics for ought-statements that would invalidate the agglomeration principle is ethical. Unless there is an alternative that is unknown to me, the only ethically plausible interpretation of moral systems that exclude agglomeration is van Fraassen's—that they are systems of commands by appropriate authorities. In such systems, provided that a command is in proper form and has been given by an appropriate authority, its moral validity is assured. However, although there are systems of this kind (divine-command systems being the most common), rationalists reject them as false in principle. Their position is that the only thing that can make a command a moral one is that it is imposed by practical reason. The commands God addresses to human beings as such are indeed morally binding; but that is because they express the infinite rationality of the divine essence, in which human rationality participates. To depict God as imposing on human beings commands contrary to practical reason is not only blasphemous but also absurd.

A moral theory according to which the ultimate moral authority gives commands that cannot be agglomerated conceives the moral universe as analogous to the U.S.S. Caine in Herman Wouk's *The Caine Mutiny*, and the moral authority as analogous to Captain Queeg. Even in the U.S.S. Caine, Kant's principle that ought implies can holds: a command to do the impossible is not a genuine command. However, two distinct commands, each of which can be obeyed, will each be legitimate, even if the situation is such that they cannot both be obeyed. True, at a court martial, it would be a perfect defense against a charge of disobedience that, having obeyed one of the conflicting commands, it thereby became impossible to obey the other. But, as long as Captain Queeg was the sole judge, one can imagine that this perfect defense would be rejected, as St. Gregory the Great imagined God rejecting a parallel defense to the charge of failing to obey conflicting divine commands. From the point of view of the lower deck, the universe of the U.S.S. Caine is absurd and unjust, but it is not inconsistent. And if the relation of human beings to moral authority is that of the lower deck to Captain Queeg, morality is absurd and nasty (we cannot say "unjust"!) but it is not inconsistent.

It is of the essence of rationalism to repudiate any conception of the relation of human beings to moral authority as analogous to that of the lower deck on the U.S.S. Caine to Captain Queeg. For according to rationalism, genuine moral requirements are requirements of practical reason on beings who themselves possess practical reason. Moral requirements may be asserted by authorities outside the individual moral agent, for example, the state (e.g., in criminal law). But no external requirement can be a moral requirement unless an adult of sound mind and normal education in a morally decent society, if he wishes to learn, can be brought to see its necessity for himself. Those who are under the moral law

are therefore autonomous. It is as though Captain Queeg were unable to give any commands that did not belong to a set which, as a whole, the entire lower deck could be brought to acknowledge to be reasonable. In the moral universe, human beings stand to their moral authorities—the state, religious institutions, public opinion—not only as the lower deck stood to Captain Queeg, but as did the brother officials and equals who tried him at his court martial. And just as a court martial will judge a commander incompetent if he has made a practice of giving commands that must be ruled invalid when agglomerated, so autonomous moral agents will reject a moral system as ill constructed if there are situations to which its precepts apply, but in which their agglomeration would be invalid.

For this reason, the only semantics of ought-statements that appears to make sense of abandoning the agglomeration principle is ethically impossible. How, then, can situations occur at all in which moral obligations conflict? Among recent philosophers, the late E. J. Lemmon appears to have been the first to draw the inevitable conclusion: that such situations can occur is "a refutation of the principle that 'ought' implies 'can.' "[11] But Lemmon's treatment was cavalier. The Kantian principle is too deeply entrenched in ethical thought to be dismissed outright. Not only rationalists are apt to be bewildered by what a moral obligation could be, if there should admittedly be no question of doing what one is morally obliged to do. Ruth Barcan Marcus, however, has recently proposed a revised version of the Kantian principle which promises both to make sense of moral obligations and to allow for the possibility of situations in which they conflict.[12]

The idea underlying Marcus's revision of the ought-implies-can principle originates in model theory. A set of meaningful sentences is consistent, she points out, provided only that it is possible for all the members of the set to be true: provided that there is a model, or possible world, in which they are all true. "Analogously," she goes on to say, "we can define a set of rules as consistent if there is some possible world in which they are all obeyable in all circumstances in *that* world" (238). If a moral system is consistent provided only that there is a possible world on which all its precepts are obeyable in all circumstances, the principle that ought implies can must be reformulated as two distinct principles, a first-order one and a second-order one. The first-order principle is that each and every nonagglomerated ought implies can: if you ought to do something, that something not being itself an agglomeration of things you ought to do, then you can do it. The second-order principle is that each agglomerated ought, if it cannot be obeyed in all circumstances in the actual world, must be such that one can try to bring about a world in which it can be obeyed in all circumstances, and one ought to try. But this principle is regulative only. As Marcus puts it:

One ought to act in such a way that, if one ought to do x and one ought to do y, then one can do both x and y. But the second-order principle is regulative. This second-order 'ought' does *not* imply 'can'. There is no reason to suppose, this being the actual world, that we can, individually or collectively, however holy our wills or rational our strategies, succeed in wholly avoiding . . . conflict [of obligations]. It is not merely failure of will, or failure of reason [that produces such conflict]. It is the contingencies of this world (242).

The semantics for the moral ought by which Marcus elucidates her revision of the ought-implies-can principle, like that by which van Fraassen gave sense to the negation of the agglomeration principle, is logically unobjectionable. And it has ethical attractions. Confronted with situations in which they cannot do what seems to be for the best unless they violate some moral principle they embrace, moralists have always been tempted to find fault with the contingencies of the world rather than with their moral thinking. When Cicero lamented to Atticus that Cato seemed to think that he lived in Plato's republic, and not in the cesspool of Romulus, he was objecting, not to Cato's principles, but to his rustic notion that principles were to be acted on.[13]. Is morality not an ideal, after all? How can we be blamed for falling short of our ideal when a flawed world puts its attainment beyond our reach? However often the ideal we should like to be able to live up to is violated by the best we can actually do, it remains our ideal; we are remorseful at having done what we had to do, and we strive (without much hope, it is true) to bring about a world in which we shall no longer have to do it.

Like Cato, rationalists have always rejected this Ciceronian position. Morality, as they conceive it, is a system of precepts defining the limits imposed on human action by practical reason; and human action takes place in the actual world—in Cicero's cesspool of Romulus. But no human being knows completely either that part of the course of events constituting the actual world which bears upon his own actions or the causal principles that obtain in it. Hence, while an adequate rationalist theory of morality is not concerned with mere fantasy worlds, it must lay down what practical reason requires of human beings not only in the actual world, but in any possible world that, for all they know, may turn out to be actual. According to the moral tradition that has descended to us, through Christianity, from Greek philosophy and Jewish religion, rational beings act freely in a course of events in which everything except the actions of rational beings forms part of a lawful natural order.[14]

I do not think that Davidson, or Williams, or Marcus, or any of the phalanx of distinguished contemporary philosophers who, by maintaining the reality of moral conflict implicitly reject the possibility of an acceptable rationalist moral theory, would deny that such a theory would be desirable if it were possible. Why are they convinced that it is not? Why does it seem to them virtually beyond question that some moral conflicts, at least, are not illusions symptomatic of the failure of thought, but genuine discoveries?

To judge by the examples they offer, most critics of rationalism appear to follow Henry Sidgwick in holding that no rationalist theory of the duty of keeping promises can fail to generate moral conflicts, both by itself (conflicts between promises) and in relation to other parts of morality (conflicts between promise-keeping and other duties). An example of the first kind is described by Marcus, when she points out that I may "make two promises in all good faith and reason that they will not conflict" and yet find that they do conflict "as a result of circumstances that were unpredictable and beyond my control" (241)—as when, having a thousand dollars in my office safe and five hundred in my pocket, and owing Smith and Jones five hundred dollars each, I promise each that I will repay my debt at my office tomorrow, only to find next day that I cannot do so, because overnight my safe has been emptied by a burglar. An example of the second kind has already been touched on in discussing the agglomeration principle. I have promised to transact some business with an associate in his office at noon; but on my way I pass two cars that have collided, and am begged by paramedical officers to help them to treat the injured, because otherwise at least one will die. In this unforeseeable contingency, I cannot both save the life of the injured person and keep my promise.

Although some rationalists have treated promising less competently than others, most of them agree that no genuine conflict of duties occurs in cases of either of these kinds, and many agree also on the principles by which this can be shown. The fundamental principle is that *it is morally wrong to make a promise unless you can keep it and it is morally permissible for you to keep it.*[15]

By itself, this principle would be self-defeating. With respect to most promises that matter, promiser and promisee alike know that unforeseeable contingencies can occur that would make it either impossible or wrong for the promiser to keep his word. If, therefore, it were wrong to make a promise unless one knew that no contingencies would

occur that would make it either impossible or wrong to keep it, promising would almost always be wrong. But it is not. How is that possible? I submit that it is because most of us are willing to accept a promise provided that we trust the promiser and understand him to have acceptable reason to believe that he can and may do what he promises. True, we recognize that acceptable reasons may not be sufficient reasons: owing to unforeseeable contingencies it may turn out to be impossible or wrong to keep the promise. Since we accepted the promise on the understanding that things might so turn out, should they do so we would not be entitled to demand that it be kept, although, depending on circumstances, we might be entitled to amends for the breach. Hence we have a second principle: *most promises are made and accepted on the twofold condition that the promiser has acceptable reason to believe that he can and may do what he promises, and that if nevertheless it turns out that he either cannot or may not, the promisee will not be entitled to performance.* If the promiser fails to satisfy his part of this twofold condition, he does wrong in making the promise, and his consequent moral difficulties are his fault, not the fault of the circumstances or of the moral system. If the promisee disregards the condition on what he is entitled to, and demands that the promiser keep his promise even though, through no fault of his own, he either cannot or may not keep it, the promiser may reject that demand as contrary to a condition on which his promise was accepted. This twofold condition on the collaborative act of making and accepting a promise, unlike internal conditions which vary from promise to promise, is virtually universal, and hence is normally unexpressed.

A difficulty, however, remains. It sometimes happens that, although a promise is given and accepted on the condition just described, the promisee would not consider acceptable the reason upon which the promiser believes that he can and may keep his word. This disagreement may not appear when the promise is made, because a promisee normally does not ask the promiser what his reason is for believing that he can and may keep his word. This difficulty is resolved by a third principle: that *it is wrong for a promiser to make a promise on any condition on which he does not believe the promisee to understand him to make it.* As William Whewell pointed out,[16] it cannot be seriously maintained, even by disgruntled promisees, that a promiser binds himself to do more than he believes the promisee, in accepting the promise, takes him to bind himself to do.

When I find myself in the fix that if I do something I will break my word to Lavinia and that if I do not I will break my word to Lolita, then according to the first of these principles, there is some reason to presume that, in view of my promise to Lolita, it was wrong to make to Lavinia the promise I did. But what if I had reason to believe that I could keep my promises to both? Then, according to the third principle, I must ask whether I believed that Lavinia, had she known of my promise to Lolita, would have thought my reason for believing that I could also keep my word to her to have been acceptable. If I did not, then I wrongly made Lavinia a promise on a condition on which I did not believe she understood me to have made it. On the other hand, if I did, then by the second principle, since there was a condition on my giving my word to Lavinia that has not been fulfilled, I am not bound to do what I promised her, although I may have amends to make for not doing it. It will be obvious how the three principles apply to the examples given of the two kinds of alleged conflict of duties to which promising gives rise.

Promising survives as an important institution, and not merely as an amiable ritual, because promiser and promisee can often be confident, whether from a shared culture or from personal intimacy, that they would agree about the acceptability or unacceptability of any reason that might be put to them for believing that a particular promise could be kept. You show that giving your word is a serious matter by your scrupulousness in ensuring that those to whom you give it understand the conditions on which you do so and in keeping it when those conditions are fulfilled, not by irrational guilt at breaking it when they are not.

I do not imply that before now any rationalist moralist has resolved in exactly this way conflicts of duties allegedly generated by the institution of promising. But I do contend that many rationalist theories contain the elements of this way of resolving them: in particular, the principle that it is wrong for anybody to make a promise unless he can keep it and it is morally permissible for him to keep it; and the related principle that besides the internal conditions on what is promised, there are normally other conditions, usually unexpressed, on the act of promising itself. In view of that, I further contend that even if a given rationalist theory fails to exclude the possibility of situations in which morally permissible promises could generate irresoluble conflicts of duties, it can nevertheless, along the lines I have proposed, be so revised as to exclude it.

Yet there is an objection of principle to the idea underlying this way of resolving conflicts of duties arising from promises. That idea is that no genuine conflict of duties can be generated by a promise it was wrong to make. But is that true? Even conceding that it is wrong to promise to do what you cannot do or what it would be wrong to do, can a promiser plead that wrong as justifying his breaking his word? Has not the promisee reason to complain: "You should have thought of that when you gave me your word, which I accepted in good faith on the conditions on which you gave it; but it does not follow, because you did wrong to give it, that you do not also do wrong in breaking it"? This seems unanswerable; and if it is, those who wrongly give their word may entangle themselves in genuine conflicts of duties.

The rationalist reply to this objection, which was first clearly worked out by St. Thomas Aquinas, concedes its point, but deprives it of force by a distinction.[17]. The doctrine that there can be no genuine conflict of duties is ambiguous. If it means that all the precepts of a true moral system are obeyable in all situations to which it applies, then it is true. But taken in this sense, it does not imply that somebody who violates some of its precepts in some situations will be able either to obey all its other precepts in those situations or all its precepts in other situations. And cases of conflicts of duty arising from wrongful promises show that it is false if it is taken in a stronger sense in which it would imply that not even wrongdoing can give rise to situations in which the wrongdoer is entangled in a conflict of duties.

Aquinas classically expressed this point by distinguishing two kinds of conflict of duties, or, as he called it, two kinds of "perplexity": perplexity *simpliciter* and perplexity *secundum quid* (*ibid.*). A moral system allows perplexity (or conflict of duties) *simpliciter* if and only if situations to which it applies are possible, in which somebody would find himself able to obey one of its precepts only if he violated another, even though he had up to then obeyed all of them. For reasons already given, Aquinas held that any moral system that allows perplexity *simpliciter* must be inconsistent. By contrast, a system allows perplexity (or conflict of duties) *secundum quid* if and only if situations to which it applies are possible in which, as a result of violating one or more of its precepts, somebody would find that there is a precept he can obey only if he violates another. With regard to perplexity *secundum quid* Aquinas remarked that there is nothing logically wrong (*inconveniens*) with a moral system according to which a person in mortal sin can find himself perplexed.[18]

Since not all rationalists have perceived the distinction between conflicts of duty *simpliciter* and conflicts of duty *secundum quid,* not all have been in a position to draw the conclusion that a moral system may be consistent and yet allow conflicts of duty *secundum quid*—conflicts that themselves arise out of violations of duty. And, despite a note in G. H. von Wright's *Essay in Deontic Logic* that contains everything essential,[19] neither Aquinas's distinction nor its implication appears to be well known. It is therefore hard to estimate how far the prevalent opinion that rationalist systems of morality must be inconsistent because they generate moral conflicts proceeds from the error that systems that generate moral conflicts *secundum quid* must be inconsistent. However, once cases of conflict *secundum quid* are excluded as irrelevant to the question of consistency, plausible cases of moral conflict generated by sophisticated rationalist systems become hard to find.

Most of the remaining cases that appear in recent philosophical discussion have a common genus. And light is thrown on that genus by Marcus's claim to have derived, from the analogy of Buridan's ass, a principle that can be relied upon to generate moral conflict even within moral systems having only one fundamental principle, like Kant's. She writes:

> . . . it can be seen that the single-principle solution is mistaken. There is always the analogue of Buridan's ass. . . . The lives of identical twins are in jeopardy, and, through force of circumstances, I am in a position to save only one. Make the situation as symmetrical as you please. A single-principled framework is not necessarily unlike the code with qualifications or priority rule, in that it would appear that, however strong our wills or complete our knowledge, we might be faced with a moral choice in which there are no moral grounds for favoring doing x over y (236–7).

I take it that Kant, and most rationalists, would object that the question which child is to be saved is not a moral question at all, if *ex hypothesi* the moral considerations are symmetrical; and that it seems to be a moral question only if it is falsely assumed that any practical question about what to do in a situation in which morality places restrictions on what we may do must be a moral question.

Where the lives of identical twins are in jeopardy and I can save one but only one, every serious rationalist moral system lays down that, whatever I do, I must save one of them. By postulating that the situation is symmetrical, Marcus herself implies that there are no grounds, moral or nonmoral, for saving either as opposed to the other.

Why, then, does she not see that, as a practical question, Which am I to save? has no rational answer except "It does not matter," and as a moral question none except "There is no moral question"? Certainly there is no moral conflict: from the fact that I have a duty to save either *a* or *b*, it does not follow that I have a duty to save *a* and a duty to save *b*. Can it be seriously held that a fireman, who has rescued as many as he possibly could of a group trapped in a burning building, should blame himself for the deaths of those left behind, whose lives could have been saved only if he had not rescued some of those he did?

Yet although there is no moral conflict in cases of this kind—no conflict between duties—there is practical conflict. The fireman has reason to help, and wants to help, every one of those who beg him to; and he is torn when he can act on one such reason only if he does not act on another equally strong. This is one of those conflicts of grounds of obligation which Kant distinguished from genuine conflicts of obligation.[20] If there were only one person in the burning building, his need for help would hold the field as a ground binding to a duty (*Verpflichtungsgrund*); but since there are other grounds of the same force and it is impossible to act on them all, none of them holds the field as a ground binding to a duty, and the fireman's only duty or obligation is to act on as many of them as possible, it does not matter which. Still, although in this situation none of the various grounds binds to a duty, they remain grounds and they are in conflict. Practical conflict between considerations that have force, especially when in other circumstances one or another of them would give rise to a moral obligation, is readily mistaken for moral conflict.

The reason many philosophers at the present time are convinced that no acceptable moral theory can exclude the possibility of moral conflict *simpliciter* appears to be that, like Marcus, they assume that the question, What shall I do? in any situation in which moral considerations are relevant, must be a moral question. Davidson's remark, for example, "I do not believe that any version of the "single principle" solution [of the problem of moral conflict], once its implications are understood, can be accepted: principles, or reasons for acting, are irreducibly multiple" (34), would miss the point if the irreducibly multiple reasons for acting were not moral. But rationalists insist that for the most part they are not.

If, as rationalists maintain, morality is the sum of those conditions on human action which are unconditionally required by practical reason, then for the most part moral considerations will not suffice to answer the question, What shall I do? They will in exceptional cases. For example, if I have made a binding promise to mail a letter by today's last collection, and half a minute before that collection am at the post office letter in hand, then moral considerations do suffice to answer the question, What shall I do in the next half minute? But such cases are not the rule. In Kant's rationalist theory, for example, of those human actions which are morally permissible, very few discharge perfect duties; the larger number, but still few, that discharge the imperfect duties of self-culture and beneficence allow room for inclination and, hence, are partly determined by nonmoral considerations; but most, including many of those we think about hardest and find it hardest to decide on (such as those raising questions like, Shall I rebuild my house on Malibu beach? Shall I abandon the doctoral program in Assyrian and apply to business school? and Shall I propose marriage to Bathsheba?) have little or nothing to do with morality.

It is true that, in many situations, the considerations I may have to weigh in answering the question, What shall I do? are irreducibly multiple: considerations of desire, convenience, affection, indignation, and courtesy—along with those of morality. The rationalist position is that, in most cases, moral considerations do not suffice to answer the question, What shall I do? What they do suffice to answer is the very different question, What conditions are imposed by practical reason on what I may do? Davidson's premise is true: the reasons that bear on what we are to do are irreducibly multiple. And his conclusion follows from it: in human praxis generally, conflicts of reasons for acting are inescapable. But, since not all practical principles are moral principles, practical conflicts are not necessarily moral conflicts; and rationalists maintain that they never are.

The argument of this paper is simply that the rationalist position that moral obligations never collide has not been shown to be false and that the prevalent impression that it has been springs from three sources: confusion of practical conflict generally with moral conflict; overlooking the distinction between moral conflict *simpliciter* and moral conflict *secundum quid;* and neglect of the casuistical resources of the various rationalist ethical traditions. I do not contend that any rationalist theory of morality yet produced is completely acceptable either morally or logically; but I do contend both that several such theories (among which I number those of Aquinas and Kant) are, in essence, serious options for moralists, and also that, if they should prove inconsistent, their inconsistency will turn out to result from corrigible blemishes rather than from radical incoherence.

NOTES

The first version of this paper was presented to Donald Davidson's seminar at the University of Chicago in Winter 1981, the second was a Matchette lecture at the University of Wisconsin at Madison in November 1981, and substantially the present version was the Donald J. Lipkind Memorial Lecture at the University of Chicago in May 1982. For detailed criticism, I owe much to the audiences on those occasions; and also to members of colloquia at the branches of the University of California at Santa Cruz, Riverside, Irvine, and Los Angeles, at Texas A & M University, at the California Institute of Technology, and at Marquette University, Milwaukee, to all of which versions were read.

1. *Essays on Actions and Events* (New York:

Oxford, 1980), pp. 2/3, 34. Parenthetical page references to Davidson are to this book.

2. Ross, *The Right and the Good* (New York: Oxford, 1930); Broad, *Five Types of Ethical Theory* (London: Routledge & Kegan Paul, 1930); for a recent endorsement, Robert Nozick, "Moral Complications and Moral Structures," *Natural Law Forum,* xiii (1968):1–50.

3. I have reversed the order of Davidson's sentences in presenting what he says.

4. Louis Infeld, trans. (New York: Harper & Row, 1963), pp. 226–228.

5. Königsberg: 2nd ed., 1798, p. 24 (Ak. ed., vol. 6, p. 224). John Ladd's translation is the basis of that given here, but I have altered it in three places. The German text corresponding to the fourth sentence of my English version is: "wenn zwei solcher Gründe einander widerstreiten, so sagt di praktische Philosophie nicht: dass die stärkere Verbindlichkeit die Oberhand behalte (*fortior obligatio vincit*), sondern der stärkere Verpflichtungsgrund behält den Platz (*fortior obligandi ratio vincit*)."

6. *Grundlegung zur Metaphysik der Sitten* (Riga: 2nd ed., 1786), p. 53n. (Ak. ed., vol. 4, p. 421n).

7. New York: Oxford, 1971.

8. "Ethical Consistency," in *Problems of the Self* (New York: Cambridge, 1977), p. 175. [This paper originally appeared in *Proceedings of the Aristotelian Society,* supp. vol. xxxix (1965).]

9. van Fraassen, "Values and the Heart's Command," *Journal of Philosophy,* lxx, 1 (Jan. 11, 1973): 15–19. I use only van Fraassen's "initial" interpretation of ought, which clearly reveals his fundamental idea, and not his final and more sophisticated formulation, which enables him to deal with complexities foreign to the subject of the present paper.

10. St. Gregory's position is set out in Kenneth E. Kirk, *Conscience and Its Problems* (London: Longman, 1927), p. 322. See also my *The Theory of Morality* (Chicago: University Press, 1977), p.144.

11. "Moral Dilemmas," *Philosophical Review,* lxxi, 2 (April, 1962): 139–158.

12. "Moral Dilemmas and Consistency," *Journal of Philosophy,* lxxvii, 3 (March 1980): 121–136, esp. 133–135. Parenthetical page references to Marcus will be to this paper.

13. "... ille optimo animo utens et summa fide nocet interdum rei publicae; dicit enim tanquam in Platonis πολιτεία, non tanquam in Romuli faece sententiam" (*Epistulae ad Atticum,* II, 1, 8).

14. By contrast, for example, with the morality of Hinduism; see my *Theory of Morality, op. cit.*, pp. 32–36, for a brief discussion.

15. In *A Theory of Reasons for Action* (New York: Oxford, 1971), pp. 164/5, David A. J. Richards has attempted to formulate the "generally accepted critical attitudes concerning the use . . . of expressions like 'I promise' " on which the existence of promising as a social institution depends. Most rationalists would endorse his formulation as approximately right.

16. *The Elements of Morality*, 4th ed. (Cambridge: Deighton Bell, 1864), sec. 280, p. 155.

17. *Summa Theologiae*, I–II, 6 *ad* 3; II–II, 62, 2; III, 64, 6 *ad* 3; *de Veritate*, 17, 4, *ad* 8.

18. *de Veritate*, 17, 4 *ad* 8.

19. Amsterdam: North Holland, 1968, p. 81 n. 1. As far as I know, this is the first reference to Aquinas's distinction in print by a recent philosopher: von Wright himself acknowledges that P. T. Geach drew his attention to the relevant passages in Aquinas's writings.

20. See note 5 above.

27
THE SUBJECTIVITY OF VALUES

J. L. Mackie

1. MORAL SCEPTICISM

There are no objective values. This is a bald statement of the thesis of this chapter, but before arguing for it I shall try to clarify and restrict it in ways that may meet some objections and prevent some misunderstanding.

The statement of this thesis is liable to provoke one of three very different reactions. Some will think it not merely false but pernicious; they will see it as a threat to morality and to everything else that is worthwhile, and they will find the presenting of such a thesis in what purports to be a book on ethics paradoxical or even outrageous. Others will regard it as a trivial truth, almost too obvious to be worth mentioning, and certainly too plain to be worth much argument. Others again will say that it is meaningless or empty, that no real issue is raised by the question whether values are or are not part of the fabric of the world. But, precisely because there can be these three

From *Ethics,* (Penguin Books, 1977). Reprinted by permission.

different reactions, much more needs to be said.

The claim that values are not objective, are not part of the fabric of the world, is meant to include not only moral goodness, which might be most naturally equated with moral value, but also other things that could be more loosely called moral values or disvalues—rightness or wrongness, duty, obligation, an action's being rotten and contemptible, and so on. It also includes non-moral values, notably aesthetic ones, beauty and various kinds of artistic merit. I shall not discuss these explicitly, but clearly much the same considerations apply to aesthetic and to moral values, and there would be at least some initial implausibility in a view that gave the one a different status from the other.

Since it is with moral values that I am primarily concerned, the view I am adopting may be called moral scepticism. But this name is likely to be misunderstood: 'moral scepticism' might also be used as a name for either of two first order views, or perhaps for an incoherent mixture of the two. A moral sceptic might be the sort of person who says 'All this talk of morality is tripe,' who rejects morality and will take no notice of it. Such a person may be literally rejecting all moral judgements; he is more likely to be making moral judgements of his own, expressing a positive moral condemnation of all that conventionally passes for morality; or he may be confusing these two logically incompatible views, and saying that he rejects all morality, while he is in fact rejecting only a particular morality that is current in the society in which he has grown up. But I am not at present concerned with the merits or faults of such a position. These are first order moral views, positive or negative: the person who adopts either of them is taking a certain practical, normative, stand. By contrast, what I am discussing is a second order view, a view about the status of moral values and the nature of moral valuing, about where and how they fit into the world. These first and second order views are not merely distinct but completely independent: one could be a second order moral sceptic without being a first order one, or again the other way round. A man could hold strong moral views, and indeed ones whose content was thoroughly conventional, while believing that they were simply attitudes and policies with regard to conduct that he and other people held. Conversely, a man could reject all established morality while believing it to be an objective truth that it was evil or corrupt.

With another sort of misunderstanding moral scepticism would seem not so much pernicious as absurd. How could anyone deny that there is a difference between a kind action and a cruel one, or that a coward and a brave man behave differently in the face of danger? Of course, this is undeniable; but it is not to the point. The kinds of behaviour to which moral values and disvalues are ascribed are indeed part of the furniture of the world, and so are the natural, descriptive, differences between them; but not, perhaps, their differences in value. It is a hard fact that cruel actions differ from kind ones, and hence that we can learn, as in fact we all do, to distinguish them fairly well in practice, and to use the words 'cruel' and 'kind' with fairly clear descriptive meanings; but is it an equally hard fact that actions which are cruel in such a descriptive sense are to be condemned? The present issue is with regard to the objectivity specifically of value, not with regard to the objectivity of those natural, factual, differences on the basis of which differing values are assigned.

2. SUBJECTIVISM

Another name often used, as an alternative to 'moral scepticism,' for the view I am discussing is 'subjectivism.' But this too has more than one meaning. Moral subjectivism too could be a first order, normative, view, namely that everyone really ought to do whatever he thinks he should. This plainly is a (systematic) first order view; on examination it soon ceases to be plausible, but that is beside the point, for it is quite independent of the second order thesis at present under consideration. What is more confusing is that different second order views compete for the name 'subjectivism.' Several of these are doctrines about the meaning of moral terms and moral statements. What is often called moral subjectivism is the doctrine that, for example, 'This action is right' *means* 'I approve of this action,' or more generally that moral judgements are equivalent to reports of the speaker's own feelings or attitudes. But the view I am now discussing is to be distinguished in two vital respects from any such doctrine as this. First, what I have called moral scepticism is a negative doctrine, not a positive one: it says what there isn't, not what there is. It says that there do not exist entities or relations of a certain kind, objective values or requirements, which many people have believed to exist. Of course, the moral sceptic cannot leave it at that. If his position is to be at all plausible, he must give some account of how other people have fallen into what he regards as an error, and this account will have to include some positive suggestions about how values fail to be objective, about what has been mistaken for, or has led to false beliefs about, objective values. But this will be a development of his theory, not its core: its core is the negation. Secondly, what I have called moral scepticism is an ontological thesis, not a linguistic or conceptual one. It is not, like the other doctrine often called moral subjectivism, a view about the meanings of moral statements. . . .

It is true that those who have accepted the moral subjectivism which is the doctrine that moral judgements are equivalent to reports of the speaker's own feelings or attitudes have usually presupposed what I am calling moral scepticism. It is because they have assumed that there are no objective values that they have looked elsewhere for an analysis of what moral statements might mean, and have settled upon subjective reports. Indeed, if all our moral statements were such subjective reports, it would follow that, at least so far as we are aware, there are no objective moral values. If we were aware of them, we would say something about them. In this sense this sort of subjectivism entails moral scepticism. But the converse entailment does not hold. The denial that there are objective values does not commit one to any particular view about what moral statements mean, and certainly not to the view that they are equivalent to subjective reports. No doubt if moral values are not objective they are in some very broad sense subjective, and for this reason I would accept "moral subjectivism" as an alternative name to "moral scepticism." But subjectivism in this broad sense must be distinguished from the specific doctrine about meaning referred to above. Neither name is altogether satisfactory: we simply have to guard against the (different) misinterpretations which each may suggest.

3. THE MULTIPLICITY OF SECOND ORDER QUESTIONS

The distinctions drawn in the last two sections rest not only on the well-known and generally recognized difference between first and second order questions, but also on the more controversial claim that there are several kinds of second order moral questions. Those most often mentioned are questions about the meaning and use of ethical terms, or the analysis of ethical concepts. With these go questions about the logic of moral statements: there may be special patterns of moral argument, licensed, perhaps, by aspects of the meanings of moral terms—for example, it may be part of the meaning of moral statements that they are universalizable. But there are also ontological, as contrasted with linguistic or conceptual, questions about the nature and status of goodness or rightness or whatever it is that first order moral statements are distinctively about. These are questions of factual rather than conceptual analysis: the problem of what goodness is cannot be settled conclusively or exhaustively by finding out what the word 'good' means, or what it is conventionally used to say or to do.

Recent philosophy, biased as it has been towards various kinds of linguistic inquiry, has tended to doubt this, but the distinction between conceptual and factual analysis in ethics can be supported by analogies with other areas. The question of what perception is, what goes on when someone perceives something, is not adequately answered by finding out what words like 'see' and 'hear' mean, or what someone is doing in saying 'I perceive . . .', by analysing, however fully and accurately, any established concept of perception. There is a still closer analogy with colours. Robert Boyle and John Locke called colours 'secondary qualities', meaning that colours as they occur in material things consist simply in patterns of arrangement and movement of minute particles on the surfaces of objects, which make them, as we would now say, reflect light of some frequencies better than others, and so enable these objects to produce colour sensations in us, but that colours as we see them do not literally belong to the surfaces of material things. Whether Boyle and Locke were right about this cannot be settled by finding out how we use colour words and what we mean in using them. Naïve realism about colours might be a correct analysis not only of our pre-scientific colour concepts but also of the conventional meanings of colour words, and even of the meanings with which scientifically sophisticated people use them when they are off their guard, and yet it might not be a correct account of the status of colours.

Error could well result, then, from a failure to distinguish factual from conceptual analysis with regard to colours, from taking an account of the meanings of statements as a full account of what there is. There is a similar and in practice even greater risk of error in moral philosophy. There is another reason, too, why it would be a mistake to concentrate second order ethical discussions on questions of meaning. The more work philosophers have done on meaning, both in ethics and elsewhere, the more complications have come to light. It is by now pretty plain that no simple account of the meanings of first order moral statements will be correct, will cover adequately even the standard, conventional, senses of the main moral terms; I think, none the less, that there is a relatively clear-cut issue about the objectivity of moral values which is in danger of being lost among the complications of meaning. . . .

5. STANDARDS OF EVALUATION

One way of stating the thesis that there are no objective values is to say that value statements cannot be either true or false. But this formulation, too, lends itself to misinterpretation. For there are certain kinds of value statements which undoubtedly can be true or false, even if, in the sense I intend, there are no objective values. Evaluations of many sorts are commonly made in relation to agreed and assumed standards. The classing of wool, the grading of apples, the awarding of prizes at sheepdog trials, flower shows, skating and diving championships, and even the marking of examination papers are carried out in rela-

tion to standards of quality or merit which are peculiar to each particular subject-matter or type of contest, which may be explicitly laid down but which, even if they are nowhere explicitly stated, are fairly well understood and agreed by those who are recognized as judges or experts in each particular field. Given any sufficiently determinate standards, it will be an objective issue, a matter of truth and falsehood, how well any particular specimen measures up to those standards. Comparative judgements in particular will be capable of truth and falsehood: it will be a factual question whether this sheepdog has performed better than that one.

The subjectivist about values, then, is not denying that there can be objective evaluations relative to standards, and these are as possible in the aesthetic and moral fields as in any of those just mentioned. More than this, there is an objective distinction which applies in many such fields, and yet would itself be regarded as a peculiarly moral one: the distinction between justice and injustice. In one important sense of the word it is a paradigm case of injustice if a court declares someone to be guilty of an offense of which it knows him to be innocent. More generally, a finding is unjust if it is at variance with what the relevant law and the facts together require, and particularly if it is known by the court to be so. More generally still, any award of marks, prizes, or the like is unjust if it is at variance with the agreed standards for the contest in question: if one diver's performance in fact measures up better to the accepted standards for diving than another's, it will be unjust if the latter is awarded higher marks or the prize. In this way the justice or injustice of decisions relative to standards can be a thoroughly objective matter, though there may still be a subjective element in the interpretation or application of standards. But the statement that a certain decision is thus just or unjust will not be objectively prescriptive: in so far as it can be simply true it leaves open the question whether there is any objective requirement to do what is just and to refrain from what is unjust, and equally leaves open the practical decision to act in either way.

Recognizing the objectivity of justice in relation to standards, and of evaluative judgements relative to standards, then, merely shifts the question of the objectivity of values back to the standards themselves. . . .

6. HYPOTHETICAL AND CATEGORICAL IMPERATIVES

We may make this issue clearer by referring to Kant's distinction between hypothetical and categorical imperatives, though what he called imperatives are more naturally expressed as 'ought'-statements than in the imperative mood. 'If you want X, do Y' (or 'You ought to do Y') will be a hypothetical imperative if it is based on the supposed fact that Y is, in the circumstances, the only (or the best) available means to X, that is, on a causal relation between Y and X. The reason for doing Y lies in its causal connection with the desired end, X; the oughtness is contingent upon the desire. . . .

A categorical imperative, . . . would express a reason for acting which was unconditional in the sense of not being contingent upon any present desire of the agent to whose satisfaction the recommended action would contribute as a means—or more directly: 'You ought to dance', if the implied reason is just that you want to dance or like dancing, is still a hypothetical imperative. Now Kant himself held that moral judgements are categorical imperatives, or perhaps are all applications of one categorical imperative, and it can plausibly be maintained at least that many moral judgements contain a categorically imperative element. So far as ethics is concerned, my thesis that there are no objective values is specifically the denial that any such categorically imperative element is objectively valid. The objective values which I am denying would be action-directing absolutely, not contingently (in the way indicated) upon the agent's desires and inclinations.

Another way of trying to clarify this issue is to refer to moral reasoning or moral arguments. In practice, of course, such reasoning is seldom fully explicit: but let us suppose that we could make explicit the reasoning that supports some evaluative conclusion, where this conclusion has some action-guiding force that is not contingent upon desires or purposes or chosen ends. Then what I am saying is that somewhere in the input to this argument—perhaps in one or more of the premisses, perhaps in some part of the form of the argument—there will be something which cannot be objectively validated—some premiss which is not capable of being simply true, or some form of argument which is not valid as a matter of general logic, whose authority or cogency is not objective, but is constituted by our choosing or deciding to think in a certain way.

7. THE CLAIM TO OBJECTIVITY

If I have succeeded in specifying precisely enough the moral values whose objectivity I am denying, my thesis may now seem to be trivially true. Of course, some will say, valuing, preferring, choosing, recommending, rejecting, condemning, and so on, are human activities, and there is no need to look for values that are prior to and logically independent of all such activities. There may be widespread agreement in valuing, and particular value-judgements are not in general arbitrary or isolated: they typically cohere with others, or can be criticized if they do not, reasons can be given for them, and so on: but if all that the subjectivist is maintaining is that desires, ends, purposes, and the like figure somewhere in the system of reasons, and that no ends or purposes are objective as opposed to being merely intersubjective, then this may be conceded without much fuss.

But I do not think that this should be conceded so easily. As I have said, the main tradition of European moral philosophy includes the contrary claim, that there are objective values of just the sort I have denied. I have referred already to Plato, Kant, and Sidgwick. Kant in particular holds that the categorical imperative is not only categorical and imperative but objectively so: though a rational being gives the moral law to himself, the law that he thus makes is determinate and necessary. Aristotle begins the *Nicomachean Ethics* by saying that the good is that at which all things aim, and that ethics is part of a science which he calls 'politics', whose goal is not knowledge but practice; yet he does not doubt that there can be *knowledge* of what is the good for man, nor, once he has identified this as well-being or happiness, *eudaimonia*, that it can be known, rationally determined, in what happiness consists; and it is plain that he thinks that this happiness is intrinsically desirable, not good simply because it is desired. The rationalist Samuel Clarke holds that

these eternal and necessary differences of things make it *fit and reasonable* for creatures so to act . . . even separate from the consideration of these rules being the *positive will* or *command of God;* and also antecedent to any respect or regard, expectation or apprehension, of any *particular private and personal advantage or disadvantage, reward or punishment,* either present or future. . .

Even the sentimentalist Hutcheson defines moral goodness as 'some quality apprehended in actions, which procures approbation . . .', while saying that the moral sense by which we perceive virtue and vice has been given to us (by the Author of nature) to direct our actions. Hume indeed was on the other side, but he is still a witness to the dominance of the objectivist tradition, since he claims that when we 'see that the distinction of vice and virtue is not founded merely on the relations of objects, nor is perceiv'd by reason', this 'wou'd subvert all the vulgar systems of morality'. And Richard Price insists that right and wrong are 'real characters of actions', not 'qualities of our minds', and are perceived by the understanding; he criticizes the notion of moral sense on the ground that it would make virtue an affair of taste, and moral right and wrong 'nothing in the objects themselves'; he rejects Hutcheson's view because (perhaps mistakenly) he sees it as collapsing into Hume's.

But this objectivism about values is not only a feature of the philosophical tradition. It has also a firm basis in ordinary thought, and even in the meanings of moral terms. No doubt it was an extravagance for Moore to say that 'good' is the name of a non-natural quality, but it would not be so far wrong to say that in moral contexts it is used as if it were the name of a supposed non-natural quality where the description 'non-natural' leaves room for the peculiar evaluative, prescriptive, intrinsically action-guiding aspects of this supposed quality. This point can be illustrated by reflection on the conflicts and swings of opinion in recent years between non-cognitivist and naturalist views about the central, basic, meanings of ethical terms. If we reject the view that it is the function of such terms to introduce objective values into discourse about conduct and choices of action, there seem to be two main alternative types of account. One (which has importantly different subdivisions) is that they conventionally express either attitudes which the speaker purports to adopt towards whatever it is that he characterizes morally, or prescriptions or recommendations, subject perhaps to the logical constraint of universalizability. Different views of this type share the central thesis that ethical terms have, at least partly and primarily, some sort of non-cognitive, non-descriptive, meaning. Views of the other type hold that they are descriptive in meaning, but descriptive of natural features, partly of such features as everyone, even the non-cognitivist, would recognize as distinguishing kind actions from cruel ones, courage from cowardice, politeness from rudeness, and so on, and partly (though these two overlap) of relations between the actions and some human wants, satisfactions, and the like, I believe that views of both these types capture part of the truth. Each approach can account for the fact that moral judgements are action-guiding or practical. Yet each gains much of its plausibility from the felt inadequacy of the other. It is a very natural reaction to any non-cognitive analysis of ethical terms to protest that there is more to ethics than this, something more external to the maker of moral judgements, more authoritative over both him and those of or to whom he speaks, and this reaction is likely to persist even when full allowance has been made for the logical, formal, constraints of full-blooded prescriptivity and universalizability. Ethics, we are inclined to believe, is more a matter of knowledge and less a matter of decision than any non-cognitive analysis allows. And of course naturalism satisfies this demand. It will not be a matter of choice or decision whether an action is cruel or unjust or imprudent or whether it is likely to produce more distress than pleasure. But in satisfying this demand, it introduces a converse deficiency. On a naturalist analysis, moral judgements can be practical, but their practicality is wholly relative to desires or possible satisfactions of the person or persons whose actions are to be guided; but moral judgements seem to say more than this. This view leaves out the categorical quality of moral requirements. In fact both naturalist and non-cognitive analyses leave out the apparent authority of ethics, the one by excluding the categorically imperative aspect, the other the claim to objective validity or truth. The ordinary user of moral language means to say something about whatever it is that he characterizes morally, for example a possible action, as it is in itself, or would be if it were realized, and not about, or even simply expressive of, his, or anyone else's, attitude or relation to it. But the something he wants to say is not purely descriptive, certainly not inert, but something that involves a call for action or for the refraining from action, and one that is absolute, not contingent upon any desire or preference or policy or choice, his own or anyone else's. Someone in a state of moral perplexity, wondering whether it would be wrong for him to engage, say, in research related to bacteriological warfare, wants to arrive at some judgement about this concrete case, his doing this work at this time in these actual circumstances; his relevant characteristics will be part of the subject of the judgement, but no relation between him and the proposed action will be part of the predicate. The question is not, for example, whether he really wants to do this work, whether it will satisfy or dissatisfy him, whether he will in the long run have a pro-attitude towards it, or even whether this is an action of a sort that he can happily and sincerely recommend in all relevantly similar cases. Nor is he even wondering just whether to recommend such action in all relevantly similar cases. He wants to know whether this course of action would be wrong in itself. Something like this is the every-day objectivist concept of which talk about non-natural qualities is a philosopher's reconstruction. . . .

I conclude, then, that ordinary moral judgements include a claim to objectivity, an assumption that there are objective values in just the sense in which I am concerned to deny this. And I do not think it is going too far to say that this assumption has been incorporated in the basic, conventional, meanings of moral terms. Any analysis of the meanings of moral terms which omits this claim to objective, intrinsic, prescriptivity is to that extent incomplete; and this is true of any non-cognitive analysis, any naturalist one, and any combination of the two.

If second order ethics were confined, then, to linguistic and conceptual analysis, it ought to conclude that moral values at least are objective: that they are so is part of what our ordinary moral statements mean: the traditional moral concepts of the ordinary man as well as of the main line of western philosophers are concepts of objective value. But it is precisely for this reason that linguistic and conceptual analysis is not enough. The claim to objectivity, however ingrained in our language and thought, is not self-validating. It can and should be questioned. But the denial of objective values will have to be put forward not as the result of an analytic approach, but as an 'error theory', a theory that although most people in making moral judgements implicitly claim, among other things, to be pointing to something objectively prescriptive, these claims are all false. It is this that makes the name 'moral scepticism' appropriate.

But since this is an error theory, since it goes against assumptions ingrained in our thought and built into some of the ways in which language is used, since it conflicts with what is sometimes called common sense, it needs very solid support. It is not something we can accept lightly or casually and then quietly pass on. If we are to adopt this view, we must argue explicitly for it. Traditionally it has been supported by arguments of two main kinds, which I shall call the argument from relativity and the argument from queerness, but these can, as I shall show, be supplemented in several ways.

8. THE ARGUMENT FROM RELATIVITY

The argument from relativity has as its premiss the well-known variation in moral codes from one society to another and from one period to another, and also the differences in moral beliefs between different groups and classes within a complex community. Such variation is in itself merely a truth of descriptive morality, a fact of anthropology which entails neither first order nor second order ethical views. Yet it may indirectly support second order subjectivism: radical differences between first order moral judgements make it difficult to treat those judgements as apprehensions of objective truths. But it is not the mere occurrence of disagreements that tells against the objectivity of values. Disagreement on questions in history or biology or cosmology does not show that there are no objective issues in these fields for investigators to disagree about. But such scientific disagreement results from speculative inferences or explanatory hypotheses based on inadequate evidence, and it is hardly plausible to interpret moral disagreement in the same way. Disagreement about moral codes seems to reflect people's adherence to and participation in different ways of life. The causal connec-

tion seems to be mainly that way round: it is that people approve of monogamy because they participate in a monogamous way of life rather than that they participate in a monogamous way of life because they approve of monogamy. Of course, the standards may be an idealization of the way of life from which they arise: the monogamy in which people participate may be less complete, less rigid, than that of which it leads them to approve. This is not to say that moral judgements are purely conventional. Of course there have been and are moral heretics and moral reformers, people who have turned against the established rules and practices of their own communities for moral reasons, and often for moral reasons that we would endorse. But this can usually be understood as the extension, in ways which, though new and unconventional, seemed to them to be required for consistency, of rules to which they already adhered as arising out of an existing way of life. In short, the argument from relativity has some force simply because the actual variations in the moral codes are more readily explained by the hypothesis that they reflect ways of life than by the hypothesis that they express perceptions, most of them seriously inadequate and badly distorted, of objective values.

But there is a well-known counter to this argument from relativity, namely to say that the items for which objective validity is in the first place to be claimed are not specific moral rules or codes but very general basic principles which are recognized at least implicitly to some extent in all society—such principles as provide the foundations of what Sidgwick has called different methods of ethics: the principle of universalizability, perhaps, or the rule that one ought to conform to the specific rules of any way of life in which one takes part, from which one profits, and on which one relies, or some utilitarian principle of doing what tends or seems likely, to promote the general happiness. It is easy to show that such general principles, married with differing concrete circumstances, differing existing social patterns or different preferences, will beget different specific moral rules; and there is some plausibility in the claim that the specific rules thus generated will vary from community to community or from group to group in close agreement with the actual variations in accepted codes.

The argument from relativity can be only partly countered in this way. To take this line the moral objectivist has to say that it is only in these principles that the objective moral character attaches immediately to its descriptively specified ground or subject: other moral judgements are objectively valid or true, but only derivatively and contingently—if things had been otherwise, quite different sorts of actions would have been right. And despite the prominence in recent philosophical ethics of universalization, utilitarian principles, and the like, these are very far from constituting the whole of what is actually affirmed as basic in ordinary moral thought. Much of this is concerned rather with what Hare calls 'ideals' or, less kindly, 'fanaticism'. That is, people judge that some things are good or right, and others are bad or wrong, not because—or at any rate not only because— they exemplify some general principle for which widespread implicit acceptance could be claimed, but because something about those things arouses certain responses immediately in them, though they would arouse radically and irresolvably different responses in others. 'Moral sense' or 'intuition' is an initially more plausible description of what supplies many of our basic moral judgements than 'reason'. With regard to all these starting points of moral thinking the argument from relativity remains in full force.

9. THE ARGUMENT FROM QUEERNESS

Even more important, however, and certainly more generally applicable, is the argument from queerness. This has two parts, one metaphysical, the other epistemological.

If there were objective values, then they would be entities or qualities or relations of a very strange sort, utterly different from anything else in the universe. Correspondingly, if we were aware of them, it would have to be by some special faculty of moral perception or intuition, utterly different from our ordinary ways of knowing everything else. These points were recognized by Moore when he spoke of non-natural qualities, and by the intuitionists in their talk about a 'faculty of moral intuition'. Intuitionism has long been out of favour, and it is indeed easy to point out its implausibilities. What is not so often stressed, but is more important, is that the central thesis of intuitionism is one to which any objectivist view of values is in the end committed: intuitionism merely makes unpalatably plain what other forms of objectivism wrap up. Of course the suggestion that moral judgements are made or moral problems solved by just sitting down and having an ethical intuition is a travesty of actual moral thinking. But, however complex the real process, it will require (if it is to yield authoritatively prescriptive conclusions) some input of this distinctive sort, either premises or forms of argument or both. When we ask the awkward question, how we can be aware of this authoritative prescriptivity, of the truth of these distinctively ethical premises or of the cogency of this distinctively ethical pattern of reasoning, none of our ordinary accounts of sensory perception or introspection or the framing and confirming of explanatory hypotheses or inference or logical construction or conceptual analysis, or any combination of these, will provide a satisfactory answer; 'a special sort of intuition' is a lame answer, but it is the one to which the clear-headed objectivist is compelled to resort. . . .

Plato's Forms give a dramatic picture of what objective values would have to be. The Form of the Good is such that knowledge of it provides the knower with both a direction and an overriding motive; something's being good both tells the person who knows this to pursue it and makes him pursue it. An objective good would be sought by anyone who was acquainted with it, not because of any contingent fact that this person, or every person, is so constituted that he desires this end, but just because the end has to-be-pursuedness somehow built into it. Similarly, if there were objective principles of right and wrong, any wrong (possible) course of action would have not-to-be-doneness somehow built into it. . . .

Another way of bringing out this queerness is to ask, about anything that is supposed to have some objective moral quality, how this is linked with its natural features. What is the connection between the natural fact that an action is a piece of deliberate cruelty—say, causing pain just for fun—and the moral fact that it is wrong? It cannot be an entailment, a logical or semantic necessity. Yet it is not merely that the two features occur together. The wrongness must somehow be 'consequential' or 'supervenient'; it is wrong because it is a piece of deliberate cruelty. But just what *in the world* is signified by this 'because'? And how do we know the relation that it signifies, if this is something more than actions being socially condemned, and condemned by us too, perhaps through our having absorbed attitudes from our social environment? It is not even sufficient to postulate a faculty which 'sees' the wrongness: something must be postulated which can see at once the natural features that constitute the cruelty, and the wrongness, and the mysterious consequential link between the two. Alternatively, the intuition required might be the perception that wrongness is a higher order property belonging to certain natural properties; but what is this belonging of properties to other properties, and how can we discern it? How much simpler and more comprehensible the situation would be if we could replace the moral quality with some sort of subjective response which could be causally related to the detection of the natural features on which the supposed quality is said to be consequential.

It may be thought that the argument from queerness is given an unfair start if we thus relate it to what are admittedly among the wilder products of philosophical fancy—Platonic Forms, non-natural qualities, self-evident relations of fitness, faculties of intuition, and the like. Is it equally forceful if applied to the terms in which everyday moral judgements are more likely to be expressed—though still, as has been argued in Section 7, with a claim to objectivity—'you must do this', 'you can't do that', 'obligation', 'unjust', 'rotten', 'disgraceful', 'mean', or talk about good reasons for or against possible actions? Admittedly not; but that is because the objective prescriptivity, the element a claim for whose authoritativeness is embedded in ordinary moral thought and language, is not yet isolated in these forms of speech, but is presented along with relations to desires and feelings, reasoning about the means to desired ends, interpersonal demands, the injustice which consists in the violation of what are in the context the accepted standards of merit, the psychological constituents of meanness, and so on. There is nothing queer about any of these, and under cover of them the claim for moral authority may pass unnoticed. But if I am right in arguing that it is ordinarily there, and is therefore very likely to be incorporated almost automatically in philosophical accounts of ethics which systematize our ordinary thought even in such apparently innocent terms as these, it needs to be examined, and for this purpose it needs to be isolated and exposed as it is by the less cautious philosophical reconstructions.

10. PATTERNS OF OBJECTIFICATION

Considerations of these kinds suggest that it is in the end less paradoxical to reject than to retain the common-sense belief in the objectivity of moral values, provided that we can explain how this belief, if it is false, has become established and is so resistant to criticisms. This proviso is not difficult to satisfy.

On a subjectivist view, the supposedly

objective values will be based in fact upon attitudes which the person has who takes himself to be recognizing and responding to those values. If we admit what Hume calls the mind's 'propensity to spread itself on external objects', we can understand the supposed objectivity of moral qualities as arising from what we can call the projection or objectification of moral attitudes. This would be analogous to what is called the 'pathetic fallacy', the tendency to read our feelings into their objects. If a fungus, say, fills us with disgust, we may be inclined to ascribe to the fungus itself a non-natural quality of foulness. But in moral contexts there is more than this propensity at work. Moral attitudes themselves are at least partly social in origin: socially established—and socially necessary—patterns of behaviour put pressure on individuals, and each individual tends to internalize these pressures and to join in requiring these patterns of behaviour of himself and of others. The attitudes that are objectified into moral values have indeed an external source, though not the one assigned to them by the belief in their absolute authority. . . .

Another way of explaining the objectification of moral values is to say that ethics is a system of law from which the legislator has been removed. This might have been derived either from the positive law of a state or from a supposed system of divine law. There can be no doubt that some features of modern European moral concepts are traceable to the theological ethics of Christianity. The stress on quasi-imperative notions, on what ought to be done or on what is wrong in a sense that is close to that of 'forbidden', are surely relics of divine commands. Admittedly, the central ethical concepts for Plato and Aristotle also are in a broad sense prescriptive or intrinsically action-guiding, but in concentrating rather on 'good' than on 'ought' they show that their moral thought is an objectification of the desired and the satisfying rather than of the commanded. Elizabeth Anscombe has argued that modern, non-Aristotelian, concepts of *moral* obligation, *moral* duty, of what

is *morally* right and wrong, and of the *moral* sense of 'ought' are survivals outside the framework of thought that made them really intelligible, namely the belief in divine law. She infers that 'ought' has 'become a word of mere mesmeric force', with only a 'delusive appearance of content', and that we would do better to discard such terms and concepts altogether, and go back to Aristotelian ones.

There is much to be said for this view. But while we can explain some distinctive features of modern moral philosophy in this way, it would be a mistake to see the whole problem of the claim to objective prescriptivity as merely local and unnecessary, as a post-operative complication of a society from which a dominant system of theistic belief has recently been rather hastily excised. As Cudworth and Clarke and Price, for example, show, even those who still admit divine commands, or the positive law of God, may believe moral values to have an independent objective but still action-guiding authority. Responding to Plato's *Euthyphro* dilemma, they believe that God commands what he commands because it is in itself good or right, not that it is good or right merely because and in that he commands it. Otherwise God himself could not be called good. Price asks, 'What can be more preposterous, than to make the Deity nothing but will; and to exalt this on the ruins of all his attributes?' The apparent objectivity of moral value is a widespread phenomenon which has more than one source: the persistence of a belief in something like divine law when the belief in the divine legislator has faded out is only one factor among others. There are several different patterns of objectification, all of which have left characteristic traces in our actual moral concepts and moral language. . . .

12. CONCLUSION

I have maintained that there is a real issue about the status of values, including moral values. Moral scepticism, the denial of objective moral values, is not to be confused with any one of several first order normative views, or with any linguistic or conceptual analysis. Indeed, ordinary moral judgements involve a claim to objectivity which both non-cognitive and naturalist analyses fail to capture. Moral scepticism must, therefore, take the form of an error theory, admitting that a belief in objective values is built into ordinary moral thought and language, but holding that this ingrained belief is false. As such, it needs arguments to support it against 'common sense'. But solid arguments can be found. The considerations that favour moral scepticism are: first, the relativity or variability of some important starting points of moral thinking and their apparent dependence on actual ways of life; secondly, the metaphysical peculiarity of the supposed objective values, in that they would have to be intrinsically action-guiding and motivating; thirdly, the problem of how such values could be conse-quential or supervenient upon natural features; fourthly, the corresponding epistemological difficulty of accounting for our knowledge of value entities or features and of their links with the features on which they would be consequential; fifthly, the possibility of explaining, in terms of several different patterns of objectification, traces of which remain in moral language and moral concepts, how even if there were no such objective values people not only might have come to suppose that there are but also might persist firmly in that belief. These five points sum up the case for moral scepticism; but of almost equal importance are the preliminary removal of misunderstandings that often prevent this thesis from being considered fairly and explicitly, and the isolation of those items about which the moral sceptic is sceptical from many associated qualities and relations whose objective status is not in dispute.

28

A CRITIQUE OF ETHICAL SKEPTICISM

David O. Brink

1. INTRODUCTION

The most important kind of challenge to moral realism or moral objectivism argues that there is a *special* problem with realism in ethics. I shall defend moral realism against two influential versions of this challenge recently formulated by J. L. Mackie in his book *Ethics: Inventing Right and Wrong.*[1] According to standards of argument which Mackie himself sets, neither his argument from disagreement nor his argument from queerness shows any special problem for moral realism. Let me explain why.

Moral realism is best explained as a special case of a global realist thesis. The general thesis common to realist claims about a variety of disciplines is a two part metaphysical claim:

R: (a) there are facts of kind *x*, and
    (b) these facts are logically independent of

From *Australasian Journal of Philosophy*, Vol. 62, No 2 (1984): 111–125. Reprinted by permission.

our evidence, i.e. those beliefs which are our evidence, for them.[2]

Moral realism is then obtained by substituting 'moral' for the variable '*x*'.

MR: (a) there are moral facts, and

     (b) these facts are logically independent of our evidence, i.e. those beliefs which are our evidence, for them.

Moral realism claims that there are objective moral facts and implies that there are true moral propositions.

Moral scepticism is technically an epistemological doctrine and so is officially neutral with respect to the metaethical thesis of moral realism. Moral scepticism claims that we have no moral knowledge and this claim is compatible with the existence of objective moral facts and true moral propositions. But while moral realism and moral scepticism are compatible (we may just have no cognitive access to moral facts), the standard and most plausible reason for claiming that we have no moral knowledge is the belief that there are no moral facts. This must be why Mackie construes moral scepticism as an anti-realist thesis. I shall follow Mackie in this and treat moral scepticism as a denial of the existence of objective values.[3]

There are two basic kinds of moral sceptic. The first kind applies general sceptical considerations to the special case of morality. On his view, there are no moral facts, but neither are there any other objective facts about the world. Of course, this first sort of sceptic is quite radical and has not been terribly influential as a source of moral scepticism. The second kind of moral sceptic claims that there is a special problem about realism in ethics, a problem which does not afflict realism about most other disciplines. This clearly has been the more popular and philosophically influential version of moral scepticism. Mackie is this second kind of moral sceptic.

As this second kind of moral sceptic, Mackie complains that belief in the existence of objective values is no part of a plausible realist world-view. (E: p. 17) Mackie's sceptical arguments, therefore, cannot turn on the application of general sceptical considerations. If it can be shown that the moral realist's metaphysical and epistemological commitments are no less plausible than those of, say, the physical realist, then Mackie's sceptical arguments will have been answered.

Although it is possible to *defend* moral realism against sceptical arguments without establishing any kind of presumption in its favour, there are, as Mackie recognises, general considerations which require the moral sceptic to bear a certain burden of proof. First, this second version of moral scepticism concedes a presumption in favour of moral realism. If, as this second sort of scepticism assumes, realism is plausible about a wide range of disciplines, then there must be some special justification for taking a different view about the existence and nature of moral facts. Of course, this establishes only a very weak presumption in

favour of moral realism, but it is one which the moral sceptic must rebut.

Moreover, belief in moral realism is supported by certain features of our moral practice. In moral deliberation and moral argument we search for answers to our moral questions, answers whose correctness we assume to be independent of our means of arriving at them.[4] Of course, this presumption too is defeasible, but this takes some argument. As Mackie claims, moral scepticism must have the status of an error theory; it must explain how and why our commitment to the objectivity of moral values is mistaken. (E: p.35)

Mackie distinguishes two arguments for the second version of moral scepticism. The first turns on the apparent unresolvability of many moral disputes and so is best thought of as an argument from disagreement,[5] while the second turns on the mysterious character objective values would seem to have to have and so represents an argument from queerness. Mackie presses both of these arguments against moral realism and in favour of moral scepticism and subjectivism. In what follows, I shall examine and rebut Mackie's arguments from disagreement and queerness; I shall argue that neither argument establishes any special problem for moral realism. Although these two arguments may not exhaust the arguments for the second version of moral scepticism, they are sufficiently important both historically and philosophically that successfully rebutting them will go a long way towards defending moral realism.

2. MORAL OBJECTIVITY

Before discussing the details of the arguments from disagreement and queerness, we need to establish just which version of moral realism is or need be in question. In section 1 I described moral realism as the metaethical view that there are objective moral facts. However, in pressing the arguments from disagreement and queerness, Mackie employs a stronger or more committal version of moral realism according to which not only are there moral facts but also these moral facts are *objectively prescriptive.* (*E:* pp. 23, 26–7, 29, 40, 42; *HMT:* pp. 22, 53, 55, 134, 146; *MT:* pp. 102, 104, 115–16) Indeed, although both the argument from disagreement and the argument from queerness apply to my formulation of moral realism, some of the special appeal of the argument from queerness derives from the assumption that moral facts would have to be objectively prescriptive. (*E:* pp. 40–1; *HMT:* p. 61)

In claiming that moral facts would have to be objectively prescriptive, Mackie is claiming that moral realism requires the truth of *internalism.* Internalism is the *a priori* thesis that the recognition of moral facts itself either necessarily motivates or necessarily provides reasons for action. Internalism is an *a priori* thesis, because its proponents claim that the recognition of moral facts necessarily motivates or provides reasons for action no matter what the moral facts turn out to be. We can distinguish *motivational internalism* (MI) and *reasons internalism* (RI): MI holds that it is *a priori* that the recognition of moral facts itself necessarily motivates the agent to perform the moral action, while RI claims that it is *a priori* that the recognition of moral facts itself necessarily provides the agent with reason to perform the moral action. *Externalism,* by contrast, denies both MI and RI.

Although Mackie is unclear as between MI and RI,[6] he clearly thinks that some version of internalism is required by moral realism. Both MI and RI make exceptionally strong claims. MI claims that—whatever the moral facts turn out to be and regardless of the psychological make-up of the agent—the mere recognition of a moral fact necessarily provides some motivation to perform the moral action, while RI claims that—whatever the moral facts turn out to be and regardless of the agent's interests or desires—the mere recognition of a moral fact necessarily provides the agent with at least some reason to perform the moral action. These claims are quite implausible,

and it is unclear why moral realism is committed to either of them.

It is unlikely that the recognition of moral facts *necessarily* motivates or provides reasons for action; it is very unlikely that the recognition of moral facts *alone* necessarily motivates or provides reasons for action; and the mere recognition of moral facts almost certainly does not necessarily motivate or provide reasons for action *regardless of what the moral facts turn out to be.* Whether the recognition of moral facts motivates certainly depends upon what the moral facts are, and, at least on most plausible moral theories, whether recognition of these facts motivates is a matter of contingent (even if deep) psychological fact about the agent. Whether the recognition of moral facts provides reasons for action depends upon whether the agent has reason to do what morality requires. But this, of course, depends upon what morality requires, i.e. upon what the moral facts are, and, at least on standard theories of reasons for action, whether recognition of these facts provides reason for action will depend upon contingent (even if deep) facts about the agent's desires or interests. So, internalism is false; it is not something which we can know *a priori,* i.e. whatever the moral facts turn out to be, that the recognition of moral facts alone either necessarily motivates or necessarily provides reasons for action.

It is hard to see why moral realism should be committed to the truth of internalism. Mackie claims both that moral realists have traditionally been internalists (*E:* p. 23) and that internalism is part of common sense moral thinking. (*E:* p. 35) But both claims seem false and would carry relatively little weight, even if true. Once we make clear the strength of the internalist claim—that we know *a priori* that *mere* recognition of moral facts *necessarily* motivates or provides reasons for action—it is less clear that the tradition of moral realism is a tradition of internalism. In particular, although I cannot argue the claims here, I doubt that Plato, Hume, or Sidgwick is, as Mackie claims, an internalist. And, of course, even if many moral philosophers have thought that internalism is true, it would not follow that they were right. Nor does common sense moral thinking seem to support belief in internalism; in fact, it seems extremely unlikely that any belief so recherche could be part of common sense moral thinking. Even if belief in internalism were part of common sense moral thinking, it would be revisable, especially if it could be shown that belief in internalism plays a social role such that it would persist even if mistaken.

So no good reason has been produced for thinking that internalism is true or for thinking that moral realism requires internalism. This means that the moral realist can defend externalism. In particular, determination of the motivational and reason-giving power of moral facts will have to await specifications of the moral facts and of the desires and interests of agents. In defending moral realism against the arguments from disagreement and queerness, I will offer what I call a functionalist theory of moral value according to which moral facts are facts about human well-being and flourishing as a model specification of moral realist claims. This account illustrates the kind of justification of morality which the externalist can provide, for this functionalist theory implies that moral facts will *as a matter of fact at least typically* provide agents with reasons to do the morally correct thing.

3. THE ARGUMENT FROM DISAGREEMENT

Mackie claims that the best explanation of inter- and intra-societal ethical disagreement is that there simply are no moral facts, only differences of attitude, commitment, or decision. (*E:* pp. 36–7) Of course, disagreement does not entail scepticism. Mackie recognises that we do not infer from the fact that there are disagreements in the natural sciences that the natural sciences are not objective disciplines. Nor do we make what might appear to be the more modest inference from the fact that there is a specific

dispute in some subject that there is no fact of the matter on the particular issue in question. For example, no one concluded from the apparently quite deep disagreement among astronomers a short while ago about the existence of black holes that there was no fact of the matter concerning the existence of black holes. Mackie's claim is that disagreement in ethics is somehow more fundamental than disagreement in other disciplines. In particular, realism about a discipline requires that its disputes be resolvable at least in principle, and, while most scientific disputes do seem resolvable, many moral disputes do not.

Mackie imagines the moral realist replying that moral disputes are resolvable, because deep moral disagreements are not really cases of disagreement. Rather, they are cases in which 'disputants' apply antecedently shared moral principles under different empirical conditions. (*E:* p. 37) The resulting moral judgments are about different action types, so the 'disagreements' in question are really only apparent.

Mackie issues two rejoinders to this realist reply. His first rejoinder is that this realist response commits the realist to (a) claiming that necessity can only attach to general moral principles and (b) accepting the following counterfactual: ' . . . if things had been otherwise, quite different sorts of actions would have been right'. (*E:* p. 37) (a) and (b), Mackie claims, imply that many action types will be right or wrong only contingently.

Although this rejoinder does raise some interesting questions about the modal status of moral facts, it in no way threatens moral realism. First, certainly some moral facts are contingent, and, even if this realist reply requires the contingency of some moral facts, this shows nothing about how many moral facts the realist must regard as contingent. But, secondly and more importantly, Mackie's modal issue is a red herring. The truth of moral realism turns on the existence of moral facts, not their modal status.

Mackie's second rejoinder to the realist reply is simply that some moral disputes are real disputes. Not all putative moral disagreements can be explained away as the application of antecedently shared moral principles in different circumstances. (*E:* p. 38)

Mackie is right that many moral disputes are genuine, and, if the realist had no account of these disputes, Mackie would have a strong argument against moral realism. But the realist can account for moral disputes.

As we have seen, not every apparent moral disagreement is a genuine dispute. But the realist need not maintain even that all genuine moral disputes are resolvable. He can maintain that some moral disputes have no uniquely correct answers. Moral ties are possible, and considerations, each of which is objectively valuable, may be incommensurable. [7] So the moral realist need only maintain that most genuine moral disputes are resolvable. [8]

Indeed, the realist can plausibly maintain that most genuine moral disputes are in principle resolvable. Mackie's discussion of the realist's reply shows that Mackie thinks moral disagreement is resolvable if and only if *antecedent* agreement on general moral principles obtains. This claim presupposes a one-way view of moral justification and argument according to which moral principles justify particular moral judgments but not vice versa. However, this view of moral justification is defective. As Goodman, Rawls, and other coherentists have argued, justification proceeds both from general principles to particular cases and from particular cases to general principles. [9] Just as agreement about general moral principles may be exploited to resolve disagreement about particular moral cases, so agreement about particular moral cases may be exploited to resolve disagreement about general moral principles. Ideally, trade-offs among the various levels of generality of belief will be made in such a way as to maximise initial commitment, overall consistency, explanatory power, etc. A coherentist model of moral reasoning of this sort makes it much less plausible that

disagreements over moral principles are in principle unresolvable. [10]

Moreover, a great many moral disagreements depend upon disagreements over the non-moral facts. First, many disagreements over the non-moral facts result from culpable forms of ignorance of fact. Often, for moral or non-moral reasons, at least one disputant culpably fails to assess the non-moral facts correctly by being insufficiently imaginative in weighing the consequences for the relevant people of alternative actions or policies. This sort of error is especially important in moral disputes, since thought experiments (as opposed to actual tests) play such an important part in the assessment of moral theories. Thought experiments play a larger role in moral methodology than they do in scientific methodology, at least partly because it is often (correctly) regarded as immoral to assess moral theories by realising the relevant counterfactuals.

Secondly, many moral disagreements result from reasonable but nonetheless resolvable disagreements over the non-moral facts. The correct answers to moot moral questions often turn on certain non-moral facts about which reasonable disagreement is possible and which may in fact be known by no one. Correct answers to moral questions can turn at least in part upon correct answers to non-moral questions such as 'What (re)distribution of a certain class of goods would make the worst-off representative person in a particular society best-off?', 'Would public ownership of the means of production in the United States lead to an increase or decrease in the average standard of living?', 'What is the correct theory of human personality?', and 'What kind of life would my severely mentally retarded child lead (if I brought the pregnancy to term and raised the child), and how would caring for him affect my family and me?'. However difficult and controversial these questions are, the issues which they raise are in principle resolvable. Moral disputes commonly do turn on disagreement over issues such as these, and, insofar as they do, moral disputes are clearly resolvable in principle.

Mackie argues that if moral realism were true, all moral disputes should be resolvable, and since many seem irresolvable, he concludes that moral realism is false. But the moral realist need only claim that *most genuine* moral disputes are *in principle* resolvable. Not all apparent moral disagreements are genuine, because some apparent moral disputes merely reflect the application of antecedently shared moral principles under different circumstances. Not every genuine moral dispute need be even in principle resolvable, since moral ties are possible and some objective moral values may be incommensurable. Of those genuine moral disputes which the realist is committed to treating as in principle resolvable, some depend upon antecedent disagreement over moral principles, while others depend upon disagreement over the non-moral facts. The realist can claim that antecedent disagreement over moral principles is in principle resolvable by coherence arguments and that disagreement over the non-moral facts is always in principle resolvable.[11] The moral realist gives a plausible enough account of moral disagreement for us to say that Mackie has not shouldered the burden of proof for his claim that the falsity of moral realism is the best explanation of the nature of moral disagreement.

4. THE ARGUMENT FROM QUEERNESS

The rough idea behind the argument from queerness is that objective moral facts and properties would have to be so different from the sort of natural facts and properties for which we do have evidence that we have good *a posteriori* reason to reject moral realism.[12] (*E:* pp. 38–42; *MT:* pp. 115–16) As I said in section 2, the argument from queerness is supposed to tell especially against the existence of moral facts conceived of as being objectively prescriptive. (*E:* pp. 40–1; *HMT:* p. 61) I claimed that in committing realism to objective prescriptivity Mackie is claiming that moral realism requires internalism. But

I argued that internalism is implausible and that Mackie produces no good reason for committing realism to internalism. Instead, the realist can defend externalism; determination of whether agents have reason or motive to be moral will depend upon the content of morality and facts about agents. In explaining why objective values are not queer, I will offer a model specification of moral realism, which, together with plausible empirical assumptions, implies that agents generally do have reasons to be moral.

There are two limbs to the argument from queerness: one metaphysical, one epistemological. (*E:* p. 38) I turn to the metaphysical branch of the argument first. Mackie thinks that moral realism is a metaphysically queer doctrine, because he believes that moral facts or properties would have to be ontologically simple or independent. (*E:* p. 38) The assumption is that moral properties would have to be *sui generis*, that is, ontologically independent of natural properties with which we are familiar. Although it is not inconceivable that there should be *sui generis* moral properties, we have very good *a posteriori* evidence for the truth of materialism and for the falsity of ontological pluralism.

However, Mackie's crucial assumption that moral facts and properties would have to be *sui generis* is false; moral realism does not require ontological pluralism. The moral realist has at least two options on the assumption that materialism is true: he can claim that moral properties are identical with certain physical properties, or he can claim that moral properties supervene upon certain physical properties. Because moral properties and their instances could be realised in non-physical as well as a variety of physical ways, neither moral properties nor their instances should be identified with physical properties or their instances.[13] For this reason, it is best for the moral realist to claim that moral properties supervene upon physical properties.

Mackie recognises the realist's claim about the supervenience of moral facts and properties on physical facts and properties but claims that the alleged supervenient relation is also metaphysically queer:

Another way of bringing out this queerness is to ask about anything that is supposed to have some objective moral quality, how this is linked with its natural features. What is the connection between the natural fact that an action is a case of deliberate cruelty—say, causing pain just for fun—and the moral fact that it is wrong? It cannot be an entailment, a logical or semantic necessity. Yet it is not merely that the two features somehow occur together. The wrongness must somehow be 'consequential' or 'supervenient'; it is wrong because it is a piece of deliberate cruelty. But just what *in the world* is signified by this 'because'? (*E:* p. 41)

Although I do not think that Mackie has really motivated a metaphysical worry about moral supervenience, I shall defend moral realism against the charge of metaphysical queerness by adopting the strategy which Mackie mentions of finding partners in guilt—although once it is clear what sort of company the realist is keeping it would only be perverse to regard them as partners in *guilt*.[14] I shall argue that the supervenient relation which the realist claims obtains between moral properties and natural or physical properties is neither uncommon nor mysterious.

Although it is an interesting question what the precise relation is between property identity and supervenience, it is fairly clear that one property can supervene upon another without those two properties being identical.[15] A supervenient relation obtains between two properties or sets of properties just in case the one property or set of properties is causally realised by the other property or set of properties; the former property or set of properties is the supervening property or set of properties, and the latter property or set of properties is the base property or set of properties. Supervenience implies that no change can occur in the supervening property without a change occurring in the base property, but it also asserts a claim of ontological dependence. Assuming, as Mackie does,

that materialism is true, all properties ultimately supervene on material or physical base properties.[16] Physical properties are basic then in the sense that all other properties are nothing over and above physical properties. Biological, social, psychological, and moral properties are all realised physically; they are simply different *kinds* of combinations and arrangements of matter which hang together explanatorily.[17]

Supervenience is a relation of causal constitution or dependence. There is nothing strange and certainly nothing unique about the supervenience of moral properties on physical properties. Assuming materialism is true, mental states supervene on physical states, yet few think that mental states are metaphysically queer (and those that do do not think that supervenience makes them queer). Social facts such as unemployment, inflation, and exploitation supervene upon physical facts, yet no one supposes that social facts are metaphysically queer. Biological states such as being an organism supervene on physical states, yet no one supposes that organisms are queer entities. Macroscopic material objects such as tables supervene on micro-scopic physical particles, yet no one supposes that tables are queer entities. In short, it is difficult to see how the realist's use of supervenience in explaining the relationship between moral and physical properties makes his position queer. Moral properties are not ontologically simple or independent; but then neither are mental states, social facts, biological states, or macro-scopic material objects. It is unlikely that moral properties are identical with physical properties; moral properties could have been realised non-materially. But there is every reason to believe that in the actual world moral properties, like other natural properties, are realised materially.

This realist account of supervenience discharges any explanatory obligation which the argument from metaphysical queerness imposes. The details of the way in which moral properties supervene upon other natural properties are worked out differently by different moral theories. Determination of which account of moral supervenience is best will depend upon determination of which moral theory provides the best account of all our beliefs, both moral and non-moral. Although I obviously cannot do here what is needed to defend a particular account of moral supervenience, I will now offer a *model* specification of the moral realist's metaphysical claims.

When trying to determine the way in which moral properties supervene upon other natural properties, one might start by looking at plausible theories about other kinds of properties. Functional theories provide plausible accounts of a wide variety of kinds of properties; the nature of biological, psychological, social, and economic properties is profitably viewed in functional terms. Consider functionalist theories of mind as an example. Although functionalism is not without its critics,[18] it is fair to say that there are no rival *theories* in the philosophy of the mind today.[19] What is essential to any particular mental state type, according to functionalism, is the causal role which that mental state plays in the activities which are characteristic of the organism as a whole. Mental states are identified and distinguished from other mental states in terms of the causal relations which they bear to sensory inputs, behavioural outputs, and other mental states. To take a hoary example, functionalist theories of mind claim that pain is identified and distinguished from other mental states by virtue of its tendency to result from tissue damage, to produce an injury-avoidance desire, and to issue in the appropriate injury-avoidance behaviour. The physical states which realise this functional state are the physical states upon which pain supervenes.

Similarly, the moral realist might claim that moral properties are functional properties. He might claim that which is essential to moral properties is the causal role which they play in the characteristic activities of human organisms.[20] In particular, the realist might claim that moral properties are those which bear upon the maintenance and flourishing of human organisms. Maintenance and flourishing presumably consist in

necessary conditions for survival, other needs associated with basic well-being, wants of various sorts, and distinctively human capacities. People, actions, policies, states of affairs, etc. will bear good-making moral properties just insofar as they contribute to the satisfaction of these needs, wants, and capacities. People, actions, policies, states of affairs, etc. will bear bad-making moral properties just insofar as they fail to promote or interfere with the satisfaction of these needs, wants, and capacities.[21] The physical states which contribute to or interfere with the satisfaction of these needs, wants, and capacities are the physical states upon which, on this functionalist theory, moral properties ultimately supervene.

Although I cannot and do not need to defend here this functionalist model, it is worth pointing out how this model addresses two issues of concern to Mackie, namely, the justifiability of morality and the decidability of moral disputes. In section 2 I argued that internalism is implausible and that determination of whether agents have motivation or reason to be moral depends upon the content of morality and facts about agents. If this functionalist account of moral value which I have proposed as a realist model is plausible, then there is reason to think that moral facts will at least typically provide agents with reasons for action. Everyone has reason to promote his own well-being, and everyone has reason to promote the well-being of others at least to the extent that his own well-being is tied up with theirs. Presumably, any plausible theory of human needs, wants, and capacities will show that the satisfaction of these desiderata for any given individual will depend to a large extent on the well-being of others. People have needs and desires for friendship and love and for the benefits of cooperative activity; they also have capacities for sympathy, benevolence, and social intercourse. In order to satisfy these social needs, desires, and capacities, agents must develop and maintain stable social dispositions, and this means that they will often have reason to benefit others even when they do not otherwise benefit by their action. So, although there may be cases in which maintaining or promoting human well-being involves no benefit to the agent, there is good reason to suppose that human well-being and agent well-being will by and large coincide. As this functionalist theory of value illustrates, externalism allows a strong justification of morality.

This functionalist theory of moral value also helps to explain the nature of moral disagreement. Common sense and attention to the argument from disagreement tell us that moral disputes can be extremely difficult to resolve. This functionalist specification of moral realism explains why many moral disputes which are in principle resolvable are nonetheless so difficult to resolve even under favourable conditions. Because facts about human well-being and flourishing depend at least in part upon facts in such complex and controversial empirical disciplines as economics, social theory, and psychology, even disputants who share something like the functionalist theory of value and are well informed will often disagree about what morality requires.

In addition to the metaphysical complaint about 'what in the world' a supervenient relation is, Mackie lodges an epistemological complaint about how we could know when the appropriate supervenient relation obtains. (*E:* p. 41) We may know that certain natural facts or facts under a non-moral description obtain, but how do we know or go about finding out whether these physical facts realise any moral facts and, if so, which? Mackie claims that we could gain this kind of moral knowledge only if we had special faculties for the perception of moral facts of the sort ethical intuitionism ensures. But, Mackie argues, although moral intuitionism could have been true, there are good *a posteriori* grounds for believing that no such faculties exist. Therefore, barring the cognitive inaccessibility of moral facts, moral realism must be false. (*E:* pp. 38–9)

The epistemological belief that moral realism is committed to intuitionism rests at least in Mackie's case on the mistaken metaphysical assumption that moral values would have to be ontologically *sui generis*. If and only if moral facts were queer kinds of entities would we need some special faculty for cognitive access to them. But the realist denies that moral facts are *sui generis;* moral facts supervene on natural facts. One goes about discovering which natural facts moral facts supervene on by appeal to moral theories. (Of course, appeal to a particular moral theory is justified only in that theory coheres well with other moral and non-moral beliefs we hold.) For example, if the functionalist account of moral value sketched above can be defended, than we do know how to set about ascertaining which if any moral facts supervene on a particular set of natural facts. We ascertain whether the natural facts in question contribute to, interfere with, or are neutral with respect to the maintenance and promotion of human well-being. Granted, in many cases this will be no easy task, since completion of the task will depend in part upon answers to controversial empirical questions in such fields as economics, social theory, and psychology. But all this shows is that moral knowledge is sometimes hard to come by, not that it is queer or mysterious.

Mackie might complain that both acceptance and application of moral theories must be guided by other moral commitments. Not only does acceptance of the functionalist theory of value depend upon its coherence with, among other things, other moral beliefs, but also the findings of such disciplines as economics, sociology, and psychology cannot fully determine the extension of 'human well-being and flourishing'. Even if the special sciences can tell us something about human needs, wants, and capacities, and the effective ways of realising them, these sciences cannot rank these components of the good or adjudicate conflicts among them. Some irreducibly normative questions must be answered in determining what constitutes human well-being and flourishing.

But if the fact that some or all of our moral judgments are theory-dependent in this way is supposed to present a genuine epistemological problem for the moral realist which is not simply the result of applying general sceptical considerations to the case of morality, Mackie must claim that theory-dependence is a feature peculiar to moral methodology. Is this claim at all plausible?

Here, as before, the moral realist can find quite respectable partners 'in guilt'. It is a commonplace in the philosophy of science that scientific methodology is profoundly theory-dependent. Assessments of theoretical simplicity and theory confirmation as well as standards of experimental design and instrument improvement require appeal to the best available background theories in the relevant disciplines. For example, in theory confirmation there is an ineliminable comparative component. Theories count as well confirmed only if they have been tested against relevant rivals, and determination of which alternative theories are relevant or worth considering requires appeal to background bodies of accepted theory. Acceptance of normal scientific observations and judgments, as well as application of general methodological principles, is also theory-laden. For example, judgments about the acidity or alkalinity of a substance which are based on the results of litmus paper tests pre-suppose belief in the normality of the test conditions and acceptance of the relevant chemical theories explaining how litmus paper detects pH and how pH reflects acidity and alkalinity.

The fact that scientific method is heavily theory-dependent shows that science and ethics are on a par in being theory-dependent. Thus, the fact that moral commitments must be appealed to in the acceptance and application of moral theories poses *no special* epistemological problem for moral realism. Of course, although most of us do not draw non-realist conclusions from the theory-dependence of scientific method, one may wonder how the profoundly theory-dependent methodologies in science and ethics can be *discovery* procedures. The answer is that theory-dependent methodologies are discovery procedures just in case a sufficient number of background theories in

the disciplines in question are approximately true.[22] And I have been arguing that Mackie has provided no good reason for doubting that some of our moral background theories are approximately true.

Mackie might respond that the moral and scientific cases are not in fact on a par and that there is reason to doubt the approximate truth of our moral theories, because while there is a good deal of consensus about the truth of the scientific theories appealed to, say, in the making of pH judgments, there is a notable lack of consensus about which moral theories to appeal to in making moral judgments. There are at least three reasons, however, for dismissing this response. First, this response probably overstates both the degree of consensus about which scientific theories are correct and the degree of disagreement about which moral theories are correct.[23] Secondly, the response probably also overstates the amount of antecedent agreement necessary to reach eventual moral agreement. Finally, this response just raises from a different perspective the argument from disagreement, and we say that the moral realist has a plausible account of moral disputes.

These considerations show that moral realism is committed to nothing metaphysically or epistemologically queer. The realist holds that moral facts supervene upon other natural facts and that moral knowledge is acquired in the same theory-dependent way that other knowledge is. Moral realism is plausible enough both metaphysically and epistemologically to allow us to say that Mackie has again failed to shoulder the burden of proof.

5. CONCLUSION

Mackie follows an important sceptical tradition in attempting to show that there is a special problem about realism in ethics. He recognises that it is the sceptic who bears the burden of proof but claims that his arguments from disagreement and queerness satisfy this burden. I argued, however, that neither argument provides good reason for disbelieving moral realism; certainly neither argument successfully bears the sceptic's burden of proof. The moral realist has various resources with which to account for moral disputes, and neither his account of the supervenience of moral facts nor his account of the theory-dependence of moral knowledge is queer or uncommon. I also introduced and developed a functionalist theory of moral value according to which moral facts are facts about human well-being and flourishing. Although the truth of this functionalist theory is not essential to the defense of moral realism, it does provide a plausible model for a realist program in ethics. Mackie's arguments from disagreement and queerness do not exhaust the sceptical challenges to moral realism. But both arguments are sufficiently important that by successfully rebutting them we have gone a long way towards defending moral realism. [24]

NOTES

1. J. L. Mackie, *Ethics: Inventing Right and Wrong* (New York: Penguin Books, 1977) (hereinafter *E*). Mackie further discusses a number of features of these two arguments in *Hume's Moral Theory* (Boston: Routledge & Kegan Paul, 1980) (hereinafter *HMT*) and *The Miracle of Theism* (New York: Oxford University Press, 1982) (hereinafter *MT*). Parenthetical references in the text to *E*, *HMT*, or *MT* are to pages in these books.

2. Cf. Michael Devitt, 'Dummett's Anti-Realism' *Journal of Philosophy* 80 (1983), pp. 75—6. For obvious reasons, the kind of dependence asserted in R is logical, not causal.

3. The simple denial of the existence of moral facts, accompanied by no positive account of the nature of moral values, is moral nihilism. But Mackie, like most moral sceptics, not only denies the existence of objective values but also adopts a constructivist or subjectivist position about the nature of value according to which we make or choose moral value.

4. See Thomas Nagel, 'The Limits of Objectivity' in S. McMurrin (ed), *The Tanner Lectures on Human Values I* (Salt Lake City: University of Utah Press, 1980), p. 100. Cf. *E:* pp. 35, 48–9; *HMT:* pp. 34, 70–5, 136.

5. Mackie himself refers to this argument as 'the argument from relativity'. (*E:* p. 36) But this label is at least misleading and on a natural reading of 'relativity' begs the question, since the argument in question alleges that moral relativity (or at least the denial of moral realism) is the best explanation of the facts about moral disagreement.

6. *E:* pp. 23, 40, 49; *HMT:* pp. 22, 53; and *MT:* p. 102 require MI, while *MT:* p. 115 explicitly requires RI.

7. Of course, the mere absence of a single fact or set of facts *in virtue of which* both considerations are valuable does not establish incommensurability.

8. A realist *could* maintain that most or even all genuine moral disputes are unresolvable, as long as he was willing to claim that moral ties and incommensurable values occurred frequently enough. Although these claims are compatible with his position, reliance on them would weaken his reply to the argument from disagreement.

9. See, *e.g.*, Nelson Goodman, *Fact, Fiction, and Forecast* (Indianapolis: Hackett, 1979), p. 66; John Rawls, *A Theory of Justice* (Cambridge, MA: Harvard University Press, 1971), pp. 20, 46–51; Rolf Sartorius, *Individual Conduct and Social Norms* (Encino, CA: Dickenson, 1975), pp. 31–3; and Norman Daniels, 'Wide Reflective Equilibrium and Theory Acceptance in Ethics' *Journal of Philosophy* 76 (1979), pp. 256–282.

10. Although a coherentist theory of moral truth would be incompatible with moral realism, this part of the realist's reply requires only a coherence theory of moral justification.

11. Actually, the argument from disagreement presupposes that disagreement over non-moral facts is always in principle resolvable.

12. As Mackie himself observes (*MT:* p. 116), the queerness argument is *a posteriori* and not *a priori* as R. M. Hare, *Moral Thinking* (New York: Oxford University Press, 1981), pp. 82–6, insists.

13. Cf. Saul Kripke, 'Identity and Necessity' reprinted in S. Schwartz (ed), *Naming, Necessity, and Natural Kinds* (Ithaca, NY: Cornell University Press, 1977), pp. 76, 98–9 and *Naming and Necessity* (Cambridge, MA: Harvard University Press, 1980), p. 148; and Richard Boyd, 'Materialism without Reductionism: What Physicalism Does Not Entail' in N. Block (ed), *Readings in Philosophy of Psychology I* (Cambridge, MA: Harvard University Press, 1980).

14. Also, recall that Mackie advocates a selective and not a general kind of scepticism.

15. Cf. Boyd, 'Materialism without Reductionism: What Physicalism Does Not Entail'; and Jaegwon Kim, 'Causality, Identity, and Supervenience in the Mind-Body Problem' *Midwest Studies in Philosophy IV* (1979), pp. 31–49.

16. Supervenience is a transitive relation.

17. Although Mackie does not press Moore's open question argument or any of its cognates against moral realism, it is worth pointing out that property supervenience does not require any kind of syntactic or linguistic reductionism. Just as property identity does not require property predicate synonymy, so property supervenience does not require synonymy or meaning implications between supervening property predicates and base property predicates. For instance, whether or not human pains supervene on C-fiber firings, the truth of this claim does not depend upon whether there are synonymy relations or meaning implications between 'human pain' and 'C-fiber firing'. Thus, although biological, social, psychological, and moral properties all supervene on physical properties, biological, social, psychological, and moral terms need not be definable in the language of particle physics. This explains how moral realism can be true even if there are no reductive definitions of moral terms.

18. See, *e.g.*, Ned Block, 'Troubles with Functionalism' reprinted in N. Block.

19. The functionalist literature is quite extensive; I rely principally upon the following: David Armstrong, *A Materialist Theory of Mind* (Boston: Routledge & Kegan Paul, 1968); Ned Block, 'What is Functionalism?' in N. Block; Ned Block and Jerry Fodor, 'What Psychological States Are Not' reprinted in N. Block; Richard Boyd, 'Materialism without Reductionism: What Physicalism Does Not Entail'; Austen Clark, *Psychological Models and Neural Mechanisms* (New York: Oxford University Press, 1980); Jerry Fodor, 'Materialism' in D. Rosenthal (ed), *Materialism and the Mind-Body Problem* (Englewood Cliffs, NJ: Prentice-Hall, 1971); Gilbert Harman, *Thought* (Princeton: Princeton University Press, 1973); Hilary Putnam, *Mind, Language, and Reality* (New York: Cambridge University Press, 1975), chapters 14, 16, 18, 20–2; and K. V. Wilkes, *Physicalism* (Boston: Routledge & Kegan Paul, 1978).

20. A functionalist moral realist might claim that moral properties are properties which play a certain role in the activities which are characteristic of *sentient* organisms.

21. When suitably developed, this functionalist theory of moral value might be quite similar *in content* to the moral theory which Mackie himself defends in part II of *E*. However, Mackie and I would still disagree about *the status* of this theory. I am suggesting that it might be true; he is presumably doing something like recommending the adoption of his theory.

22. Boyd argues that because of the profound theory-dependence of scientific methodology, the instrumental reliability of scientific method can *only* be explained by assuming the truth of scientific realism. See Richard Boyd, 'Realism, Underdetermination, and a Causal Theory of Evidence' *Nous* 7 (1973), pp. 1–12 and 'Scientific Realism and Naturalistic Epistemology' *PSA 1980 Volume 2* (East Lansing, MI: Philosophy of Science Association, 1981).

23. Cf. Alan Gewirth, "Positive 'Ethics' and Normative 'Science' " reprinted in J. Thomson and G. Dworkin (eds), *Ethics,* (New York: Harper & Row, 1968).

24. I would like to thank Tom Arner, Richard Boyd, Norman Dahl, T. H. Irwin, David Lyons, John McDowell, Alan Sidelle, Nicholas Sturgeon, and readers for the *Australasian Journal of Philosophy* for helpful comments on earlier versions of this paper.

29
ETHICS AND OBSERVATION
Gilbert Harman

1. THE BASIC ISSUE

Can moral principles be tested and confirmed in the way scientific principles can? Consider the principle that, if you are given a choice between five people alive and one dead or five people dead and one alive, you should always choose to have five people alive and one dead rather than the other way round. We can easily imagine examples that appear to confirm this principle. Here is one:

You are a doctor in a hospital's emergency room when six accident victims are brought in. All six are in danger of dying but one is much worse off than the others. You can just barely save that person if you devote all of your resources to him and let the others die. Alternatively, you can save the other five if you are willing to ignore the most seriously injured person.

From *The Nature of Morality: An Introduction to Ethics* by Gilbert Harman. Copyright © 1977 by Oxford University Press. Reprinted by permission.

It would seem that in this case you, the doctor, would be right to save the five and let the other person die. So this example, taken by itself, confirms the principle under consideration. Next, consider the following case.

You have five patients in the hospital who are dying, each in need of a separate organ. One needs a kidney, another a lung, a third a heart, and so forth. You can save all five if you take a single healthy person and remove his heart, lungs, kidneys, and so forth, to distribute to these five patients. Just such a healthy person is in room 306. He is in the hospital for routine tests. Having seen his test results, you know that he is perfectly healthy and of the right tissue compatibility. If you do nothing, he will survive without incident; the other patients will die, however. The other five patients can be saved only if the person in Room 306 is cut up and his organs distributed. In that case, there would be one dead but five saved.

The principle in question tell us that you should cut up the patient in Room 306. But in this case, surely you must not sacrifice this innocent bystander, even to save the five other patients. Here a moral principle has been tested and disconfirmed in what may seem to be a surprising way.

This, of course, was a "thought experiment." We did not really compare a hypothesis with the world. We compared an explicit principle with our feelings about certain imagined examples. In the same way, a physicist performs thought experiments in order to compare explicit hypotheses with his "sense" of what should happen in certain situations, a "sense" that he has acquired as a result of his long working familiarity with current theory. But scientific hypotheses can also be tested in real experiments, out in the world.

Can moral principles be tested in the same way, out in the world? You can observe someone do something, but can you ever perceive the rightness or wrongness of what he does? If you round a corner and see a group of young hoodlums pour gasoline on a cat and ignite it, you do not need to *conclude* that what they are doing is wrong; you do not need to figure anything out; you can *see* that it is wrong. But is your reaction due to the actual wrongness of what you see or is it simply a reflection of your moral "sense," a "sense" that you have acquired perhaps as a result of your moral upbringing?

2. OBSERVATION

The issue is complicated. There are no pure observations. Observations are always "theory laden." What you perceive depends to some extent on the theory you hold, consciously or unconsciously. You see some children pour gasoline on a cat and ignite it. To really see that, you have to possess a great deal of knowledge, know about a considerable number of objects, know about people: that people pass through the life stages infant, baby, child, adolescent, adult. You must know what flesh and blood animals are, and in particular, cats. You must

have some idea of life. You must know what gasoline is, what burning is, and much more. In one sense, what you "see" is a pattern of light on your retina, a shifting array of splotches, although even that is theory, and you could never adequately describe what you see in that sense. In another sense, you see what you do because of the theories you hold. Change those theories and you would see something else, given the same pattern of light.

Similarly, if you hold a moral view, whether it is held consciously or unconsciously, you will be able to perceive rightness or wrongness, goodness or badness, justice or injustice. There is no difference in this respect between moral propositions and other theoretical propositions. If there is a difference, it must be found elsewhere.

Observation depends on theory because perception involves forming a belief as a fairly direct result of observing something; you can form a belief only if you understand the relevant concepts and a concept is what it is by virtue of its role in some theory or system of beliefs. To recognize a child as a child is to employ, consciously or unconsciously, a concept that is defined by its place in a framework of the stages of human life. Similarly, burning is an empty concept apart from its theoretical connections to the concepts of heat, destruction, smoke, and fire.

Moral concepts—Right and Wrong, Good and Bad, Justice and Injustice—also have a place in your theory or system of beliefs and are the concepts they are because of their context. If we say that observation has occurred whenever an opinion is a direct result of perception, we must allow that there is moral observation, because such an opinion can be a moral opinion as easily as any other sort. In this sense, observation may be used to confirm or disconfirm moral theories. The observational opinions that, in this sense, you find yourself with can be in either agreement or conflict with your consciously explicit moral principles. When they are in conflict, you must choose between your explicit theory and observation. In ethics, as in science, you sometimes opt for theory, and say that you made an error in observation or were biased or whatever, or you sometimes opt for observation, and modify your theory.

In other words, in both science and ethics, general principles are invoked to explain particular cases and, therefore, in both science and ethics, the general principles you accept can be tested by appealing to particular judgments that certain things are right or wrong, just or unjust, and so forth; and these judgments are analogous to direct perceptual judgments about facts.

3. OBSERVATIONAL EVIDENCE

Nevertheless, observation plays a role in science that it does not seem to play in ethics. The difference is that you need to make assumptions about certain physical facts to explain the occurrence of the observations that support a scientific theory, but you do not seem to need to make assumptions about any moral facts to explain the occurrence of the so-called moral observations I have been talking about. In the moral case, it would seem that you need only make assumptions about the psychology or moral sensibility of the person making the moral observation. In the scientific case, theory is tested against the world.

The point is subtle but important. Consider a physicist making an observation to test a scientific theory. Seeing a vapor trail in a cloud chamber, he thinks, "There goes a proton." Let us suppose that this is an observation in the relevant sense, namely, an immediate judgment made in response to the situation without any conscious reasoning having taken place. Let us also suppose that his observation confirms his theory, a theory that helps give meaning to the very term "proton" as it occurs in his observational judgment. Such a confirmation rests on inferring an explanation. He can count his making the observation as confirming evidence for his theory only to the extent that it is reasonable to explain his

making the observation by assuming that, not only is he in a certain psychological "set," given the theory he accepts and his beliefs about the experimental apparatus, but furthermore, there really was a proton going through the cloud chamber, causing the vapor trail, which he saw as a proton. (This is evidence for the theory to the extent that the theory can explain the proton's being there better than competing theories can.) But, if his having made that observation could have been equally well explained by his psychological set alone, without the need for any assumption about a proton then the observation would not have been evidence for the existence of that proton and therefore would not have been evidence for the theory. His making the observation supports the theory only because, in order to explain his making the observation, it is reasonable to assume something about the world over and above the assumptions made about the observer's psychology. In particular, it is reasonable to assume that there was a proton going through the cloud chamber, causing the vapor trail.

Compare this case with one in which you make a moral judgment immediately and without conscious reasoning, say, that the children are wrong to set the cat on fire or that the doctor would be wrong to cut up one healthy patient to save five dying patients. In order to explain your making the first of these judgments, it would be reasonable to assume, perhaps, that the children really are pouring gasoline on a cat and you are seeing them do it. But, in neither case is there any obvious reason to assume anything about "moral facts," such as that it really is wrong to set the cat on fire or to cut up the patient in Room 306. Indeed, an assumption about moral facts would seem to be totally irrelevant to the explanation of your making the judgment you make. It would seem that all we need assume is that you have certain more or less well articulated moral principles that are reflected in the judgments you make, based on your moral sensibility. It seems to be completely irrelevant to our explanation whether your intuitive immediate judgment is true or false.

The observation of an event can provide observational evidence for or against a scientific theory in the sense that the truth of that observation can be relevant to a reasonable explanation of why that observation was made. A moral observation does not seem, in the same sense, to be observational evidence for or against any moral theory, since the truth or falsity of the moral observation seems to be completely irrelevant to any reasonable explanation of why that observation was made. The fact that an observation of an event was made at the time it was made is evidence not only about the observer but also about the physical facts. The fact that you made a particular moral observation when you did does not seem to be evidence about moral facts, only evidence about you and your moral sensibility. Facts about protons can affect what you observe, since a proton passing through the cloud chamber can cause a vapor trail that reflects light to your eye in a way that, given your scientific training and psychological set, leads you to judge that what you see is a proton. But there does not seem to be any way in which the actual rightness or wrongness of a given situation can have any effect on your perceptual apparatus. In this respect, ethics seems to differ from science.

In considering whether moral principles can help explain observations, it is therefore important to note an ambiguity in the word "observation." You see the children set the cat on fire and immediately think, "That's wrong." In one sense, your observation is that what the children are doing is wrong. In another sense, your observation is your thinking that thought. Moral observations might explain observations in the first sense but not in the second sense. Certain moral principles might help to explain why it was *wrong* of the children to set the cat on fire, but moral principles seem to be of no help in explaining *your thinking* that that is wrong. In the first sense of "observation," moral principles can be tested by observation—

"That this act is wrong is evidence that causing unnecessary suffering is wrong." But in the second sense of "observation," moral principles cannot clearly be tested by observation, since they do not appear to help explain observations in this second sense of "observation." Moral principles do not seem to help explain your observing what you observe.

Of course, if you are already given the moral principle that it is wrong to cause unnecessary suffering, you can take your seeing the children setting the cat on fire as observational evidence that they are doing something wrong. Similarly, you can suppose that your seeing the vapor trail is observational evidence that a proton is going through the cloud chamber, if you are given the relevant physical theory. But there is an important apparent difference between the two cases. In the scientific case, your making that observation is itself evidence for the physical theory because the physical theory explains the proton, which explains the trail, which explains your observation. In the moral case, your making your observation does not seem to be evidence for the relevant moral principle because that principle does not seem to help explain your observation. The explanatory chain from principle to observation seems to be broken in morality. The moral principle may "explain" why it is wrong for the children to set the cat on fire. But the wrongness of that act does not appear to help explain the act, which you observe, itself. The explanatory chain appears to be broken in such a way that neither the moral principle nor the wrongness of the act can help explain why you observe what you observe.

A qualification may seem to be needed here. Perhaps the children perversely set the cat on fire simply "because it is wrong." Here it may seem at first that the actual wrongness of the act does help explain why they do it and therefore indirectly helps explain why you observe what you observe just as a physical theory, by explaining why the proton is producing a vapor trail, indirectly helps explain why the observer observes what he observes. But on reflection we must agree that this is probably an illusion. What explains the children's act is not clearly the actual wrongness of the act but, rather, their belief that the act is wrong. The actual rightness or wrongness of their act seems to have nothing to do with why they do it.

Observational evidence plays a part in science it does not appear to play in ethics, because scientific principles can be justified ultimately by their role in explaining observations, in the second sense of observation—by their explanatory role. Apparently, moral principles cannot be justified in the same way. It appears to be true that there can be no explanatory chain between moral principles and particular observings in the way that there can be such a chain between scientific principles and particular observings. Conceived as an explanatory theory, morality, unlike science, seems to be cut off from observation.

Not that every legitimate scientific hypothesis is susceptible to direct observational testing. Certain hypothesis about "black holes" in space cannot be directly tested, for example, because no signal is emitted from within a black hole. The connection with observation in such a case is indirect. And there are many similar examples. Nevertheless, seen in the large, there is the apparent difference between science and ethics we have noted. The scientific realm is accessible to observation in a way the moral realm is not.

4. ETHICS AND MATHEMATICS

Perhaps ethics is to be compared, not with physics, but with mathematics. Perhaps such a moral principle as "You ought to keep your promises" is confirmed or disconfirmed in the way (whatever it is) in which such a mathematical principle as "5 + 7 = 12" is. Observation does not seem to play the role in mathematics it plays in physics. We do not and cannot perceive numbers, for example, since we cannot be in causal contact with them. We do not even understand what it would be like to be in causal contact with the number 12, say. Relations among numbers cannot have any more of an effect on our perceptual apparatus than moral facts can.

Observation, however, *is* relevant to mathematics. In explaining the observations that support a physical theory, scientists typically appeal to mathematical principles. On the other hand, one never seems to need to appeal in this way to moral principles. Since an observation is evidence for what best explains it, and since mathematics often figures in the explanations of scientific observations, there is indirect observational evidence for mathematics. There does not seem to be observational evidence, even indirectly, for basic moral principles. In explaining why certain observations have been made, we never seem to use purely moral assumptions. In this respect, then, ethics appears to differ not only from physics but also from mathematics. . . .

30
MORAL EXPLANATIONS

Nicholas L. Sturgeon

There is one argument for moral skepticism that I respect even though I remain unconvinced. It has sometimes been called the argument from moral diversity or relativity, but that is somewhat misleading, for the problem arises not from the diversity of moral views, but from the apparent difficulty of *settling* moral disagreements, or even of knowing what would be required to settle them, a difficulty thought to be noticeably greater than any found in settling disagreements that arise in, for example, the sciences. This provides an argument for moral skepticism because one obviously possible explanation of our difficulty in settling moral disagreements is that they are really unsettleable, that there is no way of justifying one rather than another competing view on these issues; and a possible further explanation for the unsettleability of moral disagreements, in turn, is moral nihilism, the view that on these issues there just is no fact

From "Moral Explanations" ed. David Copp and David Zimmerman, *Morality, Reason and Truth* (Rowman and Littlefield, 1985): 49–71. Reprinted by permission.

of the matter, that the impossibility of discovering and establishing moral truths is due to there not being any.

I am, as I say, unconvinced: partly because I think this argument exaggerates the difficulty we actually find in settling moral disagreements, partly because there are alternative explanations to be considered for the difficulty we do find. Under the latter heading, for example, it certainly matters to what extent moral disagreements depend on disagreements about other questions which, however, disputed they may be, are nevertheless regarded as having objective answers: questions such as which, if any, religion is true, which account of human psychology, which theory of human society. And it also matters to what extent consideration of moral questions is in practice skewed by distorting factors such as personal interest and social ideology. These are large issues. Although it is possible to say some useful things to put them in perspective, it appears impossible to settle them quickly or in any a priori way. Consideration of them is likely to have to be piecemeal and, in the short run at least, frustratingly indecisive.

These large issues are not my topic here. But I mention them, and the difficulty of settling them, to show why it is natural that moral skeptics have hoped to find some quicker way of establishing their thesis. I doubt that any exist, but some have of course been proposed. Verificationist attacks on ethics should no doubt be seen in this light, and J. L. Mackie's recent "argument from queerness" is a clear instance. The quicker response on which I shall concentrate, however, is neither of these, but instead an argument by Gilbert Harman designed to bring out the "basic problem" about morality, which in his view is "its apparent immunity from observational testing" and "the seeming irrelevance of observational evidence."[1] The argument is that reference to moral facts appears unnecessary for the *explanation* of our moral observations and beliefs.

Harman's view, I should say at once, is not in the end a skeptical one, and he does not view the argument I shall discuss as a decisive defense of moral skepticism or moral nihilism. Someone else might easily so regard it, however. For Harman himself regards it as creating a strong *prima facie* case for skepticism and nihilism, strong enough to justify calling it "the problem with ethics."[2] And he believes it shows that the only recourse for someone who wishes to avoid moral skepticism is to find defensible reductive definitions for ethical terms; so skepticism would be the obvious conclusion to draw for anyone who doubted the possibility of such definitions. I believe, however, that Harman is mistaken on both counts. I shall show that his argument for skepticism either rests on claims that most people would find quite implausible (and so cannot be what constitutes, for *them*, the problem with ethics); or else becomes just the application to ethics of a familiar *general* skeptical strategy, one which, if it works for ethics, will work equally well for unobservable theoretical entities, or for other minds, or for an external world (and so, again, can

hardly be what constitutes the distinctive problem with *ethics*). I have argued elsewhere, moreover, that one can in any case be a moral realist, and indeed an ethical naturalist, without believing that we are now or ever will be in possession of reductive naturalistic definitions for ethical terms.

I. THE PROBLEM WITH ETHICS

Moral theories are often tested in thought experiments, against imagined examples; and, as Harman notes, trained researchers often test scientific theories in the same way. The problem, though, is that scientific theories can also be tested against the world, by observations or real experiments; and, Harman asks, "can moral principles be tested in the same way, out in the world?"

This would not be a very interesting or impressive challenge, of course, if it were merely a resurrection of standard verificationist worries about whether moral assertions and theories have any testable empirical implications, implications statable in some relatively austere "observational" vocabulary. One problem with that form of the challenge, as Harman points out, is that there are no "pure" observations, and in consequence no purely observational vocabulary either. But there is also a deeper problem that Harman does not mention, one that remains even if we shelve worries about "pure" observations and, at least for the sake of argument, grant the verificationist his observational language, pretty much as it was usually conceived: that is, as lacking at the very least any obviously theoretical terminology from any recognized science, and of course as lacking any moral terminology. For then the difficulty is that moral principles fare just as well (or just as badly) against the verificationist challenge as do typical scientific principles. For it is by now a familiar point about scientific principles—principles such as Newton's law of universal gravitation or Darwin's theory of evolution—that they are entirely devoid of empirical implications when considered in isolation.[3] We do of course base observational predictions on such theories and so test them against experience, but that is because we do *not* consider them in isolation. For we can derive these predictions only by relying at the same time on a large background of additional assumptions, many of which are equally theoretical and equally incapable of being tested in isolation.

A less familiar point, because less often spelled out, is that the relation of moral principles to observation is similar in *both* these respects. Candidate moral principles—for example, that an action is wrong just in case there is something else the agent could have done that would have produced a greater balance of pleasure over pain—lack empirical implications when considered in isolation. But it is easy to derive empirical consequences from them, and thus to test them against experience, if we allow ourselves, as we do in the scientific case, to rely on a background of other assumptions of comparable status. Thus, if we conjoin the act-utilitarian principle I just cited with the further view, also untestable in isolation, that it is always wrong deliberately to kill a human being, we can deduce from these two premises together the consequence that deliberately killing a human being always produces a lesser balance of pleasure over pain than some available alternative act; and this claim is one any positivist would have conceded we know, in principle at least, how to test. If we found it to be false, moreover, then we would be forced by this empirical test to abandon at least one of the moral claims from which we derived it.

It might be thought a worrisome feature of this example, however, and a further opening for skepticism, that there could be controversy about which moral premise to abandon, and that we have not explained how our empirical test can provide an answer to *this* question. And this may be a problem. It should be a familiar problem, however, because the Duhemian commentary includes a precisely corresponding point about the scientific case: that if we are

at all cautious in characterizing what we observe, then the requirement that our theories merely be *consistent* with observation is a very weak one. There are always many, perhaps indefinitely many, different mutually inconsistent ways to adjust our views to meet this constraint. Of course, in practice we are often confident of how to do it: if you are a freshman chemistry student, you do not conclude from your failure to obtain the predicted value in an experiment that it is all over for the atomic theory of gases. And the decision can be equally easy, one should note, in a moral case. Consider two examples. From the surprising moral thesis that Adolf Hitler was a morally admirable person, together with a modest piece of moral theory to the effect that no morally admirable person would, for example, instigate and oversee the degradation and death of millions of persons, one can derive the testable consequence that Hitler did not do this. But he did, so we must give up one of our premises; and the choice of which to abandon is neither difficult nor controversial.

Or, to take a less monumental example, contrived around one of Harman's own, suppose you have been thinking yourself lucky enough to live in a neighborhood in which no one would do anything wrong, at least not in public; and that the modest piece of theory you accept, this time, is that malicious cruelty, just for the hell of it, is wrong. Then, as in Harman's example, "you round a corner and see a group of young hoodlums pour gasoline on a cat and ignite it." At this point, either your confidence in the neighborhood or your principle about cruelty has got to give way. But the choice is easy, if dispiriting, so easy as hardly to require thought. As Harman says, "You do not need to *conclude* that what they are doing is wrong; you do not need to figure anything out; you can *see* that it is wrong" (p. 4). But a skeptic can still wonder whether this practical confidence, or this "seeing," rests in either sort of case on anything more than deeply ingrained conventions of thought—

respect for scientific experts, say, and for certain moral traditions—as opposed to anything answerable to the facts of the matter, any reliable strategy for getting it right about the world.

Now, Harman's challenge is interesting partly because it does not rest on these verificationist doubts about whether moral beliefs have observational implications, but even more because what it does rest on is a partial answer to the kind of general skepticism to which, as we have seen, reflection of the verificationist picture can lead. Many of our beliefs are justified, in Harman's view, by their providing or helping to provide a reasonable *explanation* of our observing what we do. It would be consistent with your failure, as a beginning student, to obtain the experimental result predicted by the gas laws, that the laws are mistaken. But a better explanation, in light of your inexperience and the general success experts have had in confirming and applying these laws, is that you made some mistake in running the experiment. So our scientific beliefs can be justified by their explanatory role; and so too, in Harman's view, can mathematical beliefs and many commonsense beliefs about the world.

Not so, however, moral beliefs: they appear to have no such explanatory role. That is "the problem with ethics." Harman spells out his version of this contrast:

You need to make assumptions about certain physical facts to explain the occurrence of the observations that support a scientific theory, but you do not seem to need to make assumptions about any moral facts to explain the occurrence of the so-called moral observations I have been talking about. In the moral case, it would seem that you need only make assumptions about the psychology or moral sensibility of the person making the moral observation. (p.6)

More precisely, and applied to his own example, it might be reasonable, in order to explain your judging that the hoodlums are wrong to set the cat on fire, to assume "that the children really are pouring gasoline on a cat and you are seeing them do it." But there is no

obvious reason to assume anything about "moral facts," such as that it is really wrong to set the cat on fire. . . . Indeed, an assumption about moral facts would seem to be totally irrelevant to the explanation of your making the judgment you make. It would seem that all we need assume is that you have certain more or less well articulated moral principles that are reflected in the judgments you make, based on your moral sensibility. (p. 7)

And Harman thinks that if we accept this conclusion, suitably generalized, then, subject to one possible qualification concerning reduction that I have discussed elsewhere, we must conclude that moral theories cannot be tested against the world as scientific theories can, and that we have no reason to believe that moral facts are part of the order of nature or that there is any moral knowledge (pp. 23, 35).

My own view is that Harman is quite wrong, not in thinking that the explanatory role of our beliefs is important to their justification, but in thinking that moral beliefs play no such role. I shall have to say something about the initial plausibility of Harman's thesis as applied to his own example, but part of my reason for dissenting should be apparent from the other example I just gave. We find it easy (and so does Harman [p. 108]) to conclude from the evidence not just that Hitler was not morally admirable, but that he was morally depraved. But isn't it plausible that Hitler's moral depravity—the fact of his really having been morally depraved—forms part of a reasonable explanation of why we believe he was depraved? I think so, and I shall argue concerning this and other examples that moral beliefs very commonly play the explanatory role Harman denies them. Before I can press my case, however, I need to clear up several preliminary points about just what Harman is claiming and just how his argument is intended to work.

II. OBSERVATION AND EXPLANATION

(1) For there are several ways in which Harman's argument invites misunderstanding. One results from his focusing at the start on the question of whether there can be moral *observations*. But this question turns out to be a side issue, in no way central to his argument that moral principles cannot be tested against the world. There are a couple of reasons for this, of which the more important by far is that Harman does not really require of moral facts, if belief in them is to be justified, that they figure in the explanation of moral observations. It would be enough, on the one hand, if they were needed for the explanation of moral beliefs that are not in any interesting sense observations. For example, Harman thinks belief in moral facts would be vindicated if they were needed to explain our drawing the moral conclusions we do when we reflect on hypothetical cases, but I think there is no illumination in calling these conclusions observations. It would also be enough, on the other hand, if moral facts were needed for the explanation of what were clearly observations, but not moral observations. Harman thinks mathematical beliefs are justified, but he does not suggest that there are mathematical observations; it is rather that appeal to mathematical truths helps to explain why we make the physical observations we do (p. 10). Moral beliefs would surely be justified, too, if they played such a role, whether or not there are any moral observations.

So the claim is that moral facts are not needed to explain our having any of the moral beliefs we do, whether or not those beliefs are observations, and are equally unneeded to explain any of the observations we make, whether or not those observations are moral. In fact, Harman's view appears to be that moral facts aren't needed to explain anything at all: though it would perhaps be question-begging for him to begin with this strong a claim, since he grants that if there were any moral facts, then appeal to other moral facts—more general ones, for exam-

ple—might be needed to explain *them* (p. 8). But he is certainly claiming, at the very least, that moral facts aren't needed to explain any non-moral facts we have any reason to believe in.

(2) Other possible misunderstandings concern what is meant in asking whether reference to moral facts is *needed* to explain moral beliefs. One warning about this question I have dealt with in my discussion of reduction elsewhere;[4] but another, about what Harman is clearly *not* asking, and about what sort of answer I can attempt to defend to the question he is asking, I can spell out here. For Harman's question is clearly not just whether there is *an* explanation of our moral beliefs that does not mention moral facts. Almost surely there is. Equally surely, however, there is *an* explanation of our commonsense non-moral beliefs that does not mention an external world: one which cites only our sensory experience, for example, together with whatever needs to be said about our psychology to explain why with that history of experience we would form just the beliefs we do. Harman means to be asking a question that will lead to skepticism about moral facts, but not to skepticism about the existence of material bodies or about well-established scientific theories of the world.

Harman illustrates the kind of question he is asking, and the kind of answer he is seeking, with an example from physics that it will be useful to keep in mind. A physicist sees a vapor trail in a cloud chamber and thinks, "There goes a proton." What explains his thinking about this? Partly, of course, his psychological set, which largely depends on his beliefs about the apparatus and all the theory he has learned; but partly also, perhaps, the hypothesis that "there really was a proton going through the cloud chamber, causing the vapor trail, which he saw as a proton." We will *not* need this latter assumption, however, "if his having made that observation could have been equally well explained by his psychological set alone, without the need for any assumption about a proton" (p. 6).[5] So for reference to moral facts to be *needed* in the explanation of our beliefs and observations, is for this reference to be required for an explanation that is somehow *better* than competing explanations. Correspondingly, reference to moral facts will be unnecessary to an explanation, in Harman's view, not just because we can find some explanation that does not appeal to them, but because *no* explanation that appeals to them is any better than some competing explanation that does not.

Now, fine discriminations among competing explanations of almost anything are likely to be difficult, controversial, and provisional. Fortunately, however, my discussion of Harman's argument will not require any fine discriminations. This is because Harman's thesis, as we have seen, is *not* that moral explanations lose out by a small margin; nor is it that moral explanations, though sometimes initially promising, always turn out on further examination to be inferior to nonmoral ones. It is, rather, that reference to moral facts always looks, right from the start, to be "completely irrelevant" to the explanation of any of our observations and beliefs. And my argument will be that this is mistaken: that many moral explanations appear to be good explanations, or components in good explanations, that are not obviously undermined by anything else that we know. My suspicion, in fact, is that moral facts are needed in the sense explained, that they will turn out to belong in our best overall explanatory picture of the world, even in the long run, but I shall not attempt to establish that here. Indeed, it should be clear why I could not pretend to do so. For I have explicitly put to one side the issue (which I regard as incapable in any case of quick resolution) of whether and to what extent actual moral disagreements can be settled satisfactorily; but I assume it would count as a defect in any sort of explanation to rely on claims about which rational agreement proved unattainable. So I concede that it *could* turn out, for anything I say here, that moral explanations are all defective and should be discarded. What I shall try to show is merely that many moral

explanations look reasonable enough to be in the running; and, more specifically, that nothing Harman says provides any reason for thinking they are not. This claim is surely strong enough (and controversial enough) to be worth defending.

(3) It is implicit in this statement of my project, but worth noting separately, that I take Harman to be proposing an *independent* skeptical argument—independent not merely of the argument from the difficulty of settling disputed moral questions, but also of other standard arguments for moral skepticism. Otherwise his argument is not worth separate discussion. For *any* of these more familiar skeptical arguments will of course imply that moral explanations are defective, on the reasonable assumption that it would be a defect in any explanation to rely on claims as doubtful as these arguments attempt to show all moral claims to be. But if *that* is why there is a problem with moral explanations, one should surely just cite the relevant skeptical argument, rather than this derivative difficulty about moral explanations, as the basic "problem with ethics," and it is that argument we should discuss. So I take Harman's interesting suggestion to be that there is a *different* difficulty that remains even if we put other arguments for moral skepticism aside and *assume*, for the sake of argument, that there are moral facts (for example, that what the children in his example are doing is really wrong): namely, that these assumed facts *still* seem to play no explanatory role.

This understanding of Harman's thesis crucially affects my argumentative strategy in a way to which I should alert the reader in advance. For it should be clear that assessment of this thesis not merely permits, but *requires*, that we provisionally assume the existence of moral facts. I can see no way of evaluating the claim that *even if* we assumed the existence of moral facts they would still appear explanatorily irrelevant, without assuming the existence of some, to see how they would look. So I do freely assume this in each of the examples I discuss in the next section. (I have tried to choose plausible examples, moreover, moral facts most of us would be inclined to believe in if we did believe in moral facts, since those are the easiest to think about; but the precise examples don't matter, and anyone who would prefer others should feel free to substitute her own.) I grant, furthermore, that if Harman were right about the outcome of this thought experiment—that even after we assumed these facts they still looked irrelevant to the explanation of our moral beliefs and other nonmoral facts—then we might conclude with him that there were, after all, no such facts. But I claim he is wrong: that once we have provisionally assumed the existence of moral facts they *do* appear relevant, by perfectly ordinary standards, to the explanation of moral beliefs and of a good deal else besides. Does this prove that there *are* such facts? Well of course it helps support that view, but here I carefully make no claim to have shown so much. What I *show* is that any remaining reservations about the existence of moral facts must be based on those *other* skeptical arguments, of which Harman's argument is independent. In short, there may still be a "problem with ethics," but it has *nothing* special to do with moral explanations.

III. MORAL EXPLANATIONS

Now that I have explained how I understand Harman's thesis, I turn to my arguments against it. I shall first add to my example of Hitler's moral character several more in which it seems plausible to cite moral facts as part of an explanation of nonmoral facts, and in particular of people's forming the moral opinions they do. I shall then argue that Harman gives us no plausible reason to reject or ignore these explanations; I shall claim, in fact, that the same is true for his own examples of the children igniting the cat. I shall conclude, finally, by attempting to diagnose the source of the disagreement between Harman and me on these issues.

My Hitler example suggests a whole range of extremely common cases that appear not to have occurred to Harman, cases in which we cite someone's moral character as part of an explanation of his or her deeds, and in which that whole story is then available as a plausible further explanation of someone's arriving at a correct assessment of that moral character. Take just one other example. Bernard DeVoto, in *The Year of Decision: 1846*, describes the efforts of American emigrants already in California to rescue another party of emigrants, the Donner Party, trapped by snows in the High Sierras, once their plight became known. At a meeting in Yerba Buena (now San Francisco), the relief efforts were put under the direction of a recent arrival, Passed Midshipman Selim Woodworth, described by a previous acquaintance as "a great busybody and ambitious of taking a command among the emigrants."[6] But Woodworth not only failed to lead rescue parties into the mountains himself, where other rescuers were counting on him (leaving children to be picked up by him, for example), but had to be "shamed, threatened, and bullied" even into organizing the efforts of others willing to take the risk; he spent time arranging comforts for himself in camp, preening himself on the importance of his position; and as a predictable result of his cowardice and his exercises in vainglory, many died who might have been saved, including four known still to be alive when he turned back for the last time in mid-March.

DeVoto concludes: "Passed Midshipman Woodworth was just no damned good" (1942, p. 442). I cite this case partly because it has so clearly the structure of an inference to a reasonable explanation. One can think of competing explanations, but the evidence points against them. It isn't, for example, that Woodworth was a basically decent person who simply proved too weak when thrust into a situation that placed heroic demands on him. He volunteered, he put no serious effort even into tasks that required no heroism, and it seems clear that concern for his own position and reputation played a much larger role in his motivation than did any concern for the people he was expected to save. If DeVoto is right about this evidence, moreover, it seems reasonable that part of the explanation of his believing that Woodworth was no damned good is just that Woodworth *was* no damned good.

DeVoto writes of course with more moral intensity (and with more of a flourish) than academic historians usually permit themselves, but it would be difficult to find a serious work of biography, for example, in which actions are not explained by appeal to moral character: sometimes by appeal to specific virtues and vices, but often enough also by appeal to a more general assessment. A different question, and perhaps a more difficult one, concerns the sort of example of which Harman concentrates, the explanation of judgments of right and wrong. Here again he appears just to have overlooked explanations in terms of moral character: a judge's thinking that it would be wrong to sentence a particular offender to the maximum prison term the law allows, for example, may be due in part to her decency and fairmindedness, which I take to be moral properties if any are. But do moral features of the action or institution being judged ever play an explanatory role? Here is an example in which they appear to. An interesting historical question is why vigorous and reasonable widespread moral opposition to slavery arose for the first time in the eighteenth and nineteenth centuries, even though slavery was a very old institution; and why this opposition arose primarily in Britain, France, and in French- and English-speaking North America, even though slavery existed throughout the New World. There is a standard answer to this question. It is that chattel slavery in British and French America, and then in the United States, was much *worse* than previous forms of slavery, and much worse than slavery in Latin America. This is, I should add, a controversial explanation. But as is often the case with historical explanations, its proponents do not claim it is the whole story, and many of its opponents grant that there may be some truth in these comparisons, and that they may after all form a small part of a larger explanation. This latter concession is all I require for my example. Equally good for my purpose would be the more limited thesis which explains the growth of antislavery sentiment in the United States, between the Revolution and the Civil War, in part by saying that slavery in the United States became a more oppressive institution during that time. The appeal in these standard explanations is straightforwardly to moral facts.

What is supposed to be wrong with all these explanations? Harman says that assumptions about moral facts seem "completely irrelevant" in explaining moral observations and moral beliefs (p. 7), but on its more natural reading that claim seems pretty obviously mistaken about these examples. For it is natural to think that if a particular assumption is completely irrelevant to the explanation of a certain fact, then that fact would have obtained, and we could have explained it just as well, even if the assumption had been false. But I do not believe that Hitler would have done all he did if he had not been morally depraved, nor, on the assumption that he was not depraved, can I think of any plausible explanation for his doing those things. Nor is it plausible that we would all have believed he was morally depraved even if he hadn't been. Granted, there is a tendency for writers who do not attach much weight to fascism as a social movement to want to blame its evils on a single maniacal leader, so perhaps some of them would have painted Hitler as a moral monster even if he had not been one. But this is only a tendency, and one for which many people know how to discount, so I doubt that our moral belief really is overdetermined in this way. Nor, similarly, do I believe that Woodworth's actions were overdetermined, so that he would have done just as he did even if he had been a more admirable person. I suppose one could have doubts about DeVoto's objectivity and reliability; it is obvious he dislikes Woodworth, so perhaps he would have thought him a moral loss and convinced his readers of this no matter what the man was really like. But it is more plausible that the dislike is mostly based on the same evidence that supports DeVoto's moral view of him, and that very different evidence, at any rate, would have produced a different verdict. If so, then Woodworth's moral character is part of the explanation of DeVoto's belief about his moral character.

It is more plausible of course that serious moral opposition to slavery would have emerged in Britain, France, and the United States even if slavery hadn't been worse in the modern period than before, and worse in the United States than in Latin America, and that the American antislavery movement would have grown even if slavery had not become more oppressive as the nineteenth century progressed. But that is because these moral facts are offered as at best a partial explanation of these developments in moral opinion. And if they really *are* part of the explanation, as seems plausible, then it is also plausible that whatever effect they produced was not entirely overdetermined; that, for example, the growth of the antislavery movement in the United States would at least have been somewhat slower if slavery had been and remained less bad an institution. Here again it hardly seems "completely irrelevant" to the explanation whether or not these moral facts obtained.

It is more puzzling, I grant, to consider Harman's own example in which you see the children igniting a cat and react immediately with the thought that this is wrong. Is it true, as Harman claims, that the assumption that the children are really doing something wrong is "totally irrelevant" to any reasonable explanation of your making that judgment? Would you, for example, have reacted in just the same way, with the thought that the action is wrong, even if what they were doing *hadn't* been wrong, and could we explain your reaction equally well on this assumption? Now, there is more than one way to understand this counterfactual question, and I shall return below to a reading of it that might appear favorable to Harman's

view. What I wish to point out for now is merely that there is a natural way of taking it, parallel to the way in which I have been understanding similar counterfactual questions about my own examples, on which the answer to it has to be simply: it depends. For to answer the question, I take it, we must consider a situation in which what the children are doing is not wrong, but which is otherwise as much like the actual situation as possible, and then decide what your reaction would be in that situation. But since what makes their action wrong, what its wrongness *consists* in, is presumably something like its being an act of gratuitous cruelty (or, perhaps we should add, of intense cruelty, and to a helpless victim), to imagine them not doing something wrong we are going to have to imagine their action different in this respect. More cautiously and more generally, if what they are actually doing is wrong, and if moral properties are, as many writers have held, supervenient on natural ones,[7] then in order to imagine them not doing something wrong we are going to have to suppose their action different from the actual one in some of its natural features as well. So our question becomes: Even if the children had been doing something else, something just different enough not to be wrong, would you have taken them even so to be doing something wrong?

Surely there is no one answer to this question. It depends on a lot about you, including your moral views and how good you are at seeing at a glance what some children are doing. It probably depends also on a debatable moral issue; namely, just *how* different the children's action would have to be in order not to be wrong. (Is unkindness to animals, for example, also wrong?) I believe we can see how, in a case in which the answer was clearly affirmative, we might be tempted to agree with Harman that the wrongness of the action was no part of the explanation of your reaction. For suppose you are like this. You hate children. What you especially hate, moreover, is the sight of children enjoying themselves; so much so that whenever you see children having fun, you immediately assume they are up to no good. The more they seem to be enjoying themselves, furthermore, the readier you are to fasten on any pretext for thinking them engaged in real wickedness. Then it is true that even if the children had been engaged in some robust but innocent fun, you would have thought they were doing something wrong; and Harman is perhaps right[8] about you that the actual wrongness of the action you see is irrelevant to your thinking it wrong. This is because your reaction is due to a feature of the action that coincides only very accidentally with the ones that make it wrong. But, of course, and fortunately, many people aren't like this (nor does Harman argue that they are). It isn't true of them, in general, that if the children had been doing something similar, although different enough not to be wrong, they would still have thought the children were doing something wrong. And it isn't true either, therefore, that the wrongness of the action is irrelevant to the explanation of why they think it wrong.

Now, one might have the sense from my discussion of all these examples, but perhaps especially from my discussion of this last one, Harman's own, that I have perversely been refusing to understand his claim about the explanatory irrelevance of moral facts in the way he intends. And perhaps I have not been understanding it as he wishes. In any case, I agree, I have certainly not been understanding the crucial counterfactual question, of whether we would have drawn the same moral conclusion even if the moral facts had been different, in the way he must intend. But I am not being perverse. I believe, as I have said, that my own way of taking the question is the more natural one. And, more importantly: although there is, I grant, a reading of that question on which it will always yield the answer Harman wants—namely, that a difference in the moral facts would *not* have made a difference in our judgment—I do not believe this reading can support his argument. I must now explain why.

It will help if I contrast my general approach with his. I am approaching questions about the justification of belief in the spirit of what Quine has called "epistemology naturalized."[9] I take this to mean that we have in general no a priori way of knowing which strategies for forming and refining our beliefs are likely to take us closer to the truth. The only way we have of proceeding is to assume the approximate truth of what seems to us the best overall theory we already have of what we are like and what the world is like, and to decide in the light of *that* what strategies of research and reasoning are likely to be reliable in producing a more nearly true overall theory. One result of applying these procedures, in turn, is likely to be the refinement or perhaps even the abandonment of parts of the tentative theory with which we began.

I take Harman's approach, too, to be an instance of this one. He says we are justified in believing in those facts that we need to assume to explain why we observe what we do. But he does not think that our knowledge of this principle about justification is a priori. Furthermore, as he knows, we cannot decide whether one explanation is better than another without relying on beliefs we already have about the world. Is it really a better explanation of the vapor trail the physicist sees in the cloud chamber to suppose that a proton caused it, as Harman suggests in his example, rather than some other charged particle? Would there, for example, have been no vapor trail in the absence of that proton? There is obviously no hope of answering such questions without assuming at least the approximate truth of some quite far-reaching microphysical theory, and our knowledge of such theories is not a priori.

But my approach differs from Harman's in one crucial way. For among the beliefs in which I have enough confidence to rely on in evaluating explanations, at least at the outset, are some moral beliefs. And I have been relying on them in the following way.[10] Harman's thesis implies that the supposed moral fact of Hitler's being morally depraved is irrelevant to the explanation of

Hitler's doing what he did. (For we may suppose that if it explains his doing what he did, it also helps explain, at greater remove, Harman's belief and mine in his moral depravity.) To assess this claim, we need to conceive a situation in which Hitler was *not* morally depraved and consider the question whether in that situation he would still have done what he did. My answer is that he would not, and this answer relies on a (not very controversial) moral view: that in any world at all like the actual one, only a morally depraved person could have initiated a world war, ordered the "final solution," and done any number of other things Hitler did. That is why I believe that, if Hitler hadn't been morally depraved, he wouldn't have done those things, and hence that the fact of his moral depravity is relevant to an explanation of what he did.

Harman, however, cannot want us to rely on any such moral views in answering this counterfactual question. This comes out most clearly if we return to his example of the children igniting the cat. He claims that the wrongness of this act is irrelevant to an explanation of your thinking it wrong, that you would have *thought* it wrong even if it wasn't. My reply was that in order for the action not to be wrong it would have had to lack the feature of deliberate, intense, pointless cruelty, and that if it had differed in this way you might very well *not* have thought it wrong. I also suggested a more cautious version of this reply: that since the action is in fact wrong, and since moral properties supervene on more basic natural ones, it would have had to be different in *some* further natural respect in order not to be wrong; and that we do not know whether if it had so differed you would still have thought it wrong. Both of these replies, again, rely on moral views, the latter merely on the view that there is *something* about the natural features of the action in Harman's example that makes it wrong, the former on a more specific view as to which of these features do this.

But Harman, it is fairly clear, intends for us *not* to rely on any such moral views in

evaluating his counterfactual claim. His claim is not that if the action had not been one of deliberate cruelty (or had otherwise differed in whatever way would be required to remove its wrongness), you would still have thought it wrong. It is, instead, that if the action were one of deliberate, pointless cruelty, but this *did not make it wrong*, you would still have thought it was wrong. And to return to the example of Hitler's moral character, the counterfactual claim that Harman will need in order to defend a comparable conclusion about that case is not that if Hitler had been, for example, humane and fairminded, free of nationalistic pride and racial hatred, he would still have done exactly as he did. It is, rather, that if Hitler's psychology, and anything else about his situation that could strike us as morally relevant, had been exactly as it in fact was, but this had *not constituted moral depravity*, he would still have done exactly what he did.

Now the antecedents of these two conditionals are puzzling. For one thing, both are, I believe, necessarily false. I am fairly confident, for example, that Hitler really was morally depraved; and since I also accept the view that moral features supervene on basic natural properties,[11] I take this to imply that there is no possible world in which Hitler has just the personality he in fact did in just the situation he was in, but is not morally depraved. Any attempt to describe such a situation, moreover, will surely run up against the limits of our moral concepts—what Harman calls our "moral sensibility"—and this is no accident. For what Harman is asking us to do, in general, is to consider cases in which absolutely *everything* about the nonmoral facts that could seem morally relevant to us, in light of whatever moral theory we accept and of the concepts required for understanding that theory, is held fixed, but in which the moral judgment that our theory yields about the case is nevertheless mistaken. So it is hardly surprising that, using that theory and those concepts, we should find it difficult to conceive in any detail what such a situation would be like. It is especially not surprising when the cases in question are as paradigmatic in light of the moral outlook we in fact have as is Harman's example or is, even more so, mine of Hitler's moral character. The only way we could be wrong about this latter case (assuming we have the nonmoral facts right) would be for our whole theory to be hopelessly wrong, so radically mistaken that there could be no hope of straightening it out through adjustments from within.

But I do not believe we should conclude, as we might be tempted to, that we therefore know a priori that this is not so, or that we cannot understand these conditionals that are crucial to Harman's argument. Rather, now that we have seen how we have to understand them, we should grant that they are true: that if our moral theory were somehow hopelessly mistaken, but all the nonmoral facts remained exactly as they in fact are, then, since we do *accept* that moral theory, we would still draw exactly the moral conclusions we in fact do. But we should deny that any skeptical conclusion follows from this. In particular, we should deny that it follows that moral facts play no role in explaining our moral judgments.

For consider what follows from the parallel claim about microphysics, in particular about Harman's example in which a physicist concludes from his observation of a vapor trail in a cloud chamber, and from the microphysical theory he accepts, that a free proton has passed through the chamber. The parallel claim, notice, is *not* just that if the proton had not been there the physicist would still have thought it was. This claim is implausible, for we may assume that the physicist's theory is generally correct, and it follows from that theory that if there hadn't been a proton there, then there wouldn't have been a vapor trail. But in a perfectly similar way it is implausible that if Hitler hadn't been morally depraved we would still have thought he was: for we may assume that our moral theory also is at least roughly correct, and it follows from the most central features of that theory that if Hitler hadn't been morally depraved, he wouldn't have done what he did. The *parallel* claim about

the microphysical example is, instead, that if there hadn't been a proton there, but there *had* been a vapor trail, the physicist would still have concluded that a proton was present. More precisely, to maintain a perfect parallel with Harman's claims about the moral cases, the antecedent must specify that although no proton is present, absolutely *all* the non-microphysical facts that the physicist, in light of his theory, might take to be relevant to the question of whether or not a proton is present, are exactly as in the actual case. (These macrophysical facts, as we may for convenience call them, surely include everything one would normally think of as an observable fact). Of course, we shall be unable to imagine this without imagining that the physicist's theory is pretty badly mistaken; but I believe we should grant that, *if* the physicist's theory were somehow this badly mistaken, but all the macrophysical facts (including all the observable facts) were held fixed, then the physicist, since he does accept that theory, would still draw all the same conclusions that he actually does. That is, this conditional claim, like Harman's parallel claim about the moral cases, is true.

But no skeptical conclusions follow; nor can Harman, since he does not intend to be a skeptic about physics, think that they do. It does not follow, in the first place, that we have any reason to think the physicist's theory *is* generally mistaken. Nor does it follow, furthermore, that the hypothesis that a proton really did pass through the cloud chamber is not part of a good explanation of the vapor trail, and hence of the physicist's thinking this has happened. This looks like a reasonable explanation, of course, only on the assumption that the physicist's theory is at least roughly true, for it is this theory that tells us, for example, what happens when charged particles pass through a supersaturated atmosphere, what other causes (if any) there might be for a similar phenomenon, and so on. But, as I say, we have not been provided with any reason for not trusting the theory to this extent.

Similarly, I conclude, we should draw no skeptical conclusions from Harman's claims about the moral cases. It is true that if our moral theory were seriously mistaken, but we still believed it, and the nonmoral facts were held fixed, we would still make just the moral judgments we do. But *this* fact by itself provides us with no reason for thinking that our moral theory *is* generally mistaken. Nor, again, does it imply that the fact of Hitler's really having been morally depraved forms no part of a good explanation of his doing what he did and hence, at greater remove, of our thinking him depraved. This explanation will appear reasonable, of course, only on the assumption that our accepted moral theory is at least roughly correct, for it is this theory that assures us that only a depraved person could have thought, felt, and acted as Hitler did. But, as I say, Harman's argument has provided us with no reason for not trusting our moral views to this extent, and hence with no reason for doubting that it is sometimes moral facts that explain our moral judgments.

I conclude with three comments about my argument.

(1) I have tried to show that Harman's claim—that we would have held the particular moral beliefs we do even if those beliefs were untrue—admits of two readings, one of which makes it implausible, and the other of which reduces it to an application of a general skeptical strategy, a strategy which could as easily be used to produce doubt about microphysical as about moral facts. The general strategy is this. Consider any conclusion C we arrive at by relying both on some distinguishable "theory" T and on some body of evidence not being challenged, and ask whether we would have believed C even if it had been false. The plausible answer, *if* we are allowed to rely on T, will often be no: for if C had been false, then (according to T) the evidence would have had to be different, and in that case we wouldn't have believed C. (I have illustrated the plausibility of this sort of reply for all my moral examples, as well as for the microphysical one.) But the skeptic of course

intends us *not* to rely on T in this way, and so rephrases the question: Would we have believed C even if it were false *but* all the evidence had been exactly as it in fact was? Now the answer has to be yes; and the skeptic concludes that C is doubtful. (It should be obvious how to extend this strategy to belief in other minds, or in an external world.) I am of course not convinced: I do not think answers to the rephrased question show anything interesting about what we know or justifiably believe. But it is enough for my purposes here that no such *general* skeptical strategy could pretend to reveal any problems peculiar to belief in *moral* facts.

(2) My conclusion about Harman's argument, although it is not exactly the same as, is nevertheless similar to and very much in the spirit of the Duhemian point I invoked earlier against verificationism. There the question was whether typical moral assertions have testable implications, and the answer was that they do, so long as you include additional moral assumptions of the right sort among the background theories on which you rely in evaluating these assertions. Harman's more important question is whether we should ever regard moral facts as relevant to the explanation of nonmoral facts, and in particular of our having the moral beliefs we do. But the answer, again, is that we should, so long as we are willing to hold the right sorts of *other* moral assumptions fixed in answering counterfactual questions. Neither answer shows morality to be on any shakier ground than, say, physics, for typical microphysical hypotheses, too, have testable implications, and appear relevant to explanations, only if we are willing to assume at least the approximate truth of an elaborate microphysical theory and to hold this assumption fixed in answering counterfactual questions.

(3) Of course, this picture of how explanations depend on background theories, and moral explanations in particular on moral background theories, does show why someone already tempted toward moral skepticism on other grounds (such as those I mentioned at the beginning of this essay)

might find Harman's claim about moral explanations plausible. To the extent that you already have pervasive doubts about moral theories, you will also find moral facts nonexplanatory. So I grant that Harman has located a natural symptom of moral skepticism; but I am sure he has neither traced this skepticism to its roots nor provided any independent argument for it. His claim that we do not *in fact* cite moral facts in explanation of moral beliefs and observations cannot provide such an argument, for that claim is false. So, too, is the claim that assumptions about moral facts seem irrelevant to such explanations, for many do not. The claim that we *should* not rely on such assumptions because they *are* irrelevant, on the other hand, unless it is supported by some independent argument for moral skepticism, will just be question-begging: for the principal test of whether they are relevant, in any situation in which it appears they might be, is a counterfactual question about what would have happened if the moral fact had not obtained, and how we answer that question depends precisely upon whether we *do* rely on moral assumptions in answering it.

My own view I stated at the outset: that the only argument for moral skepticism with any independent weight is the argument from the difficulty of settling disputed moral questions. I have shown that anyone who finds Harman's claim about moral explanations plausible must already have been tempted toward skepticism by some other considerations, and I suspect that the other considerations will typically be the ones I sketched. So that is where discussion should focus. I also suggested that those considerations may provide less support for moral skepticism than is sometimes supposed, but I must reserve a thorough defense of that thesis for another occasion.[12]

NOTES

1. Gilbert Harman, *The Nature of Morality: An Introduction to Ethics* (New York: Oxford University Press, 1977), pp. vii, viii. Parenthetical page references are to this work.

2. Harman's title for the entire first section of his book.

3. This point is generally credited to Pierre Duhem; see *The Aim and Structure of Physical Theory*, trans. Philip P. Wiener (Princeton, N. J.: Princeton University Press, 1954).

4. In the longer paper from which this one is abridged. The salient point is that there are two very *different* reasons one might have for thinking that no reference to moral facts is needed in the explanation of moral beliefs. One—Harman's reason, and my target in this essay—is that no moral explanations even *seem* plausible, that reference to moral facts always strikes us as "completely irrelevant" to the explanation of moral beliefs. This claim, if true, would tend to support moral skepticism. The other, which might appeal to a "reductive" naturalist in ethics, is that any moral explanations that *do* seem plausible can be paraphrased without explanatory loss in entirely nonmoral terms. I doubt this view, too, and I argue in the longer version of this paper that no ethical naturalist need hold it. But anyone tempted by it should note that it is anyway no version of moral skepticism: for what it says is that we know *so much* about ethics that we are always able to say, in entirely nonmoral terms, exactly which natural properties the moral terms in any plausible moral explanations refer to—that's why the moral expressions are dispensable. These two reasons should not be confused with one another.

5. It is surprising that Harman does not mention the obvious intermediate possibility, which would occur to any instrumentalist: to cite the physicist's psychological set *and* the vapor trail, but say nothing about protons or other unobservables. It is *this* explanation, as I emphasize below, that is most closely parallel to an explanation of belief about an external world in terms of sensory experience and psychological makeup, or of moral beliefs in terms of nonmoral facts together with our "moral sensibility."

6. Bernard DeVoto, *The Year of Decision: 1846* (Boston: Houghton Mifflin, 1942), p. 426; a quotation from the notebooks of Francis Parkman. The account of the entire rescue effort is on pp. 424—444.

7. What would be generally granted is just that *if* there are moral properties they supervene on natural properties. But, remember, we are assuming for the sake of argument that there are. I think moral properties *are* natural proper-

ties; and from this view it of course follows trivially that they supervene on natural properties: that, necessarily, nothing could differ in its moral properties without differing in some natural respect. But I also accept the more interesting thesis usually intended by the claim about supervenience—that there are more basic natural features such that, necessarily, once they are fixed, so are the moral properties. (In supervening on more basic natural facts of some sort, moral facts are like *most* natural facts. Social facts like unemployment, for example, supervene on complex histories of many individuals and their relations; and facts about the existence and properties of macroscopic physical objects—colliding billiard balls, say— clearly supervene on the microphysical constitution of the situations that include them.)

8. Not *certainly* right, because there is still the possibility that your reaction is to some extent overdetermined, and is to be explained partly by your sympathy for the cat and your dislike of cruelty, as well as by your hatred for children (although this last alone would have been sufficient to produce it).

We could of course rule out this possibility by making you an even less attractive character, indifferent to the suffering of animals and not offended by cruelty. But it may then be hard to imagine that such a person (whom I shall cease calling "you") could retain enough of a grip on moral thought for us to be willing to say he thought the action *wrong,* as opposed to saying that he merely pretended to do so. This difficulty is perhaps not insuperable, but it is revealing. Harman says that the actual wrongness of the action is "completely irrelevant" to the explanation of the observer's reaction. Notice that what is in fact true, however, is that it is *very hard* to imagine someone who reacts in the way Harman describes, but whose reaction is *not* due, at least in part, to the actual wrongness of the action.

9. W.V.O.Quine, "Epistemology Naturalized," in *Ontological Relativity and Other Essays* (New York: Columbia University Press, 1969), pp. 69–90. In the same volume, see also "Natural Kinds," pp. 114–38.

10. Harman of course allows us to assume the moral facts whose explanatory relevance is being assessed: that Hitler was depraved, or that what the children in his example are doing is wrong. But I have been assuming something more—something about what depravity *is,* and about what *makes* the children's action wrong. (At a minimum, in the more cautious version of my argument, I have been assuming that *something* about its more basic features makes it wrong, so that it could not have differed in its moral quality without differing in those other features as well.)

11. It is about here that I have several times encountered the objection: but surely *supervenient* properties aren't needed to explain anything. It is a little hard, however, to see just what this objection is supposed to come to. If it includes endorsement of the conditional I here attribute to Harman, then I believe the remainder of my discussion is an adequate reply to it. If it is the claim that, because moral properties are supervenient, we can always exploit the insights in any moral explanations, however plausible, without resort to moral *language,* then I have already dealt with it in my discussion of reductionism: the claim is probably false, but even if it is true it is no support for Harman's view, which is not that moral explanations are plausible but reducible, but that they are totally implausible. And doubts about the causal efficacy of supervenient facts seem misplaced in any case, as attention to my earlier examples illustrates. High unemployment causes widespread hardship, and can also bring down the rate of inflation. The masses and velocities of two colliding billiard balls causally influence the subsequent trajectories of the two balls. There is no doubt some sense in which these facts are causally efficacious *in virtue of* the way they supervene on—that is, are constituted out of, or causally realized by—more basic facts, but this hardly shows them inefficacious. (Nor does Harman appear to think it does: for his *favored* explanation of your moral belief about the burning cat, recall, appeals to psychological facts [about your moral sensibility], a biological fact (that it's a cat) and macrophysical facts [that it's on fire]—supervenient facts all, on his physicalist view and mine.) If anyone does hold to a general suspicion of causation by supervenient facts and properties, however, as Jaegwon Kim appears to (see "Causality, Identity, and Supervenience in the Mind-Body Problem," *Midwest Studies in Philosophy* 4 (1979), pp. 31–49, it is enough to note that this suspicion cannot diagnose any special difficulty with *moral* explanations, any distinctive "problem with ethics." The "problem," arguably, will be with every discipline but fundamental physics. On this point, see Richard W. Miller, "Reason and Commitment in the Social Sciences," *Philosophy and Public Affairs* 8 (1979): 252–55.

12. This essay has benefited from helpful

discussion of earlier versions read at the University of Virginia, Cornell University, Franklin and Marshall College, Wayne State University, and the University of Michigan. I have been aided by a useful correspondence with Gilbert Harman; and I am grateful also for specific comments from Richard Boyd, David Brink, David Copp, Stephen Darwall, Terence Irwin, Norman Kretzmann, Ronald Nash, Peter Railton, Bruce Russell, Sydney Shoemaker, and Judith Slein. Only after this essay had appeared in print did I notice that several parallel points about *aesthetic* explanations had been made by Michael Slote in "The Rationality of Aesthetic Value Judgments," *The Journal of Philosophy* 68 (1971): 821–39; interested readers should see that paper.

Suggested Readings

BLACKBURN, SIMON. "Moral Realism," in *Morality and Moral Reasoning*, edited by John Casey, 101–124. Methuen: London, 1971.

BRINK, DAVID O. *Moral Realism and the Foundations of Ethics*. Cambridge: Cambridge University Press, 1988.

COPP, DAVID, AND ZIMMERMAN, DAVID. *Morality, Reason and Truth*. Totowa: Rowman & Littlefield, 1985.

GILLESPIE, NORMAN, ED. *Moral Realism*, Vol. XXIV, Supplement, *The Southern Journal of Philosophy* (1980).

GOWANS, CHRISTOPHER, ED. *Moral Dilemmas*. New York: Oxford University Press, 1987.

HARMAN, GILBERT. "Metaphysical Realism and Moral Relativism." *Journal of Philosophy* 79 (1982):568–75.

HARRISON, JONATHAN. "Mackie's Moral 'Skepticism'." *Philosophy* 57 (1982):173–191.

HONDERICH, TED, ED. *Morality and Objectivity*. London: Routledge & Kegan Paul, 1985.

LOVIBOND, SABINA. *Realism and Imagination in Ethics*. University of Minnesota Press: Minneapolis, 1983.

MACKIE, J. L. *Persons and Values*. Oxford University Press: New York, 1985.

MACKIE, J. L. "Anti-Realisms." In *Logic and Knowledge*, 225–45. Oxford University Press: Oxford, 1985.

McDOWELL, JOHN. "Virtue and Reason." *Monist* 62 (1979):331–50.
　"Values and Secondary Qualities." In *Morality and Objectivity*, edited by Ted Honderich, 110–29. Routledge and Kegan Paul: London, 1985.

RAILTON, PETER. "Moral Realism," *Philosophical Review* 95 (1986):163–207.

RAWLS, JOHN. "The Independence of Moral Theory." *Proceedings of the American Philosophical Association* 48 (1975):5–22.

RUSSELL, BRUCE. "Moral Relativism and Moral Realism." *Monist* 67 (1984):435–51.

SAYRE-MCCORD, GEOFFREY, ED. *Essays on Moral Realism*. Ithaca: Cornell University Press, 1988.

SAYRE-MCCORD, GEOFFREY. *Moral Dilemmas*. Cambridge: MIT Press, 1988.

SINNOTT-ARMSTRONG, WALTER. "Moral Dilemmas and Incomparability." *American Philosophical Quarterly* 22 (1985):321–29.

SOLOMON, DAVID. "Moral Realism and Moral Knowledge." In *Proceedings of the American Catholic Philosophical Association* 59 (1984):41–57.

WERNER, RICHARD. "Ethical Realism." *Ethics* 93 (1983):653–79.